V. Y. Mudimbe
Undisciplined Africanism

Contemporary French and Francophone Cultures

Series Editors

EDMUND SMYTH
Manchester Metropolitan University

CHARLES FORSDICK
University of Liverpool

Editorial Board

JACQUELINE DUTTON
University of Melbourne

LYNN A. HIGGINS
Dartmouth College

MIREILLE ROSELLO
University of Amsterdam

MICHAEL SHERINGHAM
University of Oxford

DAVID WALKER
University of Sheffield

This series aims to provide a forum for new research on modern and contemporary French and francophone cultures and writing. The books published in *Contemporary French and Francophone Cultures* reflect a wide variety of critical practices and theoretical approaches, in harmony with the intellectual, cultural and social developments which have taken place over the past few decades. All manifestations of contemporary French and francophone culture and expression are considered, including literature, cinema, popular culture, theory. The volumes in the series will participate in the wider debate on key aspects of contemporary culture.

Recent titles in the series:

13 Mireille Rosello, *The Reparative in Narratives: Works of Mourning in Progress*

14 Andy Stafford, *Photo-texts: Contemporary French Writing of the Photographic Image*

15 Kaiama L. Glover, *Haiti Unbound: A Spiralist Challenge to the Postcolonial Canon*

16 David Scott, *Poetics of the Poster: The Rhetoric of Image-Text*

17 Mark McKinney, *The Colonial Heritage of French Comics*

18 Jean Duffy, *Thresholds of Meaning: Passage, Ritual and Liminality in Contemporary French Narrative*

19 David H. Walker, *Consumer Chronicles: Cultures of Consumption in Modern French Literature*

20 Pim Higginson, *The Noir Atlantic: Chester Himes and the Birth of the Francophone African Crime Novel*

21 Verena Andermatt Conley, *Spatial Ecologies: Urban Sites, State and World-Space in French Cultural Theory*

22 Lucy O'Meara, *Roland Barthes at the Collège de France*

23 Hugh Dauncey, *French Cycling: A Social and Cultural History*

24 Louise Hardwick, *Childhood, Autobiography and the Francophone Caribbean*

25 Douglas Morrey, *Michel Houellebecq: Humanity and its Aftermath*

26 Nick Nesbitt, *Caribbean Critique: Antillean Critical Theory from Toussaint to Glissant*

27 Edward Welch and Joseph McGonagle, *Contesting Views: The Visual Economy of France and Algeria*

28 Rosemary Chapman, *What is Québécois Literature?: Reflections on the Literary History of Francophone Writing in Canada*

PIERRE-PHILIPPE FRAITURE

V. Y. Mudimbe

Undisciplined Africanism

LIVERPOOL UNIVERSITY PRESS

First published 2013 by
Liverpool University Press
4 Cambridge Street
Liverpool
L69 7ZU

Copyright © 2013 Pierre-Philippe Fraiture

The right of Pierre-Philippe Fraiture to be identified as the author of this book has been asserted by him in accordance with the Copyright, Designs and Patents Act 1988.

All rights reserved. No part of this book may be reproduced, stored in a retrieval system, or transmitted, in any form or by any means, electronic, mechanical, photocopying, recording, or otherwise, without the prior written permission of the publisher.

British Library Cataloguing-in-Publication data
A British Library CIP record is available

ISBN 978-1-84631-894-8 cased

Typeset by Carnegie Book Production, Lancaster
Printed and bound by CPI Group (UK) Ltd, Croydon CR0 4YY

À ma mère. Merci.

Contents

Acknowledgements	ix
List of Abbreviations	xi
Introduction: 'Multidirectional Memory'	1
1 'Mission Impossible?'	16
2 'The Invention of Otherness'	50
3 'The West or the Rest?'	79
4 'Changing Places'	113
5 'Independences?'	147
Conclusion: 'The Return of the Unhomely Scholar'	182
Notes	190
Select Bibliography	234
Index	255

Acknowledgements

Thank you to Alison, as always, and to our two daughters, Manon and Ella.

I would like to express my gratitude to Valentin Mudimbe for being so helpful and available throughout this project.

I would like to thank the following people for providing extremely useful comments on the first draft of the manuscript: Charles Forsdick, Claire Griffiths, David Murphy, Paul O'Carroll, and Daniel Orrells; Anthony Cond for being such an encouraging editor; Michael Syrotinski for supporting my British Academy Mid-Career Fellowship; Sue Barnes, the production editor and Paul Smith the copy editor; Patrick Crowley for commenting on earlier publications which have indirectly contributed to this book; the two anonymous readers for their useful comments on the manuscript; the members of the research group ConceptAfrica led by Bo Stråth and Axel Fleisch from the University of Helsinki; Gary Gutting; Bernard Porter. I would also like to thank the following individuals for inviting me to deliver papers on V. Y. Mubimbe: Maurice Amuri, Gurminder Bhambra, Erika Carter, Dominique Combe, Ferdinand De Jong, Donatien Dibwe dia Mwembu, Lieve Spaas, Jane Hiddleston, David Johnson, and Bill Marshall. Thank you to Hannah Grayson and Nicolas Martin-Granel for contributing to 'V. Y. Mudimbe: Past and Present Africa' (March 2012).

My deepest gratitude goes as well to Peter Larkin from the Warwick University Library; to the staff of the Vere Harmsworth Library in Oxford: Jane Rawson, Judy Warden, Johanna O'Connor, and Martin Sutcliffe; and the staff of the Archives de la littérature (Bibliothèque Royale, Brussels): Saskia Bursens, Paul-Étienne Kisters, Marc Quaghebeur, Yves De Bruyn, and Jean Danhaive.

I would also want to thank the University of Warwick for granting me a study leave (October–December 2010) which enabled me to start this project; and, finally, I would like to express my gratitude to the British Academy for funding a research visit to Lubumbashi (September 2010) and granting me a very generous 'Mid-Career Fellowship' (October 2011–June 2012) which enabled me to complete this book.

Abbreviations

I refer to Mudimbe's major works using the following abbreviations. All translations are mine unless otherwise stated.

AF   *L'Autre Face du royaume: Une introduction à la critique des langages en folie* (Lausanne: L'Age d'homme, 1973)

BI   *Le Bel immonde*; translation used here: *Before the Birth of the Moon*, translated by Marjolijn de Jager (New York: Simon & Schuster, 1989 [1976])

CA   *Carnets d'Amérique, septembre–novembre 1974* (Paris: Éditions Saint-Germain-des-Prés, 1976)

CB   *Cheminements: Carnets de Berlin (avril–juin 1999)* (Quebec: Humanitas, 2006)

CG   *Les Corps glorieux des mots et des êtres: Esquisse d'un jardin africain à la bénédictine* (Paris and Montreal: Présence africaine/Humanitas, 1994)

É   *L'Écart*; translation used here: *The Rift*, translated by Marjolijn de Jager (Minneapolis: Minnesota University Press, 1993 [1979])

Entre   *Entre les eaux* (Paris: Présence africaine, 1973)

Idea   *The Idea of Africa* (Bloomington and Indianapolis: Indiana University Press, 1994)

IoA   *The Invention of Africa: Gnosis, Philosophy, and the Order of Knowledge* (Bloomington and Indianapolis: Indiana University Press, 1988)

Nation   *Autour de la 'Nation': Leçons de civisme. Introduction* (Kinshasa and Lubumbashi: 'Objectifs 80', Éditions du Mont Noir, 1972)

OAF On African Fault Lines: Meditations on Alterity Politics (Scottsville, South Africa: University of KwaZulu-Natal Press, 2013)

OP L'Odeur du père: Essai sur des limites de la science et de la vie en Afrique noire (Paris: Présence africaine, 1982)

P&F Parables and Fables: Exegesis, Textuality and Politics in Central Africa (Madison: University of Wisconsin Press, 1991)

Speech The Surreptitious Speech: Présence africaine and the Politics of Otherness, 1947–1987 (University of Chicago Press, 1992)

SII Shaba Deux: Les Carnets de Mère Marie-Gertrude (Paris: Présence africaine, 1989)

TF Tales of Faith: Religion and Political Performance in Central Africa (London and Atlantic Highlands, NJ: The Athlone Press, 1997)

Introduction: 'Multidirectional Memory'

Over 100 days, BBC Radio 4 set out to present, in a series of short programmes broadcast from 18 January to 22 October 2010, 'a history of the world in 100 objects'. What was noteworthy about this enterprise was the use of the indefinite article – 'a' history – as it would nowadays indeed be a little presumptuous to embark on *the* history of the world, a bold project which has nonetheless tempted historians in the not too distant past. Interestingly, all the objects selected to testify to this notional 'history of the world' come from the British Museum, a much-admired institution and seat of knowledge which was like its European and North-American counterparts in Paris, Brussels, Berlin, and New York closely associated with the many ethnographic ventures that accompanied the colonial expansion of the West in Asia, Africa, Australia, and the Americas. However ethically sensitive the museum may have subsequently become, the fact remains that many of the artefacts exhibited were dubiously acquired – indeed, some are known to have been stolen from their places of origin. I do not intend though to apportion blame here as I believe that the relation between ethnography as a discipline and the development of colonial projects in the nineteenth and twentieth centuries is not absolute.[1] Early ethnographers and travellers had also, as Johannes Fabian argues, to be 'out of their minds' and reach a type of 'ecstasis', which in many respects negated the strict positivist foundation of their nineteenth-century upbringing and its 'regime of hygiene',[2] in order to connect with hitherto completely foreign environments:

> in their first or early contacts with unfamiliar cultures, the emissaries of imperialism [...] permitted themselves to be touched by lived experiences. [...] those instances involved them in [...] moral puzzles and conflicting

demands. What I find striking [...] is that explorers frequently overcame these intellectual and existential problems by stepping outside [...] the rationalized frames of exploration, be they faith, knowledge, profit, or domination. This 'stepping outside' or 'being outside' is what I call the ecstatic.[3]

The British Museum, as any other museums created in the midst of the colonial age, bears witness to the troubled legacy of a discipline which was complicit in the essentialism of imperial projects and their pretention to classify non-European cultures along rational criteria. Indeed, ethnographic museums were set up to carry out a very didactic mission, that of reconstituting the life and the culture of the non-Western 'primitive'. Ironically, however, these public spaces were, as in the case of the Pitt Rivers Museum in Oxford or the Museum of Central Africa in Brussels – especially before their recent overhauls – often haphazardly configured and were therefore not the most persuasive examples of the scientific and taxonomical spirit that had guided earlier explorers. They were the material traces of the very conditions in which ethnographic encounters took place. These were predominantly scientific as imperial emissaries adhered to 'a "pure" science of other peoples based on the ideals of positivism';[4] but they were also 'ecstatic' and reflecting these travellers' fetishism: 'the premise of African fetishism had its counterpart in the explorer's accumulating "curios", a preoccupation that in some cases did become "fetishistic" in its obsessiveness'.[5] In this sense, ethnography and its underlying 'ecstasis' decentred the positivist and linear trajectory of the colonial project.

'A history of the world in 100 objects' is also the product of this decentring, which, as we shall see throughout this book, is reminiscent of Valentin Mudimbe's focus on historical discontinuities and his own attempt to debunk the myth of reason and cultural holism upon which the development of ethnography had been predicated. Interestingly, 'A history of the world in 100 objects' is predominantly informed by a series of objects belonging to what was once referred to as the exotic domain of Western art history and anthropology.[6] The Sudanese Slit Drum is one of those artefacts; its presence at the British Museum reflects the difficult relationship between Africa and the West. The drum originates from Central Africa, in southern Sudan, where it was revered as a sacred object symbolising the authority of a powerful Bantu chief and where it was used as a musical instrument to mark significant community events. More prosaically, it was also employed as a means of communication to transmit important messages over long distances. The drum, however, testifies to history as well as indigenous African tradition. The history of Sudan is complex and has been marked by conflicts between the Muslim North and the animist (and since colonisation increasingly Christian) South. After one of the many skirmishes between northern and southern warriors, the drum was seized in the 1870s by an Islamic chief and turned into a Muslim object – the flanks of the calf-shaped instrument being re-carved to accommodate Koranic verses. This addition altered the original tonality of the drum, which, in an ironic twist of fortune, became an emblem of the Mahdi rebellion and the short-lived Mahdi domination over Sudan in the 1880s. When Lord Kitchener successfully 'pacified' Sudan after the battle of Omdurman in 1898, the drum then became a symbol of Victorian supremacy in Eastern Africa. The Sudanese Slit Drum therefore conveys a multiplicity of meanings and resonates with conflicts cutting across the North–South axis and religious divides. The involvement of Lord Kitchener adds a geopolitical dimension to this already intricate web of memories as he is – beyond the well-documented role that he played during the First World War as his Majesty's main recruiting agent – chiefly remembered as the artisan of an African *Entente cordiale* and the settling, in the wake of the Fashoda incident (1898), of Franco-British territorial disputes in Africa. The drum therefore tells many stories and – especially in the wake of Sudan's recent partition – may yet again have other tales to tell and may even recount, to use a phrase first coined by the German historian Reinhart Koselleck, the 'futurity' of the past.[7]

V. Y. Mudimbe's treatment of Africa displays a similar 'multidirectional' quality. The adjective has been used by Michael Rothberg in *Multidirectional Memory*.[8] This book explores, via a corpus of authors and film directors such as Hannah Arendt, W. E. B. Du Bois, Aimé Césaire, Marguerite Duras, Jean Rouch, and Michael Haneke, the memory of the Holocaust in conjunction with that of decolonisation. Rothberg argues that memory is not an exclusive process. He rejects two central claims: 'that a straight line runs from memory to identity' and 'that the only kinds of memories and identities that are [...] possible are ones that exclude elements of alterity and forms of commonality with others.'[9] This non-exclusive understanding of memory and identity has been, as I shall demonstrate in this book, central to Mudimbe's thought since the end of the 1960s, a period which coincided with the emergence, or the re-assertion, of exclusive identity politics not only in sub-Saharan Africa but also in black diasporas worldwide. For Mudimbe, memories and identities are indeed negotiated at the crossroads between cultures and politics. What is true of Sudan is also true of his native Congo, a country which has, since its independence in 1960, been threatened in the geographical boundaries inherited from the former colonial regime and first delineated at the Berlin Conference in 1884–85 (*CB*, 168–71).

Mudimbe has devoted a significant portion of his research career to the study of ideologies. He is therefore aware of the elusiveness of cultural identity and memory. Places, monuments, individuals, and texts are pliable materials that can be reinvented and ascribed new meanings and functions. The premise that no archive is sacred lies at the heart of his reading and writing practice. This perspective also characterises his interpretation of colonial modernity and its real and symbolic impact on contemporary Congo. In *The Idea of Africa*, Mudimbe assesses various ways in which the Congolese space could be interpreted and linked to antagonistic memories. The approach adopted by the author is – as often in this *œuvre* infused with Sartrean themes and phraseology – phenomenological and autobiographical (see also *CG*, 35–46). He, for instance, remembers a walk that he took in Kapolowe, a small city between Likasi and Lubumbashi, in Katanga, on 30 June 1960 (Congo's Independence Day) when he was still a seminarian. What is significant here is the focus on the 'body': the author suggests that the sensorial response generated by this experience is ultimately more significant than historicist attempts to identify ruptures and discontinuities between a colonial *before* and a postcolonial *after*:

> I walked slowly. I was *in situ* and continued forward, glad to be able to name the concrete links between, on the one hand, the order imposed by the conquest and the metamorphosis of the area I was crossing and, on the other hand, the marks and signs of a past (*un avant*) which ought to be able to repeat and to recite that night their otherness, which is that of violated experiences. In the name Belgian Congo the adjective which disappeared is a symbol. The empty space which it left behind will be inscribed in the history that was just beginning. Nevertheless, it is clear that evidence of the rupture, if indeed there was one, is not to be found in the disappearance of the adjective nor in the new signs generated by its suppression. The body which lives or survives as the transcript of the metamorphosis is still that which testifies to the break. (*Idea*, 135)

Kapolowe's topographic configuration, and its planning across a North–South axis, serves as an example to illustrate the conflict of memories inherited by post-independence Congo and already experienced during the colonial period by the locals. It is also used to evoke other sites, notably Mpala and Elisabethville (Lubumbashi), where this conflict was imprinted in the very fabric of the urban topography.[10] Mudimbe remarks that all indigenous settlements, the 'centres extra-coutumiers', run by white staff and missionaries and built during the colonial era, reiterated urbanistically, as it were, the politics of conversion that was taking place in other spheres (religion, education, language policies, and labour practices). With its church, school, and workshops located at the northern end of the axis, the 'centre extra-coutumier' signified a clear rupture with the 'pagan' and pre-literate past. This sense of disjuncture with the original village, situated at the southern end, is further accentuated by the presence, between the two areas, of 'an empty space' (*Idea*, 135). This space is ambiguous because it separates but also implies the possibility of a future synthesis:

> It is neither a garden nor a forest. It is not a collection of flowerbeds, nor is it a complete disorder. It is annoying because of what it reveals: separation. It is tactical. It repeats and illustrates in a concrete manner the classic division of a colonial city, as in the case of Elisabethville: Limits-Sud Avenue. The symbolism of this distance and this separation of black and white areas seem to evoke, paradoxically, a connection between the two extremities. In other words, the south might one day become the north, which is to say that it might one day, by modelling itself on the north, reflects the order and values contained therein. We know that this is geographically impossible. But the ideology of development lies in this ambiguous space, as a dream and a challenge. (*Idea*, 135)

Colonisation and its aftermath did not create stable (pure) identities and sites of memory. The now outmoded idea of a 'clash' between 'tradition' and 'modernity' is unable to capture the complexity of the situation. Mudimbe has since the 1970s abandoned this phrase in favour of a more nuanced appraisal of memory and cultural identity. If modernity means Christianity, he contends that its emergence and development are multidirectional and non-linear. There is very concrete historical evidence to support this claim: centuries before the arrival of the White Fathers in 1879 on the western coast of Lake Tanganyika, the Kingdom of Kongo (located in West Central Africa, on an area including portions of Angola, Cabinda, the Republic of Congo, and the Democratic Republic of the Congo) was evangelised by Portuguese settlers who in 1491 renamed the capital city from Mbanza-Kongo to San Salvador.[11] With regards to the colonisation of sub-Saharan Africa by the West, he argues that it was 'isomorphic with a conversion to Christianity' (*Idea*, 118), a view that can be applied to Belgium's colonial expansion in Central Africa. This isomorphic process is, however, far from being unproblematic because evangelisation was undertaken by different religious orders such as the White Fathers, the Jesuits, the Dominicans, the Benedictines, the Scheutists, or the Redemptorists, who had divergent objectives (see *TF*, 40–41) and *modi operandi*.[12] The modernity that this ecclesiastical occupation generated is multifaceted and does not reflect the separation that traditionally prevailed between regular and secular orders:

> [T]he ordinary life of the Catholic Church in the West, at the parish level, was not in the hands of religious Orders or, to use the technical expression, of Regulars; rather, the secular clergy, the clergy who do not submit to monkish vows [...] attend to parish matters. (*Idea*, 108–09)

Paradoxically, therefore, the 'modernity' introduced in the Belgian Congo is reminiscent of a type of organisation pre-dating the French Revolution and in which regular orders were in charge of worldly affairs. Mudimbe notes that what he calls the 'Central African political nightmare' can partly be ascribed to the division, in 1911, of the Congo into ten ecclesiastical prefectures (*Idea*, 109). This focus on religion is significant, not least because the author himself was once a Benedictine seminarian. He regards the Congo as an 'interesting experiment' because '[i]ts geography had been turned into a kind of spiritual checkerboard on which each unit or square was occupied by a definite religious style' (*Idea*, 109–10). Modernity is often associated with the emergence of nationalism which, in turn, conjures up ideas of homogenisation, assimilation, and unity.[13] European colonisation of the last quarter of the nineteenth century was predicated upon an analogous set of ideas. The supposed fragmentation of African political entities was often evoked – as in, for instance, speeches by Jules Ferry or Leopold II – to legitimise colonial enterprises. Mudimbe argues that political scientists ascribe too much significance to 'tribal' (*Idea*, 109) and ethnic factors to account for the disintegration of the Congolese state. He contends that the impact of the ecclesiastical 'idiosyncrasies' mentioned above should be taken more seriously since 'most politicians of the 1960s throughout Central Africa were former seminarians' (*Idea*, 109). With regards to his native Congo, he speaks of the enduring legacy of this 'socioreligious' (*Idea*, 110) reconfiguration of the national geography and shows that some of the most influential politicians of the early 1960s – Kasa-Vubu, Albert Kalondji, and Cardinal Malula, among others – used 'to meet regularly as "former students of Scheutists" and share between them a "common" language, despite their ideological differences' (*Idea*, 110; see also *CG*, 77–78).

This explanation does not invalidate the ethnic argument – the 'invention of the Indigène'[14] – as a major factor in the making of contemporary Congo but merely demonstrates that the aforementioned 'Central African political nightmare' cannot be solely attributed to the resurgence of some pre-colonial ethnically inspired fragmentation. The religious and ethnic memories do not cancel one another. They are, to return to Rothberg's terminology, two of the different facets of a 'multidirectional memory' and, as such, are 'subject to ongoing negotiation, cross-referencing […] borrowing' and are thus 'productive and not privative'.[15] In his patient exegesis of the factors that have contributed to the *invention* of Africa, Mudimbe seldom disagrees categorically with his interlocutors but highlights, more often than not, the partial truth of their views. What is a truthful account? How can Africa be truthfully represented? These are some of the fundamental questions running through Mudimbe's work from the late 1960s to the present day, that is, the period that will be examined in this book. Between sub-Saharan Africa and its representation lies a major stumbling block or a type of disfiguring device that definitively postpones the emergence of the truth. Indeed, this 'will to truth' becomes highly questionable when, 'converted into a dominating knowledge and actualized as an imperialist project' as it invariably transforms itself into a 'will to "essentialist" prejudices, divisions, and destruction' (*Idea*, 213). This device is ideology: every textual intervention about Africa is, as he argues, ideologically driven and results – the titles of his major essays are in this respect very significant – in 'inventions', 'parables', 'fables', and' tales'. Mudimbe's critical work is primarily concerned with recovering the logic behind this complex nexus of stories about Africa, or 'knowledges', which, he remarks, 'seem to function like fiction for me' (*Idea*, 208). This is a formidably difficult task and one that has been carried out with the proverbial patience of the Benedictine seminarian that he was and has remained despite his effective dissociation with the religious order of his youth (*CG*, iii; *CB*, 125). This patient exercise is premised on the Foucault-inflected idea that knowledge has a subconscious: 'I have been trying to understand the powerful yet invisible epistemological order that seems to make possible, at a given period, a given type of discourse about Africa' (*Idea*, xiv). He remarks that the history of science describes not only 'scientific consciousness' but also recovers what escapes this consciousness: 'the influences that affected it, the implicit philosophies that were subjacent to it […] the unseen obstacles […] This unconscious is always the negative side of science – that which resists it […] or disturbs it' (*Idea*, xiv). The deciphering of the many layers underpinning this epistemological subconscious does not reveal the African *chose du texte*, for, as he would often argue, 'African discourses have been silenced radically or, in most cases, converted by conquering Western discourses' (*Idea*, xiv).

Mudimbe's *œuvre* is above all concerned with the discursive history of Africanism in France and in Belgium. Until the early years of the twentieth century, Africanism remained an amorphous and *undisciplined* field.[16] The term referred to a dispersed body of writings, ideas, and representations about sub-Saharan Africa. Africanism is therefore the African equivalent of Orientalism, as this notion was examined by Edward Said. The word 'Africanist' was indiscriminately used in relation to the accounts of early travellers, ethnographers, novelists, and painters. In Belgium, Africanism became an academic discipline in the wake of the foundation of the Museum of Tervuren in 1910;[17] in France, the creation of the 'Institut d'ethnologie' at the Sorbonne in 1925 gave a decisive impetus to the development of Africanist anthropology and to the emergence of 'Negro-African' responses in the fields of politics and culture (literature, anthropology, and philosophy). Mudimbe's use of the term, as we shall see in this book, reflects this polysemy and, what is more, is not limited to modernity as it also extends to the *longue durée*, that is, the Renaissance and the Greco-Latin Antiquity. Africanism is thus studied in its chronological, spatial, and ethnic/racial complexities. Mudimbe's approach exposes the multi-layered memory of Africanism and evokes therefore the multidirectional perspective mentioned above:

> Memories are not owned by groups – nor are groups 'owned' by memories. Rather the borders of memory and identity are jagged; what looks at first like my own property often turns out to be a borrowing or adaptation from a history that initially might seem foreign or distant. Memory's anachronistic quality – its bringing together of now and then, here and there – is actually the source of its powerful creativity, its ability to build new worlds out of the materials of older ones.[18]

Structure, Aims, and Corpus

This book charts the intellectual history of Valentin Yves Mudimbe from the late 1960s to the present day. This journey from Elisabethville/Lubumbashi to Louvain, Nanterre, and Duke University, traces Mudimbe's trajectory against major debates on decolonisation, anthropology, and postcolonial representations. This exploration of the macro-critical context in which Mudimbe's thought has unfolded underscores, via close readings of his most influential texts, the discursive strategies that he has developed to recover the epistemological basis underlying the 'invention' of past and present sub-Saharan Africa. The term 'Africanism', as referred to in the title, is used here to locate more precisely his main object of study, which is less Africa *per se* than the many discourses formulated about Africa since Antiquity. In his many books, Mudimbe has undertaken the *archaeology* of the links between colonial power and Africanist knowledge. He argues, very critically, that Africanist anthropologists were often mobilised to gather intelligence, which, ultimately, contributed to the consolidation of imperial regimes and continued to shape African consciousness after independence. Mudimbe belongs therefore to this generation of thinkers for whom Africanism was a dirty word and a discipline forever contaminated by colonial ideology. This book, however, contends that he paradoxically *can* be regarded as an Africanist of sorts or, to put it differently, that he has remained throughout his career fascinated by colonial and missionary Africanists such as Marcel Griaule,[19] Melville Herskovits, and Placide Tempels and their tendency to construct Africa from a variety of disciplinary angles. Mudimbe is difficult to categorise; his work sits at the cross-roads between several disciplines: Greco-Latin philology, history, sociology, theology, social anthropology, and philosophy. His 'undisciplined' erudition and methodological posture open up therefore the possibility of exploring, beyond ethnic divides and historical ruptures, the various memorial sites of Africanist anthropology and its more recent attempts to act as an emancipating force in sub-Saharan Africa.

There is a large body of secondary sources on Mudimbe[20] and several monographs in French by Bernard Mouralis,[21] Justin Bisanswa,[22] Jean-Christophe Kasende,[23] and Kasereka Kavwariheri.[24] This book has benefited from their perspectives, that is, their ability to expose the transgeneric coherence of Mudimbe's multifarious production (Mouralis, Kasereka, Kasende) and debunk (Bisanswa) the hagiographic attempts on the part of many readers and critics to mythologise the Congolese author. The existing literature in English is, on the other hand, not as extensive. This is a surprising fact if one considers that Mudimbe has spent nearly half of his life in the United States and that his work – its focus on unequal modes of 'production' in the field of knowledge, its exploration of the colonial archive and neo-colonial representations – resonates with analogous endeavours by critics such as Edward

Said, Homi K. Bhabha, Gayatri C. Spivak, and Dipesh Chakrabarty to 'unthink Eurocentrism'.[25] Indeed, there is for Neil Lazarus a paradox as Mudimbe enjoys 'immense prestige within *African* Studies' but 'continues to occupy only a modest status in the contiguous but relatively distinct field of *postcolonial* Studies'.[26] This lack of engagement with Mudimbe – 'his work tends to be acknowledged perfunctorily, if at all'[27] – is for Lazarus a reflection of the 'disproportionate weighting' in postcolonial studies 'towards South Asian culture and society',[28] and, I would add, towards the Caribbean (and the Maghreb) in Francophone postcolonial studies.

Mudimbe's work has nonetheless attracted the attention of many critics in the Anglo-American academia, in the form of journal articles and book chapters.[29] Although this material is mostly dispersed, there have also been, in the past twenty years, three notable attempts to reflect in book-length publications on some of the issues raised by Mudimbe's main works. Manthia Diawara edited a special issue of *Callaloo* on Mudimbe in 1991.[30] This journal issue is the first substantial scholarly overview of Mudimbe's career in English. In addition to interviews with Mudimbe (by D. A. Masolo and Faith Smith), a 'portrait' of the author (by Gaurav Desai), and a selective bibliography, it also provides close readings of his *œuvre* (by Bogumil Jewsiewicki, Kenneth Harrow, and Benetta Jules-Rosette), excerpts from *L'Écart* and *Shaba Deux* in English, and a short essay on translating Mudimbe by Marjolijn de Jager.

In 2005, Kai Kresse, the German anthropologist then based at the University of St Andrews in the United Kingdom, edited another special issue on Mudimbe for the *Journal of African Cultural Studies*.[31] The contributors to this volume were all Africanists: Kai Kresse, Louis Brenner, Wim van Binsbergen, and Neil Lazarus, who added a postcolonial twist to the discussion by suggesting, as mentioned above, the contiguity between African *and* postcolonial studies. What is noteworthy about this publication is the effort to treat Mudimbe as an object of study but also as a scholar who has developed critical (and dynamic) tools to investigate other objects of study. This tendency is most evidently pursued in Kresse's own contribution. In this article, he argues that Nicholas Brown's discussion of a didactic Swahili poem by Ahmed Sheikh Nabhany, albeit Mudimbian in its premise (that is, based on the assumption that Nabhany cannot escape a Eurocentric power-knowledge problematic) fails to register the more positive implications of Mudimbe's work, the 're-construction of an [African] epistemological framework', thereby obstructing 'the focus on the complex internal power-knowledge relationships within Africa and its multiple and multi-layered social histories'.[32]

Michael Syrotinski's *Singular Performances* (2002)[33] is predicated upon an analogous ambition to study Mudimbe's main novels and essays and 'apply' Mudimbian concepts to a contemporary corpus of African writers and film-makers such as Bernard Dadié, Ousmane Sembène, Tierno Monénembo, Véronique Tadjo, Werewere Liking, and Sony Labou Tansi. *Singular Performances* is, strictly speaking, not a book *on* Mudimbe but a study that is nonetheless overwhelmingly informed and shaped by the theoretical implications of Mudimbe's thinking, in addition to providing close readings of some of Mudimbe's essays and novels. The overall articulation of the book, which starts and ends with Mudimbe, explores the possibilities of Mudimbe's work, that is, as implied by the brief focus on Kresse's own 'application' of Mudimbian paradigms in his reading of a reading, its ability to be used as an instrument to trace the origins and multifarious manifestations of Eurocentrism, its Derridean tendency to defer meanings,[34] but also to produce an arena for the re-inscription of an African subjectivity and epistemology.

The present book, *V. Y. Mudimbe: Undisciplined Africanism*, is indebted to these earlier studies. It aims to explore the tension between Mudimbe's worldliness and critical positions; it proposes, as suggested by the abstract that follows, to approach Mudimbe as the reader, and writer, of other readers.

Chapter 1, 'Mission Impossible?', examines the relationship between Mudimbe's intellectual training among the Benedictines and his subsequent critique of the colonial and neo-colonial orders. What is at issue here is his ability to mobilise creatively the 'old' knowledge of the 'colonial library' – biblical exegesis, religious and missionary history and ethnography, and Greco-Latin philology and mythology – to deconstruct the historical and political myths that have since the Renaissance contributed to the idea of Africa *and* the construction of sectarian identity politics in contemporary Congo-Zaire. Via a selection of essays and perspectives from *L'Autre Face du royaume* (1973), *Entre les eaux* (1973), *The Invention of Africa* (1988), *Parables and Fables* (1991), *The Idea of Africa* (1994), *Les Corps glorieux* (1994), *Tales of Faith* (1997), and *Carnets de Berlin* (2006), the investigation appraises the Foucauldian strategies employed by the author to retrieve the discourses underpinning African evangelisation and the Church's relentless ambition to 'enlighten' the proverbial *Other* of Western modernity (the 'savage', the 'pagan', or the 'primitive'). By way of the famous disputation between Lévi-Strauss and Sartre with regards to the respective role and function of history and anthropology,[35] the second part of the chapter focuses on ethnic violence in Mudimbe's fourth novel, *Shaba Deux* (1989), and in his Lévi-Straussian examination of Luba mythical figures in *Parables and Fables*. The third part provides a critical overview of Mudimbe's recurrent tendency to engage with the Classics and to defend the view that Antiquity belongs as much to Africa as it belongs to the West. 'Hérodote le menteur', an essay from *L'Autre Face du royaume,* is explored to demonstrate that, fifteen years before Martin Bernal's *Black Athena* (1988), Mudimbe used a Greek text – in this case Plutarch's reception of the ancient Greek historian and ethnographer Herodotus – to show that ancient Greek literary culture was already questioning itself, and *that* is its value for Congolese modernity under Mobutu.

Chapter 2, 'The Invention of Otherness', focuses on the political context of Congo-Zaire in the period immediately after independence; it also examines V. Y. Mudimbe's career in the early 1970s and the author's creative decision to embrace abstruseness against didacticism. Part I explores the political situation that led to the creation of the Second Republic in 1965 and to the renaming of the country from 'République Démocratique du Congo' to 'République du Zaïre' in the wake of Mobutu's political programme of authenticity ('Zairianisation'). The discussion highlights the significance of the 'Manifeste de la Nsele', the party political manifesto on which Mobutu's one party system founded its legitimacy. The origin of the document is controversial and there are good reasons to believe that it was written in the first place by Mobutu's political opponent Pierre Mulélé whom Mobutu had assassinated in 1968. This would explain the socialist overtones of this document, which was universally praised for its ambition to put an end to the predatory system that had prevailed during the First Republic (1960–65). Part II is devoted to a close reading of Mudimbe's little-studied *Autour de la 'Nation': Leçons de civisme* (1972). In this collection of essays, Mudimbe, who engages here in 'scribal politics' as this phrase was developed by Chris Bongie,[36] reflects upon the emergence of a Zairian national culture from which political *praxis* would be generated as the essay can be read as an attempt, on Mudimbe's part, to explore the legacies of dialectical materialism and the advent, under the aegis of Althusser, of scientific Marxism. In this reading, I evaluate Mudimbe's essay against *Discours sur l'authenticité* (1973) by his Congolese contemporary Kutumbagana Kangafu and appraise the two authors' discussion on nation-building and the development of an autonomous cultural sphere on the basis of Jean-Luc Nancy's *The Inoperative Community* (1991).

Chapter 3, 'The West or the Rest?', focuses on the development of Mudimbe's epistemological commitment from his collections of essays in French, *L'Autre Face du royaume* and *L'Odeur du père*, and his third novel, *L'Écart*, up to the present day in the soon-to-be-published *On African Fault Lines*. Throughout his career, Mudimbe has argued that the conditions presiding over the practice and the production of knowledge in Africa and the Third World have alienated local people from their own *chose du texte* and that they therefore need to be less reliant upon the West in terms of funding, concepts, and methodologies. Part I teases out the Marxian dimension of Mudimbe's militancy and demonstrates that it is directly indebted to Sartre's various attempts in the immediate post-war period to come to terms with the racist ideologies underpinning the Holocaust and colonialism. In this discussion, special emphasis is placed on *Portrait of the Anti-Semite* (1948) as this essay can be regarded as a sort of Ur-text from which Mudimbe has been able, via concepts such as the 'look', freedom, and authenticity, to develop his own examination of African epistemological subjugation. Part II studies Mudimbe's recurrent exploration of social anthropology. It is argued that his scholarship possesses also a political and indeed an ethical dimension as he has always promoted the idea that anthropological research – in which the subject of the investigation was traditionally treated as mere data – should be conducted on a more equitable and inter-subjective basis. Mudimbe's evaluation of anthropology is examined against that of Johannes Fabian, in *Time and the Other: How Anthropology Makes its Objects* (1983), and Benoît Verhaegen, the originator of 'histoire immédiate', as they both advocate the transformation of anthropological *praxis*. Part III focuses on Geert Hofstede's *Cultures and Organizations: Software of the Mind* (2005), read by Mudimbe in his forthcoming *On African Fault Lines*, and identifies Mudimbe's attempt to connect this recent bestseller of organisational anthropology to evolutionist paradigms.

Chapter 4, 'Changing Places', is devoted to Mudimbe's crucial move to the American academia in the late 1970s. This transfer had far-reaching consequences on his work, not least because he had to change language and redefine his role as an African scholar in an academic context, which had become increasingly receptive to the 'proto-postcolonial' claims of rewriting history from its hitherto neglected ethnic and gender 'margins'. Mudimbe's deep familiarity with Foucault's thinking facilitated his introduction in this new critical arena where Foucault-friendly figures, such as Said, were not uncommon. Part I analyses *Carnets d'Amérique, septembre–novembre, 1974* (1976), a travelogue that Mudimbe produced after visiting the United States as an official emissary of the Zairian government to gather information on the pedagogical practices of some leading American universities such as Columbia and Princeton. This highly personal and subjective book can be considered as the prelude to his definitive transatlantic relocation. A mere six years after Martin Luther King's assassination, Mudimbe explores his own dependency and alienation as an African scholar, but is also eager, here and there, to register the signs of America's own racial *decolonisation* and to map out, in Harlem, Atlanta, New Orleans, and in Afro-American institutions such as Howard University (where he interviewed Léon Gontran Damas), the gradual memorialisation of African American cultures. Part II focuses on *The Invention of Africa* and teases out the Foucauldian apparatus of the essay. This critical influence is illustrated through Mudimbe's reading of pre-classical and classical artists such as Hieronymus Bosh and Pierre Paul Rubens and their respective epistemological (in)ability to accommodate similitude and difference in their representations of blackness. This indebtedness to Foucault is also examined via Mudimbe's critical appraisal of Senghor's consecration of E. W. Blyden as the precursor of negritude. Part III closely examines Foucault's 'constituent models' as developed in *The Order of Things* to account for the genesis of the human sciences in the wake of the French Revolution. These models, 'functions/norms', 'conflict/rules', and 'significations/system', are paramount as they enabled Mudimbe to conduct his survey of African 'Gnosis' in *The Invention* (from Placide Tempels, Alexis Kagame to Paulin Hountondji and Engelbert Mveng) and understand its development as a series of successive epistemological shifts.

Chapter 5, 'Independences?', considers decolonisation as a process, which started before 1960 but which, more than fifty years on, has not been completed yet in the former colonies *and* in the old *métropoles*. This last chapter assesses not so much the legacy of Mudimbe's thought as the way in which it resonates, often indirectly, with the idea that decolonisation in Africa has failed to deliver its promises. In this discussion, two sub-Saharan African thinkers from the diaspora, Achille Mbembe and Patrice Nganang, are examined as they share with Mudimbe an ability to cross the boundaries between literature, philosophy, and the social sciences and have both displayed a tendency to analyse the African present from their own autobiographical standpoints. Part I focuses on Mbembe's essay *Sortir de la grande nuit* (2010) and appraises its Fanonian/Sartrean and Mudimbian subtext, that is, its ambition to call for the emergence of a 'new' African subject who would surmount dialectically his/her present but also reflect on the 'futurity' of the past, a point also made by Mudimbe in 'Ut Recte Valeant: the Politics of Languages in Third-Century Roman Africa' (2005), which is briefly assessed here. Part II explores Nganang's *Manifeste pour une nouvelle littérature africaine* (2007) and examines the strategy that the critic chooses to adopt so as to dismiss the historicist dimension of Sartre's understanding of political and literary commitment in favour of a negative dialectics, as this notion was developed by Theodor Adorno after the Holocaust. It is here that Nganang and Mbembe overlap. Indeed, Nganang's *Manifeste* is heavily indebted to two essays previously published by Mbembe, 'African Modes of Self-Writing' (2002) and 'Necropolitics' (2003), in which it is argued that African thought (and thus Mudimbe as one of its arch-representatives) has failed, a deficiency all the more evident in the period after the Rwandan genocide (1994), to analyse the significance of the survivor figure. Part III tests this claim in two novels by Mudimbe unfolding against the backdrop of ethnic violence and heteronormative gender politics – *Entre les eaux* (1973) and *Le Bel immonde* (1976) – and provides therefore a sort of retroactive response to the attacks levelled by Nganang and Mbembe. Finally, the discussion examines Mudimbe's 'Reprendre' (*The Idea of Africa*), an essay in which he teases out attempts on the part of Congolese and African painters to offer creative examples of survivals rooted in daily practices and everyday-life violence.

I

'Mission Impossible?'

> The Egyptians who live in the cultivated parts of the country, by their practice of keeping records of the past, have made themselves much the most learned of any nation of which I have had experience. I will describe some of their habits: every month for three successive days they purge themselves, for their health's sake, with emetics and clysters, in the belief that all diseases come from the food a man eats; and it is a fact – even apart from this precaution – that next to the Libyans they are the healthiest people in the world.
>
> Herodotus[1]

V. Y. Mudimbe famously referred to Jean-Paul Sartre as 'an African philosopher' (*IoA*, 83) and a 'philosophe nègre' (*CB*, 69). This unilateral africanisation of the Paris-born phenomenologist compels the reader to pause and think about the many fault lines but also intellectual and imaginary overlaps between Africa and Europe. Where does the former start and where does the latter stop? There are of course objective geographical facts and undeniable ethnic markers to corroborate the idea that Africa and Europe are distinct entities with neatly defined boundaries. Mudimbe has, however, shown that human exchanges have the ability to upset the patient labours of geographers and cartographers (*CB*, 169–70).[2] He is interested in real maps and has devoted the bulk of his career to the notion of space and to the task of 'Mapping the Margins' (*Idea*, 72–80) and African 'beliefs' (*TF*, 72). Space, however concrete it may be, is also constructed by imaginary and discursive (and therefore largely subconscious) processes, which do not comply with the rules of physical geography. Mudimbe's geography is the 'geography of a discourse' (*IoA*, 187–200), that is, 'imaginative geography', to use a phrase coined by Gaston Bachelard[3] and subsequently used by Edward Said in his own mapping out of Orientalism.[4] This distinction between the space conjured up by imagination and discourses, on the one hand,

and 'l'espace indifférent du géomètre' [the surveyor's indifferent space][5] allows us to ask whether Mudimbe, the Congo-born author who has been shaped by a very traditional Western-style education, is not, after all, *also* a European philosopher. The investigation will rely on this premise and favour a number of texts – novels, essays, and autobiographies – where a critical engagement with European corpora is most noticeable. It will be attempted here to tease out Mudimbe's relationship to Western culture and to review the strategies that he has adopted to make undisciplined use of the 'Western library' – the Christian tradition, Africanist anthropology (the 'colonial library'), and Greco-Roman scholarship – not only to mount his critique of the West but also to propose routes out of dependency. Western culture plays therefore a very ambiguous role as it is, at the same time, crucified *and* called upon as a repository of knowledge and wisdom that will, it is hoped, facilitate the resurrection of Africa.

The first part of this chapter will interrogate Mudimbe's main essays in order to delineate the way in which he has accounted for the role of Christianity in the making of sub-Saharan African modernity; in the second part, the focus will move onto *Shaba Deux*, a novel in which the violated body of the female narrator is used to symbolise Congolese chauvinism and, by analogy, the devastating effects of ethnic prejudices and violence in a war-stricken Katanga; I shall then examine, via Lévi-Strauss's reading of Sartre's *Critique of Dialectical Reason* in *The Savage Mind*, the strategies employed by Mudimbe to accommodate myths and history in order to excavate, from Luba mythology (and from *Une Bible noire*[6]), a Luba-Katanga/Kasai historiography; finally, the analysis will shift to Mudimbe's appropriation of Greek myths and historical culture, and more specifically of Herodotus, to comment on the production of *true* historical accounts in Antiquity and *in the present day*.

A Christian Library

The Christian faith – explored for its own sake but also, as suggested by Wim van Binsbergen, as a means of 'autobiographical self-definition'[7] – is one of the most enduring concerns of Mudimbe's writing,[8] and one, as we shall see here, which should not be limited to the last two hundred years:

> Three historical waves initiated three different Christianities: first, the conversion of North East Africa from the apolostic era and since the sixth century and their relation to Islam. The second wave, which began in the

fifteen and sixteenth century, parallels European imperialism; and finally, the nineteenth century, the period of conquering colonial Christianity.[9]

The ubiquity of the faith should not surprise as missionary thought and action had a profound effect on the development of early modern and modern colonialism in sub-Saharan Africa and elsewhere and 'against the apparent fragility of oral traditions [...] have affected almost all social structures'.[10] The circumstances under which the Belgian Congo came into being offer in this respect an interesting example because missionary orders such as the White Fathers, Scheutists, Redemptorists, Capucins, Jesuits, Trappists, Dominicans, and, of course, Benedictines (*Idea*, 108; *TF*, 40) were given a great deal of autonomy by Leopold II in the early days of the conquest and were able until the independence and after to retain a predominant role in the field of education.[11] The multifarious overlaps between evangelisation, colonisation, education, and knowledge production about Africa, notably in social and cultural anthropology, constitute Mudimbe's main field of investigation. In his numerous studies, explorers, colonial administrators, Christian missionaries, and anthropologists are often (but not always as will be shown) treated as interchangeable figures, that is, as spokespersons of a system whose rules lie hidden in the epistemological unconscious of the West: 'With a *bel ensemble*, missionaries, anthropologists, and colonizers expounded means and techniques of changing the African context and transforming it according to both Western and Christian standards' (*P&F*, 32) and he notes that in this process 'God's desire for the conversion of the world' is understood 'in terms of cultural and socio-political regeneration, economic progress and spiritual salvation' (*IoA*, 47). For this reason, he has consistently defended the idea that professional ethnographers and Christian missionaries did belong to the same archaeological milieu, shared analogous conditions of possibility, and fashioned 'an idea of Africa' that was more revealing of the observers than of the 'objects' under their scrutiny. His analysis of imperialism over the *longue durée* is motivated by the ambition to appraise the effects of colonial legacies on contemporary Africa in order to comprehend the mechanisms that have presided until today over the invention of the African Other. The Church, as the first global agency of modern times, is ascribed a major role in this 'othering' process.

Mudimbe's exploration of the impact that the Church has had over Africa and former colonies in Latin America rests upon the tripartite segmentation of historical time (Renaissance, Classical age, and modernity) that Michel Foucault had developed in *Les Mots et les choses*.

This said his examination is not consistently Foucauldian inasmuch as he is of the view that from the Renaissance until the 1950s the Church has remained doggedly focused on the dissemination of the faith. There is therefore a tendency in these analyses to favour epistemological continuity over sudden and radical ruptures. Mudimbe is therefore using Edward Said's less historical model of Orientalism with Foucault's brand of historicism. This does not mean, however, that Mudimbe does not register in this very long historical period subtle changes in the way in which Christian clerics have adapted their *modus operandi* to increase the number of worshippers in Europe's newly conquered colonial dominions and indigenise biblical messages (*IoA*, 44–64). The emergence of the Other in the field of the Same did not rely on one single logic that mechanically reproduced itself over all perceptual, cognitive, and material areas. Mudimbe shows, by way of Margaret Hodgen,[12] that the first *feitiços* brought back to Europe by Portuguese sailors in the late fifteenth century were, by and large, considered as culturally neutral and were not immediately perceived within the boundaries of a dualistic logic: 'Because of their shapes and styles, sometimes a bit terrifying, they account for the mysterious diversity of the Same' (*IoA*, 10). This inclusive gesture, and the belief that human differences were the many facets of God's image, is an application of Foucault's intuition in his *Histoire de la folie à l'âge classique* regarding the status of madness before the 'Great Confinement'. Mudimbe, in line with Foucault's idea that the Classical age was marked by an epistemological rupture (captured, according to E. C. Eze, by the publication of Georg Hornius's first ethnic world atlas in 1653[13]) adds that the perception of the *feitiços* changed over time and that they became the expression of an *Other* aesthetics: 'it is not until the eighteenth century that, as strange and "ugly" artefacts, they really enter into the frame of African art' (*IoA*, 10).

On the other hand, Mudimbe contends that the logic behind the evangelisation of Africa and the Americas crystallised earlier on and acquired *fairly* definite contours at the age of the great discoveries. The need for imperial expansion was reflected by an ambition to propagate the faith and, over time, the two objectives became indistinguishable. As new territories were annexed in the new world, the papacy, in a famous bull (*Inter Coetera*, 1493) demanded 'that barbarous nations be overthrown and brought to the faith itself' (*Idea*, 30; see also *OP*, 106; *IoA*, 45; and *CB*, 107). The territories inhabited by pagans were declared '*terra nullius*', or no man's land, a concept, which, as Mudimbe explains, gave the right to Spanish and Portuguese settlers 'to dispossess [...] non-Christians of all their goods (mobile and immobile) [...] to invade and conquer these peoples' lands, to expel them from it, and, when necessary, to fight them and subjugate them in a perpetual servitude' (*Idea*, 33). This basic opposition between Christians and pagans (later civilised and primitives), as Mudimbe argues, would in the next centuries, in fact until the interwar period, underpin the relationship between the West and its colonies and provide a justificatory basis for the indigenous populations' concrete but also moral, psychological, and epistemological expropriations.

This last suggestion is nonetheless nuanced and substantiated by a number of concrete case studies demonstrating that behind this very real continuum, which constituted the common horizon of European racism for more than 400 years, Christianisation was also shaped by circumstantial factors, regional conditions, and time-specific singularities. In *The Invention*, he shows that Christian evangelists in Africa, whether they were Westerners or Africans, submitted their missionary vocation to the 'authrority of the truth', that is, 'a normative discourse already given, definitely fixed, clearly meant in "a vital connection between Christianity and Western culture as a whole"' (*IoA*, 47). Via three representative figures from *Ancien Régime* to the period immediately preceding African decolonisation, Mudimbe illustrates that, although missionaries invariably considered themselves as agents of a superior civilisation and envoys of God in not yet fully Christianised realms, their ecclesial *praxis* went through a number of significant epistemological transformations. The first cleric is the Italian seventeenth-century Catholic priest Giovanni Romano. Romano contributed, as shown by Elisabeth Mudimbe-Boyi,[14] to the evangelisation of the kingdom of Kongo from 1645 onwards and produced a relation of his experiences among the newly converted noblemen of the Kongo royal court and the mass of local pagans. Romano's stance illustrates the fact that no blanket theory can fully account for the encounters between Westerners and their Others. Indeed, his attitude does not quite comply with the papal instruction mentioned earlier but rather confirms (cautiously) the epistemological segmentation conceived by Foucault. Mudimbe implies here that the notion of 'Classical Age' (or 'Age of Reason') cannot be understood too rigidly: Romano, a seventeenth-century man, operates as a pre-classical evangelist as his style is said to be reminiscent of that of Saint Boniface who spread Christianity in the Frankish Empire in the middle of the eighth century (*IoA*, 48). His understanding of Kongo society is mediated through feudal socio-economic categories: 'dukes', 'earls', 'barons', and, at the other end of this strictly dualistic social configuration, 'poor and pagan people' (*IoA*, 48). In his ethnographic descriptions, Romano does not use derogatory terms to account for local mores and practices, which are 'neither bizarre nor curious' (*IoA*, 48) but rather located, like the *feitiços* referred to before, within the human possibilities as permitted by divine creation. If Romano is determined to achieve conversion and eradicate the presence of 'Satan' in the African 'field of Christianity', Mudimbe also argues that at the heart of the cleric's conviction 'lies the desire for the universality of God's law' (*IoA*, 49). Paganism, rather than blackness *per se*, thus, is the issue around which Romano's 'Missionary Theology of Salvation' (*IoA*, 53) is articulated. The term 'pagan', as Christopher Miller argues about Rimbaud's 'Mauvais sang' (in *Une Saison en enfer*) is ambiguous but conveys an open-endedness that reflects Romano's conception of God's creation in Europe and elsewhere:

> The word has tended to project the image of an Other within the realm of the same, of a European having all beliefs or no beliefs but understood as being *prior* to true belief in a monotheistic god. The pagan [...] is not 'stuck' in a 'perpetual childhood' [...] he is on his way to conversion.[15]

The second cleric considered in this discussion is Samuel Ajayi Crowther, a native of Yorubaland, who, in addition to being a noted classicist and linguist,[16] became in 1864 the first black Anglican bishop of Nigeria. His relation to paganism rests upon a much more racially based set of principles than Romano's. Mudimbe contends that Crowther is the 'sign of an episteme' (*IoA*, 49). By this he means that he wholeheartedly embraced the nineteenth-century worldview with regards to racial hierarchies and subordinate status of Africa and adopted, in his appraisal of future converts, a tendency to conflate ideas of 'paganism, nakedness, and cannibalism' (*IoA*, 49; see also *P&F*, 37–38). Placide F. Tempels is the third ecclesiastical model presented here. Like Crowther and Romano, the Belgian Franciscan, who from the 1930s worked among the Baluba-Katanga,[17] is shown to be the product of very specific conditions of possibility, those of Europe in the interwar period. Tempels was of the view that 'Christianity is the only possible consummation of the Bantu ideal' (*IoA*, 54) and argued, a point that would later outrage thinkers such as Aimé Césaire[18] and Paulin Hountondji,[19] that he, rather than the Bantu themselves, was equipped to expose the features of Bantu ontology.[20] Although primarily driven by the 'authority of the truth' and a 'dualistic anthropology' (*IoA*, 53), his vocation reflects, at the same time, the epistemological shift that revolutionised missionary and anthropological practices after the First World War. In 1919, the papacy published the *Maximum Illud* encyclical letter in which it was argued that Catholic evangelisation in overseas territories had entered a new phase and that European missionaries needed now to focus their energy on calling up vocations among indigenous converts in order to lay down the foundations of future local clergies.[21] This new approach was premised on the idea that the pagan was in actual facts not as 'Other' as it had originally been thought. Interestingly, Pope Benedict XV, the author of this encyclical, encouraged missionaries to learn local languages and to identify in autochtonous religions cornerstones on which indigenised versions of Christianity would be able to be developed. The French phrase 'pierres d'attente de la foi' [stepping stones of the faith] captures this objective of discovering in African religions – 'African beliefs' was the preferred (and derogatory) designations (*IoA*, 76) – the traces of what Wilhelm Schmidt – linguist, anthropologist, Roman Catholic priest, and founder of *Anthropos* – famously called *Urmonotheismus* (primitive monotheism).[22] Schmidt contended that monotheism had constituted the first forms of religion and human civilisations had only in subsequent phases turned to polytheism. According to Mudimbe, Schmidt's concept gave legitimacy 'to what was formerly called pagan and polytheist belief' and opened up the possibility of reconciling God with the gods:

> One of the major assumptions of Schmidt's method is the existence of a universal theory or 'philosophy' that each human community expresses in its own way and according to its own needs The philosophy would be always and everywhere particular in its religious, cultural, and historical manifestations, but universal in its essence. (*IoA*, 58)

The idea was seized upon by missionaries such as Tempels, who in the wake of *Maximum Illud* endeavoured to excavate and, as it were, resurrect the dormant Christian God from the Bantu pantheon and system of thought:

> All that Christianity is about is to find our *bumuntu* (being man). We shall find the *bumuntu* if we realize that it is based on three aspirations: *uzima* (life-force), *uzazi* (fecundity), and *mapendo* (love-unity). Having found our *bumuntu* we shall be able to transcend all the barriers that separate husband from wife, young from old, white from black, Luba from Lunda, priests from believers – we all shall be 'one thing', *kintu kimoja*.[23]

This discursive shift, which coincides with the emergence of more relativist practices in anthropology and the birth of written literature from sub-Saharan Africa, prefigures decolonisation (*P&F*, 34–35; *CG*, 55). Ironically, it also marks the return of the early modern attitude towards paganism: however differently it may express itself, it remains the singular and local manifestation of a higher, that is, universal, truth that the Christian God is thought to embody: 'The "pagan culture" is considered and analysed as an abandoned field in which God's signs already exist' (*IoA*, 56). This is where the major divergence between Crowther and Tempels lies. Whereas the former was epistemologically linked to the evolutionary practices and principles of the 'Missionary Theology of Salvation' and contributed thus to the 'confinement' (Foucault) of African pagans, Tempels embodies the 'Theology of Indigenization' (or 'inculturation'[24]) and the systematic development of a local clergy conceived as the accommodation of local signs within a Christian framework: 'The emphasis he gave to Bantu ontology […] means that he had faith in the possibility of bringing about a "new Christian civilization" without destroying Bantu values or their underlying major principles' (*IoA*, 53).[25]

These three individuals, Romano, Crowther, and Tempels, are treated here as the spokespersons of time-specific discourses. By way of a methodology, which largely relies on Foucault's archaeology, Mudimbe privileges therefore subconscious processes over subjective agency. Nonetheless, it is important to add that his excavation of theological and missionary discourses focuses, sometimes affectionately, on the input and significance of specific voices. Mudimbe often goes beyond the aridity of epistemological examinations. This applies, for instance, to Tempels. He is presented here as the 'sign of an episteme' but, on the other hand, Mudimbe cannot help to comment, often admiringly, on the bravery of the Flemish Franciscan who, after the publication of *La Philosophie bantoue*, was threatened by the Bishop of Katanga Jean-Félix de Hemptinne and faced the possibility of excommunication, a measure that was ultimately not applied (*IoA*, 137). Tempels is an ambiguous figure. He is the representative of the colonial order but his *Bantu Philosophy* also prefigures the reflection conducted later by Central African thinkers and theologians such as Alexis Kagame,[26] Vincent Mulago,[27] Fabien Eboussi-Boulaga,[28] Oscar Bimwenyi,[29] John Mbiti,[30] F.-M. Lufuluabo,[31] Meinrad Hebga,[32] Engelbert Mveng,[33] and, of course, Mudimbe himself, who all, sometimes ambiguously as in the case of Kagame and Mulago, broke away with the principles of the 'Theology of Indigenization' to advocate the necessity of a 'Theology of Incarnation', that is, an 'adaptation theology' driven by an ambition to 'raise the African Deus Absconditus [hidden God] to his fulfilment into the Deus Christianorum' [God of the Christians] (*P&F*, 13–14):

> The emphasis is [...] put on new premises: négritude, blackness, African heritage and experience. It tends to present conversion in terms of critical integration into Christianity; that is [...] asserting cultural autonomy and [...] defining Christianization as a way of accomplishing in Christ a spiritual heritage authentically African. (*IoA*, 60)

In *The Surreptitious Speech*, and in many other essays,[34] Mudimbe talks of 'the ambiguity of Tempels' *Bantu Philosophy* vis-à-vis the colonial system' (*Speech*, xiv). This said, Tempels would have, in the main, subscribed to the objectives listed in this definition of the 'Theology of Incarnation'. It is indeed important to remember that *Bantu Philosophy* was published by Présence africaine (in French and in English) and that the Jamaa movement, a hybrid European-African Church set up in the 1950s, was initiated as a response to Tempels's teaching in the mining region of Kolwezi in South Katanga.[35] Johannes Fabian argues that in the atmosphere of 'estrangement', 'alienation', and 'social/cultural anomy' that characterised daily life in Black industrial areas in the last years of colonial rule, Tempels's message offered the hope 'for a better world'[36] akin to those disseminated by charismatic and revolutionary (anti-colonial) movements such as Kitawala and Kimbanguism,[37] and Pierre Landu's (failed) attempt, in the novel *Entre les eaux*, to prove that there is only one God and that the Christian God is not white (*Entre*, 95).

Men such as Tempels have never stopped intriguing Mudimbe because they are dialectical figures who cannot be easily labelled away: 'Tempels' *Bantu Philosophy* (1959) achieves and negates Lévy-Bruhl' (*P&F*, 11). Tempels arrived in Katanga in 1933 and left in 1962. The ambivalence resides in the fact that the Flemish missionary gradually moved away from the prejudices of his education and became an African thinker of sorts. His active involvement in 'adaptation theology', in the 'Decentering of God's Signs' (*P&F*, 15–31), in an African context enabled him to transcend racial differences. In this respect Mudimbe argues that the distinction of speeches from a geographical perspective – 'speech from without and speech from within' – is no longer pertinent to account for the reinvention of African Christianity in the years 1940–60 (*P&F*, 14). He notes the ironic attempt, on the part of the Congolese theologian Vincent Mulago (to whom *Parables and Fables* is dedicated), 'to bring back to an orthodox line the spiritual experience of the controverted

Jamaa movement created by Tempels' (*P&F*, 60). Tempels's trajectory, he is between languages, between Katanga and Europe, during colonial rule but also after (he died in 1977), mirrors in many respects Mudimbe's own trajectory. Beyond the very important theological points that the references to Tempels generate, his presence in Mudimbe's essays often possesses a quasi-autobiographical dimension, an argument, which can, for that matter, be extended to other ecclesiastical figures explored in his *œuvre* such as Victor Roelens, Bernard Mels in *The Idea of Africa* (*Idea*, 110–129; *TF*, 47–51), and Alexis Kagame in *Les Corps Glorieux* (*CG*, 49–51; *TF*, 135–45).

Born in 1941 in the southern Katangese mining city of Jadotville (now Likasi), where his father was a skilled worker at the Union Minière du Katanga, Mudimbe was from the age of ten educated by European Benedictine missionaries first in Kakanda and then in Mwera, near Lubumbashi (*P&F*, 94; *TF*, 48–49). As a *de facto* member of the *évolué* class, he was destined to embrace priesthood, one of the very few prestigious careers available to natives, at a time when the higher education sector for Congolese was still in its infancy.[38] In 1959, he became under the name of Frère Mathieu (*CG*, 25) a Benedictine monk in the monastery of Gihindamuyaga in Rwanda: 'I was then almost eighteen, completely Francophonized, submitted to Greco-Roman values and Christian norms' (*P&F*, 94; see also *TF*, 48–50). In 1961, the year after the independence, he returned to secular life as a student at the University of Kinshasa and 'fifteen years later, after several turns in my life, I was serving as the dean of Faculty of Philosophy and Letters at the Lubumbashi campus of the national University of Zaire' (*P&F*, 94–95). Behind the apparent rupture that this mini biography suggests – Mudimbe left, however, Rwanda because he was outraged by the 'scandalous' attitude adopted by the Catholic Church with regards to the ethnic conflict between the Hutus and the Tutsis (*CG*, 75) – the story of his return to secular life is also one of continuity. The French word 'clerc' springs to mind as it both means 'cleric' (in the religious sense) *and* intellectual (scholar and learned), as in Julien Benda's famous *La Trahison des clercs*, subsequently translated as *The Treason of the Intellectuals*.[39] In this passage from religious to secular life, Mudimbe remained a *clerc* – Wim van Binsbergen very aptly talks of his 'clerical intellectualism'[40] – and has since this moment been conscious of the fact that the learned professor will never be able to part from Frère Mathieu and suppress the *rule* of his youth and his former masters' daily injunction: '*Ora et Labora*' [pray and work] (*CG*, 15; *CB*, 125).

Shaba Deux

Mudimbe's own attempt to explore the question 'suis-je, vraiment, un lien entre le passé africain et la modernité de l'Europe chrétienne?' [am I, really, a link between African past and the modernity of Christian Europe?] (*CG*, 54) is also at the centre of *Entre les eaux* and *Shaba Deux: Les carnets de Mère Marie-Gertrude*. The former is better known as it has been translated into English[41] and examined by a number of critics.[42] The latter, on the other hand, has not benefited from the same exposure, particularly in the English-language scholarship,[43] although Michael Syrotinski has provided, by way of a comparison with *Le Bel immonde*, an analysis of the gender politics underpinning the novel.[44] Indeed, via a focus on the lesbian subtext of these two novels, Syrotinski demonstrates that Mudimbe's exploration of epistemic violence – Africa, as Europe's invented, 'primitive', and 'abject' 'body' – is given new expression here and opens up the possibility of positing homoerotic desire as a practice, which destabilises 'the socially constructed contours of the allegedly "natural" body'.[45] I shall return to this issue in Chapter 5 in my own reading of *Le Bel immonde*.

Both novels focus on Catholic figures: Pierre Landu, a priest, in *Entre les eaux* and a Franciscan nun, Mère Marie-Gertrude, in *Shaba Deux*. Beyond this common dimension, the two books are very different. *Entre les eaux* is, as will be shown again in Chapter 5, rooted in real historical events and depicts the political turmoil brought about by armed rebellions during the transition from the First to the Second Congolese Republic. The book, however, presents itself above all as the illustration, through fictional material, of a thesis, that is, Landu's *bad faith*, ineffectual commitment, and inability to choose between Jesus and Marx. Landu appears as the West's 'being-for-others', a category used by Sartre in *L'Être et le néant*,[46] and then later in more overtly political texts such *Réflexions sur la question juive*[47] and 'Orphée noir'[48] to describe the way in which the 'look' congeals and reified identities. Landu's Weltanshauung has been shaped by the Catholic Church. This condition blinds him and, although he is very aware of his situation, he cannot escape, in the same way as Mudimbe is not really able to move away from Frère Mathieu, from what he *is* for the others. He is the black priest wearing white masks and every attempt to redefine his role is caught up in the vicious circle created by the Western-style education of which he is the most accomplished product as he holds a doctorate in theology from the pontifical Angelicum University. The book is peppered with cultural references – Gentile Bellini's and Hieronymus Bosch's art, Mozart, Bach, Miguel Hernández's poetry, European mystics – which indicate that Landu's grasp of Africa and endeavours to reach his fellow Africans to fight the Church's 'injustice institutionnalisée' (*Entre*, 14) is forever contaminated and hindered by this culture of adoption. Significantly, he admits not to be able to contemplate God but through 'les vitraux des cathédrales européennes' [the stained glass windows of European cathedrals] (*Entre*, 96).

Even though the two novels are very close from a structural point of view, notably with regards to the use of very subjective narrative voices interweaving present and past events via a complex network of flashbacks,[49] Marie-Gertrude is an altogether different character as her commitment is more clearly identifiable and Kavwahirehi is right to argue that the distance between *Entre les eaux* and *Shaba Deux* reflects the passage from 'la mauvaise foi à l'authenticité' [bad faith to authenticity].[50] This is not to say that she does not share traits with Landu as she often doubts about the solidity of her faith and cannot suppress a deep sense of guilt and helplessness, neatly captured by the implicit comparison that she establishes between her own fate and that of Jean-Baptise Clamence in Camus's *La Chute* (*SII*, 120). As a nurse and a Franciscan, she is, however, better equipped than Landu, who often retains the stiffness of an allegory, to serve the disenfranchised, poor, and sick members of her local community during a short-lived but brutally repressed civil war in Kolwezi (Katanga/Shaba). The form of the novel, a series of diary entries from 28 May to 29 June, contributes to reducing the distance between the readers and Marie-Gertrude who is the first-person narrator of a story, which is also *her* story, a very significant point since the novel explores the possibility, as indicated by the author in the preface, of rewriting, from the perspective of the 'sans-pouvoir' [powerless] (*SII*, 10), the sequence of historical events that led to the Shaba II crisis in 1978. The constant shift from daily-life issues to philosophical, theological, and literary digressions is reminiscent of Mudimbe's own style in his autobiographies, *Carnets d'Amérique*, *Les Corps glorieux*, and *Carnets de Berlin*. Marie-Gertrude, however, does not conclude her story as she is abruptly removed and silenced by inquisitive soldiers from the national army. Her final entry is followed by an 'épilogue' (151–52) in which the reader is informed that after leaving the monastery on 30 June for what seemed a routine administrative matter, her horribly mutilated body was found in the local river.

It is probable that this novel, which was written at the end of the

1970s but only came out in 1989 when Mudimbe had relocated in the United States, would not have been allowed to be distributed and sold in Mobutu's Zaire, had it been released after the Shaba II events. The narrative presents itself as an indictment of ethnic violence. It loosely chronicles the sinister role that the national army played, with the support of foreign troops from France and Belgium, to manipulate regional differences in order to keep the upper hand and defeat the Katangese insurgents during the Shaba II operation. Despite the author's initial disclaimer in the 'Avertissement' that the novel is an 'invention' (*SII*, 9), this book, much more explicitly so than in Mudimbe's other three novels, is set against the backdrop of recognisable historical events. Nearly thirty years after the independence of the Congo, Mudimbe reopens the issue of Zaire's national unity and hopes that his own 'invention' will have the power of challenging the 'fables' that have been spread in the Congolese savannah to uphold 'l'histoire des puissants' [the history of the powerful] and the 'immodestie diabolique des politiques' [the diabolical immodesty of politicians] (*SII*, 9–10). Marie-Gertrude's Franciscan monastery is used here to very good effect to symbolise the nation, the threat of partition, and the role of prayers, religious meditation, theological thought (and by analogy scholarship) in times of war and political unrest.

Marie-Gertrude, as a character, is employed to conduct a reflection upon the links between religion and human suffering. By extension, she appears also as a narrative ploy to explore Mudimbe's own predicament as an intellectual *and* an African. The novel exposes therefore the extent to which prayers, theological, and philosophical contemplation have a real place in areas such as Central Africa where the rule of law has been suspended, where a permanent state of exception has become the rule, where the neo-colonial 'sovereign' and his subalterns, as in Achille Mbembe's 'Aesthetics of Vulgarity', has a right to abuse and kill,[51] and where, crucially, human existence has been reduced to a fight for survival and a crude choice between 'bare' life and death.[52] This question haunts Marie-Gertrude and is constitutive of her ambiguity and recurring hesitations between the contemplative and secular requirements of her vocation as a Franciscan. She oscillates between the figures of 'Marie' (contemplation) and 'Marthe' (action) and although she accepts that her calling rests upon an equilibrium between the two she is of the view that in some critical circumstances one has, in order to contribute to the survival of one's community, to *choose* (the alternative to this would be 'bad faith') to serve others and fight for their lives (*SII*, 35). In the midst of the crisis, she is paradoxically ordered to look after the convent library and is reduced to wipe dust off bookshelves and 'ordonner des objets de luxe lorsque je pourrais [...] sauver la vie de quelques hommes' [catalogue luxury items when I could save the lives of a few men] (*SII*, 77). This passage sums up Marie-Gertrude's dilemma as it questions the relevance and the usefulness of scholarship (symbolised here by books) in the face of death and human destruction. Via this character, Mudimbe, in an act of self-critique announcing Patrice Nganang's assault on the 'patience of philosophy' (see Chapter 5), seems to doubt the significance of his life-long determination to explore the 'colonial library'. Whilst war is raging in the outside world, Marie-Gertrude compares her retreat in the peaceful environment of the library to 'une étrange obscénité' [strange obscenity] (*SII*, 77–78).

If Landu appeared as a voice to denounce the ethnocentric arrogance of the Church (and hence of Western culture as a whole), Marie-Gertrude, for her part, is driven by an ambition to bring down scholars from their pedestals – she says that she is a 'fausse intellectuelle' (*SII*, 39) – in order to promote resistance from below and a return to a type of faith closer to the needs of her indigenous parishioners. Her fleeting references to *Vie du père Lebbe*[53] (*SII* 27, 29), a book on the life of a Belgian missionary whose work was the major inspiration behind *Maximum illud*, demonstrates her commitment to the indigenisation/incarnation of Catholicism. Frédéric Lebbe, who worked as a Lazarist father in China from the beginning of the twentieth century to 1940,[54] took the Chinese citizenship towards the end of his life and was throughout his apostolate an indefatigable advocate of the creation of a local clergy and of the sinicisation of Catholic rites. Father Lebbe's action symbolises therefore the ability of *some* clerics to transcend racial and cultural differences, to take on board local variations, and reject dogmatism in favour of an everyday appropriation of the faith by local Christians. Her quasi dismissal of Eboussi-Boulaga – she argues that *La Crise du muntu* is 'trop difficile pour moi' [too difficult for me] and decides to return it to the library (*SII*, 69) – is in this respect somewhat surprising as the Cameroonian theologian has been one of the foremost analysts of the inculturation of Christianity in Africa. In *Christianity without Fetishes*,[55] he argues that African Christianity needs to free itself from the 'fetishes', used here metaphorically as a synonym for ideas or worldviews, produced in the West and transposed in Africa. This point coincides with Mudimbe's critique of 'adaptation theology' – it remains ethnocentric and often fails to be a 'theology of incarnation dominated by the notion of the uniqueness of each human experience' (*P&F*, 67) – and, by analogy, with his examination of Africa's epistemological subservience.⁵⁶ Interestingly, *Christianity without Fetishes* is also, as indicated by the subtitle of the essay, an endeavour to 'recapture' Christianity. This objective overlaps with Mudimbe's many attempts to *reprendre* (reprise, re-appraise)⁵⁷ what has in African religious, artistic, and epistemological manifestations been captured by Western rules, canons, and procedures but also, as indigenisation is an inevitable consequence, what has been recaptured, displaced and bricolaged by local imaginations and practices through a 'kind of performative reeinscription [...] that is, an activity that is both singular and reduplicative, that both takes up again an interrupted tradition and also reworks it within a contemporary sociopolitical context'.⁵⁸ Marie-Gertrude's reference to Father Lebbe's work suggests that she subscribes to the idea that the universality of the Christian message does not imply uniformity of rites. Her decision to return Eboussi-Boulaga's essay to the library indicates that she has little time for the luxury goods of contemporary African philosophy. Her thoughts are elsewhere and, true to the Franciscan tradition, she admits that her heroes in real life are 'les pauvres' [the poor] (*SII*, 56) and martyrs and mystics such a Joan of Arc, Teresa of Avila, and Sister Anwarite (*SII*, 56),⁵⁹ who, in the face of persecution, accepted to sacrifice their lives.⁶⁰

Marie-Gertrude's convent is also, as mentioned earlier, a metaphor for the Congolese nation and its endemic divisions. The civil war provokes the gradual disintegration of the community and leads to her assassination, which symbolically takes place on the anniversary of independence, an ironic reversal if one considers that women figures were often used to symbolise the nation in anti-colonial struggles.⁶¹ Marie-Gertrude's presence in the local community and allegiance to the Church is a reminder of the complexity of modern Congo. The subtle differences existing between the different missionary orders, metaphorically hosted at the end of the novel under one single roof (and under Marie-Gertrude's precarious authority), suggest the idea that the religious dimension needs to be given as much weight as gender, racial, and ethnic arguments in the examination of Congolese history (*SII*, 145, 148). Marie-Gertrude is very aware of her skin colour, feels objectified (in a Sartrean sense) by her white sisters' gaze – she is 'la petite négresse du groupe' [the group's little negress] (*SII*, 40) – but she is also conscious that the notion of race is one of the elements among other no less significant factors that defines her as an African today. This recognition

'Mission Impossible?'   31

that race is not the only prism through which one's position in the world can be examined is also to be found in Mudimbe's posture as a reader and interpreter of texts. The many detours that he adopts in his essays are signs of his openness and refusal to be pigeonholed as a black philosopher. It is also, ultimately, a position adopted in the name of intellectual integrity as notions of races, in the context of the decolonisation of Congo, were invariably exploited to fabricate exclusive theories, *fables*, *tales*, taxonomic tables, and 'cannibalist farces' (*BI*, 203), such as that of authenticity and zairianisation (see Chapter 2) developed in the early years of Mobutu's rule. Mudimbe, close to Mabika Kalanda's *La Remise en question*,[62] argues that attempts to decolonise knowledge, but also mentalities and prejudices, must be predicated upon a critical interrogation of all values, whether expressed by Africans, Westerners, colonialists, and advocates of authenticity (*IoA*, 167–69; *P&F*, 47).

Une Bible noire

Mudimbe's examination of *Une Bible noire* in 'Genesis and Myth' (*P&F*, 86–123) bears witness to this exegetic openness, off-beat style, and ability to move away from dualistic categories and to salvage from oblivion sections of the colonial library. Published in 1973, this book rests upon ethnographic data collected among Luba people by Fourche and Morlighem, two Belgian amateur anthropologists, in the Kasai province from 1923 to 1947 (*P&F*, 93). The interesting fact here is the delay between the time when the fieldwork was carried out during the colonial period and the publication of the book, after the decolonisation of Africa *and* anthropology. Mudimbe identifies the methodological flaws of the study and regrets that the two authors partly failed to expound in greater depth the context in which they operated, the type of relationship they established with their Luba informants, and the strategies used to transcribe the interviews (*P&F*, 100), even though he is quick to add that the scientific credibility of anthropological work cannot always be guaranteed by self-analyses about fieldwork (*P&F*, 101). He is also suspicious of 'the rigorous completeness of the narrative and its intellectual systematicity' (*P&F*, 100). Besides, he contends that, however thoroughly the study may have been conducted, it 'obeys the authors' authority' (*P&F*, 105), remains a 'reconstruction', a '*patched* narrative', a 'translation' underpinned by a 'silent grid' and resulting from 'an elaborate work of intellectual rearrangement […]

of the primordial discourse' (*P&F*, 104). The argument is typically Mudimbian (but also, as will be shown in Chapter 5, inspired by Michel de Certeau's opposition between 'place and 'space'[63]) and reflects the epistemological foundation of his analytical approach.[64] His critique of the *Bible noire* is nonetheless relative and is certainly not final as he argues that the two authors' achievement is in fact 'remarkable' (*P&F*, 106) and can be, in terms of quality and reception, compared to the works of towering figures such as Leo Frobenius, Marcel Griaule, and Tempels who all operated during or immediately after the interwar period (*P&F*, 101, 106). In this assessment, Mudimbe argues that it would be unfair to reproach 'an old man' – he uses the singular because Fourche died many years before the publication – for remaining faithful to the methods and techniques of his time' (*P&F*, 101). This last point is expressed to pre-empt the repetition with regards to the *Bible noire* of the 'dishonest' critiques to which Griaule's work had been exposed – he talks in this respect of 'Griaule-bashing' (*P&F*, 101) – and the allegations that his 'translation' of the Dogon myths had simply been a 'lie' rather than an 'arrangement' (*P&F*, 101).

The *Bible noire* is a translation, that is, a new text, which does not reproduce the pre-text. Mudimbe shows that its production is reliant upon a logic of appropriation/re-appropriation as described by Michel de Certeau in the introduction of *The Practice of Everyday Life* whereby consumers and users of cultural goods and services are described as creative and *inventive* agents of a 'hidden' '*poiēsis*'. Certeau uses a linguistic analogy to describe this 'secondary production hidden in the process of […] utilization'.[65] He remarks that the connection between primary and secondary production is reminiscent of the way in which speakers use, perform, and therefore transform a language and its '*established* vocabulary and syntax':

> The act of speaking (with all the enunciative strategies that implies) is not reducible to the knowledge of a language. By adopting the point of view of enunciation […] we privilege the act of speaking; according to that point of view, speaking operates within the field of a linguistic system; it effects an appropriation, or reappropriation, of language by its speakers; it establishes a *present* relative to a time and place; and it posits a *contract with the other* (the interlocutor) in a network of places and relations.[66]

The hermeneutic process underlying the passage from the pre-text to the *Bible noire* generates an 'invention'. In *Les Corps glorieux*, in an examination of analogous translations by Henri Maurier and

Kwasi Wiredu, Mudimbe reminds his readers that the word needs to be understood as the etymon of the Latin *inventio*: 'De *in* + *venire* comme croisement, rencontre avec; et aussi, comme découverte et appropriation de ce que feu Michel de Certeau a joliment appelé le contrat avec un autre être' [From *in* + *venire* as in coming across, encountering; and also discovering and appropriating of that which the late Michel de Certeau elegantly called the contract with another being] (CG, 175–76). In a very rare reference to Jacques Derrida, and more specifically to 'Edmond Jabès and the Question of the Book' in *Writing and Difference*,[67] Mudimbe argues, quoting Derrida, that

> The difference between the horizon of the original text and the exegetic writing makes the difference between the rabbi and the poet irreducible. Forever unable to reunite with each other, yet so close to each other, how could they ever regain the *realm*. (P&F, 105)

The difference between Fourche, Morlighem, and their Luba informant is as irreducible. Despite the 'violence' of their exegetic operation and the 'sovereignty of [their] analytical reason' (P&F, 104–05), the two anthropologists succeed, according to Mudimbe, in producing a quasi 'authentic' account wherein they demonstrate their ability to render 'an African configuration to the point of speaking almost perfectly the language of an unrecorded history and its fantasies' (P&F, 106). The fact that local intellectuals and experts in Luba culture and theology such as Mabika Kalanda and Marcel Tshiamalenga praised the book for its scientific validity and ability to convincingly capture the tone and style of Luba cosmogony is another reason for taking the *Bible noire* seriously (P&F, 102, 106). Mudimbe adds also, although he does not ascribe any scientific weight to the anecdote, that the narrative is 'faithful to local memories' and reflects his own initiation in the Luba-Songye tradition, which took place in 1949 in his father's birth village in Kasai (P&F, 94–95, 102–03).

The most noteworthy and novel merit of the *Bible noire*, however, is, as Mudimbe argues, its aptitude to invalidate 'any disjunction between mythical and historical spaces', discard the traditional opposition between oral and written cultures (P&F, 95), and, hence, move away from the conceptual framework (the prelogical versus logical antinomy) that had hitherto largely informed colonial anthropology. Mudimbe's reading of Morlighem and Fourche's study is based on the Lévi-straussian premise in *La Pensée sauvage*,[68] and notably in the chapter 'History and Dialectic' in which he develops a discussion on Sartre's *Critique of Dialectical*

Reason, that philosophers such as Sartre 'have valued history above the other human sciences and formed an almost mystical conception of it'.[69] This argument translates Lévi-Stauss's attempts in the 1950s and early 1960s to raise the institutional profile of anthropology, which in terms of academic recognition still lagged far behind history and sociology.[70] More importantly, however, his attack is directed towards the residual humanist assumptions of traditional history, that of the 'great man' of Western historiography, in order to demonstrate that the idea of historical continuity, qualified by Lévi-Strauss as 'the last refuge of a transcendental humanism',[71] is a human construct modelled after the 'supposed (and he argues unrealistic) totalizing continuity of the self'[72] and 'secured only by dint of fraudulent outlines'.[73] Lévi-Strauss contends here that the cult of progress, which presided over the construction of Western historiography, mirrors the way in which individuals perceive their own diachronic development. History, Lévi-Strauss remarks, is always partial, that is, 'biased' and 'incomplete',[74] and 'historical facts are no more *given* than any other',[75] for history as a discipline is forever constrained, at the expense of a 'multitude of psychic movements', to select 'regions, periods, groups of men and individuals in these groups and to make them stand out as discontinuous figures, against a continuity barely good enough to be used as a backdrop'.[76] If historical continuity is a fiction, then history is 'never history, but history-for'.[77] With this Sartrean/Heidegerrian formula, Lévi-Strauss suggests that Western historiography (of which Sartre is a key proponent) is Eurocentric as it invariably celebrates – the biased selection mentioned earlier – stories, moments, events, and characters at the expense of others, arbitrarily perceived as secondary. Lévi-Strauss argues that Sartre's philosophy and the recognition of the 'fundamental opposition he postulates between myself and other',[78] results in rejecting the Other within, and by extension the exotic Other, in an a-historic realm: 'what can one make of peoples "without history" when one has defined man in terms of dialectic and dialectic in terms of history?'[79]

Lévi-Strauss's dismissal of history is predicated upon the idea that, in its 'biased' and 'incomplete' pursuit to seek 'men' and their singularities, it fails to find 'man'[80]: 'Ethnographic analysis tries to arrive at invariants beyond the empirical diversity of human societies'.[81] This does not mean that structuralism completely bypasses history, as attested by the works of figures such as Fernand Braudel and Lucien Febvre who welcomed structuralist paradigms. In *The Savage Mind*, but also in previous and subsequent writings and interviews,[82] Lévi-Strauss has often advocated the complementarity of the two sciences, conjuring up the figure of the two-faced Janus to express this solidarity:

> The fundamental difference between the two disciplines is not one of subject, of goal, or of method. They share the same subject, which is social life; the same goal, which is a better understanding of man; and, in fact, the same method, in which only the proportion of research techniques varies. They differ, principally, of complementary perspectives: History organizes its data in relation to conscious expressions of social life, while anthropology proceeds by examining its unconscious foundations.[83]

In his reading of *Une Bible noire*, Mudimbe takes on board this solidarity between the two disciplines in order to demonstrate that a structuralist examination of Luba cosmogony can shed light on the development, over time and space, of a Luba historical narrative and the emergence of a Luba-inspired political and cultural order in Katanga. The bible, which has Christian overtones, proposes an in-depth examination of Luba mythology, including the emergence of an all-powerful god (Maweja), the constitution, under his authority (actually through his own metamorphoses), of a large pantheon of lesser gods and spirits, and the creation of the earth and heavens. 'Genesis and Myth' stands out when considered against the background of Mudimbe's whole *œuvre* as he is here less interested in delineating the 'geography of a discourse' as he is in *doing* structuralist anthropology. Although he was in direct contact with the material under scrutiny – as mentioned about his own initiation in Kasai in 1949 – the approach that he adopts is typically Lévi-straussian. Lévi-Strauss's aversion for fieldwork is well-documented.[84] The time that he spent on data-collecting expeditions is short when compared to his formidably long career. This imbalance shaped the nature of his work as it relied heavily upon ethnographic descriptions and observations made by other fieldworkers. Lévi-Strauss, paradoxically, remained an armchair anthropologist whilst inventing modern anthropology, a discipline that gained its scientific credibility by favouring fieldwork over positivist speculation, a trend forcefully advocated by Franz Boas, one of Lévi-Strauss's life-long models.[85] The *textual* quality of his analyses, and his encyclopaedic ability to leap from Amerindian myths to Poussin and Rimbaud,[86] Chopin,[87] and Wagner,[88] depends upon a methodology consisting in comprehending human creations (this *com-prehension* is for Mudimbe the mark of Lévi-Strauss's ethnocentrism and 'super-rationalism' (*IoA*, 34)) as a repository of *signs* dialectically responding to one another.

Mudimbe's exegesis of *Une Bible noire* is premised upon Lévi-Strauss's (Saussurian and Jakobsonian) idea that the analysis of language provides an analogical model to classify the building blocks (mythemes) and the deep structures of Luba culture and, as indicated above about the opposition between history and anthropology, its 'unconscious foundations' for 'language, an unreflecting totalization, is human reason, which has its reasons and of which man knows nothing'.[89] *Une Bible noire* is shaped into a narrative of sorts and records the way in which magic-religious ('magico-religieuses') conceptions, beliefs, and practices are expressed in Luba populations of Central Zaire.[90] The two authors provide, via numerous footnotes and thick descriptions, a wealth of information about theological, cosmogonic, linguistic, and etymological issues encountered during their collections of local myths and stories. Mudimbe does something completely different as he uses this 'œuvre indigène' [indigenous work][91] to re-arrange it scientifically, treat it as a 'logic game' (*P&F*, 116), break it down into a number of limited but recurrent patterns and figures and, hence, reveal through a series of binary oppositions and intermediary subcategories the hidden grammar, themes, and transformations of the Luba cosmogony. Mudimbe is therefore able to bring the narrative to a higher level of abstraction and identify from Fourche and Morlighem's empirical translation variants of the same myth and, ultimately, universal invariants that illuminate past and present political and religious practices in Congo-Zaire and beyond.

The worldview generated by the self-created god Maweja is highly codified. In his reading, Mudimbe boils the myth down to a series of dichotomies – male/female, Earth/Heavens, dark/light, good/evil, life/death, dry season/rainy season, red/white – and provides, via synoptic tables and diagrams, a precise inventory of the themes and motives, that is, mythemes, that has enabled the myth to be further reinvented and transformed. The genesis induced by Maweja's self-creation, and the subsequent schizogenesis (splitting) resulting from it, present themselves as a series of connected myths echoing one another and recycling one another's materials through a dialectical logic of inversion:

> The first creation [...] concerns spirits [...] and heavenly things. The second creation is structurally opposed to the first. It gives life to terrestrial beings [...] During the dry season principal and elder terrestrial creatures appear; during the rainy season, junior beings and things. The creation itself is completed on earth when Maweja brings to existence new entities through schizogenesis, thanks to already created species. [...] The code of the second creation produces a balance between its order and

that of the first creation. It brings about primordial binary oppositions: dry season versus rainy season, terrestrial elder things versus terrestrial junior things. (P&F, 110)

The Luba worldview as expressed in the *Bible noire* and decoded by Mudimbe is, however, also conveyed by a number of intermediary subcategories, which relativize the absoluteness of the binary logic implied by this excerpt and complexify the original formula allowing thus an unlimited proliferation of related mythical combinations. Mudimbe shows that the notion of gender does not comply with a male *or* female logic but allows, as often in mythology, the creation of male *and* female beings: 'the body of Maweja's creatures is always hermaphroditic' (P&F, 112). The male/female opposition is therefore not absolute. In fact, it is invariably nuanced by another order, that presiding over elders and juniors, as females always possess a junior male side and males a discreet female aspect. However, males take precedence over females on the basis of their qualities, which are 'aggressiveness and imperiousness; fullness, toughness, and sharpness; violence and strength' whereas female qualities are 'passivity and fecundity; roundness, hollowness, and welcoming; and mildness and beneficence' (P&F, 112).

Mudimbe also demonstrates that the use of colours in the Luba tradition is predicated upon a logic whereby intermediary subcategories and symbolically meaningful hues play a significant role against the backdrop of a binary chromatic system. He notes that the *Bible noire* refers to two basic pairs of colours. On the one hand, white and red, which are male and elder and symbolising respectively 'strong life' and 'strong death' (P&F, 114–15). On the other, a female and junior couple of colours: black and the 'imprecise color' signifying, by opposition to the first pair, 'weaker life' and 'weaker death' (P&F, 115). By combining the terms from the different orders briefly summarised here (male, female, elder, junior, white, red, black, imprecise but also whitish, reddish, blackish, and 'absolute imprecise'), Mudimbe reveals the complexity of Luba-Kasai religious symbolism. He also posits that the *Bible noire* provides the basis for understanding historical processes and the advent of the Luba nation, a view that validates one of the chief arguments of *Parables and Fables* and the *Idea of Africa*: 'in all social formations the mythical and the historical functions seem similar'. He suggests that they are 'memories' whose 'hidden force' discloses the concatenation of events, 'successes', and 'accidents' presiding over the emergence of a culture; he also remarks that this close proximity between the historical and the mythical offers a prism to elucidate present 'political ideologies' and 'discursive practices' (P&F, 98). The *Bible noire* is thus described as an 'archival exemplum' (P&F, 99), which sheds light on the 'memory-text' (P&F, 89) of Luba history since the early fifteenth century as collected and compiled by generations of Africanists before and after independence.

Mudimbe's main primary source to conduct his analysis is one of the most widespread Bantu myths, that is, a 'historical charter' (P&F, 118), also referred to as a 'legend and a dream' (P&F, 91). Its many variants were examined and interpreted by Luc de Heusch in his now classical study *Le Roi ivre ou l'origine de l'État*, a book influenced by Lévi-Straussian methodology and which isolated from a huge mythical corpus of Luba, Kuba, Lunda (Lwena, Tchokwe) myths the invariants of Bantu culture, the processes underpinning the passage from nature to culture – 'from the Paleolithic to the Neolithic economy' (P&F, 90) – and the appearance of an organised polity in the Congolese savannah.[92] In the basic story, two main figures, Nkongolo (a Kalanga) and Ilunga Mbidi Kiluwe (a Luba), are opposed. Nkongolo is a self-made tyrant; he is ugly, violent, incestuous, unsophisticated, and rules over a territory where endogamy is the norm. The tradition refers to him as the 'red or clear skinned man who was a monstrosity' (P&F, 90). Mbidi Ilunga, on the other hand, is everything that Nkongolo is not. He is the bearer of change, the emissary of a refined civilisation, and the proverbial king who 'comes from elsewhere'.[93] He is the legitimate monarch of a hereditary and mainly exogamic dynasty; he is 'tall, lithe, handsome, and *shiningly black*' (P&F, 119). All these qualities were inherited by the son (also called Ilunga) that he conceived with Nkongolo's sister and who completed the Luba expansion.

The story of their encounter reflects the increasing political ascendency of the Luba people who from the fifteenth century onwards expanded their power from east to west, Mbidi Ilunga being known as 'the man from the East' (P&F, 90) and his son, Ilunga, 'the divider of streams of nations' (P&F, 119). In his attempt to relate the *Bible noire* to the Luba charter narrative, Mudimbe returns to the three main categories highlighted earlier: gender (male/female), seniority (elder/junior), and colour (red/white versus black/imprecise) to explain the symbolic articulation behind the passage from the primitive and arbitrary political order to civilisation. What is interesting here is that this passage from nature to culture is mediated by the weaker terms of the categories. Mbidi and his son Ilunga are black, a colour associated with 'weaker life', female, and junior attributes. The female and junior qualities of Mbidi and his son are implied by the story: Mbidi was first noticed, admired, and then introduced into Nkongolo's world by the latter's sisters (*P&F*, 119–20); Ilunga, being the son of Mbidi (the Luba king) and Nkongolo's sister, is Nkongolo's nephew and therefore his subaltern (*P&F*, 120). The new history initiated by Ilunga is made possible by the elimination of Nkongolo the red and the dismissal of the negative features that he personifies. Some variants of the myth indicate that Ilunga was also referred to as 'Kongolo Mwana', which means 'the young Kongolo', a name which implies that he 'integrates harmoniously two traditions: that of Nkongolo's light-skinned Kalanga, the first inhabitants of the region, and that of the black-skinned Luba invaders' (*P&F*, 121–22).

Through this complex and at times dense analysis, Mudimbe reflects – very aptly if one bears in mind the subtitle of *Parables and Fables* – on the links between 'exegesis, textuality, and politics in Central Africa'. This return to pre-colonial times via the exegeses of colonial and postcolonial Africanists is the sign of Mudimbe's intellectual openness and ambition to explore his own identity as a Katangese of Kasai origin. His reading seems also to suggest that beyond the illusive ruptures of a Congolese history conceived as the result of a tripartite development (pre-colonial, colonial, postcolonial), Nkongolo's and Ilunga's antagonistic political models can still contribute to a discussion on the myth of ethnic purity and the Congolese nation at the end of the twentieth century.[94]

The Ancient Library

This ability to link history and myth also informs Mudimbe's frequent exploration of the 'bibliothèque antique' [ancient library], to use an expression recently forged by Bernard Mouralis in a book examining the links between Greco-Roman cultures and Francophone sub-Saharan thought and fiction.[95] As demonstrated, for instance, by his essay 'In the House of Libya', whereby complex historical processes regarding the circumnavigation of the ancient Mediterranean and the cultural interconnectedness of Europe and Africa are traced through mythical figures such as Libya, Io, Europea, Medea, and Helen, Mudimbe's conception of Hellenism is open-ended. It is, as he suggests at the outset of his article, premised on the view that the Mediterranean has for thousands of years been 'an intercultural space created by an internal sea that connects Eur-Asia to Africa' and that 'particulars from myths, speculations, and the sciences have been testifying to a diversity that resists a reduction to a unique grid'.[96] Along other prominent African writers – Wole Soyinka, L. S. Senghor, Cheikh Anta Diop to name but a few significant figures for whom ancient civilisations played a pivotal role – Mudimbe bears witness to this ambition to recapture ('reprendre') a body of works which since the Renaissance has been hailed as quintessentially European and linked to the very genealogy and origins of a Western cultural continuum, a trend that, as Martin Bernal argued in *Black Athena*,[97] would be accentuated by nineteenth-century classical scholarship and its attempt to 'cordon off ancient Greek cultures from others on the rim of the eastern Mediterranean'.[98] Unlike Cheikh Anta Diop in his many interventions on the blackness of Ancient Egyptians and the Afro-Egyptian sources of Classical Greek culture,[99] Mudimbe does not intend to reverse, this time at the expense of Europe, this genealogical continuum. In the name of the exegetic openness that characterises his production, he refuses to order cultures along pre-established hierarchies as he is above all interested in 'les leçons qui pourraient aider notre présent africain d'où qu'elles viennent: de nos ancêtres ou des cultures les plus éloignées des nôtres' [the lessons which, whether they originate from our ancestors or from cultures most different from ours, are likely to assist our African present] (*CG*, 168). Via an expression that seems to deride the paternalistic context in which he acquired this classical expertise, he adds that 'A ce titre, la Grèce et Rome m'ont toujours paru des maîtresses magnifiques' [In this respect, Greece and Rome have always appeared to me as magnificent mistresses] (*CG*, 168). In his numerous examinations of classical authors and their commentators (Martin Bernal: *Idea*, 92–104; Cheikh Anta Diop: *IoA*: 96–97; Drusilla D. Houston, Grace H. Beardsley, Frank Snowden: *Idea*, 25–26; Paul Veyne: *AF*, 89–90; *IoA*, 17–18; Alain Bourgeois: *Idea*, 19–21; Marcel Bénabou, and Ernest Mercier[100]), Mudimbe suggests that Greco-Latin culture does not *belong* to anyone in particular and can therefore illuminate Africa's past as much as it can be used to interrogate Western history and the procedures that facilitated their respective invention, a process that, here too, needs to be conceived within the framework defined by Michel de Certeau. Mudimbe's re-appropriation of a corpus traditionally annexed by European culture has predominantly focused from the very early stages of his career, in all his main monographs but also in shorter publications, on Greek- and Latin-speaking authors such as Diodorus Siculus, Strabo, Pliny the Elder, and, as will be investigated shortly in more detail, Herodotus.

His first substantial contribution to the study of classical cultures *and* languages was the doctoral thesis that he submitted at the University of Louvain in 1970, 'Air: Étude sémantique',[101] which was subsequently published in a revised and slightly abridged version.[102] This wide-ranging lexicological work examines the evolution, from Antiquity to the twentieth century, of a semantic field comprising the Greek, Latin, and French nouns, 'ἀήρ', 'aer', and 'air'. The thesis already demonstrates all the characteristics of Mudimbe's intellectual versatility and ability to apply, in a manner, which is reminiscent of the work conducted at the same time by Alain Rey, the French leading lexicologist,[103] mathematical and statistical models but also linguistic concepts as developed by Saussure, Stephen Ullmann, Louis Hjelmslev, Pierre Guiraud, and Klaus Heger on a multilingual and trans-historic corpus.[104]

Beyond this strictly philological dimension, Mudimbe's examination of Greco-Latin corpora is above all concerned with the ambition of drawing up the boundaries of an Afro-European intellectual history. His work on early Latin-speaking African theologians is in this respect worthy of attention, particularly as it echoes with research conducted in the nineteen-seventies by African thinkers such as Engelbert Mveng[105] and Théophile Obenga[106] and prefigures, in the wake of Martin Bernal's *Black Athena*, the *rapprochement* of postcolonial studies and the classics, particularly in the Anglo-American scholarship.[107] In an article co-written with Pius Nkashama and significantly published in a Festschrift to celebrate Senghor's work as a classicist, Mudimbe investigates the writings of African prelates – Saint Augustine but also less-known characters such as Victor de Vita, Marius Victorinus, and Dracontius – in the early years of Christendom.[108] The conclusion indicates on the part of the two authors a desire to rewrite history and re-examine the respective roles played by European and African intellectual immediately before the fall of the Roman Empire (third and fourth centuries). The two authors, like Cheikh Anta Diop in his reflection on the Egyptian legacies in Greek culture,[109] contend that Latin-speaking African authors were able to shape and indeed transform the cultural and political foundations of Europe: 'Cette pensée venue d'Afrique a contribué grandement à l'édification des concepts à la fois politiques et théologiques qui sont à la base de la naissance des nouveaux États au Moyen-âge chrétien' [This thought from Africa greatly contributed to the emergence of political but also theological concepts underpinning the establishment of new states in medieval Christianity].[110] In *Les Corps glorieux*, Mudimbe would take up again an analogous argument about the Latinisation of the Roman Church under the influence of 'penseurs de l'Afrique romaine' [thinkers from Roman Africa'] such as Saint Augustine, Tertullian, and Arnobius (*CG*, 135).

Mudimbe's exploration of Greco-Roman texts also contributes to his overall epistemological project. In *Les Corps glorieux*, he reflects on his Benedictine education and the significance of this classical education for his future career as a scholar: 'Je ne m'écartais pas de ces leçons d'antan mais les reprenais [...] comme stratégie et technique pour défaire les formes des discours et du pouvoir en nos sciences humaines et sociales' [I did no reject these past lessons but recaptured them as a strategy and technique to undo the discourse and power structures informing our human and social sciences] (*CG*, 131). The verb 'défaire' is complex as it means both 'dénouer' (unknot), and implies therefore a higher level of understanding, and 'invalidate' (défaire also means to defeat), indicating that what has been undone needs to be done afresh. This complexity encapsulates Mudimbe's early plan, particularly in *L'Autre Face du royaume* as will be examined in Chapters 2 and 3, to transform the basis upon which the human sciences are practised in Africa. The lessons of his former Benedictine teachers therefore contribute – an idea, which, here too, is expressed through the verb 'reprendre' ('je reprenais') – to a better comprehension of the human sciences and the renewal of the context in which human scientists operate in Africa.

'Herodote, le menteur' (*AF*, 79–95), illustrates the strategy adopted by Mudimbe to reflect, via classical Greek authors such as Herodotus, Dionysius of Halicarnassus, Plutarch, and Thucydides, on the conditions of possibility presiding over the development of the human sciences with regards to the truth and scientific objectivity in Ancient Greece, in the French Third Republic, and in contemporary sub-Saharan Africa. As one of the first extant ethnographers of Africa, Herodotus is a figure that Mudimbe has examined several times in his publications and cautiously praised for his ability to typify, in a region stretching from the Egyptian borders to the Tritonian lake (in present Libya), a number of indigenous communities on the basis of 'some major paradigms' – such as 'habitation, social *locus*, food, physical features, and marriage' – that prefigure the classificatory studies conducted by modern social anthropologists (*Idea*, 72; see also *IoA*, 70). In 'Hérodote, le menteur', the author of *The Histories* is also considered as the first historian and Mudimbe reopens thus here 'the interminable trial that posterity continues to hold on the Herodotus case'.[111] The analysis that Mudimbe conducts is less about Herodotus *per se* than about his commentators, opponents, and supporters, in Ancient Greece and in the period from the Renaissance to the eighteenth century. The methodology that Herodotus adopted in his historical and ethnographic investigations is therefore used as a pretext to explore major questions regarding the production, and it is argued also the fabrication, on the part of historians, ethnographers, and social scientists, of *true* accounts.

Mudimbe focuses first on the way in which Herodotus' work was held by Greek historians such as Dionysius of Halicarnassus and Plutarch who respectively lived four and five centuries after Herodotus' death in 425 BC. In *On the Malice of Herodotus*, Plutarch argues that the father of history is in fact a master of trickery and a liar who behind 'an apparently simple, direct [and] clear language' secretes malignancy 'beneath a cloak of candour and sincerity' (*AF*, 85).[112] Plutarch deplores Herodotus' lack of deference towards Greek historical and mythological figures such as Io, Bacchus, Hercules, Isagoras, and Leonidas and the fact that he dismisses the Trojan War as a 'joke' (*AF*, 85–86). Above all, however, Plutarch, who was a native of Boeotia, is critical of Herodotus' tendency to glorify 'the Barbarians under the pretext of writing the history of the Greeks' (*AF*, 86) and to offend 'Boeotians and Corinthians, among many others' (*AF*, 85). Dionysius of Halicarnassus conducts a similar exercise, comparing Herodotus' methodological approach as a historian to that of Thucydides who, ultimately, is not deemed as successful as Herodotus. Unlike Plutarch, Dionysius is from the beginning until the end of his assessment very praising of Herodotus' talents and aptitude to render, in the most truthful manner, past events.

Although the two authors disagree regarding Herodotus' legacy and significance for the development of history as a science, Mudimbe contends that, in fact, they share a common goal:

> to offer an image of oneself and of one's homeland that is as pleasing as possible, if necessary by sullying one's enemies, but also by endeavouring, as much as possible and within the constraints of certain rules, to adhere to the truth as best as one can. (*AF*, 89)

Plutarch cannot countenance Herodotus' disrespectful attitude towards Boeotians, his compatriots, whereas Dionysius of Halicarnassus was in awe of Herodotus who, just like him, was a native of Halicarnassus (he is sometimes referred to as Herodotus of Halicarnassus).

By way of Paul Veyne and his influential *Comment on écrit l'histoire?*,[113] Mudimbe remarks that 'the fabric of history is […] a very human blend of material causes [...] that is far from "scientific" [...] which the historian dissects as he sees fit and in which the facts have their objective connections and their relative importance'(AF, 89–90). Fustel de Coulanges, the nineteenth-century French historian and classicist,[114] is then examined by Mudimbe to generalise onto the modern period what the Herodotus controversy had demonstrated for ancient times. In the wake of the Franco-Prussian war, patriotic sensitivities had on both sides of the Rhine reached unprecedented levels. Fustel de Coulanges, in a review of *Histoire d'Allemagne* by the French historian Jules Zeller,[115] laments his colleague's lack of patriotism and inability to praise 'the generations who preceded us' (AF, 90). Although he accepts that 'erudition should have no homeland' (AF, 91), he cannot tolerate the tendency on the part of many French historians such as Zeller to denigrate the French past and to look up for intellectual ideals outside of France.

Mudimbe uses these examples to comment on the context in which history and anthropology are conducted in the West and in Africa. The arguments used in this analysis are typically Foucauldian as he contends that the practice of science is ultimately always time-bound and the product of specific conditions of possibility:

> Although [...] researchers use renewed and ever more refined methods in an effort to express with the rigour and rationality of comprehension the apparent or effective arbitrariness of facts, debates or struggles, they also operate from an epistemological foundation which, by lending validity and meaning to their constructions, reconciles these constructions with the ultimate goals of a particular ideology. (AF, 92)

In the case of history and anthropology – two disciplines that Mudimbe, after Lévi-Strauss, presents as a two-faced Janus – the possibility of producing true accounts is compounded by what he calls 'the banality of a particular presence', that is, 'the perspective of the researcher who unearths, arranges, classifies and interprets using (sometimes) manageable norms, but also does so, consciously or unconsciously, on the basis of discreet or violent sympathies or antipathies' (AF, 92). This epistemological violence that can be traced in ancient but also contemporary texts is closely linked to the idea of ethnocentrism, a concern that, from early essays such as 'Héritage occidental de la conscience nègre'[116] to *The Invention of Africa*, fuelled Mudimbe's examination of the encounters between the West and Africa. The suggestion that any ethnographic and historical account is always shaped by a predefined cultural template subconsciously tapped into by researchers is in fact one of Mudimbe's major focuses. Echoing Edward Said's Foucault-inflected examinations of the Orient and Orientalism,[117] Mudimbe argues that this template 'raises, for the non-Westerners that we are, questions about the credibility of Western readings that concern us' (*AF*, 92). He remarks that this analysis of the epistemological basis of all intellectual endeavours goes beyond problems of methodology as it also conjures up ethical issues (*AF*, 93). He contends that researchers should handle more responsibly the truths, or so-called truths, that they disseminate and that, conversely, the recipients of these texts, who are often lured into believing that 'they are exercising their liberty as readers', should learn to challenge more readily the epistemological foundations of these documents (*AF*, 93). Mudimbe suggests that the future independence of Africa relies upon the acknowledgment that 'like historians, ethnologists – those specialists of "societies without a history" – have always lied and do so in the sense that Plutarch intended' (*AF*, 94). This lesson in humility could potentially open up a new era of greater meta-discursive awareness:

> While it may allow us to smile at those claims of absolute scientific rigour and objectivity made by certain Western Africanists, it does not dispense us Africans from asking questions about our relationship with the subject of our own research or about the type of perspective at work both in what we write and what we read. (*AF*, 94)

There is of course nothing new in the affirmation that the human sciences operate on a partly subjective basis. Mudimbe, in this essay on Herodotus' legacy is, in fact, part of long-standing debates reignited by Sartre and Lévi-Stauss – as discussed earlier – Marc Bloch and Fernand Braudel; but also by Veyne, H.-I. Marrou (a noted classicist), and Paul Ricœur, three thinkers explicitly referred to in this examination of the scientificity of the human sciences. Announcing what Veyne would argue later, Ricœur, in a chapter of *History and Truth* significantly entitled 'The Objectivity of History and the Historian's Subjectivity',[118] discusses the 'historian's craft' and remarks that through 'the *judgment of importance*' whereby 'events' and 'factors' are either deemed significant or accessory, 'the historian emphasizes the rationality of history'. This choice creates the 'continuity' of historical accounts, which are 'dependent in varying degrees upon a *popular conception of causality*'.[119] Marrou, for his part, argues that

> L'histoire nous libère des entraves, des limitations qu'imposait à notre expérience de l'homme notre mise en situation au sein du devenir à

telle place, dans telle société, à tel moment de son évolution, – et par là elle devient en quelque sorte un instrument, un moyen de notre liberté [History liberates us from the shackles and limitations imposed upon our experience of man by our situatedness within the historical process at a particular place, in a particular society, at a particular moment of its evolution – and hence it somehow becomes an instrument and a means of our freedom].[120]

What is new, however, and also liberating in Marrou's sense, is Mudimbe's use of ancient texts to 'undo' (défaire) and debunk some of the discursive fallacies, or lies, underpinning the Africanist corpus in colonial *and* post-independence times. Given the status of Greco-Latin cultures in the construction of European, and hence colonial, ideas of historical grandeur, this appropriation of Hellenism on the part of Mudimbe is the ultimate expression of his freedom as a scholar. In *Carnets de Berlin*, it is indeed in the name of freedom, resistance, and liberation that he advocates this return to Greece: 'il nous faut remonter aux Grecs, non point parce qu'ils étaient meilleurs, mais parce qu'en eux il est possible de nommer la genèse d'une parole contemporaine sur la liberté. D'où, les possibilités nouvelles des pensées de subalternité' [we need to return to the Greeks, not because they were better, but because it is possible to name through them the genesis of a contemporary discourse on freedom and, hence, new possibilities of subaltern ideas] (*CB*, 164).

This chapter has explored the power of Mudimbe's writing. It has also examined his *impossibly* difficult position, as a reader and a writer caught up between historiography and mythology, and the double bind he finds himself in, between colonial discourse and African self-expression. I began by showing how important it is for Mudimbe to historicise very carefully the presence of Christianity in Africa from the early-modern period onwards; then I moved to how fiction becomes crucial to represent contemporary Zairian history – reflecting, especially, the difficulties of excavating women's experiences in the history of contemporary Zaire; following the debate between Sartre and Lévi-Strauss, I subsequently shifted my attention to Luba mythology as a terrain offering a way of doing Luba historiography *and* anthropology; which led us, finally, to see how ancient Greek and Roman writers explicitly used myth to explore their own cultural *mentalites*.

By way of conclusion, it results from the various texts analysed here that Mudimbe's work cannot be confined to a single library, nor assigned to a single discipline. This ability to establish connections between the distant past and the present and to bring closer, via a rich web of inter-textual links, the ancient, colonial, and postcolonial libraries is predominantly the product of Mudimbe's education in the Benedictine order and his subsequent relocations in Europe and the United States. The versatility but also the many detours of his critical approach reflect the accidents and the multi-continental meanderings of an existence lived as a *scholar* – in the two meanings of the French noun 'clerc' – constantly engaged in undoing what cannot be forgotten. Asked where he was from by Régis Debray lecturing at Stanford in the late 1990s, Mudimbe replied: 'Du Congo belge, vous connaissez?' [From the Belgian Congo, have you heard of it?] (*CB*, 178). Beyond the provocation, this reply could not be closer to the truth as this remark, flippant as it may seem, reflects Mudimbe's difficulty of knowing what the (Belgian) Congo really is. Although not very politically correct, this question also conjures up a simple idea: the past cannot be erased and Mudimbe is as much from the Belgian Congo as he is from the Democratic Republic of Congo. Interestingly, *L'Autre Face* and *L'Odeur du père*, his most politically radical works, are almost entirely devoid of references to the Belgian Congo. The young Mudimbe preferred to bracket off his own past to construct, as will be examined further in the other chapters of this book, his critique of imperialism in a country, which was, with difficulty, attempting to come to terms with colonial practices. From *Parables and Fables* (1991) onwards, however, the autobiographical past has increasingly resurfaced. In the wake of Pierre Nora's *Les Lieux de mémoire* (1984–91),[121] the critical mood changed and past events and phenomena were scrutinised less for their ability to provide a reconstruction of history than for their power, in a manner reminiscent to mythical processes, to transform themselves and produce memories for subsequent generations. This new historiographical tendency constitutes a break with the idea of periodisation in the field of history. For Mudimbe, the colonial and postcolonial periods collapse into one another as he lived through the transition between the one to the other and carried forward into an elusive 'after' knowledge and memories shaped by a 'before': 'il est clair que les mémoires "africaines", les anciennes et la coloniale, loin de s'opposer se complètent plutôt. Je pense les incarner' [It is clear that 'African' memories, ancient ones and the colonial one, far from being opposed, complement one another. I believe that I embody them] (*CG*, 59).

Like other prominent postcolonial intellectuals such as Edward Said and Assia Djebar and their (cautious) praise of humanism and

Western-style education,[122] Mudimbe has explored his own double consciousness. Whereas the Western legacy is lived as a traumatic event in the early essays and novels, it has increasingly been regarded as an experience, which has engendered critical openness. For Mudimbe, 'reconnaître "mon alinénation"' [acknowledging my alienation] is, beyond the suffering and epistemological violence that he invariably examines, also the premise of a greater critical freedom:

> Je ne suis pas né fonctionnaire d'un savoir, ni porteur d'une vérité quelconque. En ma réflexion sur des conflits de lecture et d'interprétation, je m'attèle à une tâche, celle de me défaire librement de mes masques avant que la mort ne me les pulvérise à tout jamais [I wasn't born to administer a particular field of knowledge, nor to be the spokesperson of any specific thruth. In my reflection on conflicts of reading and interpretation, I endeavour to freely rid myself of my masks until death shatters them for good]. (*CB*, 69)

This posture, which echoes Richard Bjornson's idea that alienation led 'to a heightened state of awareness' (*Speech*, 149),[123] explains why Mudimbe often conducts nuanced and sympathetic appraisals, as in the case of Fathers Swartenbroekx, Lambin, Vanderyst, and Nimal (*CG*, 55–58), Augustin Planque (*TF*, 43–44), and Paul Salkin (*CB*, 172–74), of representatives of the colonial order and their occasional ability to challenge the discriminatory basis of the imperial system. By the same token, he questions the scientific validity of Adam Hoschild's portrayal of Leopoldian Congo in *King Leopold's Ghost*,[124] contending, a view that was upheld by Belgian historians of the Congo such as Jean Stengers and Jean-Luc Vellut, that not all emissaries of the King were unscrupulous and bloodthirsty psychopaths and that Hoschild should have submitted his claims to a much more rigorous methodology (*CB*, 105–106).

Ultimately, this intertwining of the ancient, colonial, and postcolonial libraries responds to a need to recapture ('reprendre') different memories, resist facile interpretations of past and present phenomena, and bring into sharper relief the interface between epistemology and politics in sub-Saharan Africa. Herodotus's malignity offers a powerful metaphor as it acts as a reminder that science can never be completely disentangled from ideology. The metaphor applies to conscious strategies implemented for centuries by the Church (and indeed churches and religious orders) to convert, in the name of *the* truth, the pagans into 'docile bodies' (*TF*, 50–56). It also provides a basis, a point that will be pursued further in Chapter 2, for a better comprehension of the circumstances underlying the difficult emergence of a nation in Congo-Zaire. On this final point, it is interesting to note that the exploration of myths (Greek but also Bantou myths) is never a gratuitous exercise and that *Shaba Deux*, a novel about modern Zaire, is also a variation on the figures of Nkongolo and Ilunga and their contemporary incarnations and epigones.

2

'The Invention of Otherness'

Quand une communauté se bat pour sauver sa peau – mur, mosquée ou tombeau de l'ancêtre – elle ne lésine pas sur les moyens: la lutte est à mort, car l'enjeu n'est plus ce qu'elle a mais ce qu'elle est.

Régis Debray[1]

This chapter will explore Mudimbe's literary and scholarly activities in the early 1970s in Congo-Zaire and pay particular attention to the hitherto little-studied collection of essays, *Autour de la 'Nation'* (1972),[2] in which the author reflects on the newly introduced ideology of Zairianisation, a process whereby the former name of the country was changed to Zaire in the wake of the Mobutu-led politics of authenticity.[3] In the maturation of the author, and in the process that eventually led to his international recognition and prominence, this period is of the utmost significance. In many ways, the corpus that resulted from this very prolific decade provided a basis and a blueprint for future intellectual endeavours, and for the conceptualization of ideas that would be developed, nuanced, and reinterpreted later. The term 'reinterpretation', as will be discussed here, reflects one of the core aspects of his work, that is, its open-endedness and ability to approach reading and exegesis as a dynamic and *unfinishable* process. One thing is certain: his work will remain unfinished precisely because this *unfinishability* is at the very heart of his writing project. The word 'polymath' also springs to mind as this corpus comprises poetry, novels, prefaces and forewords, academic essays, and policy-making reports disseminated in a great variety of journals in Zaire and elsewhere,[4] as well as collections of essays, the two most outstanding ones being *L'Autre Face du royaume* and *L'Odeur du père*: the latter text, although it came out in 1982 after he moved permanently to the United States to take up his first (American) professorial position at Haverford College, belongs to the Zairian decade.

Zairianisation

Zairian culture during the 1970s was deeply paradoxical: the country was run by a totalitarian regime, which not only controlled cultural productions but also attempted to promote the idea of an *authentic* national culture, and yet it was at its most creative and prolific during this period, notably in the fields of music, dance,[5] and literature.[6] This paradox applies to Mudimbe too: how was he allowed to express artistic and academic freedom if one accepts the premise that his production – on the surface a critique of the epistemological basis of Western domination over sub-Saharan Africa in all areas of knowledge – could have conceivably been read as an indirect and implicit plea for more political freedom for the citizens of Zaire? This criticism was, to my knowledge, never levelled against his writings during the 1970s.[7] I would want to contend, however, that his use of the word 'insurrection' in the coda of *L'Autre Face du royaume* (*AF*, 154), is perhaps less innocuous than it may seem. As his work is not outwardly political (although, ultimately, it is, as will be demonstrated in this chapter), it is reasonable to think that if censors read it at all, they read it for what it proclaimed to be, that is, as a critical exploration of the practice of the social sciences in sub-Saharan Africa. Had they read it for what is was really – and I cannot stress enough the hypothetical nature of the exercise that I am conducting here as very few academic works have explored head on the practice of censorship in Zaire[8] – they would have most probably banned it.[9] Mudimbe announces in the introduction of this book that his focus on social anthropology – he uses the French term 'ethnologie' – is but a 'pretext' (*AF*, 10) to initiate a debate that would encourage Africans (he does not say Zairians) to 'entreprendre chez eux un discours théorique qui soit producteur d'une pratique politique' [formulate in Africa a theoretical discourse that would generate a political practice] (*AF*, 10). He argues throughout this book – he is in this respect, a point that will be examined in more detail in Chapter 3, very close to Fabian's analysis of the 'denial of coevalness' in *Time and the Other*[10] – that anthropology continues to be informed by principles and procedures of thought established in the West (and for the West). If this focus on social anthropology is a 'pretext', it is reasonable to argue that his critique has in fact a much wider scope and is also directed towards the regime's totalitarian propensity. He contends, after all, that African scholars in the social sciences operate on the basis of dualistic, self-exclusive, and therefore totalitarian sets of propositions – science versus ideology, savagery versus civilization, civilization versus traditional culture (*AF*, 153–54) – which blind them to the possibility of what he calls, rather cryptically, 'un subtil usage de l'intersection' [a subtle use of the intersection], a principle, which can 'permettre une insurrection' [generate an insurrection] (*AF*, 154). Their totalitarianism, and failure to approach science other than in purely Manichean terms, reflects thus metonymically (the part is indicative of the whole) the shortcomings of a political programme that also conceptualised change dualistically. Ultimately, and this is the reason why the term 'insurrection' should be taken in its usual (and more common) political sense, he exposes the regime's inability to break away from neo-colonialism and to establish what Mobutu and his *Mouvement Populaire de la Révolution* (MPR) leadership obsessively referred to as an *authentically* Zairian nation.

Mudimbe's trajectory is, overall, quite classical and mirrors that of some of his contemporaries such as Georges Ngal, Kadima-Nzuji, and Pius Nkashama, to name but three prominent Congolese figures who also embraced literary and scholarly careers. His education straddles indeed not only the chronological divide between the colonial and the postcolonial periods but also the boundaries between Africa and Europe. After completing his doctorate, he returned to his native country where he quickly rose to academic and literary fame and became the most celebrated Congolese writer of the decade. By 1970, Mobutu, however, had become a very notorious figure and the ruthless nature of his leadership was a well-documented fact. As far back as 1966, that is, only a few months after Mobutu's successful military *coup* on 24 November 1965, Césaire had portrayed in *Une Saison au Congo*[11] a barely disguised but clearly identifiable commander in chief of the Congolese army (named 'Mokutu') as a brutish, remorseless, and power-thirsty advocate of a new African *Realpolitik*. Césaire's play very deftly captured the political opportunism of a man who orchestrated Lumumba's liquidation in 1961 and decided subsequently to turn him into a national hero after eventually securing absolute power for himself with the institution of the Second Republic in 1965.[12] Later, one of Mobutu's victims (and former political ally during the Kasa-Vubu presidency[13]) in exile would publish an indictment of the regime significantly subtitled as 'les crimes de Mobutu' [Mobutu's crimes].[14] That this book was published by François Maspero, a publisher traditionally sympathetic to anti-colonial causes and newly independent countries, is indicative of the disrepute into which the Congolese dictator had fallen.

The paradox that will be explored in this chapter is that Mudimbe, who was clearly very aware of this situation, was able to survive and even flourish under the Mobutu dictatorship despite the fact that some of his work became increasingly critical of the regime's excesses and its pretentions that Zairian culture constituted an authentic totality, or an 'immanent community', to use an expression by Jean-Luc Nancy to which I shall return.[15] The paradox can partly be explained through Mobutu's personality and own journey from obscurity to political prominence. Although not university educated, it is worth pointing out that Mobutu was no philistine, that he never adopted a completely anti-intellectual stance, and that his actions, albeit driven by a high degree of pragmatism (the *Realpolitik* alluded to earlier), were not deprived of idealism. As a matter of fact, he had from the outset of his political career, that is, as early as September 1960 in the midst of the Lumumba 'affair', displayed an ability to rally intellectuals to his cause and to seek advice and guidance among the newly constituted elite of the nation.[16] When he seized power in 1965 as a result of a bloodless military *coup*, which gave him a five-year mandate to reorganise the country (he eventually stayed in power until 1997), his action was welcomed by the 'Union générale des étudiants congolais' (UGEC), the main Congolese students' organisation, which would play a key role in the formulation of the ideological tenets of the one-party system constituted under the aegis of the *Mouvement populaire de la révolution* (MPR) in 1967 in Nsele.[17] The Congolese historian Isidore Ndaywel è Nziem goes even as far as to argue that Mobutu – who interestingly held a life-long fascination for North Korea and Communist China[18] – was until 1967 seduced by the Marxist–Leninist rhetoric and objectives of the UGEC.[19] Ndaywel identifies two main reasons behind this fact: first Mobutu had been influenced by the Marxism-inflected 'leçons politiques anticolonialistes apprises naguère en compagnie de Lumumba' [anticolonialist political lessons previously learnt in the company of Lumumba];[20] secondly, and more opportunistically, this rhetoric presented the advantage of countering vigorously and unambiguously the capitalist tendency that had informed the short-lived premiership of (the still popular) Moïse Tshombe, the very man that the *coup* had successfully driven away from power.[21] In spite of this obvious influence, Mobutu opted for a less extreme route and the founding document of the MPR and of the one-party system – the 'Manifeste de la Nsele' (named after the place where it was drafted near Mobutu's fiefdom in Mbandaka) – indicates that the new regime would above all focus on the restoration of a

Congolese national identity. The sudden resurrection of Lumumba, a move first suggested by the more radical UGEC,[22] was evidently part and parcel of this plan to create a new national order. Interestingly, however, the terms 'nationalisme' and then 'nationalisme congolais authentique' were dropped in favour of 'authenticité'.[23] This semantic operation constitutes a discursive shift, which benefited Mobutu, the new leader, at the expense of Lumumba who was still widely associated with the idea of Congolese nationalism. Similarly, the authors of the 'Nsele Manifesto' have been accused of plagiarism as the document is allegedly a copy of a constitutional revision drafted (but never implemented) in 1964.[24] It has also been argued in relation to this Manifesto that it was composed on the basis of another document, first written and then lost by Pierre Mulélé, the Congolese Maoist revolutionary leader who fought against the Congolese army, the 'Armée nationale congolaise' (ANC), during the First Republic, after serving in Lumumba's cabinet as minister of education.[25] Ndaywel contends that, although this hypothesis has hitherto not been proven, it is highly plausible and would certainly account for the Manifesto's socialist overtones. If Mulélé's authorship were to be confirmed, this would indicate, according to Ndaywel, that the Manifesto could be regarded as a type of conciliatory 'national pact'[26] representing the views and aspirations of all Congolese, that is, not only the ruling and intellectual elite that rallied around Mobutu but also, and more crucially, the vast majority of Congolese from rural areas. From 1963 onwards, Pierre Mulélé, ideologically and militarily trained in China after Lumumba's assassination in January 1961, organised rural militias to pursue, with and on behalf of the people abandoned by this ruling *bourgeoisie* (and their Western acolytes), the interrupted Lumumbist revolution and attempt to achieve a proletarian 'second independence'.[27] Despite some very significant military successes and the establishment of a short-lived 'République Libre du Congo' [Free Republic of Congo] in Stanleyville (now Kisangani), Lumumba's hometown, Mulélé's revolutionary movement gradually abated after Mobutu's accession to power in November 1965. The fact that Mobutu also claimed Lumumba's revolutionary legacy – *Mouvement populaire de la révolution* could indeed be mistaken for a Marxist appellation – contributed to blur the divide between their respective programmes.[28] In 1968, Mulélé was lured into Kinshasa under the pretence that he would be granted amnesty and was brutally executed – an event that 'cracked the veneer of stability and reconciliation under which Mobutu has lately ruled'.[29] I shall come back in Chapters 3 and 5 to the Mulelist revolution, notably through Benoît Verhaegen's *Rébellions au Congo*[30] and Mudimbe's *Entre les eaux*, a novel published in 1973 but written in 1966[31] against the backdrop of this left-wing popular guerrilla warfare (the Kwilu rebellion),[32] in which this failed attempt to bring about a 'second independence' is implied.

Mudimbe's literary and academic career was fashioned and conditioned by the inception of the Second Republic after the military *coup* of 1965. The new regime was eager to encourage the promotion of a recognisable Congolese and (from 1971 onwards) Zairian culture. Like other budding talents from his generation, he was sent to Europe, where he spent his time between the universities of Leuven-Louvain, Nanterre, and Besançon to perfect his education, mainly in the fields of linguistics, anthropology, and philosophy. On his return, he was able to reap the benefits of this prolonged stay abroad and actively to participate, as a senior member of the national university establishment, in the shaping of a new cultural era. He edited, for instance, to mention a book often overlooked by Mudimbe critics, *La Dépendance de l'Afrique et les moyens d'y remédier*, a voluminous collection of essays that resulted from an international conference of Africanists held in Kinshasa in 1978 and provided a comprehensive examination of the ways in which culture, in the widest sense of the word, could contribute to African development.[33] He also authored, in a volume published in 1980 and co-edited with a group of Belgian scholars, a vast survey on the place of the social sciences in the Zairian higher education sector. In this important contribution, he establishes a compelling analogy between politics, economics, and epistemology: 'La crise de la science se réfléchit dans celle du Zaïre, de même que celui-ci est le reflet de celle qui travaille les sciences' [The crisis experienced by science mirrors that of Zaire and, similarly, Zaire is the reflection of the crisis eroding sciences].[34]

The time that coincides with his return to the Congo was characterised by a mood of euphoria and the belief that this new and favourable climate would generate the conditions for a more harmonious society and a more efficient economy, or a 'décollage' [take-off], to use a term recurrently employed in official reports.[35] This period overlapped with the implementation of the politics of authenticity, which had been formulated in the Nsele Manifesto. The appellation under which the country had been known since 1964, the Democratic Republic of Congo, was changed to the Republic of Zaire in 1971, a denomination which would remain stable until the end of the Mobutu era in 1997. For this reason, 'recours à l'authenticité' [recourse to authenticity] was also referred to as Zairianisation. Mudimbe became professor at the National University of Zaire in 1971, first at the Lovanium campus (Kinshasa) and then in Lubumbashi, in the province of Katanga (also known as Shaba as a result of Zairianisation) where he was dean of the Faculty of Letters, from 1973 to 1980, the year he permanently left the country.

Autour de la 'Nation', the collection of essays on which this chapter will focus, was published in 1972, in a series called 'Objectifs 80' founded by Mudimbe and Georges Ngal at the Éditions du Mont noir. This series responded to a desire, on the part of the regime, to initiate discussions on the notion of authenticity as a strategy to drag the country out of under-development ('Objectifs 80' was also a political slogan in use during the 1970s). Mudimbe took it upon himself therefore to reflect on, and set objectives for, the emergence of a Zairian national culture. It would thus be right to affirm with Huit Mulongo that he was at the very beginning of the first Zairian decade, not only close to the regime, but also a philosopher of authenticity of sorts.[36] *Autour de la 'Nation'*, another essay largely neglected or ignored by critics, will be scrutinised to nuance this claim as Mudimbe was evidently not a sheep-like advocate of Zarianisation. I would like to read this early essay against the work of another 'philosopher of authenticity': *Discours sur l'authenticité* by Kutumbagana Kangafu.[37]

Who was Kangafu? Mulongo counts him among the most prominent thinkers of authenticity – together with Mudimbe and alongside other less well-known figures – and argues that it would be impossible to 'réduire tous ces grands intellectuels à de simples marionnettes "orchestrées" par Mobutu' [to reduce all these great intellectuals to mere puppets manoeuvred by Mobutu].[38] Kasereka Kavwariheri, in his monograph on Mudimbe, is, on the other hand, very dismissive of Kangafu's writings and remarks that they are helpful inasmuch as they enable one to 'cartographier très rapidement "l'espace culturel mobutien"' [quickly map out the cultural space under Mobutu][39] – whereas Mulongo seemed to imply that they were intrinsically worthy of attention. Ndaywel, in his authoritative history of the Congo simply ignores him all together, and Silvia Riva, in her history of Congolese literature, mentions him only once in her bibliography. Opinions seem therefore to diverge even though Kangafu is significant enough for Mudimbe to associate him, albeit via a cursory reference, with his own first-hand experience of Zarianisation. This process is described as 'an exploitation of the tradition as a repository of signs and meanings of African authenticity' and Mudimbe remarks that '[i]n its political application it has led, at least in one case, to a notorious mystification, the Zairian policy of "authenticity" and its dubious philosophical foundations (see, e.g., Kangafu, 1973; Mbuze, 1974, 1977)' (*IoA*, 153).[40]

Mudimbe's *Autour de la 'Nation'* and Kangafu's *Discours sur l'authenticité* are borne out of the same context; they both bear witness to the climate of a nation in the making and provide, shortly after the onset of Zairianisation, a commentary on the 'Nsele Manifesto'. Even though Mudimbe, many years after, and on the other side of the Atlantic, dismisses Zairianisation as a 'notorious mystification', I would like to highlight, in a first stage, what unites the two texts, although their differences are, ultimately, more significant. Beyond the subject matter – the conditions under which a new Zairian nation can, could (or has) emerge(d) – these essays are both informed, at least on the surface, by a didactic approach: *Autour de la 'Nation'* is symptomatically subtitled as 'Leçons de civisme' [Lectures in civic education]. The philological and Greco-Latin tradition explored in Chapter 1 resurfaces here and is very concretely expressed in the way Mudimbe and Kangafu – the former being, however, more systematic and comprehensive than the latter– trace back, via their etymology and successive transformations, the fleeting meanings of key concepts and ideas – nation, revolution, ideology, development, and authenticity to name but a few – that would enable the general public to get to grips with the unfolding national revolution, although, as already hinted above, it is dubious whether the MPR was truly revolutionary. Beyond this classical heritage, the etymological exercises that they conduct in these essays result also from the very contemporary Foucaldian genealogy in which Mudimbe is known to operate and to which Kangafu admits to subscribe via a reference to *Les Mots et les choses*.[41] The two books do indeed overlap in terms of corpus of sources. This intertextuality is important, not least because it shows that the authors' reflections are underpinned by a commonality of materials, albeit used to different purposes and effects. Kangafu praises Louis-Vincent Thomas's *Le Socialisme et l'Afrique* (1966),[42] as an 'ouvrage brillant' [brilliant work][43] to make the case for the emergence of a Zairian (Herdian) *Kultur-Nation*; Mudimbe, on the other hand, refers to it to scrutinise failed attempts on the part of Socialist African leaders such as Senghor, Sékou-Touré, and Nkrumah (*Nation*, 58–59; see also *IoA*, 91–97 and *CG*, 90–93) to break away from a capitalist mode of production. I shall return later to Mudimbe's appraisal of African socialism as this reference to production is definitely not as neutral and non-committal as it may seem and could indeed be read as a signal that Mudimbe is not ready to embrace uncritically the notion of authenticity as it was advocated by the MPR. With regard to ideology they both acknowledge the historical significance of Destutt de Tracy's work on ideology, which is another tribute to Foucault since the French historian referred to Destutt de Tracy in *Les Mots et les choses*.[44] Ideology is of course another highly connoted term as its currency had been reactivated by (anticolonial) Marxists in the 1950s and 1960s. They both agree that it will play a decisive role in the promotion of the cause of authenticity. For Kangafu, however, the use of the word is unproblematic and, although he shows that its meaning has evolved since it was first introduced by Destutt de Tracy at the beginning of the nineteenth century, he seems to be content with a disarmingly naive definition: 'le nationalisme zaïrois authentique est une idéologie, entendez un ensemble d'idées, d'affirmations, de notions qui existent sous forme [...] d'une prise de position volontaire du Général Mobutu [et] d'une régulation suprême de la vie nationale entière [authentic Zairian nationalism is an ideology, that is, a set of ideas, principles, and notions emanating from a deliberate involvement on the part of General Mobutu and from a supreme regulation of the entire national life].[45] This definition seems to reflect a poorly assimilated understanding of ideology as it had been conceived by Marx and Engels in the *German Ideology*,[46] and then by anticolonial thinkers such as Cabral, Fanon, and Sartre. For this tradition, ideology is above all exploitative and the product of modes of production set in place by the ruling *bourgeoisie*, the modern capitalists who own the means of production: 'The ideas of the ruling class are in every epoch the ruling ideas: i.e. the class, which is the ruling *material* force of society is at the same time its ruling *intellectual* force'.[47] The dominant ideology is thus – for this tradition – to be overthrown by a proletarian revolution. Kangafu's definition of ideology is, additionally, too mechanistic: he uses the term as a synonym for the pledges of a party-political manifesto. He implies therefore that these ideas, once implemented, will be able to regulate the 'entire national life', a process, which, on reflection, is more evocative of *Gleichschaltung*. Finally, he ignores the fact that ideology is also linked to the development of literature, religion, and philosophy, in sum, culture, that is to say, the 'phantoms formed in the brains of men [that] are also, necessarily, sublimates of their material life-process'.[48] I highlighted above the possible relation between the Nsele Manifesto and Mulélé's original manuscript (lost and then possibly found by an ANC officer close to Mobutu) as this could explain why the Manifesto retained some Marxist features (albeit altered sometimes beyond recognition). What this focus on ideology – from Marx onwards a *materialist* concept – seeks to demonstrate is that Kangafu uses it to serve an *idealist* (romantic, communitarian) purpose. Mudimbe, on the other hand, is more cautious. Nationalism, in the form defended by the MPR, is an ideology but the term, and what it can imply, is not taken for granted. He establishes a useful distinction between ideology *tout court*, understood as a near-synonym for discourse, that is, a 'présence vivante, expression explicite ou implicite d'une organisation sociale' [living presence, explicit or implicit expression of a social organisation] (*Nation*, 27) and 'idéologie d'action' [action-driven ideology]. By way of two radically different nationalist ideologies – Machiavelli's salutary nationalism and Julius Langbehn's exclusive conception of the German nation – he argues that action-driven ideology is invariably problematic: 'Toute idéologie d'action porte en elle un problème majeur: celui de sa crédibilité comme système tolérant. C'est que toute idéologie d'action tend naturellement à s'approprier et la raison et la vérité [Every action-driven ideology has a major weakness: it lacks credibility as a tolerant system for it naturally tends to confiscate not only reason but also truth] (*Nation*, 26). As examined in Chapter 1 in his analysis of Herodotus, this focus on 'truth' and 'reason' will resurface again.

The Community

Although they both focus on the possibility of the emergence of a Zairian nation, the two authors, beyond some limited common features, approach this issue from very different angles, as demonstrated by the examination of their respective understanding of the concept of ideology. The idea of the community, as analysed by Jean-Luc Nancy in *La Communauté désœuvrée* [*The Inoperative Community*], may help us to unlock further discrepancies between Mudimbe and Kangafu. This essay, as already established by Celia Britton in *The Sense of Community in French Caribbean Fiction*,[49] offers a number of theoretical instruments to examine the ambiguities underpinning the use of the term 'community' and the ideas of 'togetherness' and 'belonging' that it usually conjures up.[50] Nancy provides, via a sustained philosophical dialogue with the works of Martin Heidegger and Georges Bataille, a reflection on communal life and a deconstructive critique of the idealist and historicist basis of Western humanism. Nancy does not lament the inefficiency of the community, as the potentially misleading word 'inoperative' could imply. The adjective 'désœuvré' carries indeed a number of very derogatory connotations in French. It is related to the noun 'désœuvrement', which conjures up ideas of idleness, powerlessness, laziness, and, on a more concrete level, unemployment. These words –'désœuvrement' and 'désœuvré' – need, however, to be understood in relation to their semantic opposites: 'œuvre' and 'œuvré'. What Nancy says is that the community, as an idea, is a construct, an invention, an *œuvre*, which has been laboured, worked, and operated on. Although it would be difficult to ascribe a specific political application to Nancy's interpretation of the community, this essay is without a doubt a critique of the ways in which this concept has been commented upon since the beginning of the nineteenth century and manipulated for political purposes. This text also provides therefore an indirect commentary on the emergence, in the wake of the French Revolution, of the mythical and communitarian basis of modern European nation states:

> We know [...] that mythology is our invention [...] And we also know that the idea of a 'new mythology', the idea of moving on to a new, poetico-religious foundation, is contemporaneous with the invention or the modern reinvention of mythology in the romantic epoch.[51]

The couple 'œuvré'/'dés-œuvré' reflects the opposition that Nancy establishes between the 'immanent community' and 'being-in-common'. The phrase 'immanent community' conveys the idea of a homogeneous – total, and Nancy argues in many respects totalitarian ('"totalitarianism" [...] might be better named "immanentism"'[52]) – identification between the community and its members. Nancy notes that in this communitarian model:

> The community is not only intimate communication between its members, but also its organic communion with its own essence. [...] it is made up principally of the sharing [...] of an identity by a plurality wherein each member identifies himself only through the supplementary mediation of his identification with the living body of the community.[53]

Nancy argues that the immanent community, invariably conveyed through 'phantasms of the lost community',[54] is the result of what he calls a 'retrospective consciousness'. He warns (an argument that could be applied to the Zairian 'immanentism' of the 1970s) that one should be suspicious of this type of consciousness, whether it 'conceives of itself as effectively retrospective or whether, disregarding the realities of the past, it constructs images of this past for the sake of an ideal or a prospective vision'.[55] He insists that this more organic and homogeneous community has never existed, it is an illusion, and that 'no *Gesellschaft* has come along to help the State, industry, and capital dissolve a prior *Gemeinschaft*'.[56] In this examination of the 'immanent community', Nancy emphasises the pivotal role of myth. Although he refers several times to the notion of myth in its anthropological and indeed mythological meanings, the concept, as explored in 'Myth interrupted' (the second chapter of the essay), is understood as a political means to found the existence and the legitimacy of the community: 'Myth is above all full, original speech, at times revealing, at times founding the intimate being of a community'.[57] The problem of this relationship between myth and the emergence of the immanent community resides precisely in the legitimising process that the myth actualises, as a 'full' and 'original speech'. Nancy is suspicious of the communion and the closure that it generates for 'myth is the opening of the mouth immediately adequate to the closure of a universe'.[58] Although what the myth resurrects or claims to resuscitate is more often than not mere invention, Nancy is eager to warn of the dangers of this type of mythology. He notes that it would be incorrect to argue that 'from the nineteenth century onward thinkers of myth are responsible for Nazism' but contends nonetheless that their thinking contributed (in the French original he talks of their 'co-appartenance'[59]) to 'the staging and setting to work – in French he very aptly uses the expression 'mise en œuvre' – of a 'Volk and of a "Reich,", in the sense that Nazism gave to these terms'.[60] For this reason, he argues against this mythical 'mise en œuvre', its tendency to generate sameness and to produce a narcissistic monologue on the community, an *œuvre* seen as complete, absolute, and definitive. In this discussion, he takes to task the 'self-consciousness of a modern world that has exhausted itself in the fabulous representation of its own power' and argues, a point that will need to be nuanced in relation to the Zairianised community examined by Mudimbe and Kangafu, that 'the idea of myth alone perhaps presents the very Idea of the West, with its perpetual […] compulsion to return to its own sources in order to re-engender itself from them as the very destiny of humanity'.[61]

Nancy puts forward a counter-model to un-work (désœuvrer) or resist the 'immanent community'. He calls it 'being-in-common' and also refers to it as the 'inoperative' or 'interrupted' community. Literature, or writing, is crucial to 'being-in-common'. Even though the 'immanent community' is radically opposed to 'being-in-common', literature, for its part, is not the complete opposite to myth. There exists indeed a link between the two in the sense that literature can become myth and perform the same communal[62] function: 'literature [is] the beneficiary (or the echo) of myth, literature has itself in a sense been thought and no doubt should be thought as myth – as the myth of the myth of mythless society'.[63] More crucially, however, literature has the power to interrupt the communion of the 'immanent community' and undo the organic relationship between the homogeneous whole and its members, that is, the self-present subjects of an equally self-present community and perfected communal identity. Nancy dismisses this unity and the metaphysical assumption that the subject, 'another, and symmetrical, figure of immanence',[64] is the 'absolute for-itself'[65] echoing the absoluteness of a community conceived as the repository of a complete and definitive meaning. Literature interrupts this completeness and fusion through a sharing ('partage') of a plurality of meanings, at times fragmentary, at times evanescent, in which the absoluteness of the opposition between 'self' and 'other' is also abolished. This type of communication, which is no longer communion (it 'does not commune'[66]), is what he calls 'literary communism': 'something that would be the sharing of community in and by its writing, its literature'.[67] The recipients and producers of this sharing are the 'singular beings' who are not the self-sufficient and immanent individuals discarded by Nancy, and referred to earlier, but beings who exist through this sharing with other singular beings. The latter, Nancy argues 'are what they are to the extent that they are articulated upon one another, to the extent that they are spread out and shared along lines of force [...] whose network makes up their being-in-common'.[68] This articulation is said to be literature and 'writing' itself or the expression of 'literary communism' as the term is understood here: 'the inscription of a meaning whose transcendence or presence is indefinitely and constitutively deferred'.[69] The interrupted community – what he also calls 'community without community' – is therefore a model of resistance: 'it is to *come*, in the sense that it is always *coming*, endlessly, at the heart of every collectivity [and] it ceaselessly resists collectivity itself'.[70]

In this reading I would like to ascertain whether the type of resistance implied in 'literary communism' is manifest in Mudimbe's didactic exploration of the nation as a concept whose understanding can ultimately contribute to 'unwork' Zairian totalitarianism. Kangafu's essay does not lend itself to this type of interpretation as it is overtly praising the new regime's effort to bring about the desired Zairianisation of national culture. It is therefore less ambiguous than *Autour de la 'Nation'* (although far from being devoid of contradictions, as we shall see). Kangafu is clearly enthusiastic about authenticity and does not miss any opportunity to pay tribute to Mobutu's role in bringing about a rejuvenated Zairian nation. In this essay, Mobutu, the nation, and authenticity are indeed the interchangeable terms that he uses to account for the existence and the making of a Zairian 'immanent community', organically constituted around a charismatic historical leader. Mobutu, who is compared to Napoleon, is said to have 'identifié au Zaïre concret au point d'en faire le drame de sa personnalité' [identified with concrete Zaire to the point of turning it into the drama of his personality].[71] Mobutu is 'essentiellement l'homme de l'Histoire' [essentially the man of History] and his action has guaranteed 'à l'histoire du Zaïre une configuration de totale libération [to the history of Zaire a configuration of total liberation].[72] In Mudimbe's essay, on the other hand, there isn't any explicit reference to Mobutu although, as said before, the book also provides an interpretation of the Nsele Manifesto, of which large passages are reproduced.

I will now turn the focus to the ways in which Kangafu and Mudimbe discuss the role of (literary) history with regards to Zairianisation. In his commentary on authenticity, Kangafu underlines the notion of 'doctrines empruntées' [borrowed doctrines].[73] He argues that the success of Zairianisation and authenticity, the two terms being used here as synonyms, will largely depend on the regime's ability to reject borrowed doctrines, such as capitalism, the civilising mission, and Christianisation, which have, Kangafu contends, maintained Zaire in poverty and underdevelopment.[74] This argument is very close to Mudimbe's critique of alienating discourses, what he called 'langages en folie' [mad languages, discourses, or speeches], and promotion of an African scientific and paradigmatic independence in, for instance, *L'Autre Face du royaume*, although he would, in his later works (see Chapter 1), favour the 'recapture' ('Reprendre') of Western legacies against their outright rejection. Kangafu associates the concept of authenticity to ideas of dignity and self-affirmation and remarks that it is also synonymous with 'être vrai [and] s'appartenir à soi-même' [being genuine and self-belonging] whereas the expression 'recours à l'authenticité' [recourse to authenticity] would mean 'rénovation de soi-même à partir du pouvoir absolu qu'est soi-même' [self-reconstruction through the absolute power emanating from the self].[75] Kangafu, via a number of quotes taken from the Nsele Manifesto but also from speeches by Mobutu himself, and from his Maoism-inspired 'Petit livre vert',[76] argues, however, that authenticity is a dynamic and non-exclusive process, which does not propose a return to traditional customs: 'il ne s'agit pas d'un chauvinisme exacerbé' [it is not meant to be exacerbated chauvinism][77] for 'le terme "traditionnel" évoque un monde figé, refermé sur lui-même: un monde fini. Il est un concept non dynamique, fixiste. Il se réfère […] à l'héritage' [the term 'traditional' suggests the idea of a fixed and introvert world: a dead world. It is a non-dynamic and rigid concept. It refers to heritage].[78] This apparent openness could suggest that Kangafu, despite what was said about his promotion of an organic relationship between the Zairian people and its leader, does not quite adhere to the notion of 'immanentism' as it was presented by Nancy, although the idea of dynamism still conveys the notion of an *œuvre* in the making.

His examination of negritude would also seem to confirm this more open and less rigid conception of the (cultural) community. Kangafu argues that Zairian authenticity and negritude are radically different. Unlike authenticity, which is throughout this essay described as an action-driven ideology, or 'idéologie opérationnelle',[79] he argues that negritude is a 'mystification grandiose' and a myth, which does not produce any tangible results.[80] Even though this particular myth is discarded, Kangafu still maintains that myths (as conceived by Nancy) are the necessary ingredients 'to found the intimate being of the community'.[81] Kangafu dismisses Senghor's *Chants d'ombre* and Césaire's *Cahier d'un retour au pays natal* as ineffective literary attempts (or myths) to reconnect with an imaginary 'Africa perennis'.[82] He argues that the movement is the product of borrowed doctrines and calls it an 'idéologie importée' [imported ideology].[83] In this discussion, Kangafu refers to contemporary thinkers who, in the wake of the Pan-African Festival of Algiers in 1969, had responded very critically and vehemently against the movement's dubious attachment to European arts and cultures. These figures are Stanislas Adotevi,[84] Marcien Towa,[85] Jean-Marie Abanda Ndengue,[86] Njoh-Mouelle Ebénézer,[87] and, last but not least, Mudimbe himself who provides a very critical analysis of negritude in *Autour de la 'Nation'*.[88] Kangafu gives – notably via Mudimbe's analysis of the movement (which he quotes here profusely) – an account of the development of negritude in the 1930s in Paris and its dissemination through *L'Étudiant noir* and *Légitime défense*. In this diatribe, Kangafu explains that the founders' ideas were fashioned by European aesthetics (Breton's surrealism) and politics (Marxism and socialism).[89] Negritude, in this perspective, is above all 'fille de l'Occident' [daughter of the West].[90] As a consequence – indeed, Kangafu's text reads here as a carefully structured demonstration – negritude needs to be replaced by a more authentically African or Zairian concept, that is, authenticity. Interestingly he justifies the definitive dismissal of negritude with the famous passage from 'Orphée noir' in which Sartre contends that negritude, being 'le temps faible d'une progression dialectique' [the weak stage of a dialectical progression], is bound to be destroyed and superseded by the emergence of a raceless society.[91] This reference to historical materialism's dialectics is intriguing in the light of what Kangafu says elsewhere about the MPR's reluctance to embrace foreign concepts; it also demonstrates the fragility of his quest for self-reliance, or worse, autarky, since he associates Mobutu's construction of a certain Zairian history with 'a configuration of total liberation'[92] and also notes that the Greek 'Authentikos' means 'pouvoir absolu' [absolute power].[93]

The ideas that Kangafu puts forward in this essay are close to arguments that Mudimbe developed in the 1970s to bring about the conditions of a deeper political and intellectual autonomy, although the latter's preference for the adjective 'African'(rather than 'Zairian') certainly suggests a more lukewarm commitment to the Zairian nationalist project. This proximity, however, is real. Mudimbe advocated in *L'Autre Face* the rejection of borrowed concepts, what he calls 'langages en folie' [alienated languages], a phrase used to indicate that some of the methodologies and procedures of thought underpinning the human sciences are dubious because they are ill-adapted to the African terrain and perpetuate, in the postcolonial present, hierarchies that were established in the colonial period. Mudimbe calls therefore for a deliverance from what he calls metaphorically 'the father's scent' (*L'Odeur du père*), although, ultimately, it is unclear who this father really is. Is it the former colonial master? Is it Mobutu, the new father of the nation? What is sure is that this deliberate ambiguity and conflation very aptly translates Mudimbe's point that political independence (as that of 1960) does not necessarily generate an epistemological revolution, or, to put it more bluntly, that the independence produced what it sought to reject, that is, neo-colonialism. This insidious smell or legacy, and their surreptitious discourses (about negritude he used the phrase 'surreptitious speech'), need thus to be eliminated for they are the fallacious discursive building blocks of the continent's invention. Kangafu links independence to authenticity and argues that this concept is the result of a genuinely Zairian set of conditions: 'Elle est le fruit d'une conscience historique spécifique. Son élaboration n'incombe ni n'est confiée à des maîtres d'autres aires culturelles' [it results from a specific historical consciousness. Its implementation is not incumbent, nor is entrusted upon masters from other cultural areas].[94] This emphasis on a specific history and geographical location is also at the core of Mudimbe's analysis of knowledge production. In *L'Autre Face*, he contends that there is only one way of conducting research in the field of social sciences in Africa: 'en demeurant *authentiquement* soi-même, situé dans le temps et l'espace réels; en étant aussi extrêmement attentif aux divers apports et à notre condition socio-historique déterminée d'intellectuel noir et africain, vivant au XXe siècle dans un pays sous-développé [by remaining authentically ourselves, located in real time and space; by being also extremely aware of the different influences and of our determined socio-historical condition of black and African intellectuals living in the twentieth century in an under-developed country] (*AF*, 135; my emphasis).

Although their views about negritude converge up to a point, there are three fundamental differences that need to be identified. First, Kangafu's analysis of this cultural phenomenon is insufficiently grounded and too one-sided in its approach. In the introduction to his essay, Kangafu reminds his readers that Africa had dominated the world until the Neolithic period and had once prosperous and industrious civilisations with complex societal structures informed by home-grown democratic principles.[95] This demonstration is reminiscent of what Nancy was arguing about the founding and legitimising discourses, or myths, underlying the construction of immanent communities. Kangafu notes that this more glorious past has been excavated, as examined in Chapter 1, by Cheikh Anta Diop and Engelbert Mveng, the two well-known scholars and classicists of the 'reconstruction de l'Afrique'.[96] Kangafu remarks that this past splendour has also been ascertained by archaeologists, historians, and ethnologists who remain, however, nameless here. Given the significance of figures such as Maurice Delafosse and Leo Frobenius in the historicisation of negritude, there is no doubt that Kangafu is implicitly referring to them in this text. In view of what he says about negritude later in the book, this acknowledgment, albeit nameless, is problematic. Indeed, Kangafu is contradicting himself and applying double standards inasmuch as he fails to register the intertextual resonances between Cheikh Anta Diop, Mveng, and their European colleagues (and predecessors). I am not intending to reintroduce through the back door, as it were, the old hierarchy of the colonial masters and their indigenous pupils (or 'pupilles'). The point I want to emphasise here is that writing, as a creative process, always involves borrowing. Diop and Mveng were intellectual towering figures of their times but they were also writing against the backdrop of specific conditions of possibility. In his analysis of negritude, Mudimbe, on the other hand, takes this complexity into account and locates negritude in a wide epistemological climate. He highlights the European origin of the movement and its dependency on the 'cadre européen' [European context] (*Nation*, 46), that of the emergence of cultural relativism in the interwar period, but adds that the idea that different cultures can nonetheless be equal is not really 'une initiative africaine' [an African initiative] (*Nation*, 47) and he refutes, as a consequence, the 'coupure Occident-Nègres qu'aurait constituée cette contestation' [the Occident-Negroes rupture, which allegedly underpinned this opposition] (*Nation*, 46). He argues – a point that he will reiterate in his encounter with Léon-Gontran Damas in America in 1974 (see *Carnets d'Amérique*, chap. 4) – that the movement, precisely because it was an offshoot of cultural relativism, was instrumental in negating the 'évidences définitives' [absolute certainties] (*Nation*, 48) on which colonialism had been erected. According to Mudimbe, negritude is a myth but a 'mythe, sans doute fécond' [perhaps a fecund myth] (*Nation*, 59) and, unlike Kangafu who attempted to promote the radical novelty of Zairianisation as a rupture from negritude, he concludes that 'c'est en tant que mythe que la négritude a pu nourrir les nationalismes africains [it is as a myth that negritude has been able to fuel African nationalisms] (*Nation*, 59).

There is another paradox, or second difference, between Mudimbe's perspective on negritude and Kangafu's interpretation of it: his insistence to ascribe not only the glorious African kingdoms and empires of the past that he mentions but also all African cultures to a 'système fondamental de pensée' [fundamental system of thought].[97] This idea of a single cultural root and principle – Glissant's well-documented 'racine unique'[98] – is ironically the very thing that Kangafu was claiming to avoid, that is, a return to some romantic 'Africa perennis'. Authenticity, defined as 'source inspiratrice de l'Afrique triomphante et industrieuse' [inspirational source of the triumphant and industrious Africa][99] is indeed reminiscent of what was extolled by Senghor and the early promoters of negritude. This movement was, as suggested by Mudimbe, a product of the brand of cultural relativism that developed in the interwar period. Fabian argues that '[r]elativism, in its functionalist and culturalist varieties, undoubtedly has its root in romantic reactions against Enlightenment rational absolutism' and, he adds – in relation to romantic exaltation of the community, Nancy referred indeed to the ill-fated 'Volk' and 'Reich' – 'that romantic ideas regarding the historical uniqueness of cultural creations were only too vulnerable to chauvinistic perversions'.[100]

This idea of an African 'fundamental system of thought' reflects also Kangafu's inability to escape the influence of 'borrowed' conceptual constructions as it is part and parcel of the 'colonial library' and the epistemological climate from which the 'invention of Africa' resulted. In this respect, it is interesting to see that Mudimbe has recurrently demonstrated that there exists an epistemological continuity between the relativist anthropology that emerged in the interwar period – for instance, Griaule's study on the Dogons or Placide Temples's Bantu philosophy – and 'the idealism of apostles of otherness' such as Cheikh Anta Diop (*IoA*, 181). Kangafu's recourse to authenticity understood as a fundamental system conjures up ideas of cultural timelessness and uniqueness, a view, which, according to Fabian, characterises a trend in post-war anthropology whereby cultures are referred to as fully integrated wholes and studied, in the name of cultural relativism, on the basis of overly systemic and totalising models and investigative methods. Fabian notes, for example, in works by Margaret Mead, Rhoda Métreaux, and Ruth Benedict of the early 1950s (and he argues that it took one generation for their 'scientific insights [...] to percolate to the level of popular consciousness'[101]), an 'intense concern for the unifying *ethos*, the common morality that accounts for regularities in the behaviour of the members of a culture'.[102] Unwittingly, it would seem, Kangafu is therefore embracing this type of 'cultural holism'[103] and the assumption that other cultures and societies can only be grasped as fully articulated organisms.[104] According to Fabian, this 'idea of totality' – the word 'organism' evokes Nancy's critique of the community as an *œuvre* – perpetuates in the present the old hierarchies, as those relating to the spatial and hence temporal distance between the anthropologist and his/her 'Others', that cultural relativism (and its recognition of the Other's culture) had set out to abolish. Seen in the context of this wider epistemological context, authenticity is unlikely to release the professed openness and dynamism.

The third difference between Kangafu and Mudimbe relates to the role of philosophy and literature. Kangafu dismisses negritude because it is allegedly too literary: it is essentially a 'mouvement littéraire' [literary movement] and, as such, it is described as a 'culte du verbe' [word-based cult], it produces a 'parole non-signifiante' [non-signifying speech] and 'définitions inopérantes' [inoperative definitions].[105] Authenticiy is a 'philosophie de l'action' [philosophy of action] and, via a passage from one of Mobutu's speeches,[106] he extols its ability to be used as a tool concretely to act upon the real world: 'Au commencement était l'action ... Le temps de la parole est passé. Nous devons maintenant passer aux actes' [In the beginning was action ... The time of the word has passed. We need now to act].[107]

Mudimbe, on the other hand, does not give credit to this opposition between words and acts. For him, literature and philosophy cannot be conceived as separate from the world of actions as reading and writing are given a transformative authority. This idea is one of the most salient arguments of *L'Autre Face*. In this collection of essays, Mudimbe contends that Africans need to think differently, that is, away from Western systems of thought internalised by African scholars, in order to be able to reorganise *differently* the African polity and *city*. *Leçons de civisme*, the subtitle of *Autour de la 'Nation'*, translates, on the part of Mudimbe, the ambition to generate an analogous dialectic between thought and political action. The essay, as mentioned earlier, has an educational dimension. Mudimbe's didacticism is, however, very different from Kangafu's as the latter establishes an unproblematic causality between the main concepts brought under his scrutiny: Mobutu has formulated an 'operational' ideology (authenticity), which will be the basis of an economic, political, and cultural revolution and will, ultimately, transform Zairian society and put an end to its former (neo) colonial dependency. This linear narrative is absent from Mudimbe's account. Throughout *Autour de la 'Nation'*, the prevailing mood is one of scepticism. The pair myth versus literature (or writing) as delineated by Nancy would seem to reflect adequately the different approaches adopted by Kangafu and Mudimbe. The former announces the glorious coronation of a benevolent sovereign; the latter dissects a number of key concepts and issues such as nation, 'cité', ideology, revolution, and development but his examination does not produce any happy ending. His didactic dissection or scepticism 'unworks' (interrupts) the totality of meaning that the myth had achieved. Mudimbe therefore engages in what Nancy names 'literary communism'. The investigation does not aim to produce a digest or an easily absorbable glossary of these terms. Mudimbe's careful unpacking reveals their polysemic nature and unpredictable metamorphoses thereby manifesting a resistance against Zairianisation. Kangafu's analysis of the emergence of a fully coherent and organically structured community is predicated upon a number of views and definitions in which generalising rules – for instance the ethnocentric depiction of Zaire – are favoured over singularities.

I would like now to turn my attention to some of the strategies whereby Mudimbe expresses this resistance. This critique doesn't possess the immediacy of a manifesto because it remains hidden behind a screen of scholarship practised here as literary camouflage. Reflecting over this period, which also coincided with his own transfer from Kinshasa to Lubumbashi, Mudimbe implies that he entered a type of intellectual *maquis* which prefigured his definitive exile of 1980:

> Today, philosophy and sociology journals and university departments have become the loci not only for academic exercises, but also for questioning the meaning of political power and interrogating all power-knowledge systems. In the school year 1968–1969, the humanist Senghor closed the University of Dakar to silence this questioning. Mobutu of Zaire, in 1971, moved the Department of Philosophy and the School of Letters two thousand kilometers from his capital. (IoA, 185)

Indeed, Lubumbashi, the second largest urban area of the country became a hotbed for political and intellectual activism and has therefore played in relation to the capital city the role of cultural 'épicentre'.[108] Some of Mudimbe's close collaborators, such as the critic and novelist Pius Ngandu Nkashama, who eventually also chose to leave Zaire, were sanctioned, displaced, or imprisoned by the regime.[109] Under these circumstances, it is not surprising that Mudimbe opted for a more abstruse style of writing to formulate his scepticism vis-à-vis Mobutu's communal project. Although primarily the stylistic mark of Mudimbe's philosophical inscription, abstruseness is also borne out of self-preservation in the face of political oppression and is therefore a tactic to undo some of the MPR's certainties. This tendency – stylistic abstruseness (a phrase used here without any derogatory connotation) – is much more pronounced in *L'Autre Face* and *L'Odeur* where didacticism, but not criticism, virtually disappeared.

Mudimbe's examination of the term 'revolution' is symptomatic of the exegetic posture that he adopts in *Autour de la 'Nation'*. He links it to the concept of 'nation' and argues that the latter gained its modern currency in the socio-political context of the French Revolution 'grâce à une opposition singulière entre la *nation* et le *roi* [thanks to a singular opposition between the nation and the king] (*Nation*, 13). Although this link between nation and revolution is quite conventional, it has also, in view of Mobutu's well-documented fascination with regal pomp,[110] a specific resonance and can be understood as a warning against the absolutist *penchant* of Mobutu, who ruled as a quasi-monarch over

Zaire for thirty-two years. In his dissection of the term (the first section is indeed entitled 'Anatomie de la révolution'), Mudimbe contends that the word has been abused and although he says that it would be illusory to establish a 'typologie assurée des faits révolutionnaires' [reliable typology of revolutionary facts] (*Nation*, 40), his intention is to discuss the intrinsic complexity of its underlying factors. The demonstration is not flawless and this is a deliberate attempt to reiterate, in the very act of writing and reading, the impossibility of creating a 'reliable typology' and a causal, and self-present sequence between the people, the nation, the leader, authenticity, and revolution. Mudimbe remains prudent throughout the analysis. He refers to 1789, 1848, 1960 (the independence of the Congo) but does not develop any specific argument about the use of the term 'revolution' in the MPR rhetoric. The analysis could therefore be read as being completely innocuous: by opening up the term, however, Mudimbe, as a good pedagogue, invites his students and readers to think beyond the boundaries of any given typology. This discussion on revolution (as that on ideology, nationalism, and development) needs to be explored against the backdrop of 'Un projet nationaliste' [A Nationalist Project, pp. 87–93], the last chapter of the book. This chapter is anything but conclusive. Here too the author practises the art of concealment mentioned above. Mudimbe lists the main articles (which he reproduces verbatim) of the Nsele Manifesto under three main subheadings ('économique', 'politique', 'idéologique') but does not provide any in-depth commentary. He recognises the merits of the manifesto but this acknowledgement is not exactly unconditional as he merely underlines, as shown in the following short passages, the potential but still hypothetical promises of the text: 'Le *Manifeste* peut être considéré comme la première expression d'un travail théorique qui penserait, en permanence et de manière critique, les exigences et les implications de la rupture' [The Manifesto can be regarded as the first expression of a theoretical attempt whereby the exigencies and implications of rupture would be permanently and critically interrogated]. He adds that 'le texte est précis: il nomme clairement les tâches qui permettraient l'établissement d'un nouveau type de rapports' [The text is precise: it clearly designates the tasks, which would enable the implementation of a new type of relationship] in the economic, political, and ideological spheres (*Nation*, 89–90). The use of the conditional is a revealing feature of this cautious endorsement.

What is problematic here is therefore not the text itself as Mudimbe argues that it *could* provide a valid blueprint for the enactment of a 'rupture' (or revolution) and the construction of a better future, but the exact status of the manifesto in relation to the MPR. Kangafu says that the manifesto *is* the MPR (itself a collective reflection of Mobutu) whereas Mudimbe implies (but does not *say*) in his examination of the concept of revolution that no neat overlap can be identified between the two. According to Mudimbe, revolutionary events require the presence of dissident voices or 'contre-sociétaires' (*Nation*, 35), as he calls them, who advocate, in the name of different economic, political, and ideological values, a counter-society. Their effort to overthrow existing power structures, however, is rarely successful because they are in most cases in the minority and do not have the resources (military, economic) seriously to threaten the established order (*Nation*, 35). Mudimbe remarks that in order to reach their aims they need to receive support from the elite for they can only succeed 'si l'élite nationale est divisée' [if the national elite is divided] (*Nation*, 35). In the context of the power shift that took place on 24 November 1965, Mobutu can hardly be described as a revolutionary 'contre-sociétaire', for he was, as commander in chief of the national army, a member of the national elite. What can be said, however, is that the elite was very divided and that Mobutu's bloodless *coup* – rather than revolution – resulted from this division at the top of the political apparatus. Mobutu capitalised on this division to sideline Kasa-Vubu and Tshombe. Interestingly, he used Mulélé's 'contre-sociétaire' discourse gradually to consolidate his authority over the country. The political elite in place since 1960 had chiefly favoured the main urban centres at the expense of rural areas and forged international links with former colonial powers. Mulélé's movement, on the other hand, had promoted the peasantry, that is, the vast majority of the country's population and the Nsele Manifesto redressed this imbalance by asserting its crucial role in the reconstruction of the nation.

On the surface, thus, Mobutu's *coup* could have been mistaken for a revolution that would have created, as Kangafu and Mudimbe indicate via a passage from the Manifesto, a 'république vraiment sociale et vraiment démocratique' [truly social and democratic republic] (*Discours sur l'authenticité*, 41; *Nation*, 91). Nonetheless, the plausibility of this proposition (and hence the likelihood of the emergence of a communitarian *œuvre*) is undermined by a number of seemingly innocuous statements. Mudimbe observes that revolution implies a series of complex mechanisms and that its main project, that is the realisation of a counter-society, is difficult to achieve (*Nation*, 37). In another statement that does not quite square up with Mobutu's track record (the assassinations of Lumumba and Mulélé being two telling examples), he notes that revolutionaries intend in general to 'corriger des excès, d'effacer des bavures [...] d'un pouvoir antérieur' [correct excesses, eradicate blunders of a previous regime] (*Nation*, 41). In the last chapter, he cites another passage from the manifesto in which it is stated that the Zairian revolution, in the spirit of the rejection of borrowed doctrines mentioned earlier, is completely different from that of Peking, Moscow, or Cuba (*Nation*, 92). In this respect, it is interesting to see that Mudimbe provides a Marxist (and Althusserian) explanation of revolutionary phenomena and contends that the emergence of a new political order depends on the thorough transformation of the social formation's infrastructure and superstructure (*Nation*, 40). It is doubtful that Mobutu ever achieved this double transformation. Despite the nationalisation of the main industries and mining resources,[111] Mobutu's regime did not genuinely transform the capitalist modes of production that had been set up under Belgian rule. Mudimbe argues that the economic domain is ultimately the dominant factor and that it can, 'en dernière instance, donner son cachet à la révolution' [in the last instance, confer its prestige to the revolution] (*Nation*, 41). The phrase 'in the last instance' is interesting and reflects Mudimbe's acquaintance with Althusser's work as he also recognises, beyond the determining importance of the economic sphere, a dialectical network of reciprocal determination between the infrastructure, or the economic foundations of society, and the superstructure (ideology and culture). The use of this phrase, 'en dernière instance', indicates on the part of Mudimbe, a willingness to assert his own intricate theoretical position and the complexity of a concept, revolution, which had been used and abused in the MPR party political rhetoric. In his conclusion, Kangafu announces, somewhat triumphantly, that authenticity, that is the new revolutionary order instigated by Mobutu, provides the only possible basis for the development of an African 'nouvel humanisme' [new humanism].[112] Mudimbe's recourse to Althusser is a strategy adopted to disqualify this facile triumphalism and its paradoxical return to humanism, a borrowed doctrine, which, ironically, had been used to legitimise colonialism.[113] In *Pour Marx*, a study that Mudimbe read carefully (*P&F*, 9), Althusser dismissed the link between humanism and revolution and argues, via a return to Marx's anti-humanism, that the study of history and hence revolution demands the examination of a complex set of factors and variables: 'In 1845, Marx broke radically with every theory that based history and politics on an essence of man'. Althusser notes that this epistemological rupture produced a 'theory of history and politics' informed by a series of 'radically new concepts' such as 'social formation, productive forces, relations of production, superstructure, ideologies, determined *in the last instance* by the economy'.[114]

Mudimbe's endorsement of Althusser's non-subjective conception of the historical process and denunciation of the cult of personality are, by way of conclusion, the lines of attack that he chooses to counter what cannot be explicitly countered, that is to say the regime's naive and definitely humanist promotion of one man (Mobutu) as the bearer of the community's destiny. This sceptical (rather than explicitly oppositional) posture is also apparent in his subsequent Zairian essays and this is the reason why *Autour de la 'Nation'* is part of an intellectual continuum that would be, as we shall see in Chapter 3, further radicalised in *L'Autre Face du royaume* and *L'Odeur du père*. Didacticism needs here to be regarded as a discursive ploy to undermine the deleterious idealism on which the regime's *raison d'être* had been erected. Didacticism is thus a manoeuvre that he chooses to combat, paradoxically, didacticism itself, that is, a pedagogical tool called upon to impart knowledge and whereby the roles and statuses of 'knowers' and 'knowees' are rigidly defined. In the French tradition, didacticism conjures up, as a teaching or communicative method, notions of clarity of expression and faith in the ability of language to act as a reliable instrument in the comprehensive transmission and systematisation of concepts and thoughts. Kangafu's exposition bears witness to this ambition to comprehend the past, the present, and the future and to capture their purported causality into a carefully orchestrated narrative. His account of authenticity, the Zairian revolution, and the birth of a new nation are reminiscent of the stages of a dialectical progression. Mudimbe's Zairian essays respond to this formidably disingenuous claim and reject its residual idealism and facile Hegelianism. This response is literary and the reflection of a concerted and meaningful stylistic posture that emphasises the provisional and the partial nature of any set of arguments. Mudimbe has primarily written essays and lately 'meditations'.[115] I would argue that his understanding of the word 'essay' is quite literal and attuned to the etymological resonance of the term: an essay is an attempt and there is thus nothing definitive about what it seeks to claim. It does not 'commune' but merely registers (shows, makes apparent, performs rather than demonstrates) in the very act of writing and reading, a resistance against any attempt to define the community too strictly. In the Foreword to *L'Odeur du père*, he reflects upon the definitely non-didactic nature of his book. He argues that the texts collected in this volume are not the results of any carefully planned strategy: 'Différents et même, apparemment, contradictoires, ils sont davantage expressions d'une interrogation attentive à la vie et au milieu vital que recherches systématiques selon les normes scolaires. Dans une certaine mesure, ils expriment mes propres contradictions d'universitaire africain' [They are different and even apparently contradictory to one another; they are not so much the products of systematically conducted research according to didactic norms as the outcomes of a cautious investigation into life and the vital *milieu*. To some extent, they express my own contradiction as an African academic] (*OP*, 14).

This statement is an act of resistance and a rejection of the mythical invention of a new but allegedly authentic Zaire and the expression of what Nancy calls 'literary communism':

> It is because there is community – unworked always, and resisting at the heart of every collectivity and in the heart of every individual – and because myth is interrupted – suspended always, and divided by its own enunciation – that there exists the necessity of 'literary communism'.[116]

And Nancy adds a little further that

> 'Literary communism' indicates at least the following: that community, in its infinite resistance to everything that would bring it to completion (in every sense of the word 'achever' – which can also mean 'finish off'), signifies an irrepressible political exigency, and that exigency in its turn demands something of 'literature', the inscription of our infinite resistance.[117]

The translator's commentary on the other meaning of the verb 'achever' (that Nancy uses in the original version of the essay in French[118]) is interesting. It conjures up ideas of finitude and death and it is in this sense that the term *unfinishability*, as used at the very beginning of this chapter in relation to Mudimbe's writings, needs to be understood. This corpus, unplanned and often contradictory as he contends, defies in its focus on 'vie' and 'milieu vital' death and the organic communion of Zairian 'immanentism' during the 1970s. Mudimbe's understanding of the relationship between the community, traditional Bantu myths and rites (and their *total* reliance on the ancestors as exposed by Placide Tempels in *Bantu Philosophy*) illustrates the same sense of finitude: myths and rites of initiation are said to offer 'une seule lecture possible, une lecture finie, achevée et absolue, celle des ancêtres' [one single reading, a finished, completed and absolute reading, that of the ancestors] (*Nation*, 68). Mudimbe's exegesis of Africa is irreverent and politically minded precisely because it advocates the sharing, in Nancy's understanding of the word, of other readings, which, in their dissemination, interrupt the absolute and 'finished' reading upon which the Bantu community had relied. In this sense, the *unfinishability* of Mudimbe's writings is close to Nancy's conception of 'inachèvemenent',[119] that is, the very principle of 'sharing':

> This sharing, this passage cannot be completed. Incompletion [inachèvement] is its 'principle', taking the term 'incompletion' in an active sense, however, as designating not insufficiency or lack, but the activity of sharing, the dynamic, if you will, of an uninterrupted passage through singular ruptures. That is to say, once again, a workless and inoperative activity. It is not a matter of making, producing, or instituting a community; nor is it a matter of venerating or fearing within it a sacred power – it is a matter of incompleting its sharing. Sharing is always incomplete [...]. For a complete sharing implies the disappearance of what is shared.[120]

This refusal to share completely is also the mark of Mudimbe's abstruse, irreverent, and resistant *essays*, for sharing completely (totally, comprehensively) would restore the myth. The focus on epistemology in most of his texts contributes to the covert sense of resistance that emanates from *Autour de la 'Nation'*, *L'Autre Face du royaume*, and *L'Odeur du père*. His ongoing critique of anthropology's reliance on methodologies and procedures of thought founded not only in the West but also during the colonial era has a transferrable quality. Attacking contemporary anthropology implicitly amounted to unravelling the shortcomings of Mobutu's totalitarian regime. In this discussion, completion – for instance, Kangafu's historicist narration of the Zairianised community – is seen as 'insufficiency or lack'. In these essays, Mudimbe regrets (an idea to which he would consistently and insistently return during those years) the ambiguous relationship between the human sciences and natural sciences.[121] He contends that the former have very little conceptual autonomy and are therefore dependent on models imported from biology or mathematics. He argues that this application is unwise, or insane (as he indeed refers to 'langages en folie'), because it simply does not attend to the very human concerns of these disciplines (anthropology, sociology, psychology, and even economy). In a discussion on development, he warns against the mystification generated by the 'calculs compliqués de l'économétrie' [complicated econometric calculations] and remarks that development cannot be left to economists alone as it also requires the attention 'du peuple entier' [of the whole of the people] (*Nation*, 86). By the same token, he notes in the Foreword of *L'Odeur du père* that the human and social sciences do not generate '"un même" inoffensif dans ses variables expressions, qui serait fidèle à lui-même – à l'instar des systèmes logiques' [an inoffensive 'same' in its variable expressions, which would be equivalent to itself – as it happens in logical systems] (*OP*, 14). The failure of anthropology, the failure of the human sciences, reflect that of the regime as there is without a doubt an analogy between social scientists' inability to break away from 'the positivist myth of a causal history' and the 'simplified and [...] lazy nineteenth-century transplantation of natural science models' (*Idea*, xvi) and Mobutu's (or Kangafu's) teleological reconstruction of an authentic Zairian community. Already in 1980, that is, at the time of his transfer to America, he allowed himself to denounce more directly the political instrumentalization of the social sciences in Zaire:

> Dans le domaine politique et administratif, des conflits d'interprétation et, éventuellement d'action, pourraient surgir et opposer le chercheur aux directives de 'l'Institut Makanda Kabobi' (IMK) dont les brochures explicitent la philosophie politique du parti, en même temps qu'elles tendent à s'ériger en instance disciplinaire et en signes d'orthodoxie pour l'interprétation et l'organisation de la vie sociale, de l'histoire du parti et de l'État [In the political and administrative domains, conflicts of interpretation and, possibly, conflicts of action are likely to emerge and oppose researchers to the guidelines issued by the 'Institut Makanda Kabobi' (IMK) whose brochures spell out the political philosophy of the party whilst attempting, at the same time, to set themselves up as disciplinary bodies and signs of orthodoxy for the interpretation and organisation of social life, the history of the party and of the State].[122]

More than twenty years after the publication of *Autour de la 'Nation'*, Mudimbe provided in *The Idea of Africa* a type of codicil to what could not have been explicitly voiced in the 1970s. This short passage, which deals explicitly with Mobutuism, is part of a wide-ranging reflection focusing, among other themes relating to the history of the region since the creation of the Congo Free State, on the long-term legacy for contemporary Zaire of missionary discourses, the birth of local faiths such as Kimbanguism, and the 'Domestication and the Conflict of Memories' (*Idea*, 105–53). He returns here to the specific period on which this chapter has focused and highlights the paradoxical nature of the 'Manifeste de la Nsele' and its 'promotion of almost socialist presuppositions for the emergence of a new society' (*Idea*, 148). This commentary, however, underscores above all the failure of the enterprise as well as the hollow and self-congratulatory narcissism of the 'Mobutuist discourse', which addressed 'itself to itself' (*Idea*, 145). According to Mudimbe, the MPR revolution never took place and this may explain why he closed (but also opened up) *L'Autre Face du royaume* with an 'invitation à l'insurrection' (*AF*, 154). He notes that, although it claimed 'absolute newness', Mobutuism used in fact 'a mixture of images that repeat[ed], in an incantatory way, desires and projects already formulated under colonial rule and during the first republic' (*Idea*, 145). This *post-scriptum* is important, not just because it enables Mudimbe to settle, once and for all, an old feud but because, ultimately, it indicates that the father merely replaced the father and that Mobutu's Zaire, in its attempt to define its own otherness, perpetuated the 'royauté normative de l'Européen' [the normative sovereignty of Europeans] (*AF*, 33) and remained the other face of the old dismissed kingdom.

3

'The West or the Rest?'

> If an inhabitant of the South Sea Island feels obliged on some ceremonial occasion to eat his grandmother, the anthropologist is attracted to examine and explain the ancient custom which caused him to do so: the practical man, on the other hand, tends to take more interest in the grandmother. The one calls it aviophagy and the other murder: it depends on the point of view.
>
> Philip Mitchell[1]

Anger, hope, Utopia, and radicalism are the four axes of V. Y. Mudimbe's work in the 1970s. There is in this corpus a marked tendency to exaggerate the West's supposed oneness and to convey the impression that the world, to use an expression first coined by Chinweizu[2] and the American anthropologist Marshall Sahlins,[3] is made up of the 'West and the Rest'. This dualistic dimension is all the more surprising given that Mudimbe advocates at the end of both *L'Autre Face* and *L'Odeur* an epistemological 'insurrection' that would reject the very dualistic basis upon which colonialism *and* neo-colonialism are predicated. The 'autre' and 'père' in the titles are signs of Mudimbe's willingness to engage with psychoanalysis (see also CG, 27–28; É, 15–16; CB, 47–50) and to establish an analogy between the construction of subjectivity and decolonisation considered in these essays as a process, which would put an end to individual and collective alienation. By way of the concept of 'aphanisis', a term borrowed by Jacques Lacan from Ernest Jones to account for the disappearance or 'fading' of the subject in the process of alienation,[4] Mudimbe argues that colonisation and alienation are governed by the same 'vel' logic (either/or)[5]:

> Ou ceci ou cela, si ceci, on perd cela; si cela, j'ai cela sans ceci [...] Un exemple plus vivant: ou votre gentille 'sauvagerie' ou la 'civilisation'. Si vous choisissez la 'sauvagerie', 'l'impérialisme vous aura [...] si vous

choisissez la 'civilisation', vous vivrez amputés de votre 'culture' [either this or that, if it is this then that is lost; if it is that, I get that without this. A more concrete example: either your lovely 'savagery' or 'civilisation'. If you choose 'savagery', 'imperialism' will get you; if you choose 'civilisation', you will live separated from your own 'culture']. (*AF*, 153–54)

Against this binarism, Mudimbe contends that alienation, as it was understood by Lacan, allows a 'subtil usage de l'intersection' [a subtle use of the intersection] (*AF*, 154) and cannot therefore be solely reduced to this painful separation from one's culture. Through this very allusive and, it must be said, undeveloped reference to Lacan, Mudimbe seems to suggest that alienation is not a dead-end but a process whereby the subject is revealed differently to him or herself; it is thus a site where new meanings emerge; its examination can, as suggested by Abiola Irele in 'In Praise of Alienation', be a means of challenging the Senghorian 'mystique of traditional forms of life' (*Speech*, 201–24 (205)). Alienation is a thorny concept because it is both a translation of the German 'Entfremdung', as used in the Hegelian and Marxist tradition, and of the French 'aliénation' (madness). Although psychological disorders result from acute cases of alienation, Lacan is, however, also of the view that the concept is partly free of its pathological connotations since it represents a necessary step in the constitution of the subject. In the mirror stage, the ego acquires an ephemeral sense of wholeness, which is subsequently challenged and destabilised by the 'field of the Other', that is, language where signifiers threaten the former sense of unity. This passage from the imaginary to the symbolic realm of language generates alienation. Lacan argues, however, that the above-mentioned 'vel' ('or' in Latin) does not, as in the statement 'la liberté ou la mort!' [freedom or death!],[6] always convey exclusive disjunctions (either/or). Aphanisis, or the experience of destitution (disappearance, fading) felt by the subject as (s)he realises that (s)he cannot conceive of her or himself but through the Other, is closely linked to the concept of separation. By way of a wordplay, which, according to Roberto Harari, 'is certainly not a divertimento',[7] Lacan demonstrates that the separation generated by alienation is an ambivalent concept that conjures up ideas of disjunction *and* parturition. Through the phonic proximity between the two Latin verbs 'separare' (separate) and 'se parere' (to beget oneself),[8] Lacan shows that alienation is also a process whereby the split subject regenerates his or herself. Mudimbe does not elaborate on his understanding of aphanisis but his sarcastic treatment of the savagery versus civilisation pair certainly indicates his intention to break away from a simplistic reading of colonial assimilation, postcolonial deliverance, and alienation.[9]

Despite Mudimbe's ability throughout his *œuvre* to look beyond fixed categories and to reappraise – 'reprendre' – the many intersections of mutually excluding traditions and memory sites, *L'Autre Face* and *L'Odeur du père* are nonetheless characterised by a certain fetishisation of the West.[10] This trend can be explained historically. Mudimbe's early writings bore witness to the very dualism of the Cold War, to decolonisation lived as an unfinished process (Viet Nam, Angola), and to the catastrophic emergence in Africa of neo-colonial states such as Zaire. In this context of acute geopolitical tensions, Marxism, which during the years leading up to decolonisation had assumed a major role in the rhetoric and praxis of liberation movements, retained its currency. *L'Autre Face* and *L'Odeur* resonate with the intellectual legacy of Marxism, a point that also applies to *Autour de la 'Nation'*, as shown in the previous chapter. The two collections of essays rely to some degree on the thought of Marx and Engels, Althusser, Maurice Godelier, Lucien Goldmann, Georg Lukász, Michel Bakounine, and, of course, Sartre, to name but a few significant figures. This Marxist apparatus is, however, not systematically deployed. Although Mudimbe addresses an imaginary 'camarade africain' towards the end of *L'Autre Face* (*AF*, 151), his engagement with Marx's followers and exegetes is more theoretical than ideological. Marxism is regarded as a useful repository of theoretical instruments and concepts to probe African decolonisation. He is 'intellectually Marxist' (*P&F*, x) and respects 'Marxism as a scientific method and discourse in its own right' (*P&F*, 183).

Beyond this interest in and even fascination for Marxism, Mudimbe has remained very critical of its applications in Africa and elsewhere in former colonised countries. In this critique, Marxist thought is stripped of its universal claims. Whether in his essays or in novels such as *Entre les eaux* and *L'Écart*, he repeats that Marxism is the product of very specific conditions of possibility, those of nineteenth-century Western Europe during the Industrial Revolution, and cannot therefore be transplanted into sub-Saharan Africa without some accommodation. By way of Césaire's famous letter to Maurice Thorez,[11] he demands, for instance, that Marxism and communism be adapted to serve the cause of black liberation movements in Africa and elsewhere and he rejects the idea that the Marxist *doxa* should prevail irrespective of its geographical transplantations (*OP*, 201). His assessment of African 'amplifications' of the Marxist doctrine is by and large extremely damning: 'African socialisms were a mystification and everyone knew it' (P&F, 183). This is particularly manifest in *The Invention of Africa*, an essay which is no longer driven by the utopian anti-colonialism, in fact, Third-Worldism, of the early essays. In a section significantly entitled 'Marx Africanized' (*IoA*, 92–97), Mudimbe praises Nkrumah's output as a political thinker.[12] He contends that the Ghanaian leader was successful in exposing 'the possibility of reconciling antagonistic forces and orienting them towards positive social change' (*IoA*, 95). He remarks, however, that he was a 'bad politician' who quickly 'turned into a dictator' and concludes that 'the best that can be said is that [Nkrumah] simply failed to put his theory into practice' (*IoA*, 95). In the same section, Ahmed Sékou Touré's attempts to reconcile socialism with Africanness in Guinea is dismissed in a very similar fashion. Mudimbe links the failures of the Africanisation of Marxism to the emergence of authoritarian regimes after 1965 and notes that this phenomenon would be increasingly fictionalised in what Patrice Nganang has called 'romans de la dictature',[13] a genre to which Mudimbe has, alongside Ahmadou Kourouma, Sony Labou Tansi, Tierno Monénembo, Tati-Loutard, and Ngugi wa Thiongo, been one of the major contributors (*IoA*, 92).

This last point is of the utmost importance. His texts are infused with Marxist phrases such as 'social formations', 'modes of production', and *praxis*, but their use, ultimately, needs to be understood as a means to eradicate authoritarianism, promote equality, and propose a counter-discourse to Mobutuism. Mudimbe is no dogmatic hardliner and his recourse to Marxism, in fact Marxianism, remains selective, idiosyncratic, and *undisciplined*. What matters is that the adoption of Marx and Althusser is seen to be beneficial to the implementation of justice and the promotion of a set of ethically sound principles in the interconnected fields of knowledge (education, cooperation, and pedagogy) and politics.

This chapter will argue that this ethical quest has remained one of the chief driving forces of Mudimbe's work from the 1970s to the present day. I shall examine here *L'Autre Face*, *L'Odeur du père*, and *L'Écart* in an attempt to demonstrate that Mudimbe privileges the notion of epistemological insurrection as a means to announce the advent of a Sartre-inflected 'new man' – and woman (see Chapters 1 and 5) – who, it is hoped, will have the ability to produce knowledge differently and reduce Africa's intellectual dependency. The first part of the analysis will contend that Mudimbe's plan to enact this epistemological deliverance strongly resonates with Sartre's post-war antiracist militancy as expressed in *Réflexions sur la question juive*. Indeed, in *L'Odeur du père*, Mudimbe remarks that this essay, alongside Césaire's position in his letter to Maurice Thorez, has enabled him to grasp the tension between freedom and inauthenticity:

> On peut estimer l'écart qui existe entre le droit à sa personnalité et les exigences de l'altérité susceptibles de conduire au racisme. Si nous reprenions [...] la réflexion de Sartre sur la question juive? Et puis, il y a Césaire qui m'a appris ceci: 'Provincialisme ? Non pas. Je ne m'enterre pas dans un particularisme étroit. Mais je ne veux pas non plus me perdre dans un universalisme décharné.' [One can appraise the gap existing between the right to one's personality and the demands for a type of alterity likely to lead to racism. What about taking up again Sartre's reflection on the Jewish question? And then, Césaire taught me this: 'Is it provincialism? No, it is not at all. I am not succumbing to narrow parochialism. But I don't want either to disappear in a lifeless universalism.']. (*OP*, 200)

In the second part of the chapter, I shall examine the way in which Mudimbe's ambition to advocate fairer practices in the human sciences also underlie his critique of social anthropology (*ethnologie*). In this discussion, Mudimbe's views will be explored against those of two contemporary Africanists, Johannes Fabian and Benoît Verhaegen, who were also based in Congo-Zaire for many years and committed to the decolonisation of anthropology; finally, the forthcoming *On African Fault Lines*,[14] a collection of 'meditations' dedicated to 'the memory of innocents, unknown millions of fellow Africans, victims of 19th and 20th century ideologies and cult of difference' (*OAF*, vi), will be assessed to observe the links between 'alterity politics' and the rise, at the beginning of the twenty-first century, of a new (but still ethnocentric) global order where knowledge practices mirror economic inequalities and power imbalances.

The *Authentic* Other

In *L'Autre Face* and *L'Odeur*, Mudimbe appears as an epistemologically committed intellectual. The two volumes are not about politics *per se* but about the interface between political sovereignty and the practice of knowledge. This latter phrase, although somewhat abstract on the surface, relates to very concrete issues as Mudimbe reminds his readers that African scholars – the two texts were published against the backdrop of intense cooperation programmes between Belgian, French, and Zairian universities – work in a conceptual framework designed in and by the West. In an oft-quoted passage, Mudimbe compares this framework to a lift operated by external agents in which African scientists find themselves trapped and unable to decide whether to go up or down (*AF*, 102–03).[15] Mudimbe establishes a very strict analogy between epistemological dependency and neo-colonialism. Political independence will not be achieved unless African scholarship frees itself from Western conceptual models. He deplores that these are uncritically adhered to and that this often subconscious compliance with the former master's discourses perpetuates in the present the old colonial rule. He has been a university professor since the late 1960s and it is therefore logical that this very professional context is used to examine the production of knowledge in newly established African universities. The fact that he is 'above all a teacher'[16] and that teachers cannot but take seriously the strategies presiding over the dissemination of knowledge has often been overlooked by his critics. The correlation between nation-building and education is a vexed issue. Mudimbe's critique of African knowledge practices, a mere decade after decolonisation, echoes the fierce polemics about the role and future of university education that took place in France and in other European countries in 1968. As a doctoral student at Louvain and an associate lecturer at Nanterre in the late 1960s, he joined in debates in which the relevance of traditional pedagogical methods was challenged and the deep disconnection between tutors and students was dismissed as a residue of the not too distant colonial period. Nineteen sixty-eight resonates with the anti-authoritarianism of decolonisation and can therefore be regarded as the culmination of an internal decolonising process whereby it was argued that the transformation of society would be achieved through the demystification of father figures and omniscient teachers.

Mudimbe is not a political activist in the truest sense of the word but from the very early days of his academic career he was driven by an ambition to develop, by way of a historical and epistemological analysis of colonialism and neo-colonialism, a socially transformative set of principles. This epistemological commitment, which is set in motion by an examination of the thought procedures underpinning the human sciences, is announced at the very outset of *L'Autre Face*. He remarks that his research intends to open up possibilities of producing a theoretical discourse from which a political practice would emerge. He adds that the human sciences are to be transformed radically and that Africans, on the basis of their own singular and concrete experiences, will take it upon themselves to achieve this epistemological renewal and will thus be able to reconcile 'pratique de la connaissance et praxis révolutionnaire' [practice of knowledge and revolutionary praxis] (*AF*, 10–11).

Mudimbe's programme, as indicated by the phrase 'praxis révolutionnaire' and the focus on the subject's singularity, resonates with Sartrean political activism and phenomenology. Until the Second World War, Sartre remained relatively apolitical. This said, it would be wrong to reduce his trajectory to a shift from ethics to politics. In fact, as argued by Noureddine Lamouchi, his thought was marked by a return to the ethical towards the end of his life.[17] After the war, however, he became increasingly aware of the necessity to move away from his former philosophical idealism in order to bridge the gap between theory and praxis and translate words into action. The Holocaust, an issue, which would haunt Sartre until his death in 1980, and decolonisation are the main historical events against which this radical politicisation crystallised. The racial question lies at the heart of this political awakening. As shown by Lamouchi, there is a continuum between *Réflexions sur la question juive*, the prefaces that Sartre produced to support books by leading intellectuals such as Senghor, Fanon, and Memmi, and the many articles published in *Les Temps Modernes* on decolonisation and liberation movements in Cuba, China, and, more generally, in the Third World. After the war, Sartre discovered history,[18] or, to be more precise, the history of the colonised Other. This discovery was predicated upon the belief that words have socially and politically transformative effects, a point that is made throughout *Qu'est-ce que la littérature*, Sartre's main theoretical work on commitment and literature: 'To speak is to act; anything which one names is already no longer quite the same; it has lost its innocence'.[19]

In this discovery of history, Sartre embraced Hegelianism and the idea that the contradiction between the thesis and the antithesis would generate change and, indeed, progress since 'man', in this conception of commitment, is regarded as an entity whose actualisation will take place in the future. In 'Orphée noir', he presents negritude as a means towards a better, in fact race-less, society and in the Preface to *Les Damnés de la terre*, violence is also conceived dialectically, that is, as an instrument to generate future liberation.[20]

Sartre's dualistic understanding of colonialism[21] is a trait that can be found in all anti-colonial thinkers but also, a mere decade after decolonisation, in Mudimbe's early works. Although Sartre's focus on colonial issues is at times very specific – it is notably the case of his Preface to *La Pensée politique de Patrice Lumumba*[22] – it remains overall subordinated to the idea that the colonial system has reached a dead-end because it rests upon two unbridgeable categories: the colonist and the native. Sartre's political analysis retained throughout this period, and until his later interventions in favour of the rights of the Palestinians in the 1970s, a very strong ethical dimension. What haunted him was the figure of the oppressed (and the counter-figure of the oppressor). In this exploration, which started in earnest with *Réflexions sur la question juive* (published in 1946 but written in October 1944[23]) and was continued during decolonisation and after, there is a clear tendency on Sartre's part to consider the Jews, blacks, colonised, African Americans,[24] and citizens from the newly (or soon-to-be) decolonised world as interchangeable categories. He would then, time and time again, establish compelling analogies between these categories, whether African Americans or Jews. Similarly, he would say that the Jew is fabricated by the anti-Semite and that the native is first and foremost an idea borne out the colonist's *situation*. The emergence of what Sartre called 'integral humanity' is reliant upon their mutual liberation, which, in turn, depends on their ability *authentically* to exercise their freedom.[25]

There is therefore a sense of continuity between *La Nausée*, *L'Être et le néant*, and Sartre's more overtly politicised works in that 'freedom', which had earlier been considered from an individual perspective, is now articulated from a collective standpoint.[26] In *Réflexions sur la question juive*, Sartre provides an analysis of anti-Semitism and, although his examination of the relationship between the anti-Semite and the Jew is reminiscent of the Hegelian Master–Slave dialectic, this essay relies chiefly on concepts, such as freedom, responsibility, situation, and (in)authenticity, developed earlier.[27] In many ways this short volume provides a lesson in existentialism, which Sartre will apply to the colonial situation and which would later be adopted by thinkers such as Fanon and Mudimbe who is the continuator of this Sartrean activism, which he has applied to his examination of anthropology *and* critique of neo-colonialism.

About the anti-Semite, Sartre argues that he operates on behalf of a 'still prelogical collectivity'.[28] Throughout the book, he insists that the anti-Semite 'subscribes to an irrationalism of fact',[29] to a lazy conceptual framework where ideas are forever set in stone and are ascribed a 'mineral permanence'.[30] The anti-Semite's 'committal'[31] is said 'not to arise from experience'.[32] This is a crucial point and one which contributes to the dismissal of the essentialist framework in which anti-Semites function. Sartre demonstrates indeed here the irrationalism of a conceptualisation in which the production of a notion (anti-Semitism) precedes experience: 'It is thus the *idea* one has of the Jew which seems to determine history, and not "historical evidence" which gives rise to the *idea*'.[33] This point, which announces the spirit presiding over the vast epistemological surveys that Mudimbe and Edward Said would conduct after decolonisation, is reinforced by the suggestion that the anti-Semites' world is devoid of any existential freedom and ruled by a set of 'petrified values'[34] for the anti-Semite is a man, as Sartre remarks, who is afraid 'of himself, of his conscience, of his freedom, of his instincts, of his responsibilities, of solitude, of change, of society and of the world'.[35] He is, and we shall return to this idea later, a man without *praxis*. His 'existence' is 'perpetually in suspense' and, in a typically Sartrean expression, he adds that the anti-Semite aspires to a life 'in which one never becomes anything else but what one already was'.[36]

Sartre's analysis of the Jew's plight is predicated upon his previous theorisation, notably in *L'Être et le néant*, of 'The Look' ('Le Regard'[37]) and (in)authenticity. Sartre contends that through the subjugating process generated by anti-Semitism, the inauthentic Jew becomes the object of the anti-Semite's consciousness and internalises, as it were, the set of petrified values in use to maintain him in a state of sub-humanity. For fear of the Other's look, the inauthentic Jew is constrained to become a mere thing. The inauthentic Jew is thus the anti-Semite's being-for-others as the former finally accepts 'with resignation the phantom being [...] which haunts him and which is none other than himself, *himself as he is for others*.[38] This alienating look, which reduces the Other to what he or she is not,[39] to an *idea* ultimately more revealing of the 'culture that produced it than [of] it putative object',[40] as Edward Said argues via a definitely Mudimbian formula, has been since decolonisation one of the most enduring concerns of anti-colonial *and* postcolonial critique. Sartre's essay also has, however, a prescriptive dimension for he argues that authentic Jews are *free* to escape their 'situation' and thus act – *praxis* mean action – on the world and transform it.

Authentic Jews, like all other authentic 'Wretched of the Earth' that Sartre would examine during his career, choose to *transcend* their own situation so as to overthrow the order that had fabricated and congealed their identity. As he would a few years later in 'Orphée noir', Sartre argues here that the introduction of a classless socialist regime would eradicate, once and for all, the factors that had allowed anti-Semitism to develop (the bourgeoisie, private property, real estate, and nationalistic chauvinism). The programme that Sartre sketches out at the end of the book is driven by an ambition to build a better future, a 'règne humain' [human reign],[41] and to call upon socialist praxis to achieve an integral humanity and generate plenitude for all.[42]

Sartre's cautious dissection of the etiology of anti-Semitism is characterised by a utopian spirit, and great deal of wishful thinking, that would become the trademarks of his activism during decolonisation and after. The demise of imperialism, like the Second World War and the Holocaust, had exposed the limits of humanism and revealed a number of possible avenues to envisage a reformed future, and 'libérer le présent du passé' [free the present from the past], to quote Régis Debray in a book on the Cuban revolution.[43] This revolution and the intervention of the Cuban Army under the leadership of Che Guevara in the years leading to the end of the First Republic in 1965 have had an enduring impact on Congolese collective memory. In his first novel, *Entre les eaux*, Mudimbe translates the highly ideological atmosphere that presided over the deployment of Marxist guerrilla fighters on Congolese soil. Cuba also played a significant role in Sartre's writings of the 1960s and in his examination of the role of praxis in Marxist revolutions. He remained deeply impressed by what he witnessed during a visit in Cuba in the early days of the newly instated Castrist regime in 1960. Lamouchi contends that this visit enabled him to confirm, via the concrete achievements of the Cuban revolutionaries, what he had exposed in his *Critique de la raison dialectique*,[44] that is, the necessary precedence of praxis over ideology,[45] or, to be more precise, the assumption that History, although largely shaped by the laws of historical materialism, is also inflected by human subjectivity, a process that Sartre described as the 'permanent and dialectical unity of freedom and necessity'.[46]

Mudimbe's early efforts to tease out the relationship between theory and praxis in the field of epistemology bears witness to Sartre's many attempts to account for the revolutionary *authenticity* of newly decolonised peoples. 'Authenticity', beyond its Sartrean conceptualisation, remains a highly suggestive and charged word in relation to Zairian independence, as examined in Chapter 2 through Kangafu's very tendentious essay, and Mudimbe is keen to remind his readers, that 'certaines philosophies du XIXe siècle européen – que l'on pense par exemple à l'Allemagne – sont des philosophies de l'authenticité' [certain nineteenth-century European philosophies – let us think about Germany for instance – are philosophies of authenticity] (*OP*, 200).

Mudimbe's frequent use of the word and its cognates is often Sartrean and, as suggested in the coda of *L'Odeur du père*, a book published after his American relocation, his recourse to this concept 'n'a rien à voir avec la "farce" zaïroise' [has nothing to do with the Zairian farce] (*OP*, 200). At the same time, however, one can assume that its very use, which in truth was subversive and insurrectional, went unnoticed, that is, was not sanctioned, precisely because of the prestige it enjoyed in Mobutu's rhetoric. By referring to authenticity, Mudimbe was therefore able to employ, in a most aptly Sartrean manner, a concept which means what it does not and does not mean what it does, a paradox which, as Mudimbe remarks, is reminiscent of Antoine Roquentin's plight in Sartre's *Nausea*, who, 'while meditating on his being and that of things [...] discovers that *he is what he is not and he is not what he is*' (*P&F*, xii; my emphasis). Mudimbe's covert critique of the regime was thus facilitated by the intrinsic *double entendre* inherent in the notion of authenticity.

Like Sartre in the fields of politics, Mudimbe advocates in *L'Autre Face* and *L'Odeur du père* a more committed, situated, and authentic practice of knowledge. He argues that the human sciences are, as it were, oppressed. Via Foucault's archaeological methodology, he shows that this state of subjugation became apparent at the very threshold of modernity when philosophy lost its ability to act as the ultimate meta-discursive arbiter, that is, its position as 'savoir synoptique' [synoptic knowledge] (*AF*, 127), of all other sciences. By way of Hermann von Helmholtz, the German physicist and historian of sciences, he shows that the end of philosophy's imperium was precipitated by the debate between Newton and Hegel and the latter's inability to produce a set of philosophical principles that would account for developments and procedures in the natural sciences (*AF*, 128). In the age of positivism the dependency grew as social scientists would increasingly rely on the natural sciences – mathematics, physics, and biology – for general laws and investigative methodologies (*AF*, p. 129). This move had, according to Mudimbe, catastrophic consequences for the human and social sciences in that it led, a point that he makes by evoking the authority of Ronald Laing (an 'anti-psychiatrist' close to Sartre), to the over-rationalisation and objectification of the human subject on whom sociological and anthropological investigations are conducted: 'se donner le social comme objet et prétendre l'expliquer signifie aussi évacuer le sujet de l'expérience, le nier radicalement' [to conceive social facts as objects and claim to elucidate them amounts to evacuate the subject of the experiment and radically to negate him] (*OP*, 52–53).

Ethnology as a Pretext

Above all, Mudimbe considers the practice of the human sciences against the backdrop of colonialism and neo-colonialism in sub-Saharan Africa. In this wide-ranging reflection, which continues to absorb his attention today, he has favoured the examination of 'ethnologie' (social and cultural anthropology). This discipline – its 'corps monstrueux' [monstruous body] (*AF*, 10) and its practitioners, the 'techniciens des sauvages' [technicians of the savages] (*AF*, 9) – is repeatedly said to be the 'pretext' of his investigation (*AF*, 10, 151; *OP*, 20, 34). By this, one needs to understand that anthropology is used as a terrain that enables Mudimbe, like several other contemporaries in the 1960s and 1970s,[47] to tease out the relationship between science and imperialism. *L'Autre Face du royaume* and *L'Odeur du père* are two volumes of essays which strictly echo one another in terms of overall thrust and conclusions. During this period, Mudimbe remains fascinated by what Robert Young would call 'Sartre's extravagances', that is, the tension between history, as a deterministic law-making process, and human subjectivity.[48] In both books, Mudimbe analyses the epistemological and historical processes responsible for the reification of sub-Saharan Africa. He shows here, a point to which he will return in his subsequent books through the application of Sartrean ontological categories (in-itself, for-itself, for-others) to the African context (see *P&F*, ix–xxii), that African scholars remained largely unaware that what they hold as knowledge is in fact 'vues réfléchies par le regard d'autrui' [views reflected by the Other's look] (*AF*, 103). Against the 'polysémie [...] pathologique' (*AF*, 126) of ethnology, he advocates therefore 'nouvelles pratiques scientifiques sur l'"un" et ses "autres"' [new scientific practices on the same and its Others] (*OP*, 203).

These two books are very close to Johannes Fabian's *Time and the Other*, which, although published in 1983, was completed in 1978.[49] There is a common focus on the underlying procedures of social and cultural anthropology during and after colonialism, a shared ability to interrogate the 'colonial library' (and particularly missionary archives and travelogues), and draw upon a multiplicity of sources cutting across several national boundaries and ranging from history, sociology, linguistics, and philosophy. Fabian, who is a practising anthropologist, has also devoted a significant part of his research to the epistemological history of the discipline.[50] Originally a Catholic priest and then an academic in the United States, Lubumbashi, and Europe, he is in terms of trajectory very close to Mudimbe who has over the years remained an important interlocutor.[51]

In *Time and the Other*, Fabian also contends that anthropological practices have a political dimension and reflect, two decades after decolonisation, the enduring hegemony of the West over its Others in the former colonies. Like Mudimbe in his early essays, he advocates the use of a liberating praxis so as to redress the balance between anthropologists and their objects. In his erudite examination of anthropological history, Fabian contends that the Other's objectification has been generated by what he calls 'allochronism' or 'denial of coevalness'. Fabian's major premise is that there is a discrepancy between ethnographic fieldwork, a subjective experience between individuals engaged in a relation of reciprocal and dialogical exchange, and anthropological writing (either ethnographic notes or theoretical studies) where the Other's presence and present are erased and denied, coevalness being the rendering of the German *Gleichzeitigkeit*. It results from this largely subconscious practice, that the Other's time is in fact *another* time, that is, 'allochronic'. This chronological distancing of the Other and the assumption that he or she remains outside Western modernity is, as Fabian deplores, an evolutionist idea which has, despite the various epistemological shifts experienced by anthropology since the early nineteenth century, retained some currency until today and can still be identified in expressions such as 'Third World'.[52] In a move that strongly resonates with Mudimbe's epistemological existentialism, Fabian argues that 'these disjunctions between experience and science' are above all the products of 'typological time',[53] that is, a conception of time relying chiefly on a number of binary oppositions such as 'preliterate versus literate', 'traditional versus modern', 'peasant versus industrial', and 'rural versus urban'. These oppositions do not measure time 'as it elapses' but map out, by way of qualities which are unequally shared by regions of the world, a new geography which exacerbates and invents the Other's time as radically different.[54] Like Mudimbe in his analysis of the modalities presiding over the production of knowledge in neo-colonial Africa, Fabian claims that allochronism is the mark of a past living on in the present: 'Earlier talk about peoples without history belongs here, as do more sophisticated distinctions such as the one between "hot" and "cold"'.[55]

Regarding this last point, it is useful to mention that the two authors were part of a critical vein for which the dismissal of neo-colonialism was formulated through a relatively negative appraisal of structuralism.

Although Foucault was (strictly speaking) not a structuralist, as he forcefully contends in the Preface of the English translation of *Les Mots et les choses*,[56] one cannot deny that his exploration of the unconscious mechanisms behind epistemological discourses is reminiscent of the methodology employed by Lévi-Strauss to delineate the structural patterns of Amerindian myths. It is therefore as a major exponent of structuralism, as a sort of omnipresent and omniscient father-figure of French thought and philosophy, that Foucault is partly rejected by Mudimbe during this period (but less so in *The Invention of Africa*). Ironically, Mudimbe uses Foucault's own words about Hegel (*OP*, 12–13) – a figure that one cannot escape and without whom philosophy cannot be conceived[57] – to make the argument that African scholars should challenge Foucault because he is, like Hegel in his time and after, the embodiment of the West and of a system of thought from which they urgently need to distance themselves: 'M. Foucault peut être considéré comme un symbole insigne de la royauté de cette pensée occidentale dont nous aimerions tant nous défaire' [M. Foucault can be considered as a prominent symbol of the sovereignty of this Western thought from which we are so determined to depart] (*OP*, 37).

At this stage of Mudimbe's career structuralism is therefore trapped in a vicious circle since it is also regarded as a salutary development, as a system offering a more scientific, less racially biased, set of approaches to analyse cultural facts. Following Ricœur in his analysis of *La Pensée sauvage*, Mudimbe objects nonetheless that Lévi-Strauss's anthropology is a 'Kantisme sans sujet transcendental' [Kantianism without a transcendental subject] (*OP*, 83),[58] that is, 'an absolute formalism', a 'philosophy' that 'would make the linguistic model an absolute'.[59] Structuralism is thus part of a continuum triggered, as argued earlier, by the demise of philosophy's imperium and by the need, on the part of social scientists, to have recourse to abstract models (tables, formulae) to account for human realities (*OP*, 83). Ricœur, in his examination of Lévi-Strauss's thought and main inspirations in the field of linguistics (Saussure and Jakobson), remarks in this respect that structural anthropology is 'a Kantian unconscious […] since we are concerned here with a categorial system without reference to a thinking subject'. And he adds: 'This is why structuralism as a philosophy will develop a kind of intellectualism which is fundamentally antireflective, anti-idealist, and antiphenomenological'.[60]

In his call for a new praxis in anthropology Fabian advocates the reintroduction of the 'thinking (and speaking) subject'. This demand is predicated upon the idea, as expressed by Ricœur, that the 'linguistic laws' favoured by Lévi-Strauss attribute too much significance to 'the nonhistorical level of the mind'.[61] Fabian's examination of Lévi-Strauss is far less conciliatory than Mudimbe's. In the Preface (but also in the last chapter[62]) of *Parables and Fables* – of course this book was published in 1991 and therefore does not quite reflect Mudimbe's earlier sensitivities – he attempted to reconcile Sartre and Lévi-Strauss whose difficult dialogue had been irremediably interrupted, as examined in Chapter 1, by Lévi-Strauss's disparaging reading of *Critique of Dialectical Reason* in *The Savage Mind*. In this piece of theoretical advocacy,[63] Mudimbe remarks that the proverbial dichotomy between agency and structure may not be as absolute as it may seem (a point made by other Sartre specialists).[64] He shows that Sartre's philosophical output is the product of a development which was inaugurated with Descartes' theorisation of the *cogito* as a self-present and self-sufficient entity. Lévi-Strauss, on the other hand, conceptualised anthropology away from Cartesianism, that is, from Rousseau's premise, a point made in the *Confessions*, that 'In truth, I am not "me" but the weakest most humble of others' (*P&F*, xiv). Despite this blatant opposition – Sartre's 'claim that we are completely free, fully responsible, and universal lawmakers and Lévi-Strauss' masterful ahistorical demonstration' (*P&F*, xi) – Mudimbe takes it upon himself to reveal points of overlap between these two competing models of subjectivity. He contends that Sartre's conception of the self – a view conveyed earlier about the relationship between the Jew and the anti-Semite – is predicated upon the notion that 'the for-itself is not fully without the for-other' (*P&F*, xii). Nonetheless, this cardinal existential principle is shown to be close to Lévi-Strauss's re-appropriation of Rousseau's view that 'there exists a "he" who "thinks" through me and who first causes me to doubt whether it is I who am thinking' (*P&F*, 178). Conversely, he argues that Lévi-Strauss is not immune to issues of agency. Indeed, Mudimbe demonstrates that Lévi-Strauss, the man, the scientist, can be read through a Sartrean grid. He notes that his scientific project, what he also calls 'Lévi-Strauss' praxis', is formulated 'within a cultural and human environment, which is an obvious practico-inert' (*P&F*, xix), that is, in the idiosyncratic Sartrean terminology, the adversity presented by the world (determining material conditions generated by former praxes) that free action strives to transcend. Further, he expands on this idea that Lévi-Strauss expresses his freedom against the backdrop of categories – 'practico-inert' and 'praxis' – that are synonymous with the in-itself/for-itself dialectic. Lévi-Strauss, a consciousness or being-for-itself, acts on the world of anthropology, makes theoretical choices in the face of its facticity (another synonym of 'practico-inert'), and brings about an epistemological revolution. Ultimately, Mudimbe's theoretical reflection appears as a means to delineate some of the parameters against which African subjectivity unfold and to comment on his own neither completely free, nor completely determined trajectory, that is, as argues Michael Syrotinski (citing Butler), his own 'vacillation between the already-there and the yet-to come'.[65]

In his appraisal of Lévi-Strauss's anthropology, Fabian is very scathing as the French anthropologist, despite his own claim of being the 'heir of the eighteenth century', is depicted as having a conception of time 'firmly rooted in nineteenth-century notions of natural history'.[66] Fabian contends that Lévi-Strauss's dismissal of Sartre's idea of history in *The Savage Mind* is duplicitous. He argues that in this attack Lévi-Strauss does not use the notions of time and space in their geographical and historical meanings as he is above all interested in defining cultural taxonomies in which time and space are contingent categories. Lévi-Strauss's space is 'tabular', that is a means to elaborate 'semiological constructs';[67] his conception of time is predicated upon a similar assumption as it does not recognise any significance to human history and subjectivity. For Fabian, Lévi-Strauss's taxonomic objectivity is 'allochronistic'. When understood within the context of ethnographic studies this focus on meaningful networks of binary oppositions favours observation over participation: for Lévi-Strauss, the ethnographer is above all a 'viewer (and perhaps a voyeur)'.[68] Here lies the main thrust of Fabian's critique as he claims that Lévi-Strauss, in privileging a contemplative idea of ethnography, shows 'utter disregard for the active, productive nature of field-*work* and its inevitable implication in historical situations and real, political contradictions'.[69] Lévi-Strauss's allochronism obfuscates the fact that ethnography is rooted in inter-subjective communication and conveys the impression that the participants are removed from the 'dialogic situation'.[70] According to Fabian, Lévi-Strauss's visualist and diagrammatic stance, which became a significant characteristic of cultural relativism (of which negritude is a product) after the Second World War, can also be traced back to the Renaissance thinker Petrus Ramus who is referred to here as one of the forefathers of European pedagogy. Ramus's style was, in the name of scientific objectivity but also of 'teachability' of knowledge,[71] predicated upon the idea that vision was the noblest of all senses. In this context, the scientist, a pedagogue who also strives for didactic intelligibility, engages in a monologue with the objects of the experiment, that is to say, observes and analyses them but does not expect anything back from them. Ramism marked, as argued by Walter J. Ong, the 'decay of dialogue' and the advent of a methodology in which 'even persons respond only as objects' and, consequently, 'say nothing back'.[72] Ramism, a stance which became, according to Fabian, synonymous with 'pedagogical method' and the 'practice of Normal Science',[73] was driven, again in the name of objectivity, to visualise and represent knowledge diagrammatically. This 'visualism' (or 'synopticism') permeated into modern anthropology as it adopted the practice of explicating other cultures through schematic visual representations or public events (illustrated travelogues, exotic fairs and exhibitions, museums, trees and tables to visualise ethnic varieties and 'primitive' cultures[74]) and consolidated thus the 'hegemony of the visual as a mode of knowing'.[75]

Visualism, as understood by Fabian, is an ethnocentric process which contributes to the idea that these other cultures scrutinised by the anthropologist are finite objects that can be exhaustively comprehended and catalogued away. This epistemological model is so powerful that it shaped anthropology from its evolutionist infancy in the early nineteenth century to cultural relativism, whereby uniquely singular cultures become 'culture gardens' in which the time of the Other is 'walled in' so that it 'cannot spill over into ours'.[76] Finally, this model also influenced structural anthropology *à la* Lévi-Strauss, even though Fabian does not do justice to Lévi-Strauss's successful attempt to challenge Western 'ocularcentrism'.[77] It is useful to remember, with regards to the connections between colonial hegemony and vision, that Sartre mentions in the very first lines of 'Orphée noir' the incredulity felt by the colonist to be looked at by the former objects of their own subjugating gaze,[78] a point developed in Mudimbe's novels such as *Le Bel immonde* and *L'Écart*. Fabian's treatment of visualism and its synonyms (allochronism, denial of coevalness, spatialization, temporalization) is therefore above all driven by an urge to link the production of knowledge to political emancipation. The context in which this activism took place is also that of Mudimbe who in *L'Odeur du père* establishes a link between the type of politically committed sociology – 'sociologie en profondeur' [in depth sociology] (*OP*, 177) – practised by Clifford Geertz and J. Fabian in the United States and Benoît Verhaegen's 'histoire immédiate'.[79]

At the time of the decolonisation of sub-Saharan Africa, African history, as an autonomous scholarly discipline, was quasi inexistent and it was not until 1960 that the first two French chairs in the history of black Africa were created at the Sorbonne.[80] The many historical publications on this region, what Mudimbe famously called the 'colonial library', had been predominantly authored by amateur anthropologists, colonial officials, and missionaries for the most part (James Frazer's 'men on the spot'[81]), who in the course of their long stays in Africa undertook to write about the peoples they were administering and evangelising. This huge historical corpus, published more often than not without the explicit support of 'metropolitan' scholarly institutions, played a crucial role in the constitution of European empires in sub-Saharan Africa. Towards the end of the 1950s, this dubious association with the colonial enterprise became a key factor in the dismissal of the 'colonial library' on the part of a new generation of historians and contributed to the emergence of a more clearly defined intellectual arena for the development of African history.[82]

Benoît Verhaegen was from 1958 onwards at the forefront of this reflection on the present and the future of historical studies in Congo-Zaire where he worked in close collaboration with Mudimbe as a university professor. Like other prominent Africanists such as Jean Suret-Canale and Georges Balandier, Verhaegen approached African history from an inter-disciplinary angle; his ambition was to contribute to the development of 'total history', that is, a type of investigation that would attempt to 'account for all aspects of a social formation and the greatest possible number of explanatory factors'.[83] Histoire immédiate[84] is, therefore, above all a collective enterprise whereby, as in Balandier's works, for instance, teams of researchers endeavour to bridge the gap between history and the social sciences in order to reincorporate 'historical analysis into the very heart of anthropological enquiry'.[85] This collective research is politically motivated and explores, in the main, the emergence of collective movements (political parties, guerrilla groups) in Congo-Zaire and significant public figures such as Lumumba and Mulélé,[86] in order to foster 'a new form of understanding contemporary political culture'.[87] It is premised on the idea that it is possible to remain intellectually rigorous whilst embracing political objectives of social transformation as he claims that histoire immédiate is 'politically committed history'.[88] Verhaegen, who was a Catholic with a Marxist inclination, took it upon himself to challenge in postcolonial Congo the enduring pedagogical elitism and the dependency syndrome inherited from the colonial period.[89] Indeed, according to Laurent Monnier, remembering the golden age of research in political science at Lovanium (the Congolese campus of Leuven University) and his encounters with figures such as Verhaegen and Mudimbe, this 'process of decolonization of knowledge [...] also implied a kind of intellectual fighting in solidarity with Congolese students and academics for the re-appropriation and change of a system of education conceived along Western patterns'.[90] The views that Mudimbe puts forwards via his metaphor of the lift, that is, African scholars operate in institutional and methodological frameworks conceived in the West as if decolonisation and May 1968 had never happened,[91] reflects Verhaegen's attempts to transform the relationship between students and their tutors, between researchers and the subjects/objects of their investigations. The meaning ascribed to 'immédiate' encapsulates the nature of Verhaegen's liberation programme. The adjective is not to be interpreted in its chronological dimension even though histoire immédiate focuses on contemporary history and recent Congolese political crises. Verhaegen's chief aspiration is to generate '"immediate" knowledge'. The term needs therefore to be understood in its 'epistemological sense' and in the context in which the researcher faces his or her informants, that is, 'when two elements (the subject and object of understanding) are brought together without intervening stages, without a third, intermediary, device'.[92] Like Mudimbe and Fabian, Verhaegen rejects intermediary devices such as objectifying procedures and allochronism which invent and invariably maintain a distance between scholars and their students. He posits thus that unmediated knowledge will emerge when these figures become equals and when the inter-subjective quality – or coevalness – of their exchange is recognised. Verhaegen is aware of the fact that total immediacy is utopian but he maintains that the 'mediating processes' should be reduced to a minimum.[93] He suggests a number of recommendations to facilitate the exchange between the 'researcher' and the 'actor' (agent) and generate thus a 'more objective understanding of history'.[94] First, the partners should trust one another and be committed to a 'compatible political project', choose 'appropriate questions', rely upon commonly shared 'categories of discourse', and communicate 'within a relatively non-directed interview'.[95] Secondly, he argues that the climate of reciprocity between the two partners is the premise upon which the political potential of the encounter can be actualised and 'the experience of the historical actor can be inserted into the collective praxis of the group'.[96] This more equitable context is, according to Verhaegen, conducive to the reciprocal transformation of the two partners involved in this process of mutual understanding: 'Historians must recognize in their counterparts not only a passive informant but a historical actor, a subject, not an object, and a colleague in knowledge as well as in action'.[97]

What is important in this programme of epistemological decolonisation is the overlap between knowledge, political action (or agency), and cultural awakening. In this text, Verhaegen applies to a former colonial country the arguments that would be used to militate for the development of a history from below and the various avatars that this broad reassessment of history has generated (social history, subaltern, women's, and postcolonial studies). His overarching contention is that the epistemologically (and hence politically) oppressed Congolese should regain his or her agency through a novel, more dialogical, less Eurocentric, practice of knowledge.

The recognition of these hitherto neglected figures echoes Fabian's belief, and of course Mudimbe's, that the imbalance between the 'Knower' and the 'Known', that is, the idea that the latter is reducible to the former's set of objectifying procedures, should be overcome.[98] What unites Mudimbe, Fabian, and Verhaegen, who belong to the same epistemological context and shaped the postcolonial Congolese higher education sector as much as they were shaped by it, is the conviction that decolonisation opens up a space where knowledge could (and should) become the vehicle of a yet to be fulfilled (political) agency. After Sartre, Mudimbe claims that the African, although determined by the European's petrifying look, is ultimately *free* to become what (s)he is not; Fabian argues that the allochronistic Other lives in fact in a time which is also hers or his and is therefore engaged in, and indeed committed to, an inter-subjective dialogue, in which, as Verhaegen contends (s)he will become the co-author and co-agent of his or her history. Viewed from today's perspective (in the second decade of the twenty-first century), their posture appears as somewhat outmoded as it bears witness to a time when social scientists spent a great deal of energy on meta-discursive issues relating to their own scientific and methodological procedures, a standpoint that Mudimbe would later deride (see *P&F*, 101). Nonetheless these reflections cannot, because of the very context in which they were formulated, be brushed aside as early expressions of political correctness. These authors were arguing, quite rightly, that anthropologists (but also social and political scientists) were perpetuating in the present, often unwittingly and as the agents of a deep-seated gnostic code, the old hierarchies upon which colonial rule had founded its legitimacy.[99] Mudimbe makes this point very clearly at

'The West or the Rest?' 99

the end of *L'Odeur du père*. He returns here to the time when he started his academic career in Zaire. This period, he argues, was still dominated by the methodological prejudices upon which 'la science coloniale' had been practiced but this haunting past was now challenged by 'un présent dans lequel B. Verhaegen, scandaleusement, tentait de vivre un pratique singulière de la science plutôt que de reproduire un "modèle"' [a present wherein B. Verhaegen was scandalously attempting to bring to life a singular practice of science rather than reproduce a model] (*OP*, 199). In this particular context, 'Histoire immédiate' captured the hope of generating 'une science engagée dans laquelle la praxis serait la clé majeure' [a committed science in which praxis would be assigned the major role] (*OP*, 199).

The discursive backdrop against which this attack against Western anthropology unfolds is not, however, without its internal ambiguities. The over-theoretical approach that Fabian, Mudimbe, and Verhaegen chose to adopt obfuscates the intended 'immediacy' of their programme and is thus partly complicit in the reifying and othering processes that they criticise and would want to overcome. This limitation of Mudimbe's work has been highlighted by various critics.[100] Although ambiguous, this attitude remains, against the Sartrean logic in which Mudimbe operates, coherent as, ultimately, he cannot be held responsible for what he is – a Westernised African – but can also transcend this *situation*. It is within these boundaries that the notion of praxis, as it is used by Mudimbe but also by Fabian and Verhaegen, must be understood. Praxis, in this context, is a tool to challenge the assumed determinism presiding over knowledge production. Praxis, a term that the three authors, however, avoid to define precisely, is used to reveal the limits of dialectical materialism against which Sartre positioned himself in his *Critique of Dialectical Reason*. The three authors refer to praxis to assert the necessity to recognise the role of human subjectivity and freedom in the process of knowledge production. Their will to contribute to the emergence of a new agent of knowledge is set against prevailing ethnocentric and paternalistic epistemological practices, that is, against an imperialist practico-inert, which is still residually affecting the present.

Although the three authors largely agree in terms of final objective, their relation to Marxism varies. Verhaegen is close to Sartre who attempted in *Critique of Dialectical Reason* to demonstrate that existentialism can be accommodated by historical materialism, that freedom (and *authenticity*) has a role to play within historical determinism. The methodology supporting histoire immédiate involves, as shown above, the former colonial object who has been promoted to the status of 'historical actor' and can now, in this sometimes confrontational dialogue with the researcher, act upon his or her own history. Nonetheless, Verhaegen is mindful to add that this encounter is a 'dialectical exchange' which makes it 'possible to understand the full significance of historical movement' (sic),[101] indicating thus that this agent is also submitted to a set of historical laws (to dialectical reason) and that the sum of individual actions will eventually generate (and tolalise themselves in), as Sartre puts it, '*one* human History, with *one* truth and *one* intelligibility'.[102]

Mudimbe is overall far less inclined, in the name of African singularity, to embrace this totalising interpretation of history even though he is of the view that the subject's praxis is limited by determining structures and challenged by the practico-inert, two concepts that, despite the well-known antagonism between structuralism and Sartrean existentialism, Sartre himself was ready to conflate.[103] Mudimbe is, however, closer to the early Sartre than Verhaegen in that he argues that Africans, as in the relation explored earlier between Jewish people and anti-Semites, are to exercise their *authenticity* in order to break away from the thingification into which they have been reduced. There is in *L'Autre Face* and *L'Odeur* a tendency to focus on the inadequacy of Western paradigms to capture African singularities. The term 'folie' in the subtitle of *L'Autre Face du royaume* is used to qualify the (mad) practice of transposing and applying uncritically 'des théories produites […] par un Ordre dans un contexte totalement différent où elles s'érigent en "dogmes", […] en "vérité absolues"' [theories produced by an Order in a completely different context where they become dogmas and absolute truths] (*AF*, 151). Similarly, in *L'Odeur du père*, Mudimbe, who has remained throughout his academic career fascinated by the transposition of conceptual systems and categories, reiterates his belief in the singularity of historical experiences, in their ability to generate their own 'normes d'intelligibilité' [norms of intelligibility] and potential to be interpreted from what they are, that is, 'sans que n'interviennent nécessairement des instruments ou des catégories privilégiés par une autre expérience' [without the necessary application of instruments or categories favoured by another experience] (*OP*, 185). Mudimbe, who is one of the precursors of epistemological commitment in Francophone sub-Saharan Africa, also carried forward into the postcolonial era a well-established tradition initiated by Sartre and indigenised, as it were, by Fanon. This legacy is acknowledged and also neatly summed up in the following quote in which Mudimbe defines his objective: '"débloquer" une pensée africaine authentique qui, d'une part rendrait compte fidèlement de l'ordre et des normes du discours africain, et d'autre part justifierait la générosité d'un F. Fanon qui affirmait: "la densité de l'histoire ne détermine aucun de mes actes. Je suis mon propre fondement."' [unblock an authentic African thought which on the one hand would truthfully account for the order and the norms of the African discourse and, on the other, justify F. Fanon's generosity when he was claiming: 'The body of History does not determine a single of my actions. I am my own foundation.'] (*OP*, 43). In this extract from *Peau noire, masques blancs*, a book which by Fanon's own admission was inspired by *Réflexions sur la question juive*, Fanon appears as the advocate of absolute singularity, a position that he justifies through an outright rejection of over-deterministic models, including Freudian archetypes. There is indeed little attempt in this essay to accommodate existentialism and dialectical reason as Fanon is definitely dialoguing with the early Sartre:

> No attempt must be made to encase man, for it is his destiny to be set free. [...] And it is by going beyond the historical, instrumental hypothesis that I will initiate the cycle of my freedom. [...] The Negro is not. Any more than the white man. Both must turn their backs on the inhuman voices which were those of their respective ancestors in order that authentic communication be possible.[104]

Fabian's rejection of allochronism is also directed towards attempts to explain non-Western cultures on the basis of all-encompassing deterministic systems. This argument echoes Mudimbe's perspectives on singular historical events and their ability to release their own 'norms of intelligibility'. As will be explored in Chapter 4, though, Mudimbe also defends, via Foucault's conceptual framework to account for the birth of scientific modernity ('functions/norms', 'conflict/rules', and 'significations/system'[105]), the view that holistic and systemic models were instrumental in the demise of racist and pseudo-scientific anthropology. Fabian does not provide any strict formula but he argues that the incorporation of coevalness into his discipline will need to be predicated upon a 'theory of praxis'.[106] This theory is inspired by Marxism, conceived as a system which can provide epistemological solutions to overcome allochronism. The key idea in this discussion is the concept of production. Throughout the study, Fabian argues that allochronistic anthropologists neglect the 'productive nature of field-*work*',[107] that is, the very real and human (subjective, auto-biographical, inter-subjective, dialogical) features of encounters which, for all intents and purposes (scientific objectivity, Ramus-inflected pedagogy and visualism), remain rooted in the materiality of *work*. Fabian opposes here Hegel and Marx. Hegel's view of the 'totality of historical forces' generated a type of anthropology that Fabian simply calls 'Hegelian'.[108] Fabian does not deny the effectiveness of such a posture but he claims that it can also miss the aims that it seeks to reach as 'holistic social science fails to provide a theory of praxis' and 'commits anthropology forever to imputing (if not outright imposing) motives, beliefs, meanings, and functions to the societies it studies from a perspective outside and above'.[109]

Conversely, Fabian praises Marx's 'presentism'[110] and identifies in his work the basis upon which a 'theory of coevalness'[111] could be achieved. Fabian's line of argument is here a little schematic as the opposition between Hegel and Marx with regard to the possibility of coevalness is built upon complex works – *Phenomenology of the Spirit*, *The German Ideology*, *The Poverty of Philosophy*, *Reading Capital* (Althusser) – that would have merited a more sustained analysis. Marx's 'presentism', that is, his recognition of the necessity of coevalness, is attributed to his belief that 'all human societies and all major aspects of a human society are "of the same age"'.[112] This idea of simultaneity is understood 'as the copresence of basic acts of production and reproduction – eating, drinking, providing shelter, clothes'.[113] To this list, Fabian adds language – the 'matter' that burdens consciousness according to Marx[114] – so as to inscribe the relevance of this notion of production (and matter) in the construction of a coeval anthropology. Language is at the heart of the anthropological praxis that he advocates because it is produced by, as much as it produces, the encounter between the Self and the Other.[115] What is meant here is that the 'production' of language and symbols does not happen in a vacuum but is generated by a 'sensuous interaction' between 'concrete organisms' and that it is thus an 'eminently *temporal* phenomenon'.[116]

This vexed relationship between time and the practice of anthropology lies at the heart of *L'Écart*,[117] in which Mudimbe continues this exploration of the strategies presiding over the allochronistic 'invention de la sauvagerie' [invention of savagery] (OP, 129). The title of the novel merits some attention. The 'gap' or the 'rift' is also the expression of the state in which anthropology is still lingering more than fifteen years after the decolonisation of the Congo. Mudimbe fictionalises here the idea that Africanism can still be defined by a lack, that is, by what it is not and has not achieved. Indeed, there is a gap between what is professed by contemporary literature for a more ethical practice of anthropology and the failure, on the part of the (sometimes well-intentioned) practitioners to translate this exigency into words. The novel attempts therefore to lay bare the discrepancy between mummified anthropological accounts and lived experiences, their material and sensuous manifestations, and the many sexual frustrations thereof. Ahmed Nara, the main character and narrator of this fiction, is an anthropologist and historian in the process of completing a thesis on Kuba civilisation. Like many francophone novels of this period by novelists such as Henri Lopès, Georges Ngal, Alioum Fantouré, Ahmadou Kourouma, and Sony Labou Tansi, the narrative, although quite clearly located in Congo-Zaire (*quite* clearly because names such as Ahmed, Salim, and Salimata could also indicate a West-African location), is set in an African country which remains nameless. Via this main character's existential predicament – Nara is Roquentin's African *Doppelgänger*[118] – the novel teases out the relationship between Africanism and the epistemological violence generated by its allochronistic practices. The narrative is divided into two unequal parts. First, a short Foreword in which a narrator announces that Nara's diary was found after his death; then the second part (called *L'Écart* by this first narrator-editor), which constitutes the bulk of the novel, that is, Nara's highly subjective and autobiographical account of the last few weeks of his life. This structure is reminiscent of the chronologically reversed narrative of the detective novel (discovery of the dead body followed by the investigation). As such, it aptly captures the hermeneutic dimension of the story and the mystery surrounding Nara's last few hours as his death is left unexplained: 'The autopsy showed nothing. Absolutely nothing' (*É*, 2). The anthropologist's diary – 'Something between a journal and a novel' (*É*, 2) – is therefore the only *corpus* on which the investigation is conducted and the only available body of clues to understand the motives behind his presumed suicide. Syrotinski shows that the 'fragmentary', 'notational', and elliptical features of *L'Écart* can be read as the difficulty on the part of the main protagonist to achieve narrative agency.[119] Nara appears here as an idealist and his reflections on Africanist scholarship echo Mudimbe's own utopian attempt to link the practice of science to revolution. He would want to contribute to the existing scholarship on Kuba culture but finds himself incapacitated by the Africanist (Belgian, Western) tradition in which he has been trained. Nara is able to identify the weaknesses and shortcomings of Africanism, the approximation of its findings and above all its over-reliance on the opposition between written and oral cultures but realises also he cannot conceptualise his own project away from these Eurocentric models:

> Virgin Africa, without archives recognized by their scholarship, is an ideal terrain for all illicit trade. The discipline I was used to, thanks to their own standards, gave me the right to demand something other than pretty embellishments concerning the civilizations of the oral tradition. A vile qualification! As if there were a single culture in existence not supported surreptitiously by the spoken word! As if the concept of archives should not coincide at all times with the specific expressions brought up to date by the short history of Europe. (*É*, 46)

The novel is also a reflection on cooperation, as that between African and European researchers during the Mobutu era, and on the new type of dependency – in fact, as Mudimbe laments elsewhere, the 'misère de la dépendance'[120] – that accompanied decolonisation in the former Belgian empire. The diary, however, plays another role as its very self-reflexive, subjective, but also dialogical nature, reveals the other side of anthropology, that is, a space where the anthropologist faces the materiality of the world and measures the fallacy or, at the very least, the limitations, of imported theoretical systems. One important aspect needs highlighting here. The novel has been apocryphally doctored by its editor who indicates in the Foreword that 'Only very rarely was I, unfortunately, not able to decipher the words' and 'I was [therefore] forced to interpret the context and submit the reading that seemed most logical to me' (*É*, 3–4). Although this disclaimer is proof of the editor's scientific rigour and integrity, it also shows the partial inadequacy of his intervention ('logical to *me*') and, by analogy, the difficulty to translate into words, and decipher, the intricacies of lived experiences. The editor's admission that the text may not be completely authentic and that his own meticulous editorial rearrangement of the original may not produce a true account does in fact serve to emphasize the *rift* between life and the human sciences; it also shows that anthropology, for all its ambition to comply with scholarly patented methodologies, remains a subjective discipline generated by the accumulation of material responses. By contrast, Nara's erratic diary opens up the possibility of a new anthropological praxis, *à la* Verhaegen and Fabian, whereby the subject is seen, heard, and spoken to as much as he sees or *inspects* the cultural group under his scrutiny. His notes appear therefore as the traces of a living laboratory wherein the ethnographer is also a self-ethnographer and in which the research cannot be kept separate from life. The historical

Kuba, the material that should normally inform Nara's investigation, are gradually overshadowed by their descendants in present-day Katanga, or in present-day Africa, as the exact location of the novel is uncertain. Nara's enquiry of sorts favours the present that he chooses to account for in a relation of coevalness with others. His notes, in which dominate sensuous responses – fear, anguish, sexual attraction, and humour – are proof that the effectiveness of the old objectivist tenets need now to be relativised and that the ascendency of the knower over the known has lost some of its former legitimacy. Although the overall tone of the novel is grave, and even somewhat solemn in places, it is interesting that the narrator uses humour to debunk, in fact ridicule, the scientific arrogance of Africanists:

> To take my mind off my card catalogue [...] I skimmed J. Dansine's book *The Ancient Kingdoms of the Kavana*. What a mess! What he writes under the pretense of scientific certainty is truly astonishing. Only in African history can the practice of silence and the art of allusion be seen as evidence of cautiousness. To make Salim laugh, I had a good time substituting the Spanish for the Lele and the Portuguese for the Kuba. This produces an enormously funny text that indicates the level of seriousness of Western scholars experienced in African matters: 'The Spanish and the Portuguese are placed under the same heading, not because they have similar political systems, far from it, but because they have a common origin, speak practically the same language, and share a same culture. The traditions of the Spanish, just like those of the Portuguese – at least of the central Portuguese – claim that these peoples go back to the same common origin and are issues of a Woot ancestor [...] Spanish tradition claims that the Spanish people, presumed to be identical to the French people, were to have come first from the southern part of the territory, then to have gone north quite slowly. But it is possible that they might have come from the west in earlier days. (*É*, 43–44)

The reference to J. Dansine, a barely disguised Jan Vansina, the author of the Africanist classic *Kingdoms of the Savannah*[121] (but also of *The Children of Woot: A History of the Kuba Peoples*[122]), indicates that the anthropological present has not completely broken away with the scientific approximations of the past. That Mudimbe should target Vansina, a scholar who contributed to the recognition of oral sources as valid historical *documents*, notably in *De la tradition orale: Essai de méthode historique*,[123] is, however, doubly ironic,[124] and demonstrates that the 'disruptive force' of the novel is played out, as often with Mudimbe, at a 'metanarrative level'.[125] This type of name corruption (Dansine for Vansina), a literary device in use in the traditional naturalistic novel, is also, on Mudimbe's part, a strategy to assert his dissociation with naturalism, a school of thought which contributed to the emergence of the omnipotent narrator, the omniscient fieldworker, and their sometimes pseudo-universal scientific premises and methodologies. This long passage uses humour, a universal device, to dismiss an ethnocentric perspective, that is, the scholar's all-powerful tendency to manipulate native raw data to infer general laws, which, when examined more closely, are more revealing of the anthropologist's praxis than of the culture under investigation. Nara's aim, ultimately, is to reiterate the singularity of historical experiences.

From Ethnology to Ethics

The singular versus universal opposition continues to inform Mudimbe's politically committed examination of the social sciences and their (in)ability to provide trans-rational tools that would enable to achieve inter-subjectivity and coevalness. *On African Fault Lines*, Mudimbe's latest collection of essays, provides a fresh attempt to deal with issues relating to knowledge, communication, and power. He reconnects here with economics, an area that would in the early days inform his analyses of Africa's dependence on the West. In *Autour de la 'Nation'* ('Exigence de l'économique: une lecture', 75–86), for instance, he ponders the significance of aid and regrets that development policies implemented and regulated by intergovernmental bodies such as the IMF are too reliant on abstract econometric factors which often leave 'the people' (as in 'le peuple') out of the equation. A very analogous concern is expressed in *On African Fault Lines* although the discussion no longer focuses exclusively on Central Africa as it has been extended to the whole world in an attempt to explore the modalities against which economic globalisation has become a reality in a context – the much discussed 'Empire' theorised by Antonio Negri and Michael Hardt[126] – in which 'the concept of a third world might have lost its transparency' (*OAF*, 3). This shift captures Mudimbe's personal evolution: 'Published twenty years ago, *The Invention of Africa* (1988), was written by a Central African francophone. The chapters of *On African Fault Lines* have been lived by an anglophone black man' (*OAF*, ix).

Fundamentally, the book is presented as a 'sceptical' and patient exercise in 'decoding rapports between alterity propositions and works on managing individuals and ideas' (*OAF*, ix). There is therefore here a clear ambition to appraise the ways in which abstract and all-encompassing paradigms (the former 'langages en folie' and 'odeur du père') are accepted, adopted, absorbed, assimilated, but also adapted, transformed, and rejected by individuals and communities who, for reasons of geography and education, are excluded from the *management* presiding over the production of these ideas. Global capitalism is also allochronistic and although the Third World has lost some of its contours – for instance, where do African and Haitian refugees belong? – its members are rarely invited to the 'banquet des pouvoirs' [banquet of powers] (Joseph Ki-Zerbo, in *OAF*, 1). The book continues to be driven by an ethical urgency as it militates for the restoration of human dignity. The geopolitical shape of the world has changed beyond recognition since the 1970s and yet Mudimbe suggests that, in terms of knowledge production, the issues that marked the neo-colonial era, are still prevalent now. A doctoral thesis on Sudanese refugees submitted in 2009 at the University of Toronto by Deepa Rajkumar is used to flesh out this sense of continuity. Mudimbe argues that this work is different from what is normally produced in the field of Refugee studies inasmuch as it is, at the same time, 'a report, an academic analysis, and an ethical statement' and could therefore be labelled as a 'testimony on testimonies' (*OAF*, 290). By this he means that the author acknowledges that her work has been shaped by the very material, 'sensuous' (as Fabian would say) conditions of her own praxis and does not try, in the name of some academic objectivity, to hide the fact that her account is a story about other stories: 'a fable or a parable about other fables' (*P&F*, xxi). In this study, she chooses indeed to consider the refugees as 'subjects in motion, in conversations, and in the research' and attempts, 'through storytelling, and a rewriting of the experience', critically to 'reformulate […] a shared responsibility' (*OAF*, 291). Mudimbe argues that this endeavour to foreground the co-responsibility of the researcher and her informants echoes Verhaegen's histoire immédiate, but also Enrique Dussel's philosophy of liberation, and their efforts to give prominence to 'intersubjectivity and interaction between alter and ego, subject and object, in the process of knowledge production and political commitment' (*OAF*, 291).

This focus on ethics lies also at the heart of Mudimbe's analysis of inter-subjectivity, that is communication rather than conversion, in the context of global capitalism. He argues, via Amitai Etzioni's sociological examination of transnational relations in the business sphere,[127] that globalisation has generated 'complex systems' of power, subordination, and 'compliances' between global and local 'actors' (*OAF*, 43) and that the shape and form of their interactions are predicated upon conflicts between economic, political, cultural, and ethical 'reasons' (*OAF*, 42–59). If reduced to the core, Mudimbe's view is not very different from the arguments that he put forward in the 1970s to endorse African singularity. Quite classically, he contends here that capitalism, and the various ways in which it is accommodated (and complied) with by local, disenfranchised, and peripheral communities, has provided since the Renaissance – in Africa, in the Americas, and elsewhere – the major blueprint to interpret the links, and the sense of continuity, between colonialism, neo-colonialism, and globalisation. In this respect, Mudimbe notes the ironic proximity of cultural and organisational anthropology. If the former was accused of serving imperialism – of orientalising the Other, inventing Africa, the Americas (Dussel[128]), and primitive societies (Adam Kuper[129]) – how can the latter's relationship to the 'reason' of the free market be conceived? The conclusion is pessimistic as this latest manifestation of anthropology is in fact said to illustrate 'the spirit of an "imperial culture"', of yet another 'claim "to defy geography"' (*OAF*, 51).

By way of Geert Hofstede's well-known study on the 'software of the mind',[130] Mudimbe proceeds to explore further the basis upon which organisational anthropology operates. Hofstede acknowledges cultural differences and argues that, as they result from a learning process occurring in early childhood, they shape the way we behave in society, in business organisations and act therefore as '*mental programmes*' or as '*software of the mind*', a phrase which is synonymous for 'culture' in its broadest, anthropological sense.[131] This basic recognition, which jeopardises the possibility of business transactions across different cultures, is the obstacle that the author sets out to overcome. The study, a self-help book of sorts which purposefully avoids 'social scientific jargon', resounds with triumphant optimism and intends to address its main 'message' to 'the intelligent lay reader' and, above all, to 'anyone who meets people from outside his or her narrow circle [...] this means virtually everybody'.[132] Although Hofstede does not refer to notions such as 'structures', 'practico-inert', and 'conditions of possibility', it must be said that like Mudimbe he argues that individuals are the products of time- and place-bound circumstances. However, Hofstede (and this is where the two authors diverge) is driven by the ambitions to identify a set of cross-cultural common denominators – dismissed by Mudimbe as 'metagrammar' (*OAF*, 56) – to lay the basis of what could be called (after Verhaegen and Fabian) 'dialogical' encounters between representatives from different (business) cultures. Hofstede's deeper grammar of human invariants is presented as a set of binary oppositions such as 'Evils versus good', 'Dirty versus clean', 'Dangerous versus safe', 'Forbidden versus permitted', 'Decent versus indecent', 'Moral versus immoral', 'Ugly versus beautiful', 'Unnatural versus natural', 'Abnormal versus normal', 'Paradoxical versus logical', and 'Irrational versus rational'.[133] Mudimbe argues that Hofstede, although ostensibly relativist in his interpretation of cultures, reproduces 'the "grand dichotomy" model without addressing its implications' (*OAF*, 56–57). By this he means that the Dutch organisational anthropologist unwittingly reconnects with the naive and mechanistic dualism of evolutionist thought. Hofstede's mission – bridging the gap between cultures to achieve (business) communication – presents according to Mudimbe another and all-together more serious caveat:

> The model transcribes, on business management agenda, an equation between economic convergence and necessary transcendence of any alterity; by this fact, it might be bypassing the equality principle between cultural systems in order to outline the requirements of a transnational organization. (*OAF*, 57)

Mudimbe is therefore of the view that Hofstede, for all his claims that differences should be respected, has sacrificed the ethical reason in the name of economic imperatives and has, in this way, confused conversion with communication. For Mudimbe, on the other hand, 'the primacy of the ethical reason over the economic, the political, and the cultural' (*OAF*, 58) is the very premise upon which inter-subjective dialogues can develop. This fundamental exigency, the 'authority of an ethics of human dignity' (*OAF*, 58), resonates with Enrique Dussel's Levinassian 'philosophy of liberation'. It is useful to recall that Dussel has devoted a significant part of his academic career to the study of the conversion of Latin America to Christianity and modernity and to the effects of globalisation. Two of his many books, *The Invention of the Americas* and *Ética de la liberación en la edad de la globalización y de la exclusión*,[134] neatly sum up Mudimbe's own concern to investigate, from *L'Autre Face du royaume* to *On African Fault Lines*, the interconnected fields of epistemology, politics, and ethics not only in Africa but also beyond.

To conclude, the authors explored here all acknowledge the rift, or the fault line, between the 'West and the Rest'. They all agree that modernity and its chief manifestations – capitalism, imperialism, neo-colonialism, and globalisation – have created zones of sub-human Others forever objectified, distanced, and mediated by omniscient 'Knowers'. Presented in these terms, this claim is of course outrageously dualistic and closer, it would seem, to conspiracy theories than to a scholarly analysis. It is, however, crucial to remember that it was formulated in times which had themselves been affected by very traumatic events and were therefore deeply polarised. Sartre's *Réflexions sur la question juive* is an attempt to explain French anti-Semitism and, beyond this domestic dimension, to elaborate the basis of an inter-subjective framework that would accommodate survivors and perpetrators in a post-Holocaust world. The basic idea underpinning Sartre's examination of the etiology of anti-Semitism is an adaptation of philosophical notions developed in *L'Être et le néant*. In a nutshell, Sartre contends that the Jew is made and invented by the anti-Semite, that he or she is, thus, the anti-Semite's 'for others'. However, Sartre also claims that Jews are free to overcome this Master–Slave dialectic and can, through a lucid assumption of their *situation*, envisage a future where they will not have to be what they *are* and will release themselves from the reified definition in which the perpetrator's *look* (or gaze) had petrified their identities. This simple but powerful idea was adopted by Mudimbe, Fabian, and Verhaegen in the field of knowledge production. Although their reflection is primarily concerned with methodological issues underlying the practice of social anthropology and history in the Congo and in the Third World, it is also, ultimately, a *pretext* to comment on the enduring presence of inequalities in the postcolonial world. Epistemology is here the vehicle for ethical and political commitment. The fraught relationship between the scholar and the 'objects' of his investigations mirrors, in the interconnected fields of knowledge, pedagogy, and cooperation, the material and hierarchical divide between sub-Saharan Africa and 'Eur-America' and it is therefore useful to remember, with Laurent Monnier, that 'Immediate History' is predominantly a 'matter of gaze'.[135] Mudimbe's intervention, but also Fabian's and Verhaegen's, however, goes beyond the description of unequal epistemological conditions. It also proposes a praxis of liberation to 'unthink' anthropology and the social sciences. Although well intentioned, it is nonetheless doubtful whether this call for a dialogical and coeval praxis has truly achieved its promises. Social anthropology has definitely decolonised its practices – it is no longer the science of the remote 'Other' – but its prejudices, the 'grand dichotomy' mentioned earlier, have infiltrated the new domain of organisational anthropology. In 'Comment on Epistemology: What is Africa', Immanuel Wallerstein captures, at one fell swoop, Mudimbe's predicament:

> In the course of the last 100 years, the concept of Africa has emerged. It is a European word, and its definition was first given by Europeans. But those so defined have struggled in recent years to take control of the defining process, or to take more control of this process, which is inherently a process that is both continuous and always reciprocal (that is, never one-sided). [...] as long as we live in a singular, hierarchical world-system, the capitalist world-economy, posing the question of whether a set of ideas, or a way of thinking, is universal (European) or African returns us only to the double bind which the system itself has created. If we are to get out of this double bind, we must take advantage of the contradictions of the system itself and go beyond it.[136]

The opening question of this chapter (the West or the Rest?) captures the paradox highlighted by Wallerstein and the double bind African intellectuals are invariably facing. It also helps to trace Mudimbe's trajectory during the most militant period of his academic life. His many attacks on the West are, however, never final, never motivated by an ambition to bracket off the West in the name of his own ethnic *reason*. His Third-Worldism is driven by an ethical need to return to raw humanity, to the poignant signs of an unfinished decolonising process, and the *bare life* of its short-changed recipients: 'Stanleyville ou Kisangani / et après Haïti et Vietnam / et ensuite? / les morts du Vietnam / les affamés des Indes / les nègres des États-Unis / les nègres émasculés d'Afrique du Sud' [Stanleyville or Kinsangani / and after Haiti and Viet Nam / and what will be next? / Viet Nam's dead / the famished of India / America's negroes / South Africa's emasculated negroes].[137] However, he is also conscious of the complexity of the responses generated, in the West and the Rest, by decolonisation. Close to Yambo Ouologuem's *Lettre à la France nègre*,[138] he fustigates the advocates of what François Furet's named the 'plébiscite du sauvage' [plebiscite of the savage].[139] According to Mudimbe, this tendency to put former colonised cultures on a pedestal is the dubious expression, on the part of some French left-wing intellectuals and ethnologists, of a postcolonial malaise, that is, a 'masochisme expiatoire' and a 'souci un peu paternaliste d'égalitarisme' [somewhat paternalistic longing for egalitarianism] (*AF*, 51–52).

The epigraph of this chapter sums up this argument and it is undeniable that Mudimbe, even when at his most utopian, remained on the side of the 'practical man'. His onslaught on the West's alienating discourses cannot be equated to an outright condemnation of the West. The subtitle of *L'Odeur du père* is helpful to relativise the position that he has adopted since the 1970s: 'essai sur *des* limites de la science et de la vie en Afrique noire' (my emphasis). The 'des' (rather than 'les') demonstrates that the disqualification is not total. To my initial question 'the West *or* the Rest?', Mudimbe would most certainly answer 'the Rest *and* the West'.

4

'Changing Places'

> A particular problem arises when, instead of being a discourse on other discourses, as it is usually the case, theory has to advance over an area where there are no longer any discourses. There is a sudden unevenness of terrain: the ground on which verbal language rests begins to fail. The theorizing operation finds itself at the limits of the terrain where it normally functions, like an automobile at the edge of a cliff. Beyond and below lies the ocean.
>
> Michel de Certeau.[1]

In 1980, V. Y. Mudimbe, who from the late 1960s onwards had also been known as Valentin Mudimbé, moved permanently to the US. The disappearance of the acute accent from his surname is the mark of a very concrete transformation as he was obliged, as will be examined in this chapter, to switch language and develop new strategies to adapt to the sociological and institutional demands of American academia. The consecration in this context came in 1988 with the publication of *The Invention of Africa*. This monograph captured the critical mood of the 1980s and resonated with other projects such as Said's *Orientalism*, Fabian's *Time and the Other*, and Spivak's 'Can the Subaltern Speak?',[2] which had all attempted to explore the links between knowledge production, representation, and imperialism. Mudimbe's first major American essay built on his previous books but the obvious Foucauldian underpinning thereof contributed to secure his position in the nascent postcolonial field, some of the leading luminaries of which, Said and Spivak, for instance, had also engaged, sometimes polemically, with Foucault's thought.

Foucault's place within postcolonial criticism is ambiguous as he never tackled colonialism directly. For some critics such as Said and Spivak themselves,[3] this absence is the mark of Foucault's inability to sever the links with a certain form of Eurocentrism, even though his *History of Sexuality*, as demonstrated by Ann Laura Stoler, provides a detailed analysis of the relationship between biopower and racial exclusions from the seventeenth century onwards.[4] Indeed, Foucault's work possesses a high degree of transferability as the connections that he establishes between discourses and power practices in the modern era provide a set of methodological premises to lay bare the 'othering' processes presiding over imperialism and challenge the permanency of some beliefs and underlying conceptual frameworks.

Mudimbe's American relocation inflected his interests and the nature of his work and forced him to rethink the place and development of Africanism beyond the exclusive relationship between Africa and Europe. Apart from an essay where he explores the confrontation between voodoo and Catholicism in Haiti,[5] the Americas are largely absent from his earlier publications. The focus on E. W. Blyden in *The Invention of Africa* constitutes therefore a major shift and reflects the ambition of considering Africanism from a transatlantic perspective. Given the fact that 'E. W. Blyden's Legacy and Questions' (*IoA*, 98–134) is the second longest chapter of the book, it is not too bold to argue that Mudimbe contributed to the invention of what Paul Gilroy – who regards Blyden as an 'especially important figure' in the history of black 'dissident intellectuals' – would later call *The Black Atlantic*.[6]

This chapter will begin by exploring the significance of *Carnets d'Amérique*, a travelogue that Mudimbe published after a journey in the United States in 1974, and which, in many ways, constitutes the intellectual prelude to his transatlantic exile. This travel diary provides an examination of the US and the American higher education sector; it also enables Mudimbe to ponder a number of issues, in the field of religion, race, and gender politics, which, whilst being intrinsically American and rooted in an American historicity, offer fascinating analogies with his native Congo. The second part of the chapter will focus on *The Invention of Africa*, tease out the intellectual basis of this volume, and explore the strategies used by Mudimbe in his excavation of African knowledge systems. The investigation will appraise the links between discourses, representations, and their conditions of possibility. In a first stage, I shall examine Mudimbe's analysis of paintings of black figures by early-modern and classical artists such as Hieronymus Bosch and Rubens; I shall then move to his critical interpretation of Senghor's canonisation of E. W. Blyden as the forefather of negritude. Finally, this discussion will explore the significance of a paradigmatic model – 'functions/norms', 'conflict/rules', and 'significations/system' – developed by Michel Foucault in *The Order of Things* to account for the development of the human sciences from the French Revolution onwards and applied in *The Invention* by Mudimbe in his chronological survey of African *Gnosis* from Blyden, Griaule, and Tempels to Paulin Hountondji and Engelbert Mveng.

Voyage in America

Like his other autobiographical books, *Carnets d'Amérique* offers precious insights into Mudimbe's personality, humour, and ability to enjoy life's simple things – even though aesthetic, intellectual, and, as we shall see, pedagogical considerations dominate the narrative. This journey of six weeks in the United States was sponsored by the African-American Institute, a cultural agency which aims to consolidate the relationship between America and African countries. The book is structured as a conventional travelogue along spatial and chronological lines, starting on 24 September in Kinshasa and finishing on 5 November in Amsterdam.[7] Between these two dates and places, the narrator provides a detailed description of his itinerary, encounters, and visits of prestigious American universities such as Columbia, Princeton, and Stanford. At the end of his mission, Mudimbe, the classicist but also future exile, is given by his guide, Mr Carter, a photocopy of the opening passage of the first ever printed version of *The Odyssey*.

This reference to Greek literature is not fortuitous as *Carnets d'Amérique* is also the diary of a learned reader. In this respect, Mudimbe's account is reminiscent of canonical travelogues such as Gide's *Voyage au Congo*,[8] of which it constitutes the African response and re-appropriation. Interestingly, the subtitle of Gide's notorious denunciation of colonial exactions in *Afrique-Équatoriale française* was 'carnets de route'. The itinerary offers many opportunities to engage in literary detours which break the monotony of the journey and enable the mind to meander away from the beaten track and its dreary routine. Like Gide in his 'carnets', taken here as the arch-example of the travel genre, Mudimbe also tends to use his eyes to remember and remind himself that he is not from *here*. Gide's observations on colonial and indigenous realities are often formulated analogically, that is, in a strict relation to France. Whenever local spectacles fail to impress him and ignite in him a much-needed exotic spark, Gide invokes the moral and aesthetic authority of France, used throughout the narrative as a yardstick to measure Africa's primitiveness or route to progress.

A similar analogical process is at work in Mudimbe's *Carnets*, although it is devoid of any ethnocentric bias. Mudimbe remains often very impressed with the technological efficiency of his hosts. The Library of Congress, with its millions of books, remarkable Africanist holdings, and formidable research tools, is described as a 'bibliothèque de rêve' [dream library] (*CA*, 35). This fascination, however, is far from being uncritical. Mudimbe's very personal account of America is, as argued by Aedín Ní Loingsigh, also a strategy to reflect upon the effects on sub-Saharan Africa of the new United States-led global order that emerged as a result of decolonisation.[9] In this respect, Ní Loingsigh contends that Mudimbe's travel is not so much a journey to the future undertaken to 'echo commonplace theories of African "backwardness"',[10] as a way to critique forcefully the technology-driven American model of progress and imperialism. Mudimbe's focus on American technological successes serves as a reminder that the American dream could not have been achieved without the cooperation of African client states such as Mobutu's Zaire and their willingness to put their natural resources at America's disposal. Can anyone for that matter ignore the fact the atomic bombs dropped on Hiroshima and Nagasaki contained Congolese uranium?

A gentle sense of irony pervades this seemingly conventional travelogue. Here too the comparison with colonial relations such as *Voyage au Congo* applies: Mr Carter, Mudimbe's guide and, as it were, local informant, is described as a 'pur Anglo-Saxon' (*CA*, 95). This ethnic descriptor is the sign of the author's ambition to parody the style of traditional ethnographic writings and their obsessions with ethno-physical annotations.[11] By the same token, the exploration of myths and cosmogonies, an area of study which lies at the very heart of ethnographic investigations, is gently derided. The foundation of Stanford University, as narrated by the author, reads as a myth of origins and is reminiscent of the style and tone usually adopted in traditional fairytales. A tripartite schema is used to structure the narrative: (1) Leiland and Jane Stanford, are famous, wealthy and beautiful, whilst being at the same time the blessed parents of a most wonderful child; (2) meanwhile, the gods, jealous as they are, cannot countenance the couple's happiness and, for this reason, use their powers to bring about the boy's premature death; (3) the parents, albeit inconsolable, decide to found a university that will be dedicated to the memory of their deceased son (*CA*, 157). What is mocked here is the naive triumphalism upon which Stanford has constructed its success story and mythology.

Beyond Stanford, where, ironically, Mudimbe would work later, this satire is, however, also aimed at the American dream *tout court*. The linear plot, the tragic crisis, and the denouement signify a facile idea of progress and its associated values of courage, resilience, and ability to 'move on'. Progress, under the neo-imperialist order that the United States embodies, has, ultimately, retained its colonial marks.

Carnets d'Amérique and the many scenes that it provides enable Mudimbe to recognise, behind American geography and politics, the face of his native Congo and signs of its ongoing dependency. He learns that Louisiana is, in terms of agricultural potential and natural resources, the richest state but also a region where the per capita income is the lowest (CA, 101). In New Orleans, he tries to retrieve the real meaning and origin of the word 'Congo', as used in 'Congo Square', but remains frustrated that the available literature on the subject is biased, seems to have been uncritically lifted from Labat's and Charlevoix's eighteenth-century relations on the Caribbean, and does not enable one to identify precisely what was understood by 'Congo' during the slave trade (CA, 113). In Atlanta, he is made aware of the segregationist dimension of the local cityscape where roads and avenues are traced to cordon off ethnic communities and reinforce the colour bar just like in the urban geography of the former Belgian Congo where the 'avenue-limite-sud' acted as the real and symbolic division between modernity and African tradition (*Idea*, 129–44; CG, 36–47).

Mudimbe's mission, like Gide's, is thus very critical. The word 'mission' needs to be clarified. Gide was operating as the official emissary of the French government. Similarly, Mudimbe's status resulted from a bilateral agreement between the American and Zairian governments. He was selected because of his expertise in modern language teaching and linguistics. This mission is therefore primarily undertaken for pedagogical reasons. At the beginning of his academic career in Zaire at the University of Lubumbashi, Mudimbe published and taught extensively in the fields of (romance and classical) philology, French grammar and applied linguistics.[12] At a time when the newly independent republic was attempting to design a set of coherent language policies in a country that has more than 300 languages, he was the Secretary-General of the Zairian Association of Linguistics (1974–76) and the director of the 'Centre for theoretical and applied linguistics' at Lubumbashi. His American mission centred therefore upon a highly sensitive issue as applied linguistics was, and still is, a nation-building/breaking instrument for a multilingual country such as Zaire.

Mudimbe's observations of American pedagogical practices in the field of applied linguistics are in the main sceptical. He refuses, as mentioned before, to put technology on a pedestal and deplores the monolingual bias of American pedagogical approaches. He argues, referring to Michel Crozier's *La Société bloquée*,[13] that the American technocratic model is also blocked (CA, 103). He recurrently reflects on the links between acculturation, knowledge transfer, and cultural alienation, what he refers to as 'folie culturelle' (CA, 127). The formulation is reminiscent of the mood that had prevailed at the time of independence among some anti-colonial intellectuals. In *Black Skin, White Masks*, Fanon had examined the Caribbean's entrapment in the other's linguistic and social worldview; in the preface to the same author's *The Wretched of the Earth*, Sartre had portrayed the *évolués*, that is local members of the emerging middle class who like Mudimbe himself had received a Westernised education, as 'walking lies'.[14] Although Fanon remains overall a relatively minor figure of Mudimbe's referential universe, the two men's utopianism, as will be argued in Chapter 5, often coincides, a point made by Robert Young in the Foreword of a translated set of essays by Sartre on colonialism.[15] In a conversation with Léon Gontran Damas at Howard University, the oldest Black university of the United States, Mudimbe, however, decides to express his partial disagreement with Fanon, a view already formulated in *L'Autre Face du royaume* (AF, 136). During this encounter his attitude towards Damas, who is traditionally regarded as one of the 'founding fathers' of negritude, is very conciliatory. Mudimbe and Damas are very conscious of the rift existing between the older generation, that of the 'founding fathers', and the younger one, that of Mudimbe, Towa, and Adotevi, with regards to negritude and its capacity to generate racial liberation. Mudimbe's stance is nonetheless one of deep respect. Unlike Fanon, he sees a continuum rather than a rupture between his intellectual work and negritude. One could say that Mudimbe, unlike many critics of negritude, does not 'fall into the trap of retrospective wisdom'.[16] He contends that thinkers of his generation would like to 'establish an African discourse about the world, a rigorous discourse that will serve as a prelude to our recognition as subjects of a culture from which we were created and which we have created' (CA, 52).[17] He adds that his own work has been driven by this very ambition: 'This is what, following in your footsteps and the footsteps of others, I try to do in *L'Autre Face du Royaume*, which I owe to you' (CA, 52). This attempt to establish a new African discourse, however, cannot happen in a vacuum and erase the common history that Africa and the West share: 'Of course this doesn't mean that we have to start everything all over again. Indeed, the ambiguities about the recommencement of History can be traced directly back to Frantz Fanon' (*CA*, 52). Fanon, notably in *The Wretched of the Earth*, had strongly criticised the essentialist dimension of negritude and advocated a revolution that would once and for all sever the links with Europe.

Mudimbe's views on pedagogy in *Carnets d'Amérique* echo therefore the underlying thesis of *L'Autre Face*, that is, the idea that some discourses can have alienating effects when applied indiscriminately. In this respect, the heated conversation with the technician of the language department of the University of California is very significant of Mudimbe's belief that pedagogy too needs to be context specific. The technician is a strong supporter of one-size-fits-all technology-assisted language pedagogy whereas Mudimbe argues, via a passing reference to the work of the American sociolinguist William Labov, that the influence of the 'substrats' [local languages], the social and geographical contexts, are to be taken into account for these factors are likely to have a clear impact on the students' experience (*CA*, 123). He remarks that the models advocated by his interlocutor would probably not have the desired effects if they were transplanted in sub-Saharan Africa which has experienced different forms of economic development and where the concept of national language does not have the same resonance as in the West. Mudimbe resents the fact that the technician thinks it conceivable to organise African countries on the basis of a rational and 'mathématisable' [able to be transcribed in mathematical concepts] model (*CA*, 126). Confronted with this assimilating discourse, Mudimbe is implicitly reminded of the dependency of his native country (*CA*, 124), and finds solace in the pre-dadaist and definitely non-didactic *Galgenlieder* and *Palmström* by Christian Morgenstern (*CA*, 126). The sudden intrusion of poetry, conceived as a realm where singular voices are free to roam, acts as an instrument against the all-encompassing claims of 'langages en folie'.

This reflection on pedagogy as a process of acculturation, and the cases of cultural alienation ('folie culturelle') that it generates, is conveyed through a short but significant reference to the works of the Franco-American ethnopsychiatrist Georges (or George) Devereux. In this passage, Mudimbe establishes a causal link between acculturation, that is, the shift from tradition to Western modernity, and psychological disorders (*CA*, 21–22) in an Africa provocatively presented as an enormous 'hôpital psychiatrique' (*CA*, 22). He argues, with Devereux, that these disorders are the products of a clash between biological, psychological, and cultural factors and the impossibility, for alienated subjects, of reconciling the contradictory demands of these different spheres in a colonial or neo-colonial context (*CA*, 22). The fragmentary structure of *Carnets d'Amérique* does not allow, however, a full development of this point but it is obvious that Mudimbe is ready to consider the therapeutic benefits of ethnopsychiatry. This hybrid field had already been alluded to in *L'Autre Face* in which Mudimbe thought it conceivable to marry the two disciplines since they are both dealing with archetypical representations as expressed in myths and dreams. In this respect, he mentioned the significant input of Géza Róheim, Marie-Cécile, and Edmond Ortigues, and Georges Devereux (*AF*, 79–81).[18] The discussion on Devereux's project is given more consideration in *L'Odeur du père*. In a chapter significantly entitled 'Un signe, une odeur' (*OP*, 19–35). Mudimbe appears at first quite sympathetic towards Devereux's ambition to bridge the gap between psychiatry and anthropology and to devise universally applicable 'concepts-clefs' [key concepts] (*OP*, 21). However, in a typically Mudimbian fashion, this focus on Devereux is said to be only a 'prétexte' (*OP*, 20) to consider not so much Devereux's book, in this instance *Essais d'ethnopsychiatrie générale*,[19] as the conditions of possibility of its production. Mudimbe's perspective is therefore above all epistemological. He argues implicitly that the possibility of a therapeutic pedagogy, that is, one that would treat the disorders caused by Western acculturation, is not to be found in ethnopsychiatry because this discipline is the product of a specific *order*: 'L'ethnopsychiatrie travaille dans un contexte socio-historique qui est singulier, utilise un langage à la fois fini et marqué par un univers culturel' [ethnopsychiatry operates in a singular socio-historical context and uses a language which is constrained and determined by a cultural environment] (*OP*, 21). This posture is symptomatic of Mudimbe's perspective. Concepts such as alienation and madness, but also tradition and modernity, are epistemological constructs and here too Mudimbe substantiates his views via arguments formulated by Foucault in *Les Mots et les choses* (1966) and *Histoire de la folie à l'âge classique* (1972). Ethnopsychiarty, for all its attempts to comprehend the ways in which alienation is perceived and treated in other cultures, remains the 'sign' of an order, that is, 'l'odeur d'un ordre, d'une région essentielle, particulière à une culture mais qui se donne [...] paradoxalement comme fondamentale à toute l'humanité' [the scent of an order, of an essential and culture-specific region which paradoxically presents itself as fundamental to the whole of humanity] (*OP*, 35). In a more recent account on the development of the discipline in the past fifty years, Didier Fassin goes much further than Mudimbe and argues that, from John Colin Carothers's *The Psychology of the Mau Mau* (1954)[20] to the works of Nathan Tobie (Devereux's disciple at the Centre Georges-Devereux in Saint-Denis), ethnopsychiatry has remained ethnocentric and has displayed, by and large, a tendency to pathologise other cultures or to exacerbate the cultural dimension of the 'African psyche'.[21] Later in this chapter, the 'ethno' in ethnophilosophy will be scrutinised not as a sign of pathologisaton but as a mark of the culturalisation of philosophy.

Mudimbe's critique of American pedagogical practices in *Carnets d'Amérique* can therefore be understood against a more wide-ranging critique of the human sciences, of which, he contends, these practices are the concrete manifestations. In this context, language teaching, which in the colonial period had been one of the chief tools to implement assimilation, is an extremely sensitive area as it also brings to the fore the very ethno-linguistic fragmentation of Mobutu's Zaire.

Carnets d'Amérique also offers the vision of a country which is slowly overcoming the legacies of the slave trade and racial discriminations. This is not to say that, as highlighted earlier about Louisiana and Atlanta, the traces of the segregationist past have disappeared. In this respect, Mudimbe's visit to the Smithsonian Institution (*CA*, 25–27), the scholarly foundation which, in conjunction with the Bureau of American Ethnology (BAE), contributed to the birth of evolutionist anthropology (notably of Amerindians), constitutes a stark reminder of the racist genesis of the United States.[22] Overall, however, it is fair to argue that only six years after Martin Luther King's assassination Mudimbe witnesses the signs of an American decolonisation of sorts and the gradual establishment of a specific African American memory. The many institutions, museums, and universities that he visits under the sponsorship of the African-American Institute bear witness to this memorialisation of Black culture. In the Renwick Gallery (Washington, DC), he is impressed by an exhibition of Nigerian contemporary artists. As will be shown again in Chapter 5, via 'Reprendre', one of his essays on African art, he is eager to highlight these artists' capacity to display what he calls 'fausse naïveté' [false naivety] (*CA*, 23), that is, their ability to parody time-honoured techniques and motifs as a means to assert their post-traditional modernity and rejection of an *invented* tradition.

His visit to the Martin Luther King Center in Atlanta captures the mood that was prevailing among black militant intellectuals in the mid-1970s. This centre, which still operates today, was created by Coretta Scott King, Martin Luther King's widow, shortly after his death in 1968.[23] Mudimbe enters in a dialogue with two researchers attached to the centre. Here, too, his attitude is sceptical and yet one is struck by the many possible analogies that can be identified between racial exploitation in America and the type of economic subjugation suffered by sub-Saharan Africans as a consequence of colonialism and neo-imperialism. The two researchers, who are both African Americans, formulate their grievances and propose solutions to generate racial equality. They argue in a manner which is reminiscent of anti-colonial movements of the preceding decades that they aim to generate a process of self-determination in order to create a solid basis for racial solidarity and restore black people's self-confidence and faith in their innate abilities to invent and act creatively (CA, 80). Their ultimate objective goes, however, beyond the black community as they would like to 'provoquer une auto-transformation de la société américaine' [generate a self-transformation of American society] (CA, 80). With its emphasis on a specific racial identity, self-pride, and creativity, this programme resonates in many ways with the Sartrean ambition to advocate the necessity of negritude as a route towards the construction of a race-less society. Mudimbe's scepticism is partly fuelled by the fact that their romanticism (CA, 86) reminds him of the utopian mood of the 1960s in Africa. The bitterness of the following remark evokes the portrayal of the Lumumba-Mobutu relationship in the epilogue of Césaire's *Une Saison au Congo*: 'Que signifie l'indépendance politique si elle est seulement un genre d'ivresse qui, à chaque anniversaire, tente de ressusciter les mythes des années 60?' [What is the point of political independence if it is only a type of intoxication, which, at each anniversary, attempts to resuscitate the myths of the 1960s?] (CA, 82–83). He warns the researchers against the confusion between class and race (CA, 82), distancing therefore himself from Sartre who had conflated the two notions in 'Orphée noir'.

The programme put forward by the two researchers at the Martin Luther King Center is characteristic of the intellectual context underpinning Black studies, which entered university curricula after Martin Luther King's assassination,[24] and the rise of postcolonial studies in the 1970s and 1980s. It would be difficult to reconstruct the exact development of this hybrid school of thought but the 1970s offer a number of clues to understand this evolution. Anti-colonial thought gradually lost its relevance during those years as it became increasingly obvious that colonialism had been replaced by a more insidious type of dependence with far-reaching consequences in the economic, political, and intellectual spheres. Mudimbe's bitterness about the shattered dreams of Congolese independence is the expression of a shift away from utopianism; it is also the recognition that yesterday's tools are no longer precise enough to measure the intricate links and fault lines between political sovereignty, economic reliance, and knowledge. It seemed suddenly that the world of Cabral, Che Guevara, the young Kenyatta, Nkrumah, Nyerere, and even Lumumba, was altogether more simple as they had above all fought for the eradication of a system articulated along a dualistic line, whereby few oppressors were faced by a mass of oppressed subjects. It would be absurd, however, to argue that the replacement of anti-colonial thought by a type of *ur*-postcolonial theory happened mechanically and that a neat and chronologically clear-cut shift took place. The word 'transition' is better suited to describe this intellectual evolution and it is in this light that Mudimbe's dismissal of Fanon's recommencement of history must be understood. Mudimbe, as is argued in Chapter 3, and his two interlocutors hesitate between direct political action and a less overtly militant, more textually driven intervention. The researchers argue that the desired emancipation must be achieved through a reappraisal of history in order to provide African Americans with the means to control the truth of their past (*CA*, 79), a point which resonates with Mudimbe's appraisal of history through the figure of Herodotus (see Chapter 1) and with the development of 'histoire immédiate' (Chapter 3) as the social scientists involved in this movement were, according to Laurent Monnier, 'deeply conscious of the ways in which the colonial system had confiscated the history of the Congolese people'.[25] This re-examination of Black history is also premised on the idea that traditional history is too heavily invested in the study of 'grands personnages' (*CA*, 79) at the expense of lesser-known figures and aspects and is, therefore, yet another 'invention' that needs urgently to be reversed in order to create the basis for liberation. In this exercise, the researchers recommend the exploration of social changes since the end of the Second World War (so, here too, the focus is on *immediate* history), the examination of Garvey's writings (*CA*, 86), and even the study of literary texts such as Margaret Walker's novel *Jubilee* (1966), given as an example to recover what has been muted by history (*CA*, 79). In this respect, it is significant to note Mudimbe's amusement when browsing the shelves of the library at Berkeley he realises that history's phallocentric tendencies are challenged by the publication of volumes catalogued under the label of 'herstory' (CA, 166). Later during his journey, he is told that some American feminists, in an attempt to emulate the spirit that had presided over the foundation of 'Black Studies' departments, are demanding the creation of departments of 'herstory' in American universities (CA, 167). Mudimbe is therefore witnessing the change that swept American liberal arts departments in the 1970s which became increasingly receptive to the 'proto-postcolonial' but also feminist claims of rewriting history from its hitherto neglected margins.[26]

At Stanford University, he met Robert McAfee Brown and carried on this reflection on the production of knowledge in the West, its consumption and mimetic reproduction, but also possible transformation in Africa and elsewhere. McAfee Brown is a well-known figure of contemporary American theology. He was a supporter of ecumenism and advocated, in the wake of the Second Vatican Council in which he sat as a Protestant observer, a rapprochement with Catholics.[27] He militated for social justice during the Civil Rights Movement, was arrested for his anti-military views during the Vietnam War, and promoted the cause of liberation theologians such as Gustavo Gutiérrez, on whom he wrote a book.[28] The discussion focuses on Christianity and its indigenisation in the United States, Latin America, and Africa. This issue of local re-appropriations of religious and philosophical constructs is, as studied in Chapter 1, central to Mudimbe's thought. He is eager to condemn culture-specific values which have gained, as a result of geopolitical hegemony, universal status but he has often argued that the idea of God must be devoid of parochial attachments. When, in *The Idea of Africa*, he explores the ways in which the Catholic Church in the Renaissance declared '*terra nullius*' large swaths of Central and South American territories, he above all condemns the Spanish and Portuguese proselytes' inability to move away from very context-specific symbols, declarations, and liturgical pronouncements. Mudimbe posits that God cannot be the vehicle for the promotion of ideological and nationalist agenda if it is to retain its universal currency. Conversely, McAfee Brown advocates the necessity of adapting and indigenise the faith to accommodate different cultures and redress world inequalities generated by wars, poverty, and colonialism (CA, 161). He remarks that new theological currents, in the United States but also in the Third World,[29] have attempted to redefine God as a 'Dieu engagé' [politically committed God] (CA, 161). Mudimbe remains sceptical and contends that the theology of liberation and other analogous movements offer solutions which are too determined by events, not removed enough from daily life and its vicissitudes; by contrast, he praises, 'la liberté magnifique du Dieu de Descartes. Un Dieu véritablement créateur, indépendant de tout principe …' [the magnificent freedom of Descartes' God. A God who is a genuine creator and does not depend on any principle …] (*CA*, 161). This said, Mudimbe's posture is not completely one-sided as he seemed to take seriously the possibility of an African theology. McAfee Brown asks him whether he thinks that this development is desirable. Mudimbe cannot hide his enthusiasm and his reply announces the spirit and hope that will pervade *The Invention of Africa*: 'Oui, dans la mesure où cela peut-être un montage extraordinaire. Imaginez une *gnose africaine* construite par des théologiens africains formés à l'école occidentale… [Yes insofar as this can be an extraordinary creation. Just imagine an African gnosis conceived by African theologians trained in a Western tradition …] (*CA*, 162; my emphasis).

An African Gnosis

The phrase 'gnose africaine' is important and goes well beyond the theological argument in which it is used, as it reflects, more fundamentally, Mudimbe's most enduring ambition to tease out the boundaries of knowledge production in the field of Africanism and to offer 'a critical synthesis of the complex questions about knowledge and power in and on Africa' (*IoA*, xi). If God defies all translations, knowledge (and knowledge on God), which traverses cultures through processes of re-appropriations and misappropriations, is perpetually an object of translation. As Mudimbe argues in the Introduction to the *Invention of Africa*, 'gnosis' has several meanings. He remarks that he prefers the phrase 'African gnosis' to 'African philosophy' for 'it is only metaphorically, or, at best, from a historicist perspective, that one would extend the notion of philosophy to African traditional systems of thought' (*IoA*, ix). He reminds that gnosis is etymologically linked to an ancient Greek verb which meant 'to know' (*IoA*, ix). The book aims therefore to explore a body of knowledge, referred to here as 'Africanism', in order to establish 'what is and what is not African philosophy' (*IoA*, ix). He contends that the methodological stance of the essay is heavily reliant on the notion of 'condition of possibility' as this was defined by Foucault in his *Archaeology of Knowledge* but also practised, it should be added, in his more historically driven investigations such as, for instance, *History of Madness*. Mudimbe's ambition is thus to show that 'discourses have not only sociohistorical origins' but also result from 'epistemological contexts' and are 'signs of something else' (*IoA*, ix). The focus of the book is to reveal the 'upstream' factors that make these discourses 'possible' (*IoA*, x). In *History of Madness*,[30] Foucault explored the development of a new discourse on madness in France's seventeenth century but also in the Europe of the Classical Age. In this slow-moving, 'patient', and scrupulously argued survey which incorporates a wealth of archival documents (court orders, medical, and legal reports) but also philosophical treaties, works of fiction, and paintings, Foucault contends that the meaning of madness changed radically from the Renaissance to the Age of Reason. The seventeenth century is marked by what he famously called the 'great confinement' (le grand renfermement), that is, by a tendency to define madness, or 'unreason' (déraison), as a socially reprehensible manifestation rather than a strictly medical disorder. There already existed before the Classical Age a dualistic perception of reason and madness but, as Foucault argues, notably via Cervantes, Shakespearian tragedies,[31] and paintings by Hieronymus Bosch,[32] madness was still regarded as a meaningful vehicle to understand human possibilities and provide insight into areas normally unavailable to reason. With the Classical Age, however, madness was 'denied the imaginary liberty that still allowed it to flourish at the time of the Renaissance',[33] and Foucault demonstrates that unreason and its cognates (madness, folly, and insanity) were increasingly used to designate and, ultimately, *confine* in the same institutions a population of socially excluded individuals such as the poor, the homosexuals, the unemployed, the libertines, and those suffering with psychological disorders. As a consequence of this epistemological rupture, unreason became, in the name of the prevailing social order, a notion to qualify, conflate, police, and exclude people who were thought to pose a threat to society:

> From the seventeenth century, a man of unreason was a real individual picked from a real social world, judged and sentenced by the society of which he was part. The key point is that madness was suddenly invested in a social world, and was granted there its own privileged and quasi exclusive place almost from one day to the next (across the whole of Europe in the space of fifty years), a clearly delimited terrain where it could be observed and denounced by all. Gone were the days when it sneaked through alleyways and hid in familiar places: now madness, and

all those who were its incarnation, could be instantly exorcised through measures of order and precautions of police.[34]

In his analysis of the representation of blackness by pre-classical and classical painters, Mudimbe applies an analogous methodology. In this discussion, which is reminiscent of Foucault's oft-quoted exploration of Velásquez's *Las Meninas* in *The Order of Things*,[35] he considers a number of European artists from the fifteenth and sixteenth centuries such as Erasmus Grasser, Hieronymus Bosch, Albrecht Dürer, and Hans Burgkmair and painters from the seventeenth century (Peter Paul Rubens, Rembrandt, and Hyacinthe Rigaud). His chief argument is that they belong to two different epistemological orders which mirror Foucault's opposition between the Renaissance and the Classical Age and their respective episteme. Renaissance painters such as Hans Burgkmair in his *Exotic Tribe* (1508) submitted African figures to aesthetic canons of their time and produced 'blackened whites' (*IoA*, 8). Mudimbe shows that this aesthetic option is, however, the expression of a 'discursive order' predicated upon the biblical idea of the monogenesis of all human beings (*IoA*, 8). This said, he adds that signs of difference such as 'nakedness, blackness, curly hair, bracelets, and strings of pearls' (*IoA*, 9) indicate that 'similitude' (*IoA*, 9) and the assimilating project underlying these painters' application of 'the *white* norm' (*IoA*, 8) can also accommodate ideas of 'distinctions', 'separations', and 'cultural distance' (*IoA*, 9). In Chapter 1, an analogous point was made about the Portuguese *feitiços* at the time of their discovery in the fifteenth century. Conversely, the seventeenth-century painters examined here relate to 'another order' because 'resemblance has been pushed out of Rubens's, Rembrandt's, and Rigaud's perceptions of blacks' (*IoA*, 9). Their representations of African figures are underpinned by a different 'epistemological foundation' (*IoA*, 9), that is, by 'theories of diversifications of beings', 'classificatory tables', and 'taxonomies' (*IoA*, 9), as developed in *The Order of Things* (chap. 5, 'Classifying').[36] Mudimbe remarks that this second and very different discursive formation played a crucial role in the 'constitution of the object of African Studies' and in 'the "Invention" of Africanism as a scientific discipline' (*IoA*, 9), but also as the manifestation of a racist ideology:

> It would be too easy to link it, *upstream*, to discursive formations about the great chain of beings and its hierarchy, and, *downstream*, first to Blumenbach's craniology and, second, to the general anti-African bias of the philosophical and scientific literature of the eighteenth and nineteenth centuries. (*IoA*, 9)

E. W. Blyden

His exploration of Edward Wilmot Blyden's work on Africa and race thinking relies also on Foucault's method and enables him, through this arch-representative of the Black Atlantic, to bridge the gap between Francophone and Anglophone Black Studies. Blyden (1832–1912) – pastor, professor of classics, politician, author, and Liberia's ambassador to Britain – is a hugely influential figure in the history of Black emancipation in Africa, in the United States, and in the Caribbean where he was born and brought up. His significance has been widely acknowledged,[37] and Mudimbe, in this critical account ('E. W. Blyden's Legacy and Questions'), interrogates Senghor's claim, in a Preface to a collection of letters by Blyden himself,[38] that Blyden is 'the foremost precursor both of *Négritude* and of the *African personality*' (IoA, 98).

In this short Preface, Senghor provides a historical précis of negritude's genesis in the early 1930s. Among other key influences, he reminds the significance of 'Negro-American' writers and thinkers such as Sterling Brown, Countee Cullen, Du Bois, and Alain Locke in the development of negritude.[39] He remarks, however, that the members of the negritude movement had failed to take on board Blyden's very significant intellectual input and argues that he had already, 'in the middle of the 19th century', formulated ideas about the 'virtues of Negritude'.[40] Senghor observes that Blyden had persistently striven to generate a 'revolution of mentalities' in order to 'lead Negro-Americans to cultivate what is "authentically" theirs', that is, 'their "African Personality"', and that he had also 'urged them to preserve their most healthy customs and even to keep their traditional dress'.[41] Senghor adds, however, that Blyden, a 'true Universal Man', had, already then, advocated 'the method which is ours today: to find ones roots in the values of Negritude, while remaining open to those of non-African civilizations'.[42] Senghor contends that his 'precursor' had long before Teilhard de Chardin 'defended the thesis that all civilisations are equal, but different'.[43] He remarks that Blyden believed that successful civilisations always resulted from 'a mixing of cultures'[44] (the phrase 'métissage culturel'[45] is used in the French version) but he regrets, however, that he was unable to repress his life-long aversion for 'racially mixed individuals' ('Métis').[46] Blyden developed indeed whilst in Liberia a dislike for the Monrovia-based Métis political elite of African-American origin and advocated, as a consequence, a return to the more authentically African 'interior'.[47]

Overall, Mudimbe does not disagree with Senghor's view of Blyden as the forefather of pan-Africanism. However there exists a major methodological difference between the two thinkers. One of Mudimbe's aims in this reading is to highlight the nature of Blyden's thought with regards to races and racial prejudices. He argues that, albeit an 'exceptional man who devoted his entire life to the cause he believed in' (*IoA*, 129), he was also the product of an *episteme* and could not escape the discursive context of his time. By the same token, he contends that 'in seeking to answer the racists in their own terms Blyden developed a theory of race, which, while vindicating the black man, derived an uncomfortably large measure of inspiration from late nineteenth-century European race-thinking' (*IoA*, 129).[48] Blyden lived in the heyday of colonialism and his ideas and rhetoric are infused with imperial phraseology. Of course, he never stopped reminding his readers and audiences of the devastating effects of slavery and European colonialism in Africa but, at the same time, he remained throughout his life a dogged advocate of the re-colonisation of Liberia by 'pure Negroes' from the United States and the Caribbean.[49] Blyden's repatriation programme was supported and funded by the American Colonization Society (ACS), an institution created in 1816 by abolitionists but also slaveholders. Whereas the former were motivated by a missionary spirit and humanitarian goals, the latter were eager to promote emancipation and deracination in order to eliminate the possible threat that 'free Negroes' could pose 'to the institution of slavery'.[50] The ACS's ambition was therefore very paradoxical as it hoped, at the same time, 'to rid the United States of both slavery and black people'.[51] In many ways, Blyden internalised this paradox, as illustrated in 'The African Problem and the Methods of its Solution', a speech that he delivered at the ACS in 1890. This speech, in which he makes a plea to intensify and accelerate the repatriation effort in Liberia, is replete with biblical metaphors, reminiscent of the missionary literature on colonisation, and driven by the idea that the settlement of Black Americans in Africa will benefit 'brethren across the deep'.[52] He contends that the enterprise has been arduous and has entered the crucial 'emigration phase' whereby 'the Negro, freed in body and mind, shall bid farewell to these scenes of his bondage and discipline and betake himself to the land of his fathers, the scene of larger opportunities and loftier achievements'. He adds, however, that '[i]t is not often given to man to labor successfully in the land of Egypt, in the wilderness and across the Jordan'.[53] Blyden, who was a keen supporter of Zionism,[54] draws a parallel between Jewish and Black diasporas and their aspiration to return to the homeland of their ancestors.[55] Announcing Cheikh Anta

Diop's cultural Pan-Africanism, he remarks that this black 'exodus' to Africa, a continent compared here to the 'gray-haired mother of civilization' whose time-honoured secrets are guarded by the 'Sphinxes',[56] is not complete but has already produced noticeable results: 'The Liberians [...] are pushing to the interior, clearing up the forests, extending the culture of coffee, sugar, cocoa [...] and training the aborigines in the arts of civilization and in the principles of Christianity'.[57]

What can be observed is that Blyden's output is marked by a number of tensions and is more complex than Senghor allows it to be. His Egyptocentric conception of the African nation is multilayered as it rests also on the notion that the Igbo people of south-eastern Nigeria, to which Blyden's ancestors belonged, were of Jewish descent.[58] Via H. Arendt's *The Origin of Totalitarianism*,[59] Mudimbe contends that Blyden's Africa was predicated upon 'romantic premises' and by the tendency, commonplace among scholars of 'the "Indo-European" or "Indo-Gemanic" culture' to confuse and amalgamate 'notions of "race", "language", "tradition", and "history"' (*IoA*, 115). This criticism helps Mudimbe to establish another analogy between Blyden and Senghor and to expose the ambiguity of the latter's racial project. Blyden's 'anti-racism' (*IoA*, 130) was also premised on the 'relativization of the supposed superiority of the categories white, civilized, and Christian' (*IoA*, 129). This parallel is useful as it helps to demonstrate a degree of continuity between the nineteenth and the twentieth centuries and show that Black activism was for a very long period unable to break away from the underlying categories of nineteenth-century ethnocentrism. This idea constitutes the intellectual backbone of Mudimbe's thesis as he often argues that the twentieth century 'could be seen as simply the continuation of a long nineteenth century'.[60]

Mudimbe's analysis shows the long-lasting influences of a specific discursive context and the many attempts to define, differentiate, and essentialise racial, national (and hence cultural) identities. His focus on Senghor's celebration of Blyden is therefore also a critique of negritude, as a revolutionary movement which did not quite manage to sever the links with ethnocentric romanticism:

> When compared to Senghor's negritude, the relevance of Blyden's commitment is still apparent, even though the concept of race is now generally considered an ideological trap. [...] Despite discrepancies due to differences of socio-political contexts, psychological situations, and philosophical references, Senghor, on the whole, pursued Blyden's ambiguous thesis. His pronouncements emphasize the African cultural

and historical identity in terms of race and consider this concept to be essential. (*IoA*, 132)

Blyden, however, is not Senghor and Mudimbe is aware that pan-Africanism and its cultural avatar, negritude, are not the only available filters to assess the significance and scope of Blyden's thought. Mudimbe's reading of Blyden is more than an overview, more than a descriptive account on the development of Ur-pan-Africanism, as it is also a strategy to criticise Senghor's humanism and lack of epistemological awareness. Mudimbe's reading has a self-reflective dimension because he also regards himself as Blyden's intellectual heir. He is indeed able to establish parallels between his own thought and Blyden's. The Liberian activist is presented as a thinker who had, 100 years before Mudimbe, conducted a sustained discussion on the discursive basis of Western colonisation in sub-Saharan Africa. Via *Christianity, Islam and the Negro Race*,[61] Mudimbe demonstrates that Blyden had also sensed that the Africa in which he was living had become an invention of the West. This realisation is significant as it complicates the relationship between Blyden and Senghorian negritude. It uncovers the limitation of any critical interpretation and the ideological bias at the heart of Senghor's reading of Blyden's legacy. It also shows, however, that Mudimbe is not immune to this type of re-appropriation as his interpretation is indeed inflected by his own intellectual and methodological agenda. Blyden needs also, according to Mudimbe, to be remembered for his ability to question the relevance (for Africa) of the theoretical basis underpinning Western social sciences. He fought for the reclamation of a suppressed cultural legacy but this objective was also informed by a desire to identify an African *gnosis*. He argues that Blyden's work rested on the 'possibility of a general criticism of social sciences' (*IoA*, 133), which, in many respects, announces his own critique:

> [Blyden] made this criticism by systematically focusing on the significance of European ethnocentrism [...] This meant, *then as now*, that an understanding of African personality or African culture cannot neglect a major dimension – the *epistemological debate*. Because of imperialism and its ideological reflections in moral and social sciences, this approach must question all discourses interpreting Africans and their culture. Blyden considered this a critical preliminary to establishing a unifying and productive rapport between African ideology and the concrete *practice of knowledge*. (*IoA*, 133; my emphasis)

The highlighted expressions demonstrate the filiation that he attempts to establish between Blyden and himself (and the intellectual tradition in which he operates). This point is made even clearer in the very conclusion of the chapter. Mudimbe argues that, thanks to Blyden, 'African intellectuals' started to realize that, in order to

> benefit from the heritage of their own history rather than remaining mere objects of or obedient participants in Western social sciences, it was their duty to master knowledge of themselves and their own culture and to open up a vigorous debate on the limits of anthropology. (*IoA*, 134)

The main point here is that this chapter on Blyden goes well beyond Mudimbe's initial question: 'in what sense can we accept Senghor's and Lynch's statements about Blyden as the precursor of negritude and "African personality?"'(*IoA*, 99). Above all, Mudimbe wants to argue that his own analysis of Africa's intellectual past is altogether less emotional and more scientific than Senghor's. Senghor's statement about Blyden's racist bias towards Mulattoes, 'no one is perfect, neither Edward Wilmot Blyden, nor the Negro-Americans who influenced us',[62] reveals the methodological rift that separates him from Mudimbe and Foucault. In *The History of Madness*, Foucault observes that the archaeological method 'means accepting the deformation imposed by our own retrospective glance'.[63] He argues that it would be tempting to believe that the conception of madness in the Classical Age was scientifically unfounded and that seventeenth-century observers had failed to recognize its true '*nature*' and missed its '*positive signs*'.[64] Rather than focusing on the 'error' that led to the '*confusion*' between criminals, blasphemers, homosexuals, libertines, and insane people, Foucault believes that it is far more fruitful to 'follow the *continuity* that our own way of thinking has broken'.[65] Senghor does not, however, take on board the 'deformation' of his own 'retrospective glance' and fails to inscribe Blyden's racial prejudice in its archaeological context.

This focus on Blyden is symptomatic of the methodological approach adopted by Mudimbe throughout *The Invention*; it also demonstrates the author's ability to reinvent himself after his relocation in the United States in 1980 even though, from *L'Autre Face* to *L'Odeur du père*, he believes that his 'major thesis has remained the same with respect to the analogical form of the social sciences and the history of Africanist discourse' (*IoA*, xi). The vast historical survey of African philosophy that *The Invention* proposes is shown to be ordered by conditions of possibilities, which, from the nineteenth century to the late twentieth century, have transformed themselves. Blyden serves therefore as a significant example to identify what Foucault called 'lignes de partage' – thresholds, dividing lines, and epistemological ruptures – first between Senghor and Mudimbe, that is, between a romantic and a more epistemologically grounded conception of Africanity, but also, and by extension, between negritude, ethno-philosophy, on the one hand, and African philosophy on the other.

Foucault and an African Order of Knowledge

The Invention of Africa is a complex book and its difficulty results from the fact that Mudimbe interrogates a very large corpus encompassing philosophy, anthropology, psychology, sociology, theology, and political thought. This apparent diversity has, however, its logic as he conducts a critique of Africanism, an area which traditionally embraced a variety of unconnected disciplines. His corpus seems amorphous precisely because Africanism was ill-defined and remained throughout the colonial era a domain in which scientific or disciplinary considerations were subordinated to a territorial logic.[66] The second factor which lends Mudimbe's project its coherence lies in the assumption that these disciplines, bar philosophy, are all 'human sciences'. The book proposes to undertake the archaeology of Africanism, considered here as a cluster of disciplines which invented *modern* Africa. In his investigations, Mudimbe focuses overwhelmingly on the nineteenth century and he attempts to explain how its legacy was absorbed and, in some instances, re-arranged, or rejected by twentieth-century Africanists and African thinkers. The book provides thus an intellectual history of African dependency and prescribes strategies to actualise epistemological independence. It is, as Michael Syrotinski remarks, both a '*prescriptive* manifesto of sorts' in addition to being 'an impressively vast *descriptive* survey of the ways in which Africa has been represented, or misrepresented'.[67]

Foucault, the 'unhappy "historian of the Same"' (*IoA*, 34), is the most significant methodological point of reference of *The Invention*, a book in which Mudimbe practises, like Spivak and Said at the same time, 'a relativization of the truth of the Same in the dispersion of history' (*IoA*, 34). For this reason, the book does not fall in the traditional category of the 'history of ideas', a genre that Foucault dismissed as 'the discipline of beginnings and ends, the description of obscure continuities, the reconstitution of developments in the linear form of history'.[68] Implicitly,

Mudimbe also demands the abandonment of the history of ideas and its 'great themes' of 'genesis', 'continuity', and 'totalization'.[69]

Mudimbe's approach is predicated upon Foucault's analysis of the development of the human sciences in the West since the end of the eighteenth century, a moment that coincided with the emergence of the modern *episteme*. In *The Order of Things* (chap. 10, 'The Human Sciences') Foucault argues that 'man', as an object of study, did not exist before the appearance of the human sciences and their focus on what would constitute 'man', that is, life, labour, and language, after the 'general redistribution of the *episteme*'.[70] By highlighting these three entities, Foucault suggests that the budding human sciences (psychology, sociology, social anthropology, literary criticism, and linguistics) 'did not inherit a certain domain, already outlined [...] which it was then their task to elaborate with positive methods and with concepts that had at last become scientific'.[71] From the very outset, their development was governed by a search for a specific scientific positivity which was achieved analogically and by means of conceptual and methodological borrowings from established empirical sciences such as biology, economics, and philology which also emerged from the modern *episteme*. Their positivity enabled 'man', caught up in the paradoxical position of being at the same time subject *and* object of knowledge, to represent himself as a living, working, and speaking subject:

> [M]an for the human sciences [...] is that living being who, from within the life to which he entirely belongs and by which he is traversed in his whole being, constitutes representations by means of which he lives, and on the basis of which he possesses that strange capacity of being able to represent to himself precisely that life.[72]

Africanist discourses were developed against the same epistemological background. In the wake of Foucault, Mudimbe suggests that the African 'man' is the product of an invention generated by this newly acquired positivity of the sciences of man. The 'site' of Africanism can therefore also 'be fixed in the vicinity, on the immediate frontiers, and along the whole length of those sciences that deal with life, labor, and language'.[73] Mudimbe, at several points in *The Invention*, but also in his other books,[74] is indeed keen to support Foucault's claim that the development of the human sciences since the early nineteenth century has been reliant upon a series of 'constituent models [...] borrowed from [...] biology, economics, and the study of languages'.[75] These models or pairs of concepts – 'functions/norms', 'conflict/rules', and 'significations/

system' – open up the possibility, according to Foucault, not only to account for the conceptual linkages and transfers between biology and psychology, economics and sociology, and philology and the study of languages (or linguistics), but also to retrace the successive epistemological shifts that have affected the science of man in the last 150 years.

Foucault defines the roles of the terms in each pair and delineates their varying importance over time. The pair 'functions/norms' pertains to the field of biology but became paramount for psychology at its nascent stage: 'man' possesses *functions* and in order to adapt, survive, and perform these functions adequately, he needs to operate within a regulatory framework that will provide 'average *norms* of adjustment'.[76] The pair 'conflict/rules' is relevant to economics and was adopted by the early sociology: 'man' has desires and ambitions which can sometimes bring him into *conflict* with other human beings and, so as to avoid these situations of conflict, he is constrained to submit his behaviour to a 'body of *rules*'.[77] The pair 'signification/system' relates to philology and will be determining in the study of myths and literature: 'man' communicates with words, signs, and gestures and all his attempts to be meaningful have a *signification* and 'constitute a coherent whole and a *system* of signs'.[78]

With regards to the chronological distribution and evolution of these terms, Foucault makes two crucial observations. Although they have all invariably inflected the shape and nature of the human sciences, these three constituent models can all be attributed to a specific timeframe. The Romantic period was marked by the 'reign of the biological model' wherein all elements that shaped 'man', that is, 'his psyche', the society in which he lived and the languages he used, were treated in terms of organic function. Then followed the 'reign of the economic model' and its analysis of human activity as a zone dominated by conflicts. Finally, 'just as Freud comes after Comte and Marx', began the 'reign of the philological model', which pursues the elucidation of 'hidden meanings', and that of the 'linguistic model' and its attempts to uncover the building blocks of 'signifying systems'.[79] Foucault adds that two additional shifts must be mentioned to account for the increasing (or decreasing) significance of these constituent models over the last century. He notices first that biological concepts and metaphors gradually gave way to 'models borrowed from language'.[80] Even more importantly, he notes that there was an overlap between this first shift and another one which permitted the second term of the 'constituent pairs' (norm, rule, system) gradually to overshadow the first term (function, conflict, signification).

Foucault suggests that this reversal from a functional to a normative model was reflected and actualised in the work of Georges Dumézil (mythology), Marcel Mauss (sociology and anthropology), and Kurt Goldstein (psychology).[81]

This latter reflection is crucial with respect to Mudimbe's archaeological project in *The Invention*. Unlike Mudimbe's previous books, *The Invention* is a monograph rather than a collection of essays. What distinguishes it from *L'Autre Face* and *L'Odeur du père* is this very homogeneous critical standpoint. In many respects, Foucault's exposition of these shifts is the matrix that allows Mudimbe to dissect the Africanist discourse. Foucault contends that the shift of emphasis from the first to the second term of the constituent models radically transformed the human sciences which hitherto had 'always extended between a positive pole and a negative pole [...] always designated an alterity'.[82] As long as the functional model prevailed over the normative one, as long as the conflict remained more determining that the rule, and the signification carried more weight than the system, it was possible to talk of 'a pathological psychology' co-existing alongside 'normal psychology' and it was accepted to speak of 'a pathology of societies' (Durkheim) and 'of irrational and quasi-morbid form of belief (Lévy-Bruhl, Blondel)'. Similarly, it was conceivable to think that some conflicts were not resolvable and could threaten society and its members. Lastly, a distinction was established between 'significant and non-significant' and it was assumed that 'there was meaning in certain domains [...] but not in others'.[83] However, as Foucault suggests, when

> the analysis was conducted from the point of view of the norm, the rule, and the system, each area provided its own coherence [...] it was no longer possible to speak of 'morbid consciousness' (even referring to the sick), of 'primitive mentalities' (even with reference to societies left behind by history), or of 'insignificant discourses' (even when referring to absurd stories, or to apparently incoherent legends). Everything may be thought within the order of the system, the rule, and the norm.[84]

This shift to the system, the rule, and the norm is of considerable importance with regards to Mudimbe's analysis as his entire investigation is predicated upon the idea that literature about Africa was submitted, from the turn of the century onwards, to a series of epistemological reversals that gradually nuanced and then transformed the evolutionary postulates that had dominated nineteenth-century discourses on races. In this respect, it is crucial to emphasise the contrast that Foucault establishes between thinkers such as Lucien Lévy-Bruhl,

Émile Durkheim, Charles Blondel, on the one hand, and Dumézil, Mauss, Goldstein, and Freud, on the other. It is unfortunate, however, that this seemingly neat contrast is not investigated further by Foucault as, to take one well-documented example, it is difficult to accept that the pair Durkheim–Mauss embodies a straightforward passage from a functionalist to a normative standpoint in sociology and social anthropology (ethnologie). It seems that Foucault, despite his critical appraisal of the history of ideas, cannot quite depart from a certain type of totalisation. A closer exegesis of Durkheim and Mauss, a task that lies beyond the scope of the present study, would reveal that Foucault's categorisation can be challenged. Durkheim, in *Les Formes élémentaires de la vie religieuse*,[85] attempts to systematise the 'rules' and 'norms' of religious manifestations. In this study, which focuses on the totemic rites of Australian Aborigines, he suggests that human behaviour and culture rest upon a coherent system made up of subsystems and that individuals are not entirely conscious of the rules that preside over their behaviour. Considered from this perspective, Durkheim's project is as 'normative' as Mauss's *Essai sur le don*,[86] a study which famously attempted, via an exploration of giving and reciprocating, to discover the governing principles of human solidarity and reveal 'ces rocs humains sur lesquels sont bâtis [les] sociétés' [those human blocks on which societies are built].[87] What needs stressing, however, is that both Durkheim *and* Mauss used terms such as 'the primitive' and 'primitiveness' and therefore did not entirely break away from the functionalist model identified by Foucault.[88]

Ultimately, Foucault is above all interested in delineating the special position of psychoanalysis and ethnology in the vast domain occupied by the human sciences because they are 'both the sciences of the unconscious'.[89] These two disciplines are more than any other concerned with the understanding of the second term of the 'constituent models' since the feature of the norm-rule-system triad in relation to the function–conflict–signification is not to be 'given to consciousness'.[90] Foucault contends that from the nineteenth century onwards the human sciences have relentlessly endeavoured to excavate 'that regions of the unconscious where the action of representation is held in suspense',[91] a trend, as he proceeds to demonstrate, that has been most manifest in the fields of psychoanalysis and ethnology.

Mudimbe's archaeology of African discourse is, in a nutshell, a survey of the consequences, for Africa, of this normative shift. In this investigation, the period that immediately follows the end of the Great War is of particular significance. This moment coincided with an epistemological dividing line and with the beginning of the end of a very long nineteenth century: 'I propose two periods and, therefore, two overlapping types of knowledge of Africa: before and after the 1920s' (*IoA*, 72). Mudimbe links this epistemological caesura to the emergence of dissenting voices on either sides of the Atlantic (Harlem Renaissance, negritude)[92] and with the development of less ethnocentric and deterministic anthropological perspectives which, albeit still reliant upon 'dubious' colonial programmes such as the 'promotion of African literature and languages', would nonetheless provide Africans with tools that would 'ultimately be used against foreign ideologies' (*IoA*, 77). He contends that the three schools of thought that had hitherto informed anthropology, that is, evolutionism, functionalism, and diffusionism, 'all repress otherness in the name of sameness, reduce the different to the already known, and thus fundamentally escape the task of making sense of other worlds' (*IoA*, 72–73). By this, he means that they were still linked to a world absorbed by the examination of the function–conflict–signification triad.

In this broad synthesis, too broad as individual voices are sometimes sacrificed at the expense of prevailing discourses and overarching tendencies, he identifies two antagonistic movements. First, the ethnophilosophical tradition represented by figures such as Evans-Pritchard, Marcel Griaule, Placide Tempels, and Alexis Kagame (but also Janheinz Jahn, Cheikh Anta Diop, John Mbiti, Vincent Mulago, Théohile Obenga, and Senghor) and, secondly, a more recent trend, to which Mudimbe belongs alongside side thinkers such as Franz Crahay, Engelbert Mveng, Marcien Towa, Paulin Hountondji, Oscar Bimwenyi, and Fabien Eboussi-Boulaga, and which defines itself against the ethnic and 'pseudo-philosophical' thrust of ethnophilosophy. Mudimbe's exploration of this development is, however, far less dualistic than it is suggested here as he often expresses, alongside other contemporary thinkers such as John Mbiti and Marcel Tshiamalenga (*IoA*, 140), his sympathy towards ethnophilosophical attempts, from the 1930s onwards, to restore the dignity of black African cultures.

The term 'ethnophilosophy' was first used by Paulin Hountondji to account for (but also critique) efforts, on the part of African and Western scholars, to describe collective philosophies of specific ethnic groups:

> That is what happens to the word 'philosophy': applied to Africa it is supposed to designate no longer the specific discipline it evokes in its Western context but merely a collective world-view, an implicit,

spontaneous, perhaps even unconscious system of beliefs to which all Africans are supposed to adhere. This is a vulgar usage of the word, justified presumably by the supposed vulgarity of the geographical context to which it is applied.[93]

Placide Tempels's famous essay *Bantu Philosophy* is widely regarded as the precursor of this ethnophilosophical vein. Mudimbe agrees with Hountondji's critique and remarks, a point convincingly made elsewhere by Tshiamalenga[94] and Eboussi-Boulaga,[95] that Tempels's concept of 'being-force' is not philosophically credible and too essentialising (*IoA*, 140–41),[96] but he concludes that the book, for all its weaknesses, would not have been the subject of so much controversy if Tempels had chosen 'a title without the term "philosophy"' (*IoA*, 141). For Mudimbe, Tempels's essay primarily needs to be located in the field of ethnography even though Tempels's ambition to identify the 'vital force' underlying Baluba 'Being' or 'ontology' seems, at first glance, to pertain to philosophy. Despite the 'fuzziness of a thought born of [...] ethnological curiosity, evangelical ambiguities, and colonial purpose' (*IoA*, 141), *Bantu Philosophy* is worthy of attention because it casts 'doubts on the greatness of the colonial venture' (*IoA*, 136), an idea also put forward by Alioune Diop in the Foreword of the Présence africaine edition of Tempels's essay in 1949. More crucially, though, *Bantu Philosophy* announces and even actualises the shift from the first term (function, conflict, signification) of the constituent models described by Foucault. Hountondji's reference to an 'unconscious system of beliefs' very aptly captures the main motive behind Mudimbe's interest in Tempels's work. In this respect, it is important to note that although Hountondji remarks that *Bantu Philosophy* was addressed to 'colonials and missionaries' rather than to Africans,[97] he is also careful to add that Tempels's study departed (a view not entirely shared by Mudimbe) from Lévy-Bruhl's 'celebrated "primitive mentality"' and was predicated upon the assumption that the African *Weltanschauung* 'rested [...] on a systematic conception of the universe which , however different it might be from the Western system of thought, equally deserved the name "philosophy"'.[98]

Marcel's Griaule work on the Dogon results, according to Mudimbe, from an analogous set of conditions of possibility. At the beginning of their career, both men, who were therefore epistemologically close to Lévy-Bruhl, subscribed to the ethnocentric idea that humanity was made up of pre-logical 'primitives' and rational Westerners. They also suggested that their theses on Bantu and Dogon ontology could be 'valid for all non-Western societies' (*IoA*, 139) and be applied to 'primitive peoples in general' (*IoA*, 142).⁹⁹ Mudimbe observes, however, that the very specific geographical focus of their studies bore witness to the possibility, opened up by Malinowski, of studying 'the epistemology and the singularity of regional cultural systems' (*IoA*, 82) from the point of view of their governing rules, norms, and systemic coherence. This wide-ranging shift, in which, Mudimbe argues, such disparate figures as Blaise Cendrar, Pablo Picasso, Wilhem Schmidt, Leo Frobenius, and Blyden played an active role, was made possible by 'the fragmentation of the notion of civilization' (*IoA*, 81). Another common factor identified by Mudimbe is that, like Tempels vis-à-vis his Baluba informants, Griaule demonstrated a high degree of '*Einfühlung*' (*IoA*, 137–44), or sympathy, towards Ogotemmêli, the Dogon sage of whom, in an ironic reversal of roles, he became the student.[100] This '*Einfühlung*' is presented as the connective thread between these early exponents of a new anthropology and the generation of thinkers to which Mudimbe himself belongs. The chapters devoted to anthropology and missionary discourses are therefore both a critique of ethnophilosophy but also a strategy whereby Mudimbe demonstrates that some of the ethnophilosophers' methodological postulates, the '*Einfühlung*', for instance, were adopted by subsequent generations of ethnologists. Mudimbe identifies thus a continuum between the 1920s and the late 1980s, between Tempels and, on the other end of the spectrum, Claude Lévi-Strauss.

His focus on Alexis Kagame's *La Philosophie bantu-rwandaise de l'être*[101] further ponders the extent to which ethnophilosphy has marked the constitution of an African gnosis. This study is a response to Tempels's thesis in that it also endeavours to unravel the significance of the concept of 'Being' among the Bantu of Central-Eastern Africa.[102] In a move which is reminiscent of (but not identical to) the works by some Anglophone African representatives of analytic philosophy such as W. E. Abraham and Kwasi Wiredu, Kagame proposes, like Mbiti and Mulago later, to describe a coherent philosophical system on the basis of a close analysis of Bantu languages. Kagame's work is rigorous and 'escapes Tempels's unsupported generalization' as 'it is now founded on a linguistic order' (*IoA*, 151). Kagame's systematisation of Bantu philosophy's deep structure is less static than Tempels's since it also considers possible transformations brought about by 'changes in present-day mentalities' (*IoA*, 151).

In this assessment, Mudimbe remains, however, very critical of the ideological dimension and catastrophic legacy of ethnophilosophy: 'Though we are now beyond Tempels's revolution, his ghost is still present' (*IoA*, 153). Tempels's philosophy was promoted 'in the name of Christian brotherhood' (*IoA*, 151) and Kagame explicitly referred in his works to 'a racial duty' (*IoA*, 151). Their 'claim to an original alterity' (*IoA*, 151) has had sinister consequences and has fuelled what Achille Mbembe calls Africa's 'necropolitics' (Chapter 5). Mudimbe deplores, in this respect, 'the cheap and easy exploitation of authenticity' by the 'Zairian government' of the early 1970s (*IoA*, 153). Later, in an affectionate but critical portrayal of Kagame, 'Alexis Kagame, Priest and Scholar' (*TF*, 135–45), Mudimbe would highlight the significance of his ethnophilosophical work but also warn of its potential danger with regards to the various genocides that have plagued recent Rwandan history. This point will be further investigated in Chapter 5.

Ethnophilosophy and its critique serve to convey a sense of epistemological continuum – characterised by the Einfülhung and shift to the second terms of the constituent models (the norm-rule-system) – but also, paradoxically, a sense of discontinuity with the more recent trends in African thought. This is where Mudimbe's survey is at its most prescriptive and where its overall coherence is also most obvious as the many names and figures listed and accumulated in the analysis are overall less significant than the wider rules, norms, and systems governing their intellectual outputs. The analysis remains linked to history and he contends, by way of Jean Copans, the crucial role played by Marxism, as seen in Chapters 2 and 3, and sociology in the recent transformation of Africanism in which a rupture with 'Griaulian idealism' (*IoA*, 176) was achieved. This transformation coincided with decolonisation and with the advent of the 'annihilation of the mythologies of the same' (*IoA*, 42). In this process, which affected the presuppositions upon which history and anthropology had hitherto relied, Mudimbe ascribes a very crucial role to Claude Lévi-Strauss who is presented throughout the *Invention* as one of the figures who facilitated an 'African amplification' (*IoA*, 35–43) of the structuralist revolution and precipitated a move away, not only from the ethnocentrism of Tempels and Kagame, but also from the more ideologically based and subject-centred writings of Fanon, Césaire, and Sartre. Mudimbe argues that the new generation of African thinkers since the 1960s, and even more so since the 1970s, have favoured 'the notion of epistemological vigilance' over 'political power and strategies for ideological succession', a point, as he remarks, neatly made by the Cameroonian philosopher Engelbert Mveng: 'if political sovereignty is necessary, the scientific sovereignty is perhaps more important in present-day Africa' (*IoA*, 36).

Lévi-Strauss's exploration of the links between mythical thought and the unconscious opens up the possibility of privileging the system over the signification. His theorisation of the incest taboo in *Les Structures élémentaires de la parenté*,[103] itself an amplification of Marcel Mauss's *Essai sur le don*, is predicated upon a new, Saussure- and Jakobson-inflected understanding of anthropology (see Chapter 1). In this context, kinship is conceived in terms of a number of oppositions between men and women (patriarchy and matriarchy), endogamy and exogamy, and, nature and culture. Kinship is therefore regarded as a strictly relational system whose structure depends upon a set of unconscious rules. Lévi-Strauss's intellectual production exemplifies the epistemological models developed by Foucault: 'the search for a discreet but essential order is what unites Foucault and Lévi-Strauss' (*IoA*, 28). The Saussurian framework of Lévi-Strauss's analysis constitutes a rupture with ethnocentrism and the racial and cultural hierarchies upon which anthropology had relied since the nineteenth century. In *Race et histoire*,[104] a work of pedagogical nature aiming to combat racial prejudices, Lévi-Strauss had advocated the equality of cultures and negated the traditional opposition between stationary and cumulative history. In *La Pensée sauvage*,[105] he would demonstrate that the 'savage' mind proceeds as logically and rationally as its 'civilised' counterpart. In this respect, it is instructive to contrast the way in which 'science' and 'magic' are analysed by Tempels and Lévi-Strauss.[106] Whereas magical thought is held by Tempels as a corruption of pure Bantu ontology, Lévi-Strauss regards magic and science as 'two parallel modes of acquiring knowledge' (*IoA*, 31).[107] This line of argument, that is, the 'rejection of the antinomy between the logical and prelogical' (*IoA*, 30), allows Mudimbe to refute the opposition between 'tradition' and 'modernity', a construct seen as yet another invention of the nineteenth century. Mudimbe argues that the autonomy of contemporary African gnosis will depend upon the ability, on the part of African thinkers, to liberate themselves from the 'primitivist strategies' (*IoA*, 195) in order to generate, like Paul Ricœur, Paul Veyne, and de Certeau in post-war France,[108] 'a critical evaluation of the history of the same' (*IoA*, 177) and reveal the 'possibility of a plural rationality and history' (*IoA*, 195).

Mudimbe is eager to contend, notably via the tension between the Self and the Other as conceived by Sartre and Lévi-Strauss (see Chapter 3), that the desired epistemological liberation is to be enacted in a zone where phenomenology and structuralism would manifest their overlaps rather than their divergences. The sympathy that Tempels, Griaule, and

Lévi-Strauss felt towards the Other of their investigations – the Baluba, the Dogon, the Nambikwara – forced them to look at themselves and to acknowledge the self-reflective quality of anthropology. The for-itself is largely defined by the for-other, and anthropology, as understood by Lévi-Strauss, is 'a means for comprehending oneself' and engaging in 'self-analytical anthropology' (*IoA*, 33). The discipline is therefore regarded as a conduit which will lead to self-knowledge. It is thus essential for African thinkers, as Mudimbe argues, to engage in a 'permanent reevaluation' of its 'limits' and 'historicity' if it is to become 'a more credible *anthropou-logos*' and if it is once and for all to relinquish its dubious status as the science of the West's Other (*IoA*, 186). The structuralist paradigm that Mudimbe chooses to favour in *The Invention* does not, however, offer any panacea despite the fact that the 'task accomplished so far is certainly impressive' (*IoA*, 186). Hountondji, Mveng, Eboussi-Boulaga, Tshiamalenga, and the many other thinkers considered in Mudimbe's essay belong to the same episteme as Lévi-Strauss and Foucault (*IoA*, 43). Mudimbe is cautious to point out that this epistemological legacy may in fact prevent them from identifying their own '*chose du texte*', that is, the very elements determining African traditions (*IoA*, 183–86). *Chose du texte*, described as 'the primordial African discourse in its variety and multiplicity' (*IoA*, 186) and elsewhere as 'zero degree discourse' (*Idea*, xiii), is a rather intriguing phrase that Mudimbe, in a typical move, does not develop but locates too loosely within the hermeneutical tradition of Ricœur and Gadamer (*IoA*, 183). A reference to Beryl Bellman's anthropological essay *The Language of Secrecy*[109] offers nonetheless some clues as to how the phrase may be understood in the specific context of *The Invention of Africa* and against the backdrop of the vexed relation between a 'text', such as Africa, and its interpreters. Bellman's study focuses on the circulations of secrets in the Poro society of West Africa. Right from the outset, Bellman highlights the 'paradox of secrecy': secrets are handed over from one generation to the next during initiations on the condition that they should remain undisclosed and yet they are routinely divulged by ways of hidden and more diffuse devices such as symbols and metaphors as used in rituals and 'deep talk' (proverbs, parables, 'dilemma tales', 'mythical narratives').[110] Bellman's aspiration is twofold: he wants to translate a regional 'text' and, at the same time, demonstrate the universal currency of some of his conclusions by calling 'attention to practices that are relevant to the communication of secrets in every culture',[111] for, as he remarks in the concluding chapter, the resolution of the 'paradox of secrecy [...] touches upon virtually every issue relevant to the study of society'.[112] This ambition to access the intimacy of a culture, that is, the very 'thing' that makes a text 'tick' does not produce, however, definitive results. Through Frank Kermode's *The Genesis of Secrecy*,[113] he suggest that the 'true meaning of a text is always elusive'[114] and, via Gadamer's *Truth and Method*,[115] he argues that 'every translation is at the same time an interpretation',[116] that is, to return to Mudimbe's idea regarding the shiftiness of the *chose du texte*, an *invention*.

Mudimbe contends that the African amplification of Western discourses such as structuralism has been a salutary development and has produced a departure from the old evolutionist views that well into the twentieth century still lingered in ethnophilosophical works and discourses of authenticity and their empirical focus on *functions*, *conflicts*, and *significations*. Structuralism provides the theoretical tools to look beyond the appearances (and into the subconscious) in order to conduct an inventory of African knowledge, delineate the order of things African, and understand the strategies implemented by Westerners and Africans to imagine, translate, and, of late, co-invent Africa. However, this book raises more questions than it provides definite answers. It is its strength and the price to pay for the 'patience of philosophy'; but it is also its limitation for it is legitimate, a point that will be picked up again in Chapter 5, to expect that some instrument would be developed to account more robustly for this concealed but yet visible African *chose du texte*. The *Invention*, ultimately, does not quite say that independence has been achieved; it suggests, however, that 'the "intelligence" of the Same' (*IoA*, 43) – structuralism, existentialism, hermeneutics – can provide the basis for a more equal and less racialised dialogue between Africans and Westerners.

To conclude, a definite continuum can be identified between *Carnets d'Amérique* and *The Invention of Africa* beyond the obvious generic differences. First, the two books are characterised by an ambition to trace the multi-continental – Africa, Europe, America – causes and effects of colonialism and slavery. Mudimbe argues that their legacy lives on but has also been increasingly memorialised. In *Carnets d'Amérique*, the young Mudimbe presents himself as the advocate of a postcolonial pedagogy and militates for the implementation, in the United States but also in his native Congo, of teaching methods that would take into account regional contexts and reject the homogenising principles of assimilation. Teaching acts therefore as a convenient pretext to promote decolonisation in a politically decolonised world, which, paradoxically, perpetuates the old colonial dichotomies between the West and the Third World. Mudimbe's idea of 'cultural madness' (folie culturelle) needs thus to be understood as a sign that the arguments of anti-colonial militancy have not lost their potency and can still be the utensils of a new global order, although he disagrees with Fanon's suggestion about the need for a recommencement of history. This expression, 'folie culturelle', resonates with the idea that the colonised were 'robbed' of their cultures and psychologically destabilised by the imposition of colonial regimes. In Fanon's and Sartre's writings, it was posited that the emergence of a 'new man' would release the untapped potentiality of the Third World and be the conduit of a much-needed political and epistemological vigilance. From an intellectual point of view, *Carnets d'Amérique* is close to *L'Autre Face du royaume* and *L'Odeur du père* in that the West is somewhat essentialised and portrayed as a homogeneous cultural entity. In this respect, it is crucial to observe that these books referred (and adhered) to the thinking of Foucault but, ultimately, held his work in deep suspicion because of his ties with an epistemological order from which Mudimbe wanted to distance himself (*OP*, 42).

The figure of the culturally alienated African remains an essential focus of *The Invention* but it is treated very differently. The approach is more dispassionate and reflects what could be named the post-revolutionary maturation of Mudimbe's thought. Marxism, in its various African avatars, is explored in *The Invention* but it is analysed as an object of knowledge rather than as a body of ideas that could reignite the revolutionary spirit of the 1950s and 1960s. The methodological apparatus presiding over this epistemological excavation acts as a screen that prevents the old utopianism to re-emerge but produces also a more austere and *patient* analysis of the ways in which Africa has been invented and re-invented in the past two centuries. The subtle reflection over the shift from the first to the second terms of Foucault's constituent models bears witness to Mudimbe's intellectual brilliance, although one is sometimes left to wonder what constitutes the *real* benefit of this intellectual strategy. In *L'Idée coloniale en France*,[117] a book that definitely belongs to the 'histoire des idées' genre as it was conceived (and dismissed) by Foucault, Raoul Girardet also argued, in a far less convoluted manner, that ideas regarding France's colonial subjects went through a number of radical transformations in the interwar period, that this shift was felt across a number of disciplines (politics, anthropology, fiction) and announced decolonisation. If considered from this perspective only, *The Invention* is somewhat disappointing. Its real contribution, however, lies in Mudimbe's ability to overcome the more partisan posture of his earlier essays and fictions. Foucault and Lévi-Strauss are not longer regarded as 'signs' of a Western episteme, as deniers of the Other's 'coevalness', but as thinkers who have contributed to the dismantlement of ethnocentrism and the creation of a more hospitable critical arena. Mudimbe's indebtedness to Foucault, Lévi-Strauss, and Sartre has often been criticised as the symbol of his dependency as a thinker[118] whereas it is proof that he has succeeded to extricate himself from the racial, national, and linguistic markers of conventional identities and all that which defined the colonial and neo-colonial situations. It would be naive, even deleterious, to confine thinking, reiterate past disciplinary gestures and demand that Africans should 'endeavor to create from their otherness a radically new social science' (*IoA*, 79).

5

'Independences?'

> We might actually say that an anthropologist 'invents' the culture he believes himself to be studying, that the relation is more 'real' for being his particular acts and experiences than the things it 'relates.' Yet this explanation is only justified if we understand the invention to take place objectively, along the lines of observing and learning, and not as a kind of free fantasy. In experiencing a new culture, the fieldworker comes to realize new potentialities and possibilities for the living of life, and may in fact undergo a personality change himself. The subject culture becomes 'visible,' and then 'believable' to him, he apprehends it first as a distinct entity, a way of doing things, and then secondly as a way in which he could be doing things. Thus he comprehends for the first time, through the intimacy of his own mistakes and triumphs, what anthropologists speak of when they use the word 'culture.' Before this he had no culture, as we might say, since the culture in which one grows up is never really 'visible' – it is taken for granted, and its assumptions are felt to be self-evident. It is only through 'invention' of this kind that the abstract significance of culture (and of many another concept) can be grasped, and only through the experienced contrast that his own culture becomes 'visible.' In the act of inventing another culture, the anthropologist invents his own, and in fact he reinvents the notion of culture itself.
>
> Roy Wagner[1]

Tradition is a contentious notion. What does it really mean? Where is the much-vaunted tradition: in the past, in the present, in the future? Its corpses are silent and demand the intervention of patient pathologists who will retrospectively reveal the time and the etiology of their deaths. The morgue is a text but, ultimately, it defies strict generalisations as the singularity of each corpse cannot be subsumed by one unifying narrative. It could be said that V. Y. Mudimbe, Achille Mbembe, and Patrice Nganang are part of a Central African tradition of writing. Interestingly, each author has devoted a significant part of their writing career to the cultural, philosophical, and political legacies of colonial and African traditions on the postcolonial here and now. A unifying narrative can indeed be traced between these three individuals on whom I shall focus in this chapter. They operate at the crossroads of several disciplines and genres: Mbembe (born 1957 in Cameroon) sits between history, political sciences, and philosophy and Nganang (born 1970 in Cameroon) is a novelist, a poet, and a cultural historian. The two Cameroonians are also from the African diaspora[2] and belong to a growing body of African intellectuals, trained in Africa and in Europe and subsequently absorbed by the American academia, which, according to Mbembe in *Sortir de la grande nuit*, an essay which will be examined here, has a 'capacité presque illimitée [...] de recycler les élites mondiales [a quasi unlimited ability to recycle world elites].[3]

Sortir de la grande nuit: Essai sur l'Afrique décolonisée by Achille Mbembe and *Manifeste d'une nouvelle littérature africaine: Pour une écriture préemptive*[4] by Patrice Nganang will be explored in this analysis to define the ways in which these two thinkers relate to V. Y. Mudimbe, the eldest member of this invented trinity. The terms 'sortir', 'décolonisée', 'nouvelle', and 'préemptive' are indicative of a shared focus on temporal ideas of shifts and transitions. The two authors attempt indeed to articulate the political (Mbembe) and the literary (Nganang) modalities of a passage to an epistemologically rejuvenated Africa which will be, according to Mbembe, 'afropolitan', 'post-racial', and, for Nganang, 'post-genocidal' and the scene of a post-Kantian subject. Beyond the differences of corpus and approaches, these two essays, ultimately, examine the concept of decolonisation of sub-Saharan Africa; they dialogue therefore, sometimes explicitly, with Mudimbe, the only representative of the trinity who is in a position to provide first-hand testimonies on the passage from the colony to the 'postcolony'.[5]

The aim of the analysis will be to assess not so much the legacy of Mudimbe's thought as the ways in which it resonates with the works of these two younger thinkers. Like Mudimbe, Mbembe and Nganang have adopted a 'writerly' style and have also practised a return to the speaking 'I' behind the scientific investigation; or, to put it differently, they have scrutinised Africa from the point of view of their own traumatic and violent experiences. In *Sortir de la grande nuit*, Mbembe recalls in a poignant chapter – 'À partir du crâne d'un mort. Trajectoire d'une vie' [From a dead man's skull. Trajectory of a life][6] – the circumstances which motivated his own exile from Cameroon.[7] Mbembe shows that the new power in place after 1960 continued to persecute members of the 'Union des populations du Cameroun' (UPC), the independence party which had been outlawed under French rule and which, from 1955 onwards, took up arms to put an end to colonialism. After defeating the UPC guerrilla fighters and assassinating its leader Ruben Um Nyobé in 1958, France gradually handed over its sovereignty to carefully selected members of the indigenous political elite.[8] Mbembe returns here to events already explored in his other books[9] but gives an altogether much more personal dimension to the repression, first by France and then by Ahmadou Ahidjo's regime, of members of the UPC. Pierre Yém Mback, one of Ruben's most immediate collaborators, was also assassinated and, in the name of the new 'fable officielle',[10] deliberately eradicated from the national memory by the newly instated postcolonial administration. Mbembe claims that this event is fundamental to understanding his own trajectory as an academic as Pierre Yém Mback, whose memory he attempts to rehabilitate in this essay, was also his aunt's husband.

Nganang, in his essay, refers to the same historical context of political and ethnic oppression in order to shed light on the links between his own life, his academic projects, and the very personal significance of the pre-emptive role that he would like to ascribe to African literature.[11] Nganang is a Bamileke and originally comes from western Cameroon, an area which from 1956 to 1970 experienced a very bloody civil war. He argues that these events amounted to a genocide jointly perpetrated by France and the dictatorial regime of Ahidjo. He recalls that the memory of this hitherto still unpunished crime was in the Cameroon of his youth a taboo subject compounded and fuelled by the fear of publicly admitting one's Bamileke ethnicity.[12] He shows that he was only able to grasp the full significance of the silence in which he grew up much later in life and abroad. First at the Bibliothèque Nationale de France and in *Main basse sur le Cameroun* by Mongo Béti;[13] but also, and above all, in Germany, the country where he studied for eight years and started his career as an author. Germany enabled him to experience a culture which 'aujourd'hui encore lutte avec les affres que peuvent causer un tel moment de chute dans la barbarie, dans l'histoire et la conscience d'un peuple' [has until today been struggling with the horrors that such a descent into barbarism may generate in the history and consciousness of a people].[14]

This self-reflexive return to a personal past to account for the foundational moments and natures of scholarly projects is therefore common to the three authors on whom this analysis focuses. For Mudimbe, the autobiography is a literary act whereby the demarcation line between life and writing becomes undistinguishable; it is also a deliberate tactic adopted by the author to undermine the sacrosanct objectivity that is supposed to govern the writing of academic essays in the human sciences. Mudimbe, as mentioned in this book, has written works that fall into the autobiographical genre, but he has, more interestingly, expressed a high degree of subjectivity in his more rigorous and academic texts. The juxtaposition of scholarship and subjectivity is unsettling from a generic perspective but it has also a political and dissident meaning: by creating this type of literary collages – Wim van Binsbergen talks of the 'kaleidoscopic effect of the intertwined use of various genres' and of 'literary collage, whose constituent elements [...] look like fragments of state-of-the-art scholarship'[15] – he also asserts his willingness to jettison an order, that of the traditional essay, its didactic norms and pretension for objectivity, lucidity, and comprehensiveness. In his analysis of the *Bible noire* (P&F, 86–123), however, this autobiographical posture responds to a need to assert, in the name of science, his 'coeval' authority. Even though Mbembe and Nganang have not as systematically as Mudimbe explored the potential of autobiography as a tool to challenge the epistemological basis of the postcolony, it is important to note that they both in their own singular ways also refuse to maintain the artificial distances between what they represent as subjects and what they pursue as scholars.

African Decolonisation Now

I would like now to turn my attention to *Sortir de la grande nuit* and *Manifeste d'une nouvelle littérature africaine* as these two texts offer a number of implicit and explicit perspectives on Mudimbe's legacy and showcase, forty years after the intellectual schism with Senghorian negritude on the part of intellectuals such as Adotevi, Towa, *and* Mudimbe, that decolonisation has generated yet another quarrel between the Ancients and the Moderns (see Mudimbe's encounter with Damas, Chapter 4). In a first stage, Mbembe's project to consider sub-Saharan Africa as the terrain of a rejuvenated humanity will be compared to Fanon's, and indeed Mudimbe's, attempts to flesh out the contours of a postcolonial world. I shall then examine how and why Mbembe and Nganang dialogue with one another, especially as Nganang's reflection, in his manifesto, relies heavily upon two other essays by Mbembe

('Necropolitics'[16] and 'African Modes of Self-Writing'[17]) which will also be considered here. Finally, the analysis will focus on Mudimbe's work – *Le Bel immonde* and *Entre les eaux*, and the author's art criticism in *The Idea of Africa* – in order to examine the way in which Mudimbe responds retroactively, as it were, to the (in my view) partly unfounded attack levelled to him by Nganang and, to a lesser extent, Mbembe.

'Essai sur l'Afrique décolonisée', the subtitle of Mbembe's text is ambiguous, and most likely deliberately so, since the author argues that the African decolonisation was a non event[18] which paved the way to the introduction of a neo-colonialist order orchestrated, in the case of francophone sub-Saharan Africa, by France itself. In this respect, Mbembe provides a catalogue of objective factors – ethnic violence, economic predation, political corruption, arbitrariness – and psychological symptoms – the Jean-François Bayart-inspired 'politics of the belly' and the African dictator's morbid sexuality and fascination with 'lower' bodily functions – to substantiate this main afro-pessimistic claim. This idea of a failed decolonisation is not new and, in fact, it predominantly informed Mudimbe's scholarly work and novels such as *Entre les eaux* and *Le Bel Immonde* from the 1970s to the publication of *The Invention of Africa*. There is therefore on the part of Mbembe an attempt to demonstrate that the past militancy of canonical thinkers and writers such as Fabien Éboussi-Boulaga, Mongo Béti, Yambo Ouologuem, Cheikh Hamidou Kane, Senghor, and, above all, Fanon, still constitutes a valid corpus to elucidate the present and probe decolonisation, a process that he regards as incomplete. This essay can also be read as a tribute to postcolonial theory and a response to the dismissive reception given to this large interdisciplinary body of texts by prominent French Africanists such as Jean-Loup Amselle[19] and Jean-François Bayart.[20] Mbembe's point of view is in many respects Saidian,[21] and therefore Foucauldian, as he explores, notably through the Haitian and Liberian cases, the extent to which these countries have remained until today subjugated by discursive and epistemic conditions established before the abolition of slavery. Mbembe, like the early Mudimbe, advocates the urgency of decolonising knowledge. He remarks that in order to 'ouvrir le futur à tous' [open up the future to everyone] it is necessary radically to critique the conditions that have perpetuated the reproduction of 'rapports de sujétion tissés sous l'Empire entre les indigènes et les colons et [...] entre l'Occident et le reste du monde' [submissive relationships developed during the imperial era between indigenous populations and colonisers and [...] between the West and the rest of the world].[22] He is of the view that the construction of the '*démocratie à venir*' [democracy yet to be] will be underpinned by a deconstruction of the 'savoirs impériaux qui, naguère, ont rendu possible la domination des sociétés non européennes' [imperial knowledge which, in the past, have made possible the domination of non European societies].[23] Mbembe contends that true liberation, that is, the passage from a 'conscience abîmée à une conscience autonome' [damaged consciousness to an autonomous consciousness][24] implies a double movement. In a manner echoing Sartre's etiology of racism, and the underlying Hegelian dialectics thereof (Chapter 3), Mbembe argues that the former slaves and colonial subjects needed to put an end to the conditions that had characterised their existence under the rule of the masters.[25] He remarks, however, that the emergence of an autonomous consciousness, or '*état de maîtrise*' [state of mastery], relies on a second abolition and implies self-abolition so as to free the self from its 'part servile constitutive' [constitutive servile part] and, in this way, generate 'l'accomplissement de soi en tant que figure singulière de l'universelle' [the achievement of the self as a singular figure of the universal].[26]

This examination of colonial servitude and focus on the transformative steps that could and, Mbembe forcefully argues, *should* form the basis for the construction of an autonomous selfhood is, as we shall see in this chapter, reminiscent of the utopian climate that prevailed in the 1950s and 1960s, in texts by Sartre and Fanon, notably, and in some of Mudimbe's early works such as *L'Autre Face*. This last comment conjures up an alternative trinity, Sartre–Fanon–Mudimbe, which deepens the complexity of the Mudimbe–Mbembe–Nganang trinity. What is surprising, perhaps outmoded, or simply the sign that the former anti-colonial militancy can still contribute to global equality and the abolition of colonial legacies and their associated psychological dependencies and complexes, is this constant focus on a symbolic rebirth of 'man', both 'singular' and 'universal'. There is here a Sartrean Leitmotiv which has been recurrently exploited by Fanon and then Mudimbe. This idea, expounded by Sartre in his *Plaidoyer pour les intellectuels*,[27] considers 'man' as a 'comme à faire' [yet to be made], that is to say as a future possibility as 'l'homme est l'avenir de l'homme' [man is the future of man] (*AF*, 136). This word, 'man', despite its gendered and masculinist connotations, needs, however, to be understood in the sense of 'human' as Mudimbe has often dismissed (see *Shaba Deux*) the misogynistic basis of his own upbringing in the Belgian Congo (*CG*, 107–21),[28] a view that also underpins his analysis of the underlying 'schizogenesis' of mythical transformations (Chapter 1), given that these transformations, and the passage to a higher form of polity, rely on the crucial interventions of female and junior 'attributes'. This new human is 'singular' because 'situated' and belongs to the universal because her or his rebirth will coincide with the emergence of a race-less humanity. Behind Mbembe's ideas, one can indeed detect the influence of the Marxism-inflected historical dialectic as it had been poeticised by Sartre in 'Orphée noir'.

Mbembe's text embraces therefore a promethean tone whose manifest traces are to be found in our second invented trinity (Sartre–Fanon–Mudimbe). *Sortir de la grande nuit* is in many respects a political manifesto. Its title is a direct tribute to Fanon's passionate revolutionary call in the conclusion of *Les Damnés de la terre*: 'La grande nuit dans laquelle nous fûmes plongés, il nous faut la secouer et en sortir'.[29] The English translation very deftly renders the sense of tragedy that the (Fanon hopes) successful orphic ascent will imply: '*We must shake off the heavy darkness in which we were plunged, and leave it behind*'.[30]

Just fifty years after decolonisation Mbembe advocates for Africa an analogous rebirth. It would be wrong, however, to consider this essay as being merely repetitious of Fanon's words and views. Mbembe's main exigency, that is, the establishment of a 'démocratie véritablement post-raciale' [truly post-racial democracy][31] retains the universal dimension promoted by Fanon but is, however, sustained by a less dualistic conception of geopolitical configurations. Mbembe's Africa is recast in a global and mostly transatlantic – the essay is dedicated to Paul Gilroy – network of exchanges. His 'Afrique décolonisée' lies at the crossroads between America, the Caribbean, Cameroon, and South Africa. The book provides also a bleak assessment of contemporary France which has not been able to shake off the discursive weight of its 'long hiver impérial' [long imperial winter].[32] The central idea here is that France has not decolonised itself. The issue of racial differences, which was the main justifying premise of French colonialism, has not been, according to Mbembe, systematically confronted by the French nation and has remained what he calls an 'impensé' [an intellectual blind spot].[33] This largely depressing portrayal of France as culturally narcissistic,[34] provincialised,[35] unable to engage self-critically with colonial repentance, and obsessed by the 'désir de frontières' [desire for frontiers][36] is not, however, just an end in itself;[37] it serves also as a pretext to examine contemporary Africa. He argues that Africa has internalised the exclusive French model. In this respect, he identifies the mimetic relationship between France's false universalism, colonial ideology, and the 'réflexe indigéniste'[38] adopted by African nationalisms after the independences, a point which reiterates the main thrust of Mudimbe's *Invention*, and, further upstream, Fanon's thoughts on the link between revolution and indigenous cultures.[39]

Mbembe, however, contends that there is more to contemporary Africa than this internalisation of imported models. The essay is a manifesto of sorts which quite programmatically seeks to map out in the present *singular* characteristics which could contribute to the underlying *universal* goal that it is pursuing. He identifies across the continent a series of signs that could constitute the building blocks of 'new cartographies', opposed in one eponymous section to the 'anciennes cartographies',[40] as he indeed announces that it is time now to 'passer à autre chose' [to move to something else].[41] These signs of the present from which, Mbembe hopes, a not too distant future will emerge, are, paradoxically, also to be found in Africa's past.

This reading strategy, in which the past is teased out to comprehend the present but, more importantly, to challenge the inevitability of present modalities, mirrors Mudimbe's recurrent attempts to examine Roman Africa in order to open up, as in 'Ut Recte Valeant',[42] 'the possibility of reconstituting regressively a configuration that can reflect back on our debates on canon and diversity issues of our contemporary multicultural contexts'.[43] He explores here the linguistic competition (between Punic, Latin, and Greek) prevailing at the time of the *Pax Romana* in North Africa and focuses on the measures implemented by the Roman administration to achieve the Romanisation and Latinisation of a vast territory stretching from Mauritania to Libya. Interestingly, however, Mudimbe argues that this process was relatively harmonious as it did not set out to suppress linguistic diversity and even created an intercultural space that connected Africa to Eur-Asia. Although Roman colonisation of North Africa contributed to the 'transmutation of a place into a space' (Michel de Certeau is, here too, the main intellectual reference), Mudimbe adds that the Roman administration and their autochtonous representatives were eager to 'preserve the *Imperium* and its ecumenicity'.[44] For Mudimbe, the Latinisation, Hellenisation, and indeed Christianisation of North Africa constitute thus a successful example of acculturation and a valid counter-model which stands in stark contrast to the French and Belgian colonial projects and their endeavours to obliterate and mummify the African *chose du texte*.

In his own analysis and examination of past models, Mbembe argues that the remapping of the continent has been aided by the gradual atomisation of the African nation-state and capitalism, two interconnected models introduced as a result of the demise of European empires. States are no longer able to impose regulatory frameworks to control the development of transnational commercial networks initiated by rich and powerful but (in theory) still non-autonomous territorial enclaves.[45] Ironically, this new post-national African modernity marks also the return of a pre-colonial model of exchange and communication and manifests therefore the 'futurity' of the past as this concept was developed by Reinhart Koselleck.[46] Like Mudimbe, Mbembe does not romanticise this former geography (the Latinisation of North Africa mentioned above) but argues, however, that African pre-colonial networks were not dependent on the idea of strict frontiers and sovereignties and had the merit of generating multi-ethnic relations.[47] Mbembe's programme is not fully developed and has in many ways a utopian and messianic dimension as he collects here and there signs indicating that the old logics that had fed and legitimised colonialism and the postcolony are receding. To qualify this new post-racial modernity, he uses the expression 'afropolitaine'. He argues that the prime site of this emerging afropolitanism is the African city and shows that South Africa constitutes the most successful example of this new trend, that is, its 'laboratoire le plus manifeste' [most evident testing ground].[48] The afropolitan city is a site of political and cultural creativity in which conventional racial markers of Africanity are challenged in favour of a more creolised political and societal project.[49] On this last point, it is significant that throughout this essay Mbembe refers to the concept of creolisation as it was examined by Édouard Glissant in the Caribbean context. Ultimately, *Sortir de la grande nuit* is driven by an idealist agenda (and also a high degree of 'wishful thinking') which championed the emergence of a 'universalisme latéral'. This type of universalism is predicated on the idea that if blacks and whites are to walk together again on the 'chemins de l'humanité' [paths of humanity], they will need to surmount – the word 'dépassement' is used here to imply this dialectical movement – 'l'opposition radicale entre le propre et l'étranger' [the radical opposition between the self and the foreigner].[50] This 'dépassement' is what the author seeks.

I have highlighted here the close relationship between Mbembe and Mudimbe and their common adherence to a type of political and epistemological militancy partly inflected – but certainly not systematically – by dialectical materialism. *The Invention of Africa*, although primarily a vast epistemological survey, is also a 'manifesto of sorts'.[51] In his conclusion, Mudimbe hopes that present signs of emancipation will provide the basis of a 'starting point', an expression which is evocative of Fanon's ambition to 'recommence' history:

> I believe that the geography of African gnosis also points out the passion of a subject–object who refuses to vanish. He or she has gone from the situation in which he or she was perceived as a simple functional object to the freedom of thinking of himself or herself as the starting point of an absolute discourse. (*IoA*, 200)

Mudimbe's survey – his 'geography of African gnosis' – measures the present against the past, and, in so doing, implicitly anticipates the shape of the future. This strategy informs Mbembe's effort to 'identifier la puissance du futur inscrite dans le présent' [identify in the present the power of the future].[52] This tactic, and its underlying teleological understanding of historical processes, is, as we shall see now, partly rejected by Patrice Nganang.

The focus on temporality is paramount in Nganang's *Manifeste*. The book proposes a complex reflection on the fleeting meanings of such concepts as past, present, and future and their (in)ability to inform African literatures and the power thereof to comment on African modernity. Nganang's text is avowedly a manifesto: it is passionate, irreverent, and impatient, as it demands, rather than hopes for, the rapid transformation of the theoretical tools that have hitherto helped scholars to read African literatures.[53] Nganang militates for the emergence of a new scholarship and, in doing so, questions performatively, that is, via a petulant, disrespectful, and sometimes incantatory style, the generic divides between scholarship and political activism. Like Mudimbe and Mbembe, he is what he writes, and *how* he writes is equally important as *what* he writes. Nganang's project is ambitious. He proposes in a loosely programmatic fashion to excavate out of a corpus paradoxically situated in the past – Soyinka, Tutuola, and Césaire are some of his authors of predilection – the contours of his new and 'pre-emptive' African writing. The enterprise amounts therefore partly to a resurrection or to an attempt to disrupt traditional concatenations – that between the African novel and its critical apparatus – genealogies, and historic-critical segmentations. The theoretical instruments used by Nganang in this manifesto are unusual. The book is indeed underpinned by a number of references to the works of canonical German philosophers such as Hegel, Nietzsche, Heidegger, Adorno, Benjamin, and Carl Schmitt, the historian of dictatorship.[54] This constant recourse to German philosophy is the effect of Nganang's autobiographical trajectory in Germany where he completed a doctoral thesis on the works of Soyinka and Brecht;[55] it also consolidates the weight and significance of the adjective 'nouvelle' in the title as Nganang's literary call to arms is also intended as an effort to break away from the habit of interpreting African novelists with francophone theorists.

This book can be read as a rejection of canonical postcolonial models and as an endeavour to constitute a 'new grammar' and take on board the new 'philosophème' of our time,[56] defined largely by the Rwandan genocide of 1994, a catastrophe which generated a 'nouvelle épistémologie'.[57] This philosopheme, a 'principe destructive-créatif',[58] Nganang calls it *tragedy*. As Adorno, who famously asked whether it was not 'barbaric' to write poetry after Auschwitz[59] – Adorno was in fact reflecting on the status of art and the relevance of modernist paradigms after the holocaust[60] – Nganang tries to ascribe a new place to novelists in a post-genocide Africa: his essay is said to be predicated upon a 'volonté de réinscription de la littérature africaine contemporaine dans le champ de l'histoire des idées' [willingness to re-inscribe contemporary African literature in the field of the history of ideas].[61] The rejection at work in this essay is explicitly directed towards the Sartre–Fanon–Mudimbe trinity. Nganang deplores that African literature and its critique have disproportionately been living 'à l'ombre de Sartre' [in Sartre's shadow].[62] African writers and thinkers, he remarks, have – this idea, of course, has been abundantly explored by the early Mudimbe – been the recipient of what he names, a 'bail transcendantal' [transcendental loan], that is, a borrowed set of conditions of possibility that have enabled them by proxy, as it were, to know the world, to write, and philosophise: 'la véritable défaite de l'Afrique sera toujours son incapacité à se penser sans l'Occident [the real failure of Africa will always be its inability to think about itself without the West].[63] What is at stake in Nganang's criticism of Sartre is the latter's examination of the necessary relation between literature and political commitment in his literary manifesto *Qu'est-ce que la littérature?*[64] Nganang argues that the role ascribed by Sartre to literature is too mimetic with regards to the real and that his influence has been such in the field of African literature that it has undermined the autonomy of African writers and prevented them from being 'original' as their relation to the real has resulted in being 'prédéfinie' by this Sartrean reading grid.[65] His interpretation of Sartre's essay is heavily indebted to Adorno's *Notes to Literature*.[66] In this collection of essays, and particularly in 'Commitment',[67] Adorno had indeed examined Sartre's thesis on literature. Adorno mostly objects to the idea that, as Sartre puts it in *What is Literature*, 'the writer deals with meanings',[68] that is, puts meanings into words which can be translated into action and which reflect meanings outside the world of literature. Adorno criticises the mechanical dimension of such a transaction; Sartre's position deprives the work of art of its indeterminacy, autonomy and, it is also argued, of its genuine ability to challenge a prescribed order. By art's autonomy, Adorno does not mean that art should be removed from society – he was never a proponent of *l'art pour l'art* – but that it is simply not there to fulfil an objective of societal utility: art is 'social primarily because it stands opposed to society. […] By congealing into an entity unto itself – rather than obeying existing social norms and thus proving itself to be "socially useful" – art criticises society just by being there'.[69] For Adorno, Sartre's 'engagement', is suspiciously philistine and compliant with the capitalist order that it paradoxically endeavours to annihilate:

> Cultural conservatives who demand that a work of art should say something, join forces with their political opponents against atelic, hermetic works of art. Eulogists of 'relevance' are more likely to find Sartre's *Huis Clos* profound, than to listen patiently to a text whose language jolts signification and by its very distance from 'meaning' revolts in advance against positivist subordination of meaning. […] Sartre's plays are vehicles for the author's ideas, which have been left behind in the race of aesthetic forms. They operate with traditional intrigues, exalted by an unshaken faith in meanings which can be transferred from art to reality. […] The combination of solid plot, and equally solid, extractable idea won Sartre great success and made him, without doubt against his honest will, acceptable to the culture industry.[70]

Nganang embraces Adorno's perspective, and 'negative dialectic'. Sartre's conception of art and literature is, according to him, 'surannée' [obsolete][71] and 'messianique'.[72] He regrets that Sartre's commitment should be so strictly linked to 'history': 'l'engagement dans l'histoire est le principe d'un art demeuré enfantin, d'un art peureux du vide par-delà l'histoire [commitment in history is the principle of a type of art which has remained childish and fearful of the emptiness beyond history].[73] In this reflection on Sartre's enduring legacy on African literature, Nganang is particularly critical of 'Orphée noir'. He wrongly argues that Sartre championed the idea of difference and authenticity[74] when the French philosopher never ascribed to negritude any coefficient of permanency since it was meant to be a stage to be dialectically surmounted. Throughout the book, Nganang takes to task Sartre's dialectic, borrowed by generations of writers and, in his eyes, unwittingly complicit in the dictatorial regimes that it nonetheless seeks to question. Like Adorno, Nganang is of the view that 'the greatness of works of art [...] consists in the fact that they give voice to what ideology hides'.[75]

Against the Sartrean conception of commitment, Nganang claims that literature should have a 'conscience prévisionnaire'[76] and become therefore an instrument to detect in the present signs of future catastrophes, and in this way, pre-empt them. This new African literature will be able to 'voir le commencement de cela qui ailleurs a creusé le puits sans fond du crime' [see the beginning of that which, elsewhere, dug the bottomless well of crime].[77] This pre-visionary perception is rooted in African reality and emerges from the 'creux morbide du cimetière de masse' [from the morbid hole of the mass graveyard] left behind by the Rwandan genocide and years of dictatorship.[78] In this respect, and in a move which reasserts the autonomy of art, he remarks aphoristically that 'l'artiste ne peint pas un arbre mais un tableau' [the artist does not paint a tree but a painting].[79] This new literature is to be found in the abyss of African negativity, that is, in a post-Kantian realm which is no longer governed by reason but ruled by life and death, the categories that Nganang borrows from Membe's 'Necropolitics',[80] an essay which 'assumes that the ultimate expression of sovereignty resides, to a large degree, in the power and the capacity to dictate who may live and who must die'.[81]

Mbembe conducts in this article a reflection on the ways in which sovereignty has been analysed by political science. He argues, a position that problematises his relation to Sartre, that too much emphasis has been placed on reason and the autonomy of the subject.[82] He questions this 'romance of sovereignty', which 'rests on the belief that the subject is the master and the controlling author of his or her own meaning'.[83] Against this schema, which, according to him, has dominated the 'philosophical discourse of modernity', he proposes to privilege 'other foundational categories that are less abstract and more tactile, such as life and death'.[84] Mbembe's development is premised on Hegel's idea in the *Phenomenology of Spirit* that becoming a subject is governed by a 'bipartite concept of negativity'.[85] First, humans negate the animal in themselves in order to gain control over nature, transform it, and create their world. In the process of this transformation, they are, in a second phase, confronted with their own death, that is, with their own negativity. Mbembe contends that 'the human being truly *becomes a subject* [...] in the struggle and the work through which he or she confronts death' and that it is 'through this confrontation with death that he or she is cast into the incessant movement of history'.[86]

Nganang argues throughout his essay that the new African literature should expose the ways in which death informs the tragedy at the heart of African everyday life. He contends that by taking this 'chemin négatif' [negative route][87] writers will retain their artistic autonomy, disclose reality, the reality of African suffering, and, beyond this particular focus, reveal human suffering in its universality. In this respect, Soyinka, Tutuola, and Césaire are described as pre-visionary and 'post-genocide'[88] writers. Césaire, for instance, was able to de-territorialise suffering.[89] His *Cahier d'un retour au pays natal*, is 'post-national' because it transcends spatial and temporal boundaries and is able to conjure up 'l'universel historique du profond désastre duquel le sujet africain se définit aujourd'hui' [the historical universal of the profound disaster against which African subjects define themselves today].[90]

With regard to the pre-visionary dissidence of these writers, Nganang adopts a number of intriguing temporal perspectives, as the most accomplished proponents of this African literature of the future are, paradoxically, in the past. He contends that their writings question conventional timelines; in their works, Nganang envisages the past from the perspective of its ability, as in Koselleck's 'contemporaneity of the non-contemporaneous', to generate conceptual blueprints for possible futurities. 'Prévisionnaire' is a neologism coined by Nganang; the new phrase exacerbates the anticipatory dimension that the word 'visionnaire' (visionary) already contains and conveys, and is therefore somewhat pleonastic. Pre-visionary writing is 'plus originaire que l'origine' [more original than the origin itself][91] and enables its readers to see the 'futur de la violence'.[92]

For all his effort to promote a 'negative route', Nganang does not quite escape the messianic and promethean path that he vehemently rejects in this manifesto. This is particularly true of the last chapter, or 'épilogue', which fails, in my view, convincingly to elucidate the meaning of the phrase 'pre-visionary'. Is it, ultimately, very different from 'visionary' since he insists that pre-visionary writers should exercise their vigilance in the present to prevent future horrors or 'suspendre l'avènement de la barbarie' [suspend the emergence of barbarism]?[93] There is also the naive and utopian move which consists in arguing that Soyinka, Césaire, and Tutuola will become the 'trinité originaire' [original trinity][94] of this new African literature. One might ask: why them, and not others? Is it merely to replace the Senghor–Césaire–Damas privileged by the historiography of negritude? Finally, Nganang's thesis does not quite manage to remain true to Adorno's negative dialectics. There is indeed in this book a marked tendency to *identify* the construction of this new African literature with subsuming concepts such as the 'Idea', 'dissidence', 'tragedy', which have the effect of ascribing, paradoxically, predefined and homogenised meanings to pre-emptive writing.

Pre-visionary consciousness needs therefore to be understood within the specific genre, the manifesto, in which it is employed. Nganang uses it also polemically to mark the divide between his 'nouvelle littérature africaine' and the (in his eyes) outmoded anti-colonial and postcolonial critique as expressed in the works of Sartre, Fanon (who is 'épistemologiquement aveugle' [epistemologically blind][95]), and V. Y. Mudimbe. With regards to Mudimbe, Nganang contends that his philosophical 'patience'[96] did not prevent the Rwandan tragedy: 'Ce n'est pas dans l'infini labyrinthe de la bibliothèque africaine que le mal est intervenu une nuit – mais dans le commun d'une rue africaine' [It is not in the limitless labyrinth of the African library that, one night, evil took place but on an ordinary African street].[97] Although Nganang highlights the scientific merits of *The Invention of Africa*, he argues that its most conclusive findings, that is, Africa is the West's discursive object, is no longer useful in a post-genocide era. Nganang also remarks, as I noted earlier in the comparison between *Sortir de la grande nuit* and *The Invention of Africa*, that Mudimbe's essay concludes on an optimistic note as he foresees in the midst of the 'geography of African gnosis' (*IoA*, 200), encouraging signs of a new discursive dawn. This 'happy ending' does not ring true with Nganang's ambition to think negatively for 'c'est dans la négation que dorénavant se trouve l'espoir' [hope resides henceforth in the negation].[98]

It would be wrong, however, to assume that Mudimbe – and there lies one of the limitations of Nganang's polemics that will be further explored here – has always been the proponent of a 'positive' dialectics. He is in many ways also a 'negator'. Nganang's analytical weakness resides in his hasty and definitely *impatient* treatment of Mudimbe's thought. Mudimbe is only a representative, albeit prominent, of African philosophy but he can hardly be regarded as its spokesperson as he has always defended the view that there are philosophers in Africa rather than a clearly identifiable 'Black African philosophy' (*Idea*, 199), reason why he prefers to use the term 'Gnosis' (Chapter 4). Nganang establishes nonetheless an irrelevant analogy between African philosophy's lack of pre-visionary capability and Mudimbe, described as the most patient of all African philosophers, who 'était endormi quand les cadavres fleurissaient dans sa cour' [was asleep when corpses were piling up in his backyard].[99]

This reductive view of the relationship between African philosophy and Mudimbe mainly results from Nganang's reading of 'African Modes of Self-Writing', another essay by Achille Mbembe, an inter-text which further complexifies the dialogue between Mudimbe and Mbembe. Nganang argues that Mbembe's exploration of African thought is altogether more dynamic and polemical than that of Mudimbe although he adds that Mbembe has remained loyal to the 'profondeur textuelle et philologique des analyses de Mudimbe' [textual and philological depth of Mudimbe's analyses].[100] Two points need to be made regarding this last statement. First, there is nothing philological about Mbembe's perspective as he identifies here the main intellectual currents and ideological trends that have inflected and above all impeded the development of African thought and philosophy. Secondly, by avoiding to qualify more accurately Mbembe's 'textual depth', he silences, in the name of the adversarial rhetoric underpinning his line of argument, the methodological strategy that Mbembe shares with Mudimbe. Like 'The Patience of Philosophy', Mbembe's essay reads indeed as a Foucault-inspired epistemological survey and critique in which, as stated in the abstract of the first version (in French) of the text, '[l]a réflexion épistémologique ouvre [...] sur le débat politique' [the epistemological reflection generates the political debate].[101] In this respect, Mbembe's appraisal of the Enlightenment with regards to the colonisation of sub-Saharan Africa is reminiscent of the way in which Mudimbe examines the role of anthropology in Africa since the French Revolution (see Chapter 4). Notions of universality, difference, assimilation are teased out by Mbembe to inventory the strategies adopted by the 'school of Enlightenment thought' – 'as exemplified by positions taken by Kant and Hegel'[102] – to exclude Black Africans from a white ontology, dominate and domesticate them, and, ultimately, convert them, 'by way of the civilizing mill of Christianity and the colonial state',[103] into enlightened citizens.

The notion of 'custom' is ascribed a central significance in this process of conversion. The examination of its ambiguity echoes indeed Mudimbe's 'textual depth' and Foucault's attempts to excavate and order the ideological and scientific foundations of discourses. Mbembe argues that the word 'custom' gained currency at the end of the nineteenth century, a time characterised by a more systematic and state-driven colonisation of sub-Saharan Africa. He suggests that this focus on 'custom' did not contradict the 'thesis of nonsimilarity' – a Foucauldian concept used by Mudimbe, notably in his examination of Renaissance artists (see Chapter 4) – but introduced, however, a 'slight slippage within the old economy of alterity'.[104] Custom is a sign of rupture but its significance needs to be nuanced and relativised since its revelation does not completely disrupt the discursive foundations of the colonial project. This is essentially what Mudimbe was positing about negritude and religious figures such as Tempels, Bernard Mels, and Alexis Kagame (see Chapter 1). *Bantu Philosophy*, for instance, was paradoxical as it 'could be understood simultaneously as an indication of religious insight, the expression of a cultural doubt about the supposed backwardness of Africans, and a political manifesto for a new policy for promoting 'civilisation' and Christianity' (*IoA*, 50).

Mbembe argues that African thought is the product of this discursive ambivalence; he also contends that in their many attempts to formulate the contours of political, economic, and cultural autonomy, African thinkers have not been able to free themselves from the very instruments that had facilitated and justified African colonisation, that is, the dualistic logic implied in the opposition between 'custom' and 'civilisation' (and its various cognates: Christianity, the State, and civil society). He also shows that African criticism has not been able to define its struggle but through 'a construction of the self understood in terms of both victimhood and mutilation'.[105] The main thrust of Mbembe's critique of African thought rests on the argument that the 'civilisation' versus 'custom' binary opposition has generated two major African discourses:

> The first of these is what might be termed *Afro-radicalism*, with its baggage of instrumentalism and political opportunism. The second is the burden of the metaphysics of difference (*nativism*). The first current of thought – which liked to present itself as 'democratic', 'radical', and 'progressive' – used Marxist and nationalist categories to develop an imaginaire of culture and politics in which a manipulation of the rhetoric of autonomy, resistance, and emancipation serves as the sole criterion for determining the legitimacy of an authentic African discourse. The second current of thought developed out of an emphasis on the 'native condition'. It promoted the idea of a unique African identity founded on membership of the black race.[106]

Mbembe ascribes to these two currents the failure of African philosophy to deal with its past and present, construct a future and yield any systematic framework to account for 'human misfortune and wrongdoing'.[107] He notes that the proponents of *Afro-radicalism* have always shied away from facing African co-responsibility for slavery and colonialism as the former was also caused by 'Africans' failure to control their own predatory greed'[108] and, the latter, was, 'in many ways', a 'co-invention',[109] or, as he said elsewhere, the product of the 'imbécillité conjuguée des Blancs et de Nègres' [combined imbecility of whites and negroes].[110] About the nativists, he remarks that their exclusive model runs counter to 'Afropolitanism' and its underlying ambition to contribute to the edification of a 'post-racial' African *polis*.

Nganang's argument is built upon analogous premises as he underscores the utter ineffectiveness of these two currents in the context of the Rwandan genocide: Afro-radicalists used the victimisation argument to prove their innocence, whereas nativists were confronted with their own shame since the identity argument had been employed by the perpetrators to legitimise ethnic massacres.[111] At this stage, it is important to point out that Mudimbe's *patient* exegesis of Africanist epistemology is linked by Nganang to the efforts of Afro-radicalists to delve into the 'dichotomies coloniales belges'[112] in order to explain the present and escape responsibility which for Nganang and Mbembe is the sign of their ongoing dependency. Nganang contends therefore that Mbembe's essay succeeded where that of Mudimbe – the reference is the *The Invention of Africa* – 's'est arrêté' [stalled].[113] He contends that, unlike Mudimbe, Mbembe is truly dissident because, via his interrogation of the present's tragedy and 'philosophème', he embraces Adorno's negative thought.[114] Although there is no explicit reference to Adorno in Mbembe's essay, Nganang's remark is valid since Mbembe refers to Jewish criticism – used here as a counter-example to African thought – and thinkers such as Hannah Arendt,[115] Dominick LaCapra,[116] and Anne Goldberg[117] and their (in his view more successful) attempts to problematise human suffering in a post-Holocaust context.

Victims and Culprits as Survivors

The rest of this chapter will probe further the opposition that Nganang establishes between Mbembe and Mudimbe with regards to 'negative thinking' and then show the way in which Mudimbe offers a sort of retroactive response in *Le Bel immonde*, *Entre les eaux*, and 'Reprendre'. There is a striking resemblance between the type of epistemological survey conducted by Mbembe in 'African Modes of Self-Writing', especially in relation to the dismissal of the two above-mentioned currents, and Mudimbe's work. In his main essays, and from the onset of his writing career,[118] Mudimbe has invariably taken to task, in the wake of Fanon's critique of negritude in *The Wretched of the Earth*, the advocates of fixed identities and those, such as Nkrumah and Nyerere, who called upon Marxism – a fundamentally internationalist doctrine – to declare the uniqueness of African nations. Given this clear overlap, it is surprising that Mbembe, and of course Nganang after him, reduces Mudimbe's philosophical input to the epistemological description of the 'colonial library', 'a pre-existing library', and its surreptitious effects on the African gnostic code:

> Africa as such exists only on the basis of the text that constructs it as the Other's fiction. This text is then accorded a structuring power, to the point that a self that claims to speak with its own, authentic voice always runs the risk of being condemned to express itself in a preestablished discourse that masks its own, censures it, or forces it to imitate. [...] it is now impossible to distinguish the 'original' from a copy.[119]

This critique is reminiscent to that levelled by D. A. Masolo against Mudimbe's work. On the one hand, Masolo acknowledges Mudimbe's ability to measure the impact of the colonial library on current African philosophy, or, to use his own words, to establish the 'diagnostic' of Africa's 'gnostic malady'; on the other, however, he regrets that no 'prognostic' of Africa's 'cure' was generated by this scholarly exercise.[120] In 'African Modes of Self-Writing', Mbembe announces his intention to go beyond this diagnostic stage and to 'propose ways out of the dead end into which [afro-radicals and nativists] have led reflection on the African experience of self and the world'.[121] Mbembe's essay is therefore also prescriptive and can be regarded as a manifesto offering tools to read the present, transform the future, and *sortir de la grande nuit*. In this reflection, Mbembe also proposes a 'negative' path through the exploration of African 'necropolitics', an area that according to him has been neglected by 'African criticism'. In this respect, he contends that the analogy between slavery, colonisation, the apartheid, and the Holocaust is entirely justified because these events 'are all characterised by an expropriation of the self by unnameable forces [...], bear witness against life itself', and 'indict life [o]n the pretext that origin and race are the criteria of any kind of valuation'.[122] Hence the fundamental question that this essay asks: 'How can life be redeemed, that is, rescued from this incessant operation of the negative?'[123] Mbembe argues that 'new

African practices of the self' must be achieved away from the former enslavement to geography and ideas of 'a lost identity that must at all costs be found again'.[124] These practices, 'whose theory and vocabulary remain to be invented' are 'sculpted by cruelty'.[125] Kourouma's *Allah n'est pas obligé*[126] constitutes, according to Mbembe,[127] an example of these new practices that Nganang locates also in *Sozaboy* by Saro-Wiwa.[128] Survivors rather than victims, these characters 'have to invent an art of existing in the midst of despoliation'.[129]

It is true that this perspective does not inform *The Invention of Africa*, which, overall, is more concerned with pre-established Western modes of thinking and meta-narratives and their impact on African scholarship throughout history until today. However, it would be erroneous to reduce Mudimbe's work to the sole excavation of the colonial library. In many respects, he has also explored the ways in which daily practices, rooted in everyday-life violence, inform the African here and now and, in some cases, offer creative examples of survivals 'in the midst of despoliation', as will be examined through *Le Bel immonde*, *Entre les eaux* and the author's art criticism. As explained in *On African Fault Lines*,[130] his most recent collection of essays, he also owes the use of the word 'invention' to *L'Invention du quotidien*.[131] In this work, Michel de Certeau and his collaborators attempt to chart, via a study of daily life and everyday situations, the ways in which ordinary people (or consumers) re-appropriate, transform, and re-invent mass culture, cityscapes, eating, cooking, and reading habits, rituals, and traditions. They argue that the consumers are also 'tactical' users or inventors of new practices which do not slavishly comply with the set of ideas that institutions and producers seek to impose upon them.[132] The survivors on whom Mbembe, Nganang (and Adorno in the figure of Schoenberg[133]) focus are inventors of novel cultural practices borne out of the horrors of wars and genocides. Mudimbe's long-standing admiration for the work of Benoît Verhaegen (as examined in Chapter 3) testifies to an analogous ambition to explore the territories where history and the practice of everyday life intersect. His *Rébellions au Congo* – that Mudimbe called 'monuments' [masterpieces] (*CA*, 133) – chronicled the development of a number of rebellions that occurred throughout the newly independent Congo in 1964 in four different regions (Kwilu, North Katanga, Maniema, and Bolobo-Mushie). What is interesting here is not so much the historical events *per se* as the way in which these poorly equipped rebels, who were eventually defeated by the Armée nationale congolaise, bricolaged new popular myths that until today have retained their currency, such as, for instance, the use of 'mai mai' (powerful water) as a means to repel the enemies' bullets.

Le Bel immonde and *Entre les eaux* bear witness to this climate of political unrest. *Le Bel immonde* (published in 1976) is set in Kinshasa in 1965 against the background of rebellions 'which did, in fact, take place', as indicated by Mudimbe in a 'Note' (*BI*, 203) in which he also mentions Verhaegen's *Rébellions au Congo*. This unambiguous chronological and spatial setting is used to explore the intricacies of political power and Congolese gender politics, notably with regards to hetero-normativity, five years after independence. A love affair between a Secretary of State, who remains nameless, and Ya, a high-class prostitute who is also involved in a lesbian relationship, is the main building block of the plot. The title of the novel captures the alienating nature, the impurity and impropriety – 'immonde' originates from the Latin adjective 'mundus' (proper) – of their relationship. 'Le Bel immonde' is used in the masculine and this could suggest that the phrase qualifies the nameless politician, his depravation, and abusive (sexual and political) tendencies to which Ya, the female character, falls victim. In this novel, as will be examined later, Mudimbe provides, like other contemporary African writers such as Ahmadou Kourouma and Sembène Ousmane, but also, more crucially, female writers such as Werewere Liking and Véronique Tadjo,[134] in their respective countries, a commentary on the misogynistic and homophobic basis of Congolese society. It appears, however, that this more straightforward interpretation in which perpetrators and victims are ascribed neatly defined roles does not do justice to the *double entendre* of the title. Throughout the narrative, Ya is called 'Belle' by her lover and, in the penultimate chapter, a police officer who fails to indict her of high treason and political espionage names her 'une immonde p__'[135] [a filthy whore] (*BI*, 195) as she chooses to accuse her lover of possible complicity with the outlawed rebels in order to save her life. When stripped of its definite article ('le'), the title conjures up the interchangeable nature of their shared impurity and responsibility. Indeed, from a phonic point of view, there is no difference between 'bel immonde' and 'belle immonde'. This indeterminacy is the sign of their complicity. The French noun 'complice', which can mean accomplice *but* also lover, reflects the ambiguous and corrupted nature of their partnership.

The novel examines daily life at the end of the First Republic and registers the signs that presided over the passage to the Second Republic. In this process, the use and abuse, on the part of the political establishment, of rhetoric as a tool to forge official fables and fake inadmissible truths is given a very prominent role.[136] The incorporation of a speech delivered by Joseph Kasa-Vubu in 1965 in front of the elected members of the Chambers provides a perfect illustration of the gap between words and deeds in the First Republic but also after under Mobutu's rule:

> Let us never forget that those who hold a public mandate are the target of all the people. It is upon the discipline which you will impose upon yourselves, upon the example which you will set, that the prestige of the Nation and the authority of the State depend. It is difficult to require our population to submit to the law if those who make the law are the first to trample it under their feet. (*BI*, 99)

The democratic principles underpinning this declaration appear to be of little avail to curb State-orchestrated torture and violence. Ya's lover is of the view that the rebels need to be dealt with once and for all: 'Direct intervention [...] is the only solution. Blood will flow. There will be casualties. That is too bad, but what can one expect? We must safeguard the integrity of the national territory at any cost' (*BI*, 164). What this last point demonstrates is that violence, *real* violence and not *just* epistemological violence, has always been, as already shown by way of *Shaba Deux* and the *Bible noire* (Chapter 1), at the forefront of Mudimbe's intellectual project. *Le Bel immonde*, which Nganang did not consider in his examination of contemporary African literature, possesses, I would argue, a 'pre-visionary' coefficient. As such the novel opens up the possibility to reflect upon African necropolitics as fictionalised, for instance, in more recent narratives about the Rwandan genocide and child soldiers in West and Central Africa.[137]

The novel also provides a vivid depiction of the capital city, Kinshasa, which is portrayed as a modern metropolis whose cartography was nonetheless shaped by the colonial experience. The fact that the 'Boulevard du 30 Juin' is shown to be flanked by 'Bata' and the 'Memling Hotel' (*BI*, 40) is proof that the Congolese capital has remained under the influence of the West and has not quite managed to sever the links with its former self (Léopoldville). The narrative thus establishes an apt analogy between the very fabric of the urban landscape and Congolese political discourse and the latter's inability to move away from the pomp and officiousness of colonial administrative language.[138] By the same token, night life is dominated by the fetishes of neo-colonialism: brands, fashion items, beverages, jazz and pop icons from postcolonial Europe and America. Ya and her lover are the consumers and the victims of this imported modernity and spectacle whose rules are laid down elsewhere. They are the participants of a system in which life itself is submitted to the laws of capitalist commodification: Ya sells her perfectly groomed body and the government minister buys it. The mercantile nature of this partnership is mediated and further reinforced by their propensity to *look* at one another, be one another's things and being-for-others.

Ya is contemplated by her lover and is forced in these inventions of her by him which resonates with Sartre's theorisation of the 'look', as seen in Chapter 3, to be what she is not in order to become what he wants her to be, that is, a sexual object and an aesthetic accessory. In the following passage, Ya reflects on the role she has been compelled to take on in order to gratify his sense of decorum and ownership:

> 'You are a living sculpture' [...] his eyes blurred, gazing upon you as if you were a statue. [...] he overwhelmed you with compliments, itemizing each physical detail, dwelling emphatically on your amber necklace, the golden bracelets that made the smallest motion of your arm sings. He had the eye of an owner looking over a new animal acquired at a steep price.
> (*BI*, 135)

In this inspection, which nullifies the traditional divide between the human and the inanimate, her body and the items jollifying it are ascribed the same value. The relationship between the minister and Ya mirrors on the sexual plane the colonial situation, and the master–slave bond thereof, as it had been analysed by Sartre and Fanon. He is the reincarnation of Bula Matari, a nickname (meaning rock breaker) originally given to H. M. Stanley to signify his superhuman ability to use explosives, and Ya is 'his Black servant, who is for the *Bula Matari* only a sexual body without an identity or a voice'.[139] Indeed, as argued by Michael Syrotinski (by way of Spivak's 'Can the Subaltern Speak'), Ya's situation dramatises the plight of African women: 'As Africans they have been the Other of colonial discourse, but as women they have been the Other of a patriarchal order that operates both internally and externally'.[140] Ya rejects, however, her lover's attempt to petrify her into a 'living sculpture'. Her refusal is also Sartrean as she uses her own eyes to defy her lover's all-encompassing gaze.

Her *look* rather than her *looks* is the crucial point here for, no pun intended, there is more to Ya than meet the *eyes*. The ethnic crisis experienced by contemporary Congo brings her own defiance into perspective. Ya is not from Kinshasa; she comes from a traditional rural area and is the daughter of a well-known rebel leader. When she is informed by members of her own tribe that her father has been assassinated and decapitated, her own story becomes the signifying fragment of a wider collective whole. Her father, 'a great man' who 'died for the cause of his people' (*BI*, 68), symbolises the return of tribal law into her own post-traditional and urbanised present. Ya and her lesbian girlfriend, euphemistically referred to as her 'sister' throughout the narrative, do not welcome this return. They reluctantly reconnect with the 'mystery of blood relationship' (*BI*, 72) and a cultural environment in which they 'instinctively' recover 'the conventional way to be womanly' (*BI*, 71). Indeed, they are reminded by their male 'brothers' of their tribal 'obligations' and the divide between what Mary Douglas called 'purity' and 'danger'[141]: 'you may neither use nor touch any object that belongs to a European [...] If you should, purify yourselves according to the law. [...] under no circumstances will you eat the liver, heart, or head of any animal whatsoever' (*BI*, 73–74). Crucially, however, Ya is ordered actively to support the rebels' fight for independence from Kinshasa and to be part of an intelligence-gathering operation targeting powerful individuals such as her lover.

The lover's scopophilia is therefore partly offset by Ya's own spying agenda. The pervasive climate of suspicion characterising this text is generated by this act of reciprocal surveillance, which, in turn, captures the mood of the Congolese dictatorship in the 1960s and 1970s. The minister is aware of the power of her gaze and knows that she sees him 'as some sort of lavish entertainment' (*BI*, 61), a phrase used here to render the French 'spectacle'.[142] Her watchful eyes also reveal the way in which he makes a spectacle of himself. There is, in this respect, a tendency on her part to focus on the zoomorphic aspects of his physique, personality, and sexuality and to compare him to stereotypically African animals (elephants, rhinoceroses, big cats). This animalisation is ambiguous because it is, at the same time, a celebration of his masculinity by way of totemic animals usually associated with power and chiefdom; on the other hand, however, these analogies are also strategies to signify his impurity and sub-human attributes. They are also the tools employed by Ya to define the contours of her own struggle and impurity.

Her father's decapitated body mirrors her decision to distance herself from the 'nativist' agenda of her 'blood' sisters and brothers and rid herself of 'l'odeur du père'.[143] What is at issue here, however, is no longer the integrity of the national territory but the stability of a phallocentric order wherein women are expected to assume, within the framework of polygamy, a strictly reproductive role so as to maintain in the present the power of the ancestors. Ya is therefore used as a vehicle to reopen the discussion on Congolese independence: if it happened at all why, asked Mudimbe who is a keen reader of Simone de Beauvoir (one of his 'glorious' bodies, see *CG*, 107–08), have Congolese women been left out of the process? Ya's impurity is polymorphous. On the one hand, she shares her lover's impurity in that she partakes in his depraved lifestyle and utter duplicity as she ends up double crossing everyone. Much more crucially, however, her *immonde* status refers to her unwillingness to abide by the heteronormative rules of Congolese society and to endorse the Bantu *philosophy* of her native village. By way of Judith Butler, herself arguing her position on the basis of Julia Kristeva's exploration of the role of the 'abject' in the constitution of the subject, Syrotinski contends that Ya is doubly 'abject' (or 'immonde'). First, in the conventional sense of the adjective given that she is a prostitute; secondly as 'a lesbian body that radically transgresses socially sanctioned gender roles'.[144] The practice of anthropology and its inability to register the deep-seated features of the Congolese cultural 'text' (the 'chose du texte') lies also at the heart of this critique that Ya embodies. The sacrificial murder of her girlfriend as part of a religious ritual practised in honour of the government minister serves as another reminder of Ya's exclusion and refusal to act as a *pure* representative of the traditional order where members are 'the fingers of a single hand, the limbs of a single body' (*BI*, 70). The fact that this event is referred to by Mudimbe in his Postface as a 'cannibalist farce' (*BI*, 203) clearly demonstrates the extent to which scientific and sexual practices are disciplined and sanctioned by a set of exclusive discourses. 'Cannibalist' is not to be understood too literally for, as pointed out by Neil Lazarus, 'the association of political dictatorship and cannibalism' was already a 'cliché' when the novel came out;[145] it indicates that Congolese knowledge has been ingested by colonialists and then digested and regurgitated by locals.[146] The 'farce' announces Nara's humorous dismissal (in *L'Écart*) of anthropological methodologies and Mudimbe's recognition that the 'Bibliothèque zaïroise' was built upon, and had to absorb, the colonial library in order to become a respectable corpus.[147]

Ya's reluctance to advocate purity is the mark of her agency as it demonstrates her ability to defy the collective anonymity of the law, and speak against tradition, an entity which remains impersonal and a-historical. It also demonstrates her willingness to challenge the very notions of purity and abjection as socially constructed and the signs of 'body politic'.[148] It is significant to add that Ya is the only character of the novel with a name: all others, including her lover, are referred to by personal pronouns and functions. Her emerging agency is further expressed by the way in which narrative voices are used throughout the novel. There too an obvious pendulum can be observed between impersonal and personal points of view as the two main characters are either addressed as 'tu'/'vous', spoken for as 'il' or 'elle', but also narrate their own stories as 'je'. The recourse to 'je' on the part of Ya cannot, however, be read too triumphantly as the last chapter marks the return of the very scene that had opened the novel: Ya sits in her favourite bar and is engaged in a conversation with a former client, an American technician who helps 'your country to develop itself' (*BI*, 202).

The circular structure of the novel and the disappearance of the first person narrator indicate the extent to which contemporary Congo is trapped in a permanent neo-colonial present. The novel as a whole, however, also demonstrates that Mudimbe cannot just be labelled as a patient philosopher. In fact, *Le Bel immonde* explores what has before and after Mobutu plagued modern Congo: ethnic violence and the necropolitics thereof.[149] Through the figures of Ya and her lover, he is also able to tease out the way in which this violence has inflected the construction of African subjects. Like Nganang's post-genocide Africans, Mudimbe's characters blur the divide between innocence and guilt, victims and perpetrators as they experience the integration of Africa into, as Nganang puts it, 'l'humanité simple, c'est-à-dire fautive' [simple but guilty humanity].[150]

Entre les eaux explores the conditions in which insurrectionists were forced to survive in a Central African country which, albeit nameless, is clearly Congo-Zaire. Although a narrative in which Sartre's notion of 'bad faith' is developed, it provides an examination of sub-Saharan 'necropolitics' and the survival of figures who are both victims and perpetrators. This novel is loosely set during the rebellions that Verhaegen investigates and it primarily focuses on the intellectual tribulation of Pierre Landu, a Catholic priest, torn between his allegiance to the Church and his desire to participate in the political transformation of his country in order to drag it out of poverty. He decides, as a consequence, to become a member of a Marxist militia group fighting the national army and sets out to reconcile his faith with his comrades' ideological agenda. His plans, however, prove unsuccessful. First, he is held in suspicion by his comrades and regarded as a 'faux prêtre' [false priest] (*Entre*, 71). Secondly, his unit is annihilated by the regular army. The ruthless method applied in the assault symbolises the return of imperialism that Mobutu until his demise would hide behind his programme of authenticity. Finally, Landu ends up in a Cistercian monastery, a place of rites and symbols solely dedicated to meditation which contrasts with his very secular attempt to embrace praxis and enact, with the support of Marx and Jesus, the transformation of Congolese society. I would like to contend that Landu's self-delusion and inability to choose, interpreted by critics,[151] and by Mudimbe himself,[152] as an attempt to fictionalise Sartrean bad faith, is much more than a philosophical subterfuge. This novel, like *L'Autre Face du royaume*, also published in 1973, examines the complex relationship between words and things, ideas and actions, theory and praxis. Mudimbe is aware that political changes will emerge at their intersections. Landu rejects dogmas, be they Catholic or Marxist, precisely because he is determined to live 'sans séparer la théorie de la pratique' [without divorcing theory from practice] (*Entre*, 26). This project results from the painful realisation that 'notre pays aujourd'hui est un enfer' [today our country has become a hellish place] (*Entre*, 53). Landu's hesitation needs to be read against the emergence at the end of the 1960s of liberation theology. He is appalled by the bloody methods of his comrades and shocked by the recognition that the Church has been acting in Africa as a banking institution (*Entre*, 106). However, he refuses to jettison Catholicism and Marxism as he is of the view that they can both offer the basis for social transformation and political emancipation in Africa. As in Gustavo Gutiérrez's influential *A Theology of Liberation*,[153] Landu argues that Jesus Christ was a revolutionary and that Christians should be 'en état permanent de révolution' [permanently in a state of revolution] (*Entre*, 27). If he models his thoughts against those of Christian mystics such as Teresa of Avila, he also remarks that his 'engagement réel' [real commitment] is based on 'méthodes objectives' (*Entre*, 103). Landu's exploration of a possible compromise between Catholicism and Marxism is therefore driven by the very practical objective of bringing about social justice, narrowing the economic gap between the haves and the have-nots, and responding creatively to the utter despoliation that Congo-Zaire was increasingly experiencing.

These very issues were at the forefront of Mudimbe's involvement with theology during the 1970s as it was thought that the southern-American context in which liberation theology had grown was comparable to that of postcolonial Central Africa. Gutiérrez's reflection (but also E. Dussel's, as briefly mentioned in Chapter 3) provided therefore a useful template for action in Zaire – but not for developing the idea of God as argued in his conversation with McAfee Brown (Chapter 4). After moving to the United States, a country where black liberation had often rhymed with black theology,[154] Mudimbe recalled the key role played by Verhaegen, 'the Belgian scholar [...] who is both a Marxist and a Catholic' (*IoA*, 178), in the dissemination of Gutiérrez's thought in Zaire:

> Verhaegen, following G. Gutiérrez's theology of liberation, proposed three genres of theological discourse: a *theology of modernity* which will link the search for social justice to the promotion of 'reason, science and progress'; a *theology of charity* which will address the issue of social inequalities and poverty and offer radically new moral solutions; and, finally, a *theology of development* which will redefine modalities of development in terms of local interests. (*IoA*, 179)[155]

This transformative programme, and its underlying focus on 'local interests', is implied in *Entre les eaux*, a novel which juxtaposes the figures of Saint Francis of Assisi (*Entre*, 111) and those of the 'prêtres ouvriers' [worker priests] (*Entre*, 148). Like Verhaegen in his re-appropriation of 'histoire immédiate', Landu argues that theory and practice will constitute the major yardsticks of social transformation, even though the following remark suggests more a precedence of the latter over the former than a real dialectical relationship: 'Debray après Castro et Guevara: d'abord une pratique [Debray after Castro and Guevara: first a practice] (*Entre*, 99). Régis Debray, the philosophy *agrégé* trained by Louis Althusser, who, however, also fought alongside Che Guevara in Bolivia, is pitted against the two Latin-American revolutionaries. With regards to (in his view) failed implementations of socialism in Africa, Landu argues that 'je me méfie des positions théoriques prises comme principes moteurs [I am suspicious of theoretical positions held as driving principles] (*Entre*, 99). These fleeting references to Latin-American revolutionary figures indicate therefore a willingness to draw an analogy between popular insurrections on the two sides of the Atlantic and to reveal, beyond their many differences, the common horizon shared by Marxists and Christians in their attempt to empower the poor and to combat global capitalism. The bearded icon Che Guevara provides thus the missing link between the figures of Marx and Jesus. In this respect, Gutiérrez remarks that Guevara, like liberation theologians, regarded Christ as a real man, with 'blood, tears [and] anguish', rather than as a remote and abstract figure.[156] He contends also that the influence is reciprocal and that the emancipation sought by his movement 'means more than overcoming economic, social, and political dependence' and will need, 'in a deeper sense', to contribute to the development of what Guevara called a 'new man', that is, to the construction of a 'qualitatively different society in which he will be free from all servitude, in which he will be the artisan of his own destiny'.[157] This Guevara-inspired creation of a 'new man', which, incidentally, resonates with the utopian militancy of the second 'trinity' identified in this chapter (Sartre–Fanon–Mudimbe), has to be, according to Gutiérrez, 'undertaken by the oppressed people themselves and [...] stem from the values proper to these people'.[158]

The important point here is that Verhaegen, Mudimbe, and Gutiérrez all advocate the necessity of overcoming a tradition which, in the spheres of scholarship, politics, and religion, continued to inform everyday practices. They all promote the rejection of parasitical intermediaries. Verhaegen, like Mudimbe, demands the abolition of the paternalistic hierarchy between scholars and informants in the human sciences and Gutiérrez, in a similar emancipating perspective, contends that ordinary people should become the theologians of their own liberation. This attempt to move away from the very landscape which had since the early 1960s characterised African (and Latin-American) neo-colonialism is formulated against dogmas and injunctions issued by agencies such as the Church or the IMF. Ultimately the aim of this operation is to challenge a geopolitical order understood in terms of centres and peripheries. Here lies one of Mudimbe's most enduring pursuits, that is, the exploration of the relationship between the global and the local, the universal and the specific. Colonialism and neo-colonialism are underpinned by processes of assimilation or by the assumption that models developed in the *metropoles*, be they academic, economic, political, and religious, can be applied to peripheries and will eventually contribute to their transformation. Mudimbe described this process of invention in *L'Autre Face du royaume* but, from *L'Odeur du père* onwards, he has argued that forced assimilation, of which he is the very product, has often failed and has become the site, before and after decolonisation, of what Mbembe called 'new African practices of the self'. The diagnostic of African maladies has therefore also been a pretext for examining the proliferation of novel cultural experiences borne out of the abyss of African negativity. Landu's trajectory is exemplary of such local re-appropriation which is neither inspired by afro-radicalists, nor nativists and what Mudimbe dismisses as their 'culte masochiste d'une altérité nègre' [masochist cult of negro alterity] (*Entre*, 99).

In 'Reprendre', a text dedicated to artistic creation in Congo-Zaire and elsewhere in sub-Saharan Africa, Mudimbe argues that a particular cult of alterity developed before decolonisation had a major impact on local artists' aesthetic sense and, ultimately, on their ability to articulate creative responses to very local events. Mudimbe does not intend here to provide a full historical overview of this aesthetic evolution: rather than focusing on 'causal successions', he remarks that his aim is to highlight 'new artistic thresholds [and] displacements of inspirations' (*Idea*, 155). The main argument made in this essay is that the 'radical reconversion of African arts' undertaken 'in the colonial settings' did not produce a neat and regimented reordering and assimilation of aesthetic practices (*Idea*, 156). This *uncanny* return of the colonial evokes Bhabha's reflections in 'Articulating the Archaic':

> [T]he repetition of the 'same' can in fact be its own displacement, can turn the authority of culture into its own non-sense precisely in its moment of enunciation. For, in the psychoanalytic sense, to 'imitate' is to cling to the denial of the ego's limitations; to 'identify' is to assimilate conflictually. It is from between them, where the letter of the law will not be assigned as a sign, that culture's double returns uncannily – neither the one nor the other, but the imposter – to mock and mimic, to lose the sense of the masterful self and its social sovereignty. It is at this moment of intellectual and psychic 'uncertainty' that representation can no longer guarantee the authority of culture.[159]

In this discussion, Mudimbe focuses notably on the significant role played by Pierre Romain-Desfossés in the mentoring, during the colonial period, of Katangese artists. It is important to point out that Mudimbe does not condemn Romain-Desfossés but presents him as a man who, albeit paternalistic in his approach, was above all pursuing an aesthetic agenda. His energy and 'missionary zeal' rested upon the conviction that local artists needed to reconnect with their African (in fact 'Nilotic') personality and move away from the 'uniformizing aesthetics of White masters' (*Idea*, 156).[160] He contended that Congolese artists were the recipients of a type of 'aesthetic unconscious', shared by all sub-Saharan Africans, and Romain-Desfossés, the father-figure of this paradoxical renewal, took it upon himself to 'awaken in his students this ancient, unchanging aesthetic memory' (*Idea*, 156). His teaching was therefore based on a cult of alterity and a belief in 'an innate African artistic imagination [...] radically different from that of Europe' (*Idea*, 159). What Mbembe, after Fanon, called 'réflexe indigéniste' became the backbone of an aesthetic philosophy which advocated the return to the primitive basis of a purer collective past. This artistic position, and above all the inverted racism that it suggests, has, however, become much more than just an instrument for the dissemination of afro-radicalist and nativist theses. 'Reprendre' is in this respect suitably ambiguous and reminiscent of Bhabha's conflictual identification. The indigenist aesthetic that Romain-Desfossés revived was adopted by his pupils but also reprised, recaptured, or adapted by subsequent generations of artists in Zaire and elsewhere on the continent. The adoption-adaptation pair renders the deliberate ambiguity contained in the French verb 'reprendre'. Mudimbe demonstrates that Romain-Desfossés's 'Nilotic etiquette' (*Idea*, 156), which echoes Cheikh Anta Diop's project, never retained any fixity and went through a number of 'displacements'.[161] This issue of displacement is central in Mudimbe's thinking and is linked to the above-mentioned relationship between the global and the local, the universal and the specific. By way of Michel de Certeau's opposition between 'place' and 'space' he often shows the ways in which the transposition and the transformation from the one to the other occur.[162] Certeau argues that

> The law of the 'proper' rules in the place: the elements taken into consideration are *beside* one another, each situated in its own 'proper' and distinct location [...] A place is thus an instantaneous configuration of positions. It implies an indication of stability.[163]

He adds that his element of order and stability is absent from 'space':

> in relation to place, space is like the word when it is spoken, that is, when it is caught in the ambiguity of an actualisation, transformed into a term dependent upon many different conventions, situated as the act of a present (or of a time), and modified by the transformations caused by successive contexts. In contradistinction to the place, it has thus none of the univocity or stability of a 'proper'.[164]

Romain-Desfossés's aesthetic order is a 'place' that became displaced or spatialised. The invention of new cultural practices results from these displacements which have affected, according to Mudimbe, the whole spectrum of art production in sub-Saharan Africa. He remarks that the notion of heritage has remained important but that artists, however, have consistently refused to define their works through this exclusive link with tradition. He contends that contemporary African artists (he refers here to an exhibition hosted by the Studio Museum in Harlem in 1990) 'consciously relate to earlier African art' but 'know how to distort it, how to submit it to their own creative process' (*Idea*, 163). Mudimbe explores also the characteristics of popular art whereby this tendency to call upon and distort tradition also operates. A popular artist such as Tshibumba Kanda-Matulu, for instance, engages with tradition, adopts its seemingly naive techniques and teases out the symbolic significance of local mythological figures such as the Mami Wata. On the surface, Tshibumba Kanda-Matulu complies with the aesthetic agenda of the Mobutu regime and its desire to promote authenticity.[165] Beyond these superficial marks of compliance, Kanda-Matulu's works nonetheless displace the stable and orderly thrust of this indigenist programme. With regards to popular artists such as Kanda-Matulu, Mudimbe argues that their works witness 'a practice of everyday life' (*Idea*, 167):

> In many respects, popular arts, mostly paintings, are structured as *histoire immédiate*, in Benoît Verhaegen's expression; they are literally a capturing of ordinary, banal stories and events (a market, a drinking party, a political event), of violence and tragedy (a civil war and assassination), or of mythological motifs [...] Here technical flaws become marks of originality. The artist appears as the '*undisciplinable*' hero, challenging social institutions, including art practices, particularly academic ones. Yet this 'deviant', who sometimes attacks both a tradition and its modern currents, incarnates clearly the locus of their confrontation. (*Idea*, 174–75; my emphasis)

Ultimately, the formal distortions that are identified here are the signs of a rebellion whereby the present is reinvented with fragments from the past *and* the present. The concept of 'invention' is therefore far from being limited to the construction of the colonial library in which Africanists would proverbially proceed to order, catalogue, and magic up their own version of Congolese culture. Mudimbe suggests that 'invention' transcends the 'tension between the within and the without' (*AOF*, 74), a point made by Roy Wagner in the epigraph opening this chapter. In his use of the concept, Mudimbe, who admits to having read Wagner's *The Invention of Culture* several times (*OAF*, 75), intends also to go beyond the simplistic opposition between creators and epigones, originals and copies and demonstrate that the 'repetition of the same' is never completely repetitious and generates its own creative displacements:

> One remembers the original meaning of *invention*, its etymological signs and values. To synthesize two axes one can find in William Freund's nineteenth-century *Dictionary of Latin* the verb *inuenio*, from *inuenire*, which means to come, to light upon a thing, find, or meet with. A second, more complex axis includes a series of values: (a) to find out, invent,

effect; (b) to discover, ascertain, learn; (c) to devise or contrive how to do a thing; (d) to acquire, get, earn. Occasionally, in a special construction, *inuenire* may signify to be at home. This rare meaning closes in on the idea supporting an expression such as the 'invention of Africa,' whose semantic play involves both the notion of processing an idea and that of a negative or positive fabrication from one's motivations. (OAF, 75)

By way of conclusion, I would like to return to the idea of Mudimbe as the 'negator', that is, to his ability to explore, express, and perform the autonomy of art as this phrase was conceived by Adorno. This ability, however, does not exclude, on Mudimbe's part, worldly (in the Saidian sense) attempts to engage with history and ideology, as demonstrated by the two novels analysed in this chapter. In this respect, it would seem that Nganang is unable, at least in this *Manifeste*,[166] to move away from an idealistic conception of literature, that is, an aesthetic position which 'often strives to discern an essential quality of literariness in admired texts' when, in fact, 'a text may appear literary, or otherwise, depending on the context in which it is regarded'.[167] Nganang, and Mbembe to a lesser extent, have a tendency to provide partial examinations of Mudimbe's work and are therefore oblivious of his attempts to engage with negative dialectics. Nganang, echoing Adorno's own criticism of Sartre's commitment, reduces Mudimbe's work to an effort to establish a mimetic relationship between history and art, politics and literature. Mbembe, although much more willing to acknowledge the legacy of the Sartre–Fanon–Mudimbe trinity, limits the scope of Mudimbe's thinking to a laudable but ultimately sterile epistemological exercise whereby African thinkers are shown to reproduce discourses created in the West. They both seem therefore to have developed a very mechanical conception of Mudimbe's work and to imply that he is the spokesperson of a stationary philosophical 'place'. They also argue that this 'place', symbolised by the figures of Sartre and Foucault, cannot be transformed into an 'immediate' (for unmediated) 'space' where the boundaries between Catholicism and Marxism are redesigned, where authenticity is parodied to reveal Mobutuism and, in turn, assert the autonomy of art through its negative for, as Adorno comments, 'art can be understood only by its laws of movement, not according to any set of invariants' and is thus 'defined by its relation to what it is not'.[168]

Finally, the two authors seem to have neglected a major point: Mudimbe's writing operates also as literary performance. It is surprising that performers and stylists such as Mbembe and Nganang have chosen to disregard this quality in Mudimbe's production. The old dichotomy between 'content' and 'form' – in French 'fond' et 'forme' – lies at the heart of this partial analysis. Mudimbe is presented as a disseminator of ideas, which he of course is, but the form and style which he adopts are overlooked at the expense of content. Mudimbe's output is not reducible to the logic of an epistemological exercise. He is also a stylist and his style often acts as a device which undoes, or interrupts, to use one of Nancy's phrases in *The Inoperative Community*, the logical concatenation that the scientific analysis had engineered. Adorno is, in the main, absent from Mudimbe's discussions. The two thinkers, however, are closer to one another than it may seem. Both have teased out the limits of the Enlightenment project through the sustained exploration of human tragedies, colonialism, and the Holocaust, which have involved them personally. There is also an issue of common stylistic posture. In his latest translation into English of *Aesthetic Theory*, Robert Hullot-Kentor reports on the difficulty of translating Adorno. He bemoans the maze-like and disorienting nature of the text and its 'paratactical' dimension. Hullot-Kentor argues that

> this paratactical style is unable [...] to refer backward or forward: Adorno never writes, 'as mentioned'. Every transition must be a transition in the object itself if it is not to unhinge the text. Thus the text is deprived of a major technique for building on what has been, or of explicitly organizing itself toward what will be, developed elsewhere.[169]

An analogous paratactical propensity can be observed in Mudimbe's works.[170] This atonal and dissonant style, which 'is not argumentative' and 'does not seek to convince',[171] offers unparalleled freedom. I talked earlier (Chapter 2) of deliberate abstruseness as a means of disavowing the didactic basis of the colonial project and its neo-colonial avatars. The paratactical tendency of Mudimbe's writing serves a similar objective as paratactical texts are 'inimical to exposition',[172] a point resonating with Wim van Bisbergen's reading of *Tales of Faith* as he suggests that the book's 'artistic originality' resides 'in the fact that it rather effectively, and deceptively, manages to conceal its literary building bricks as pieces of consistent scholarly argument'.[173] Indeed, there is a causal link between this partial dismissal of what the Enlightenment stands for and the two authors' suspicion of scholarly disciplines. Mudimbe's epistemological investigations often disclose the tyranny of all-encompassing systems of thoughts, or 'grids', in the human sciences. Disciplines – history, sociology, anthropology – are strictly regulated systems. Throughout his career, Mudimbe has remained fascinated by the attempts, on the part of thinkers such as Freud, Marx, Lévi-Strauss, and Foucault, to delve into the human psyche, to theorise the mechanisms of history, the underlying patterns of cultures, and the building blocks of knowledge. Fascination, however, does not exclude a degree of scepticism. Even at their most rigorous, the universal laws developed by the human sciences cannot escape the confrontation with specific contexts. Mudimbe's practice of the autobiographical genre is borne out of the realisation that society cannot be reduced to an 'object de raisonnement' [object of reasoning] (*OP*, 52). The practice of social sciences becomes therefore a 'deviant' exercise whereby the scholar operates outside his discipline and combats its practice of exclusion. In the introduction of *On African Fault Lines*, he admits that this book does not quite adhere to the bibliographical approach that would normally prevail in scholarly works:

> This is the moment to recognise the fact of possible forgotten sources internalised as to have lost their precise origin in the literature. By their expression, some ideas might not be mine. Yet, they had become also mine in their blurred relation to horizons of knowledge and their effects on my interrogations. Also, occasional detailed viewpoints are tacit responses to positions on alterity politics in my preceding books. (*OAF*, viii)

Mudimbe acknowledges the paradoxical nature of his trajectory as an intellectual. His focus on 'possible forgotten sources' (see also CG, 110) casts indeed a doubt on the credibility of the scholarly apparatus adopted in *On African Fault Lines*. He seems to be arguing here that his own scholarship is defined by the partial rejection of what *should* define scholarship, that is, its capacity to illuminate rather than blur the contours of knowledge. This refusal to comply reflects his ambition to perform the role of the 'undisciplinable' intellectual and to generate, alongside thinkers such as Mbembe and Nganang, a decolonisation of 'African modes of self-writing'.

Conclusion:
'The Return of the Unhomely Scholar'

'Reading Mudimbe', argues Kai Kresse, 'means engaging in an intellectual space where African studies just cannot happen in splendid isolation from other disciplines, in disjunction from the European history of the study of humanities'.[1] Indeed, V. Y. Mudimbe conjures up the image of a *fabulously* inquisitive reader sifting and collating data across disciplines. The adverb 'fabulously' is used here to reiterate the author's belief that essays and exegeses are also fables, that is, *attempts* to translate what can, at best, only be transformed. His presence at the intersection of several 'libraries' bears witness to his ambition to read Africa as an insider but also as an outsider, thereby rejecting simplistic racial, ideological, but also theoretical affiliations. In *Les Corps glorieux*, he remarks in this respect that the motto *Etiam omnes, Ego Non* [I shall do and think it even though everybody does otherwise] (*CG*, 20) has helped him from an early age onwards to value personal freedom above everything else, a stance which resonates with Fanon's 'Je suis mon propre fondement' in *Peau noire, masques blancs*. This posture has two immediate consequences. First, Mudimbe can sometimes appear as the devil's advocate who would, for instance, celebrate Lévi-Strauss's and Foucault's interventions but also, at other moments, dismiss their writings as fables about fables and denigrate the over-generalising propensity of their claims. This critical stance has also enabled him to re-open ambiguous 'texts' such as *Bantu Philosophy*, *Une Bible noire*, and Pierre Romain-Desfossé's tutelage of Katangese artists and read them as an epistemologist, that is, away from a certain form of political correctness which would tend to measure the past, and past critical positions, with instruments developed in the present. Mudimbe is an avid reader and a prolific writer and the critical brand of erudition that he has developed over the years, in fact since the beginning of his career, has been a vehicle to demonstrate that Africanism, an amorphous field that nonetheless gained scientific legitimacy and contours towards the end of the colonial rule, has always been coloured by racial assumptions.[2] He has therefore contended that statements and texts about sub-Saharan Africa during the colonial period were defined and shaped by the conditions of possibility of their production. What is interesting, however, is that he more often than not challenges this type of epistemological determinism to reveal that colonial writings are in some cases *not what they are*, or, to be more precise, more than what they are assumed to be. This position of critical independence has enabled him to transcend categories shaped by racial ideologies and to detect postcolonial inclinations well before decolonisation, in Blyden's production, for instance, and to trace colonial legacies into the twenty-first century.

The type of investigation conducted in *Autour de la 'Nation'*, *L'Autre Face du royaume*, and *L'Odeur du père* is predicated upon a refusal to embrace, through a 'subtil use of the intersection' (*AF*, 154), a completely polarised conception of the colonial/postcolonial pair. His critique of the West in these three collections of essays is abstruse – 'abstrus', 'abscons' in French – and it is interesting to note the etymological link between this adjective and the Latin verb 'abstrudere' which (like 'abscondere' to which 'abscons' is connected) means to hide or to conceal. Like Benoît Verhaegen and Johannes Fabian in their respective disciplines (history and social anthropology), he excavates in contemporary intellectual practices the remnants of a very distant past living on in the present. These statements are, however, more than belated anti-colonialist attacks as they, very crucially, *conceal* a rejection of the Zairianisation of the Congolese 'community', a self-proclaimed anti-Western project which ironically recycled outmoded nineteenth-century worldviews forged during the Romantic period to justify, often apocryphally, the birth of new nations. *Shaba Deux* examines the complexities of nation-building and gender politics in a country caught up between Lumumba's Unitarian dream – ironically *enforced* by Mobutu himself – and Katangese separatism. In a preface to a collection of essays exploring the centenary (in 2010) of the creation of Lubumbashi, Mudimbe implicitly argues that no homogenous description, and no blanket theory, of Congolese independence can be provided.[3] Mudimbe contends here by way of *Le Vocabulaire de la ville d'Élisabethville* that the binary logic behind the colonial/postcolonial pair cannot on its own capture the intricacy and the regional dynamics that presided over Congolese decolonisation. The *Vocabulaire*, as it is customarily referred to by specialists of Swahili cultures from Lubumbashi such as Johannes Fabian, who edited (through a *'re-oralization of the written original*'[4]) its first translation,[5] is a document compiled by a André Yav, a 'prête-nom' [pseudonym], according to Mudimbe, masking the involvement of several authors or 'voix d'une mémoire' [voices of a memory].[6] The *Vocabulaire* traces the history of Lubumbashi from its creation to the mid-1960s via the testimonies of individuals – Congolese servants, soldiers, and workers – who witnessed and experienced the development of this important urban and mining centre. Mudimbe argues that one cannot read the *Vocabulaire* without thinking about Ferdinand Oyono's *Une Vie de boy* inasmuch as it captures the 'invention' and the 'transformation' of a human space ('espace humain') from its social and racial margins.[7] This texts manifests therefore on the part of Congolese 'subalterns' a postcolonial ambition to produce, in Shaba Swahili and outside of their masters' (syntactic) control, a history of their city which, as Mudimbe contends, is to be situated 'dans une dialogue avec "l'histoire immediate" de Benoît Verhaegen' [in a dialogue with Benoît Verhaegen's immediate history].[8] Fabian regards also the text as a means whereby locals bypass the didactic mould of colonial servitude:

> I referred to it as an instance of 'grass-root literacy', that is, of the appropriation of a technique of writing by speakers of Shaba Swahili which was relatively free from the ideological and technical constraints that characterized literacy taught to the same speakers in other languages (French, some regional languages, and a variety of Swahili spoken by no one but considered fit for literacy). From the results – in this case the written text – we can infer that it is a literacy which works despite an amazingly high degree of indeterminacy and freedom (visible in an erratic orthography, a great disdain for 'correct' word and sentence boundaries and many other instances of seemingly unmotivated variations).[9]

The *Vocabulaire*, as he argues later, is 'a colonial history written by the colonized for the colonized'.[10] Mudimbe also argues that it is 'histoire colonial vue d'en-bas' [colonial history seen from below][11] but this statement should not be understood as proof of a straightforward reversal of the prevailing colonial logic. The passage to the postcolonial is altogether more complex. The tension between the two French verbs, 'défaire' and 'reprendre', as discussed earlier in this book, encapsulates this difficulty: to rid oneself of the colonial text implies a recapture of some of its constituents, a process which can never be a 'recommencement' of History (Fanon), a point made by Mudimbe as early as 1967.[12] The *Vocabulaire* is described as a document which here and there accounts for 'la souffrance des gens [et] le mécontentement des soldats' [people's suffering and the soldiers' discontent].[13] On the other hand, however, Mudimbe suggest that it is also a work 'qui s'insurge contre l'indépendance' [rebels against independence][14] and which holds colonisation very highly.[15] This apparent contradiction is resolved through an examination of the regional dynamics that inflected the decolonisation of Katanga, a process which, from the very outset, was seen incompatible with a wider, Unitarian Congolese nationalist project: 'Des années après l'indépendance, une forme de résistance au pouvoir de Kinshasa se traduisait ainsi au quotidien dans l'emploi du nom colonial de la ville, souvent sous sa forme abrégée d'Éville' [Years after the independence, a type of resistance to the Kinshasa power centre was expressed on a daily basis through the use of the colonial name of the city, often in its shortened form Éville].[16]

The *Vocabulaire* and the conditions underpinning its production are helpful to understand Mudimbe's relation to, and changing attitude towards, notions such as colonialism, colonial culture, and assimilation and their impact on the postcolonial present. There is a tendency in the early works to appraise the legacies of colonialism in tragic terms and to consider assimilation as an inevitable historical force that will soon empty sub-Saharan Africa of its cultures and crush its inhabitants' ability to reflect – Ahmed Nara's suicide in *L'Écart* being the most dramatic expression of this critique. Since *The Invention of Africa*, however, he has been increasingly inclined to nuance the effects of assimilation, often via autobiographical 'meditations', and tease out the ways in which it has in fact contributed to the invention – this view was the premise of Roy Wagner's anthropological classic *The Invention of Culture* – and further *unhomely* displacements, of novel, rather than imported, cultural practices. This enterprise, which echoes Homi Bhabha's idea that (colonial) culture is '*heimlich*' but also '*unheimlich*', that is, trapped in a dialectic which implies repetitions *and* transformations,[17] was also one of Michel de Certeau's points of departure in his analysis of the 'tactics' underlying *The Practice of Everyday Life*:

> [T]he ambiguity that subverted from within the Spanish colonizers' 'success' in imposing their own culture on the indigenous Indians is well known. Submissive, and even consenting to their subjection, the Indians nevertheless often *made of* the rituals, representations, and laws imposed on them something quite different from what their conquerors had in

mind; they subverted them not by rejecting or altering them, but by using them with respect to ends and references foreign to the system they had no choice but to accept. They were *other* within the very colonization that outwardly assimilated them; their use of the dominant social order deflected its power, which they lacked the means to challenge; they escaped it without leaving it.[18]

This remark applies, in the main, to modern Congo and its 'tactical' adoption/rejection of Western practices which simultaneously appear familiar *and* unfamiliar and repeat what was once there *but* also incorporate difference and transformation. In many places Mudimbe has used (or implied) the verb *reprendre* to describe this process of re-appropriation which he and, of course, many other cultural commentators of Congo-Zaire have observed in a wide spectrum of phenomena ranging from religions, architecture, the fine arts, literature, music, theology, and philosophy. Syrotinski aptly links Mudimbe's recurrent use of the term to the deconstructive nature of his work and constant attempt of 'rereading and rewriting (both Africa and the West)'.[19] A similar deconstructive operation can be observed in Romuald Hazoumè's 'masques bidon' (see the front cover of this book). 'Bidon' means 'oil canister' but also 'hoax' and indicates that Hazoumè's ironic recycling of the proverbial African mask is also meant as a critique of the postcolonial present. Reprendre is thus a notion that captures the crossovers between reading, writing, and living. Mudimbe is the *unhomely* scholar, the displaced academic who repeats, recycles, *and* transforms what cannot be quite remembered.[20] Like many other 'postcolonial' thinkers of his generation – Said, Bhabha, Spivak, and, closer to home, as it were, Mbembe and Nganang – he has experienced:

> That moment of the scattering of the people that in other times and other places, in the nations of others, becomes a time of gathering. [...] gathering in the half-life, half light of foreign tongues, or in the uncanny fluency of another's language; gathering the signs of approval and acceptance, degrees, discourses, disciplines; gathering the memories of underdevelopment, of other worlds lived retroactively; gathering the past in a ritual of revival; gathering the present.[21]

Mudimbe has lived through the downfall of a colony, experienced the slow death of a nation lured by the myths of his own apocryphal genesis but also, and more fundamentally, witnessed the gradual demise of the concept of the nation. Decolonisation, in yet another uncanny twist or return, has given way to 'Empire' (without the definite article), as this term is conceived by Michael Hardt and Antonio Negri in their eponymous essay, that is, a global space in which 'the spatial divisions of the three worlds (First, Second, and Third) have been scrambled so that we continually find the First World in the Third, the Third in the First, and the Second almost nowhere at all'.[22] The two authors suggest that the emergence of 'Empire' coincided with the collapse of European imperialism (colonial and Soviet), itself a product of 'modern sovereignty'. They argue that this type of sovereignty was predicated, an idea echoing Foucault's analysis of the modern episteme, upon a tendency to read social phenomena along an exclusive, 'Manichaean', and binary line in which races, genders, sexes, classes, 'ruler and ruled', and nationalities were ascribed rigid slots.[23] The advent of 'Empire', on the other hand, marked the development of a 'politics of difference', which 'incorporates the values and voices of the displaced, the marginalized, the exploited, and the oppressed'.[24] What is interesting here is not so much the opposition between 'modern sovereignty' and 'Empire' – it is in fact quite binary – as the argument that, 'Empire', for all its attempts to value differences, has not generated a more equitable world. The two authors contend that the passage from one form of rule to the next coincided with the deployment of global capitalism, an economic order that radically broke away with the market conditions that had prevailed until decolonisation when almighty nation-states were still regulating the world economy.[25] The decline of the sovereignty of the nation-state has therefore generated a more insidious type of centre-less sovereignty which cuts across former boundaries, bypasses the authority that was traditionally associated with them, and produces injustices – mass displacements of populations, shortages of resources and labour, genocides, and human-induced ecological cataclysms – that are as abhorrent and devastating as the catastrophes that plagued the 'modern' era.

Mudimbe, Mbembe, and Nganang have in their writings captured the articulations, fault lines, and silences implied by Hardt and Negri's historical model. Mbembe's examination of Africa, before and after *On The Postcolony*, resonates with Mudimbe's own assessment of Africa's epistemological entrapment and hope to develop the instruments of a genuine self-critique:

> There [...] arises the purely methodological question of knowing whether it is possible to offer an intelligible reading of the forms of social and political imagination in contemporary Africa solely through conceptual structures and fictional representations used precisely to deny African

societies any historical depth and to define them as radically *other*, as all that the West is not.[26]

Mbembe and Mudimbe have reflected on the transition from the colonial to the postcolonial and on the ways in which the discourses informing 'modern sovereignty' have survived and mutated to contribute to the edification of 'Empire'. Nganang has also attempted to excavate (from the past) literary voices – Soyinka, Tutuola, and Césaire – that could pre-empt cataclysms and pave the way of a future (discursive) autonomy. I am not trying to produce clear-cut oppositions between these writers but it is undeniable that 'Empire' has been until recently Nganang's main investigative terrain. His most famous novel, *Temps de Chien*, is a modern-time fable which reveals through the eyes of a dog narrator how 'Empire' is endured by the disenfranchised inhabitants of one of Yaoundé's impoverished districts. That their voices should be filtered and mediated by a dog is doubly ironic and this narrative strategy contributes to the exploration of one of the main unresolved questions posed throughout the novel: 'Où est l'homme?' [Where is man?].[27] In *Mont Plaisant*, his most recent novel, Nganang demonstrates, however, also his ability to re-examine contemporary Cameroon from the perspective of 'modern sovereignty'.[28] Bertha, the narrator, is a Cameroonian living in the United States and conducting research in her native country on the origins of Cameroonian nationalism.[29] The epigraph of the novel, a quote from Oscar Wilde, foreshadows the philosophy presiding over this research project: 'The one duty we owe to history is to rewrite it'.[30] Bertha decides indeed to bracket off Cameroonian official historiography and to save from oblivion Sultan Njoya's life before and after the Versailles Treaty (1913–33). The resurrection from the abyss of the colonial library of this significant but hitherto neglected nobleman and intellectual is Nganang's other strategy to interrogate the Cameroonian present through the excavation of its memory. In her investigation, Bertha establishes a dialogue with Sara, a ninety-year-old woman who knew the Sultan intimately. This relationship enables the researcher to reconstruct an accurate image of the Bamoun ruler, an erudite and a polyglot, who survived German, British, and French rules. The ruins of his Mont Plaisant palace, located in the deprived Nsimeyong district of Yaoundé, offer an opportunity to meditate upon contemporary Cameroon and its inability to rebuild its future upon firm cultural foundations for, as Nganang contends in an interview on *Mont Plaisant*, 'J'ai écrit pour le Cameroun qui souffre d'une stagnation historique' [I wrote for Cameroun which is suffering from historical stagnation].³¹ The forgotten palace, of which a mere few bricks have survived, constitutes also the starting point for a reflection on the invention, by Njoya himself, of a new language and alphabet as a means, in the midst of the colonial period, to overcome ethnic and linguistic fragmentation and provide an indigenous alternative to European, and Europhone, assimilation.

Beyond the theoretical detours that they choose to adopt, the dialogue between Mudimbe, Mbembe, and Nganang is predominantly inflected by this tension between the colonial and the postcolonial. Their respective tendency to privilege the one against the other, to highlight in the colonial signs of postcolonial deliverance, and to contemplate uncanny returns of the past in the present demonstrates that yesterday's exegeses and fables will continue to inform the future.

The examination of Mudimbe's writings cannot just be pursued as an end in itself. As shown in this study, V. Y. Mudimbe's thought has also been a pretext of sorts to explore various developments in African studies, and, crucially, to investigate other textual interventions beyond this loosely disciplined domain. This is not to say that his singularity can be neglected as a mere sign of a specific era. The depth of his reflection on sub-Saharan Africa relies upon a unique ability to comprehend Africa in the world, against *and* with the West and the Rest, and to tease out in the fault lines of history considered over the *longue durée* the marks of what makes us savages, *indigènes*, masters, objects ('pure' and 'abject'), subjects, bantu, women, men and, ultimately, humans. The autobiographical dimension of Mudimbe's output, finally, is also the very feature of his unhomely poetics. In the preface to *The Wretched of the Earth*, Sartre dismisses the fact that Europe 'hellenized the Asians' and invented a 'new breed' of 'Graeco-Latin Negroes'.³² Mudimbe is of course the very product of this invention which has also been at the heart of his own resourcefulness and inventiveness as an author and epistemologist:

> Postcolonialism for Mudimbe could be said to be an 'afterimage' of colonialism. An 'afterimage' is not simply what comes after the fact and it is even less a mere projection. It is a new location of possibilities where radical creativity takes effect.³³

Notes

Introduction

1 See Emmanuel Sibeud, *Une Science impériale pour l'Afrique: La construction des savoirs africanistes en France (1878–1930)* (Paris: EHESS, 'Recherches d'histoire et de sciences sociales', 2002). See also the special issue of the *African and Black Diaspora: An International Journal*, 2(2) (2009), pp. 125–269, edited by Dominic Thomas: *Museums in Postcolonial Europe* and, especially, Véronique Bragard and Stéphanie Planche, 'Museum Practice and the Belgian Colonial Past: Questionning the Memories of an Ambivalent Metropole', in Dominic Thomas (ed.), *Museums in Postcolonial Europe*, special issue of the *African and Black Diaspora: An International Journal*, 2(2) (2009), pp. 181–91.

2 Johannes Fabian, *Out of our Minds: Reason and Madness in the Exploration of Central Africa* (Berkeley: University of California Press, 2000), p. 280.

3 Ibid., p. 8.

4 Ibid., p. 274.

5 Ibid., p. 105.

6 See the book that resulted from the radio series: Neil MacGregor, *A History of the World in 100 Objects* (London: Allan Lane, 2010).

7 Reinhart Koselleck, *Futures Past: On the Semantics of Historical Time*, translated and introduced by Keith Tribe (Cambridge, Mass. and London: MIT Press, 1985), p. 77.

8 Michael Rothberg, *Multidirectional Memory: Remembering the Holocaust in the Age of Decolonization* (Stanford, Calif.: Stanford University Press, 2009).

9 Ibid., pp. 4–5.

10 See Johan Lagae, Luce Beeckmans, and Sofie Boonen, 'Decolonizing Spaces: A (Visual) Essay on Strategies of Appropriation, Transformation and Negotiation of the Colonial Built Environment in Postcolonial Congo', *HAGAR: Studies in Culture, Polity and Identities*, 9 (2) (2010), pp. 49–88.

11 Olivier de Bouveignes, *Les Anciens rois de Congo* (Namur: Grands Lacs, 1948). This study explores the development of a Central African Catholic monarchy against the background of the great discoveries in Africa and in the Americas in the late fifteenth century. See also Wyatt MacGaffey, *Modern Kongo Prophets: Religion in a Plural Society* (Bloomington: Indiana University Press, 1983).

12 See Friedrich Stenger, *White Fathers in Colonial Central Africa: A Critical Examination of V. Y. Mudimbe's Theories on Missionary Discourse in Africa* (Münster, Hamburg, and London: LIT Verlag, 2001).

13 See Anthony Giddens, *The Consequences of Modernity* (Cambridge: Polity, 1990) and Frederick Cooper, *Colonialism in Question: Theory, Knowledge, History* (Berkeley: University of California Press, 2005).

14 Mahmood Mamdani, 'The Invention of the Indigène', *London Review of Books*, 20 January 2011, pp. 31–33.

15 Rothberg, *Multidirectional Memory*, p. 3.

16 See Jean-Loup Amselle and Emmanuelle Sibeud (eds), *Maurice Delafosse: Entre orientalisme et ethnographie, l'itinéraire d'un africaniste (1870–1926)* (Paris: Maisonneuve et Larose, 1998) and also Sibeud, *Une Science impériale pour l'Afrique*.

17 I analysed this development in *La Mesure de l'autre: Afrique subsaharienne et roman ethnographique de Belgique et de France, 1918–1940* (Paris: Éditions Honoré Champion, 2007). See chap. 1, 'Savoirs ethnographiques et fictions d'empire', pp. 23–100.

18 Rothberg, *Multidirectional Memory*, p. 5.

19 See V. Y. Mudimbe, 'De la cosmologie dogon: Une méditation', *Ponti/Ponts*, 4 (2004), pp. 235–48.

20 For a relatively comprehensive list of publications in French and English (until 2003) by and on Mudimbe, see Virginia Coulon, 'Étude bibliographique de l'œuvre de V. Y. Mudimbe', in Mukala Kadima-Nzuji and Sélom Komlan Gbanou, *L'Afrique au miroir des littératures, des sciences de l'homme et de la société: Mélanges offerts à V. Y. Mudimbe* (Paris: L'Harmattan, 2003), pp. 557–89. See also 'Mukanda', the open-access electronic archive dedicated to literature from Central Africa and managed by Pierre Halen at the University of Lorraine <http://mukanda.univ-metz.fr/index.php?pg=accueil>.

21 Bernard Mouralis, *V. Y. Mudimbe ou le discours, l'écart et l'écriture* (Paris: Présence africaine, 1988).

22 Justin Bisanswa, *Conflits de mémoire: V. Y. Mudimbe et la traversée des signes* (Frankfurt: IKO-Verlag für Interkulturelle Kommunikation, 2000).

23 Jean-Christophe Kasende, *Le Roman africain face aux discours hégémoniques: Étude sur l'énonciation et l'idéologie dans l'œuvre de V. Y. Mudimbe* (Paris: L'Harmattan, 2001).

24 Kasereka Kavwariheri, *V. Y. Mudimbe et la ré-invention de l'Afrique:*

Poétique et politique de la décolonisation des sciences humaines (Amsterdam and New York: Rodopi, 2006).

25 A phrase coined by Ella Shohat and Robert Stam in *Unthinking Eurocentrism: Multiculturalism and the Media* (London: Routledge, 1994).

26 Neil Lazarus, 'Representation of Terror in V. Y. Mudimbe', in Kai Kresse (ed.), *Reading Mudimbe*, special issue on V. Y. Mudimbe, *Journal of African Cultural Studies*, 17(1) (2005), pp. 81–101 (p. 82).

27 Ibid.

28 Ibid., p. 83.

29 See, among other sources, Bernadette Cailler, 'The Impossible Ecstasy: An Analysis of V. Y. Mudimbe's *Déchirures*', *Research in African Literatures*, 24(4) (1993), pp. 15–28; Kenneth W. Harrow, *Threshold of Change in African Literature: The Emergence of a Tradition* (Portsmouth, NH and London: Heinemann/James Currey, 1994), which provides a reading of *Le Bel immonde*; Anke Granesse and Kai Kresse (eds), *Sagacious Reasoning: H. Odera Horuka in Memoriam* (Frankfurt am Main: Peter Lang, 1997), where the concept of 'Gnosis', as developed by Mudimbe, is discussed; Janice Spleth, 'The Dynamics of Power in Mudimbe's *Before the Birth of the Moon*', in Phanuel Akubueze Egejuru and Ketu H. Katrak (eds), *Nwanyibu: Womanbeing and African Literature* (Trenton, NJ: Africa World Press, 1997), pp. 69–82; Manthia Diawara, 'Reading Africa through Foucault: V. Y. Mudimbe's Reaffirmation of the Subject', in Anne McClintock, Aamir Mufti, and Ella Shohat (eds), *Dangerous Liaisons: Gender, Nation, and Postcolonial Perspectives* (Minneapolis: University of Minnesota Press, 1997), pp. 456–65; Ioan Davies, 'Negotiating African Culture: Towards a Decolonization of the Fetish', in Frederic Jameson and Masao Miyoshi (eds), *The Cultures of Globalization* (Durham NC and London: Duke University Press, 1998), pp. 125–45, in which the author analyses Mudimbe's essay 'Reprendre'; Stephen Howe, *Afrocentrism: Mythical Past and Imagined Homes* (London: Verso, 1998), where Mudimbe is mentioned in relation to negritude and ethnophilosophy; Ato Quayson, *Postcolonialism: Theory, Practice, or Process?* (Oxford: Polity, 2000); Maria Eriksson Baaz and Mai Palmberg (eds), *Same and Other: Negotiating African Identity in Cultural Production* (Stockholm: Elanders Gotab for the Nordiska Afrikainstitutet, 2001), focuses on Mudimbe's 'Reprendre'; Elias Kifon Bongmba, *African Witchcraft and Otherness: A Philosophical and Theological Critique of Intersubjective Relations* (Albany: State University of New York Press, 2001) provides a discussion on *The Invention of Africa*; George Olakunle, *Relocating Agency: Modernity and African Letters* (Albany: State University of New York Press, 2003), which partly focuses on Mudimbe's art criticism; Ali A. Mazrui, 'The Re-Invention of Africa: Edward Said, V. Y. Mudimbe, and Beyond', *Research in African Literatures*, 36(3) (2005), pp. 68–82; Andrew Apter, *Beyond Words: Discourse and Critical Agency in Africa* (University of Chicago Press, 2007), which focuses on Mudimbe and Paulin Hountondji and their examination

of ethnophilosophy; Gregg Thomas, *The Sexual Demon of Colonial Power: Pan-African Embodiment and Erotic Scheme of Empire* (Bloomington: Indiana University Press, 2007), where the author dismisses Mudimbe's reading of Martin Bernal's *Black Athena* as unconvincing and non-committal (p. 18); Pierre-Philippe Fraiture, 'V. Y. Mudimbe's "Long Nineteenth Century"', in Charles Forsdick and David Murphy (eds), *Postcolonial Thought in the French-Speaking World* (Liverpool University Press, 2009), pp. 136–46, which provides an overview of Mudimbe's work against the background of alterity politics and the legacy of nineteenth-century evolutionism; Pierre-Philippe Fraiture, 'Mudimbe's Fetish of the West and Epistemological Utopianism', *French Studies*, 63(3) (2009), pp. 308–22, in which Mudimbe's early utopian activism is explored; Jane Hiddleston, *Understanding Postcolonialism* (Stocksfield: Acumen, 2009), in which Mudimbe is compared to other 'postcolonial' thinkers such as Gayatri Chakravorty Spivak and Achille Mbembe; Aedín Ní Loingsigh, '"Alors, et l'Amérique?" Post-Independence African Travel to the United States', in *Forum for Modern Language Studies*, 45(2) (2009), pp. 129–39 and 'Agoraphobic Travel? Mudimbe's *Cheminements: Carnets de Berlin (Avril–Juin 1999)*', *Studies in Travel Writing*, 13(4) (2009), pp. 357–67, which both deal with Mudimbe's travelogs.

30 M. Diawara (ed.), *Callaloo*, special issue on V. Y. Mudimbe, 14(4) (1991), pp. 929–1035.

31 Kresse, *Reading Mudimbe*, pp. 1–129.

32 Kresse, 'Reading Mudimbe, Applying 'Mudimbe', Turning an Insider Out: Problems with the Presentation of a Swahili Poet', ibid., pp. 103–29 (p. 126).

33 Michael Syrotinski, *Singular Performances: Reinscribing the Subject in African Francophone Writing* (Charlottesville and London: University of Virginia Press, 2002).

34 On this 'oblique' Derridean dimension of Mudimbe's essays, see also Wim van Binsbergen, 'An Incomprehensible Miracle – Central African Clerical Intellectualism versus African Historic Religion: A Close Reading of Valentin Mudimbe's *Tales of Faith*', in Kresse, *Reading Mudimbe*, pp. 11–65 (p. 16 n. 6).

35 Claude Lévi-Strauss, 'History and Dialectic', in *The Savage Mind* (University of Chicago Press, 1966), pp. 245–69.

36 Chris Bongie, *Friends and Enemies: The Scribal Politics of Post/Colonial Literature* (Liverpool University Press, 2008).

Chapter One

1 Herodotus, *Snakes with Wings and Gold-Digging Ants*, translated by Aubrey de Sélincourt; translation revised by John Marincola (London: Penguin, 2007), p. 6 – extracts from *The Histories*.

2 See Vincent Bruyère, 'Mudimbe cartographe: Essai sur le corps transculturel des mots et des êtres', in Désiré K. Wa Kabwe-Segatti and Pierre Halen (eds), *Du Nègre bambara au Négropolitain: Les littératures africaines en contexte transculturel* (Metz: Centre Ecritures, 2009), pp. 31–44.

3 Gaston Bachelard, *La Poétique de l'espace* (Paris: Presses universitaires de France, 1998 [1957]).

4 Edward Said, *Orientalism: Western Conceptions of the Orient* (London: Routledge and Kegan Paul, 1995 [1978]), p. 54.

5 Bachelard, *La Poétique de l'espace*, p. 17.

6 Henri Morlighem and Tiarko Fourche, *Une Bible noire* (Paris: Max Arnold, 1973).

7 Wim van Binsbergen, 'An Incomprehensible Miracle – Central African Clerical Intellectualism versus African Historic Religion: A Close Reading of Valentin Mudimbe's *Tales of Faith*', in *Reading Mudimbe*, special issue of the *Journal of African Cultural Studies*, edited by Kai Kresse, pp. 11–65 (p. 12).

8 See Friedrich Stenger, *White Fathers in Colonial Central Africa: A Critical Examination of V. Y. Mudimbe's Theories on Missionary Discourse in Africa* (Münster, Hamburg, and London: LIT Verlag, 2001).

9 V. Y. Mudimbe and Susan Mbula Kilonzo, 'Philosophy of Religion on African Ways of Believing', in Elias Kifon Bongmba (ed.), *The Wiley-Blackwell Companion to African Religions* (Oxford: Wiley-Blackwell, 2012), pp. 41–61 (p. 42).

10 Ibid., p. 41.

11 On the educational role played by missionaries in the Congo, see Jean Pirotte, *Périodiques missionnaires belges d'expression française: Reflets de cinquante années d'évolution d'une mentalité, 1889–1940* (Louvain: Bibliothèque de l'Université, 1973); Jean Stengers, *Congo, mythes et réalités: 100 ans d'histoire* (Paris and Louvain-la-Neuve: Duculot, 1989); Isidore Ndaywel è Nziem, *Histoire générale du Congo: De l'héritage ancien à la République démocratique* (Paris and Brussels: Duculot, 1998); Michel de Schrevel, *Les Forces politiques de la décolonisation congolaise jusqu'à la veille de l'indépendance* (Louvain: Imprimerie M. and L. Symons, 1970), p. 290. See also David Van Reybrouck, *Congo, une histoire*, translated from Dutch by Isabelle Rosselin (Arles: Actes Sud, 2012).

12 Margaret T. Hodgen, *Early Anthropology in the Sixteenth and Seventeenth Centuries* (Philadelphia: University of Pennsylvania Press, 1971).

13 Emmanuel Chukwudi Eze, *On Reason: Rationality in a World of Cultural Conflict and Racism* (Durham, NC and London: Duke University Press, 2008), p. 165.

14 Elisabeth Mudimbe-Boyi, 'Testi e Immagini. La Missione del "Congo" nelle Relazioni dei Missionari Cappucini Italiani 1645–1700', unpublished thesis, Lubumbashi, 1977.

15 Christopher L. Miller, *Blank Darkness: Africanist Discourse in French* (University of Chicago Press, 1985), p. 146.

16 He translated the bible into Yoruba. On this point, see Oyèníyì Okùnoyè, ''Ewì, Yorùbá Modernity, and the Public Space', *Research in African Literatures*, 41(4) (2010), pp. 43–64 (p. 54).

17 A. J. Smet is the foremost expert on Tempels. See, among many other publications by this author, 'Placide Tempels et son œuvre publiée', *Revue Africaine de Théologie*, 1 (1977), pp. 77–128. See also Franz Bontinck (ed.), *Aux Origines de la Philosophie bantoue: La correspondance Tempels-Hulstaert (1944–1948)*, Bibliothèque du Centre d'études des religions africaines, 10 (Kinshasa: Faculté de théologie catholique, 1985).

18 Aimé Césaire, *Discours sur le colonialisme* (Paris: Présence africaine, 1950), pp. 32–33.

19 Paulin Hountondji, *African Philosophy: Myth and Reality*, translated by Henri Evans and Jonathan Rée (Bloomington: Indiana University Press, 1996 [1977]), p. 34.

20 See 'We do not claim, of course, that the Bantu are capable of formulating a philosophical treatise, complete with an adequate vocabulary. It is our job to proceed to such systematic development. It is we who will be able to tell them, in precise terms, what their inmost concept of being is', from R. P. Placide Tempels, *Bantu Philosophy*, translated by Colin King (Paris: Présence africaine, 1959), p. 25. The first French publication of the essay *La Philosophie bantoue* had been translated from Dutch by A. Rubbens (Élisabethville: Lovania, 1945) and was republished in a slightly different translation with a Preface, 'Niam M'Paya ou de la fin que dévorent les moyens', by Aloune Diop (Paris: Présence africaine, 1949).

21 On these post-First World War changes in missionary discourses, see Jean Pirotte, 'Les Armes d'une mobilisation: La littérature missionnaire de la fin du XIXe siècle à 1940', in Marc Quaghebeur, Émile Van Balberghe, et al. (eds), *Papier blanc, encre noire: Cent ans de culture francophone en Afrique centrale (Zaïre, Rwanda et Burundi)*, 2 vols. (Brussels: Édition Labor, 1992), pp. 55–103; Luc Croegaert, 'L'Action culturelle des missionnaires catholiques au Congo belge', ibid., pp. 243–69; Maurice Cheza, 'La Littérature missionnaire au Zaïre de 1945 à nos jours', ibid., pp. 381–99.

22 Wilhelm Schmidt, *Der Ursprung der Gottesidee*, 12 vols. (Münster: Aschendorff, 1926–55). There has been a long history of Urmonotheismus in European thought, notably the presence of phallic worship and fertility worship in the anti-clerical, Enlightenment imagination; histories of religion straight after the French Revolution explore in great depth original fertility/phallic/sun worships. And at the end of the nineteenth century, phallic worship became very fashionable, especially, during African explorations. So Schmidt is coming at the end of a long history on these issues – but his own angle was very different. See Whitney Davis, *Queer Beauty: Sexuality and Aesthetics from*

Winckelmann to Freud and Beyond (New York: Columbia University Press, 2010), chap. 1.

23 Johannes Fabian, 'Charisma and Cultural Change: The Case of the Jamaa Movement in Katanga (Congo Republic)', *Comparative Studies in Society and History*, 11(2) (1969), pp. 155–73 (p. 165).

24 See Edward P. Antonio, *Inculturation and Postcolonial Discourse in African Theology* (New York: Peter Lang, 2006).

25 On the way in which the missionaries used the African notion of ancestors to translate a Christian concept of God into African languages, see Paul Landau, *Popular Politics in the History of South Africa, 1400–1948* (Cambridge University Press, 2010).

26 Alexis Kagame, *La Philosophie bantu-rwandaise de l'être* (Brussels: Académie Royale des Sciences Coloniales, 1956).

27 Vincent Mulago, *La Religion traditionnelle des Bantu et leur vision du monde* (Kinshasa: Faculté de théologie catholique, 1980).

28 Fabien Eboussi-Boulaga, *La Crise du muntu: Authenticité africaine et philosophie* (Paris: Présence africaine, 1977).

29 Oscar Bimwenyi, *Discours théologique négro-Africain: Problèmes de fondements* (Paris: Présence africaine, 1981).

30 John S. Mbiti, *Concepts of God in Africa* (London: SPCK, 1970).

31 François-Marie Lufuluabo, *La Notion Luba-bantoue de l'être* (Tournai: Casterman, 1964).

32 Meinrad Hebga, *Emancipation d'églises sous-tutelle: Essai sur l'ère post-missionnaire* (Paris: Présence africaine, 1976).

33 Engelbert Mveng, *L'Afrique dans l'Église: Paroles d'un croyant* (Paris: L'Harmattan, 1986).

34 See, for example, 'Le Christianisme, une question de vie', in *OP* (pp. 58–71), where missionary work is summed up as 'réduction du "païen"' [reduction of the pagan] (p. 61); In *Idea*, he talks of the 'dangerous ethno-philosophical enterprise' of 'Placide Tempels and his disciples' (p. xiii); see also 'God's Inflections', in *TF* (pp. 1–35), in which it is argued that the early Tempels was Lévy-Bruhl's 'disciple' (p. 17).

35 Fabian, 'Charisma and Cultural Change', p. 164.

36 Ibid., p. 165.

37 On anti-colonial exegesis of the Bible in Central Africa, see, among a long list of titles, Wyatt MacGaffey, *Modern Kongo Prophets: Religion in a Plural Society* (Bloomington: Indiana University Press, 1983); Anne Mélice, 'La Désobéissance civile des Kimbanguistes et la violence coloniale au Congo Belge (1921–1959)', in *Les Temps Modernes*, 658/659 (April–July 2010), pp. 218–50; Jacques E. Gérard, *Les Fondements syncrétiques du Kitawala* (Brussels: Collection Études Africaines, 1969); Hans-Jürgen Greschat, *Kitawala: Ursprung, Ausbreitung und Religion der Watch-Tower-Bewegung in Zentralafrika* (Marburg: Elwert, 1967); Johannes Fabian, *Jamaa:*

A Charismatic Movement in Katanga (Evanston, Ill.: Northwestern University Press, 1971); Willy De Craemer, *The Jamaa and the Church: A Bantu Catholic Movement in Zaire* (Oxford: Clarendon Press, 1977).

38 According to Jean Stengers, in *Congo, mythes et réalités* (p. 194), there were, at the time of the independence of the Belgian Congo, 600 Congolese priests against only sixteen university graduates. On this, see also V. Y. Mudimbe, 'Les Intellectuels zaïrois', *Zaïre-Afrique*, 88 (1974), pp. 451–63.

39 Julien Benda, *La Trahison des clercs* (Paris: Grasset, 1927).

40 van Binsbergen, 'An Incomprehensible Miracle'.

41 V. Y. Mudimbe, *Between Tides*, translated by Stephen Becker (New York: Simon & Schuster, 1991).

42 See Bernard Mouralis, *V. Y. Mudimbe ou le discours, l'écart et l'écriture* (Paris: Présence africaine, 1988); Anthony Appiah and the pages that he dedicates to *Entre les eaux* and *L'Écart*, in his *In My Father's House: Africa and the Philosophy of Culture* (New York: Oxford University Press, 1992), pp. 152–55; Kasereka Kavwahirehi, *V. Y. Mudimbe et la ré-invention de l'Afrique: Poétique et politique de la décolonisation des sciences humaines* (Amsterdam and New York: Rodopi, 2006).

43 The novel has not been translated yet, but the journal *Callaloo*, 14(4) (1991), in a special issue dedicated to Mudimbe, offered the translation by Marjolijn de Jager, of a few pages from *Shaba Deux* (pp. 1026–32).

44 Michael Syrotinski, *Singular Performances: Reinscribing the Subject in African Francophone Writing* (Charlottesville and London: University of Virginia Press, 2002). See chap. 5, 'The Gendered Subject of Africa: Mudimbe's *Le Bel immonde* and *Shaba Deux*' (pp. 122–38).

45 Ibid., p. 129.

46 Jean-Paul Sartre, *L'Être et le néant: Essai d'ontologie phénoménologique*, corrected edn, with index by Arlette Elkaïm-Sartre (Paris: Gallimard, 2003 [1943]).

47 Jean-Paul Sartre, *Réflexions sur la question juive* (Paris: Paul Morihien, 1946).

48 Jean-Paul Sartre, 'Orphée noir', in L. S. Senghor, *Anthologie de la nouvelle poésie nègre et malgache de langue française*, Preface, 'Orphée noir', by Jean-Paul Sartre; Foreword by C.-André Julien (Paris: Presses universitaires de France, 1948), pp. ix–xliv.

49 The same technique is used in Mudimbe's third novel, *L'Écart*. On this point, see Mouralis, *V. Y. Mudimbe ou le discours* and Anthony Mangeon, 'Lumières noires, discours marrons. Indiscipline et transformations du savoir chez les écrivains noirs américains et africains; itinéraires croisés d'Alain Leroy Locke, V. Y. Mudimbe et leurs contemporains', unpublished thesis, Université de Cergy-Pontoise (France), 2004, pp. 707–08.

50 Kavwahirehi, *V. Y. Mudimbe et la ré-invention de l'Afrique*, pp. 168–78.

51 Achille Mbembe, 'The Aesthetics of Vulgarity', in *On the Postcolony* (Berkeley: University of California Press, 2001), pp. 102–41.

52 See Giorgio Agamben, *Homo Sacer: Sovereign Power and Bare Life*, translated by Daniel Heller-Roazen (Stanford, Calif.: Stanford University Press, 1998 [1995]) and Carl Schmitt, *Political Theology: Four Chapters on the Concept of Sovereignty*, translated by George Schwab (University of Chicago Press, 2005).

53 Jacques Leclercq, *Vie du Père Lebbe: Le tonnerre qui chante au loin* (Tournai: Casterman, 1955).

54 See Pirotte, *Périodiques missionnaires belges d'expression française*, p. 14.

55 Fabien Eboussi-Boulaga, *Christianity without Fetishes: An African Critique and Recapture of Christianity*, translated from French by Robert R. Barr (Maryknoll, NY: Orbis Books, 1984 [1981]).

56 For a comparative analysis of Mudimbe and Eboussi-Boulaga with regards to inculturation and adaptation theology, see Stenger, *White Fathers in Colonial Central Africa*, pp. 41–46.

57 V. Y. Mudimbe, '"Reprendre". Enunciations and Strategies in Contemporary African Arts'. First published in Susan Vogel (ed.), *Africa Explores: Twentieth-Century African Art* (New York and Munich: Center For African Art/Prestel Verlag, 1991), pp. 276–87 and subsequently expanded in *The Idea of Africa* under the same title, pp. 154–208.

58 Syrotinski, *Singular Performances*, p. 38. See also, by the same author, 'Reprendre: Mudimbe's Deconstructions', in *Deconstruction and the Postcolonial: At the Limits of Theory* (Liverpool University Press, 2007), pp. 82–97.

59 Marie-Clémentine Anuarite Nengapeta was killed in 1964 during the Simba rebellion by a Congolese officer who attempted to rape her. She was beatified by Pope John-Paul II.

60 Kasereka Kavwahirehi, in *V. Y. Mudimbe et la ré-invention de l'Afrique*, dedicates a great deal of attention to the presence of mystics and martyrs in Mudimbe's work. See, notably, pp. 132–33.

61 See Anne McClintock, Aamir Mufti, and Ella Shohat (eds), *Dangerous Liaisons: Gender, Nation and Postcolonial Perspectives* (Minneapolis: University of Minnesota Press, 1997).

62 Mabika Kalanda, *La Remise en question, base de la décolonisation mentale* (Brussels: Éditions remarques africaines, n.d. [1966]).

63 Michel de Certeau, *The Practice of Everyday Life*, translated by Steven Rendall (Berkeley: University of California Press, 1984), particularly Part III, 'Spatial Practices (pp. 91–130).

64 In 'Anthropology and Marxist Discourse' (*P&F*), he levelled a similar attack on Peter Rigby's ethnographic study *Persistent Pastoralists: Nomadic Societies in Transition* (London: Zed Books, 1985). *P&F* finishes with a chapter

in which Rigby is given the opportunity to respond to Mudimbe's critique: 'Peter Rigby's Response to "Anthropology and Marxist Discourse"' (pp. 197–203). In this piece, Rigby argues (through Johannes Fabian's concept of coevalness as developed in *Time and the Other* (see Chapter 3 of this book) that it is possible to produce an authentic cultural representation of the Ilparakuyo community and generate a '*true* dialectic between theory and practice' (p. 198) providing the anthropologist is capable of minimising the inherent inequality of the ethnographic encounter. For further discussion on this polemic, see Syrotinski's *Deconstruction and the Postcolonial: At the Limits of Theory* (Liverpool University Press, 2007) (pp. 90–97) and Lazarus's 'Representation and Terror in V. Y. Mudimbe', in Kresse, *Reading Mudimbe* (pp. 97–99). For Lazarus, Mudimbe's critique of Rigby is 'politically disenabling' (p. 98) and reductive because 'it conveys the impression that between the colonialist discourse of 'the heart of darkness' and that of Rigby, the sympathetic and competent translator-interpreter of Ilparakuyo-Maasai culture, there is, at a fundamental level, nothing to choose' (pp. 98–99). Syrotinski partly disagrees with Lazarus (and Rigby) and contends that they fail to take into account the 'deconstructive dimension of Mudimbe's work' (p. 94). He notes that Mudimbe's deliberately ambiguous use of the term representation as both 'speaking for' and 'portraying' (p. 93) is the true deconstructive (and Derridean) mark of his intervention and attempt to look beyond the 'restrictive oppositions' between 'text and life, or theory and praxis, or textual and material' (p. 95).

65 Certeau, *The Practice of Everyday Life*, p. xiii.
66 Ibid.
67 Jacques Derrida, *Writing and Difference*, translated by Alan Bass (Chicago University Press, 1978 [1967]).
68 Claude Lévi-Strauss, *La Pensée sauvage* (Paris: Plon, 1962). The translation used here is *The Savage Mind* (University of Chicago Press, 1966 [1962]).
69 *The Savage Mind*, p. 256.
70 Christopher Johnson, *Claude Lévi-Strauss: The Formative Years* (Cambridge University Press, 2003), p. 15.
71 *The Savage Mind*, p. 262.
72 Ibid., p. 256.
73 Ibid., p. 261.
74 Ibid., p. 258.
75 Ibid., p. 257.
76 Ibid.
77 Ibid.
78 Ibid., p. 249.
79 Ibid., p. 248.
80 Ibid., p. 249.
81 Ibid., p. 247.

82 See Marcello Massenzio, 'An Interview with Claude Lévi-Strauss, *Current Anthropology*, 42 (2001), pp. 419–25; Claude Lévi-Strauss (with Didier Eribon), *De Près et de loin* (Paris: Plon, 1988); Claude Lévi-Strauss, *Myth and Meaning: Cracking the Code of Culture* (New York: Schocken Books, 1995). The last was originally published in English because it comprises a series of talks that Lévi-Strauss gave in English to the Canadian Broadcasting Company (CBC).

83 Claude Lévi-Strauss, *Structural Anthropology*, vol. 1, translated by Claire Jacobson and Brooke Grundfest Schoepf (Harmondsworth: Penguin Books: 1963), p. 18.

84 See the opening sentence of Lévi-Strauss's *Tristes tropiques* (Paris: Plon, 1955).

85 On this Boasian tradition and the importance played by fieldwork in the rejuvenation of anthropology, see the classical study by James Clifford: *The Predicament of Culture: Twentieth-Century Ethnography, Literature and Art* (Cambridge, Mass. and London: Harvard University Press, 1988), p. 27.

86 Claude Lévi-Strauss, *Regarder, écouter, lire* (Paris: Plon, 1993).

87 *Tristes tropiques.*

88 Claude Lévi-Strauss, *Le Regard éloigné* (Paris: Plon, 1983).

89 *The Savage Mind*, p. 252.

90 Morlighem and Fourche, 'Introduction', in *Une Bible noire*, pp. 7–10 (p. 7).

91 Ibid., p. 9.

92 Luc de Heusch, *Le Roi ivre ou l'origine de l'État* (Paris: Gallimard, 1972). Translated as *The Drunken King or the Origin of the State* (Bloomington: Indiana University Press, 1982).

93 Luc de Heusch, 'The King comes from Elsewhere', in A. Jacobson-Widding (ed.), *Body and Space: Symbolic Models of Unity and Division in African Cosmology and Experience*, Acta Universitalis Upsaliensis, *Uppsala Studies in Cultural Anthropology*, 16 (1991), pp. 109–17.

94 Mudimbe would develop analogous ideas in V. Y. Mudimbe, 'The Idea of Luba', Afterword to M. N. Roberts and A. Roberts (eds), *Memory: Luba Art and the Making of History* (New York: Prestel and the Museum for African Art, 1996).

95 Bernard Mouralis, *Littératures africaines et antiquité: Redire le face-à-face de l'Afrique et de l'Occident* (Paris: Honoré Champion, 2011).

96 V. Y. Mudimbe, 'In the House of Libya: A Meditation', in Daniel Orrells, Gurminder K. Bhambra, and Tessa Roynon (eds), *African Athena: New Agendas* (Oxford University Press, 2011), pp. 191–209 (p. 191).

97 Martin Bernal, *Black Athena: The Afro-Asiatic Roots of Classical Civilization*, vol. 1, *The Fabrication of Ancient Greece, 1785–1995* (New Brunswick, NJ: Rutgers University Press, 1987); vol. 2, *The Archaeological and Documentary Evidence* (New Brunswick, NJ: Rutgers University Press,

1991); vol. 3, *The Linguistic Evidence* (London: Free Association Books, 2006).

98 Daniel Orrells, Gurminder K. Bhambra, and Tessa Roynon, 'Introduction' to *African Athena: New Agendas*, pp. 1–16 (p. 11).

99 See C. A. Diop, *Nations nègres et culture: De l'antiquité nègre égyptienne aux problèmes culturels de l'Afrique noire d'aujourd'hui* (Paris: Présence africaine, 1999 [1954]) in which Aesop is described as a black Egyptian (p. 398) and Diop, *Antériorité des civilisations nègres: Mythe ou vérité historique?* (Paris: Présence africaine, 1967). On Diop and his legacy, see Stephen Howe, *Afrocentrism: Mythical Past and Imagined Homes* (London: Verso, 1998).

100 These last two scholars being used in Mudimbe's 'In the House of Libya', in Orrells, Bhambra, and Roynon, *African Athena: New Agendas*.

101 Valentin Mudimbe, 'Air: Étude sémantique', thèse pour le doctorat en philosophie et lettres. Groupe Philologie romane. Présentée à la Faculté de philosophie et lettres de l'Université Catholique de Louvain, 1970.

102 V. Y. Mudimbe, *Air: Étude sémantique* (Vienna: Acta ethnologica et linguistica, 1979).

103 See Alain Rey, 'Remarques sémantiques', in *Langue Française*, 4 (1969), pp. 5–29, in which a very similar critical apparatus is used.

104 Valentin Mudimbe, 'Introduction', in 'Air. Étude sémantique', pp. 1–17.

105 Engelbert Mveng, *Les Sources grecques de l'histoire négro-africaine depuis Homère jusqu'à Strabon* (Paris: Présence africaine, 1972).

106 Théophile Obenga, *L'Afrique dans l'Antiquité: Égypte pharaonique, Afrique noire* (Paris: Présence africaine, 1973). See also, by the same author: *L'Égypte, la Grèce et l'école d'Alexandrie: Histoire interculturelle dans l'Antiquité. Aux sources égyptiennes de la philosophie grecque* (Paris: L'Harmattan, 2005).

107 With titles such as: Lorna Hardwick, *Translating Worlds, Translating Cultures* (Oxford University Press, 2000), Barbara Goff (ed.), *Classics and Colonialism* (London: Duckworth, 2005), Barbara Goff and Michael Simpson (eds), *Crossroads in the Black Aegean: Oedipus, Antigone, and Dramas of the African Diaspora* (Oxford University Press, 2007), and Emily Greenwood, *Afro-Greeks: Dialogues between Anglophone Caribbean Literature and Classics in the Twentieth Century* (Oxford University Press, 2010). On this intellectual development, see Orrells, Bhambra, and Roynon, *African Athena: New Agendas*.

108 Ngandu Pius Nkashama and V. Y. Mudimbe, 'Remarques synthétiques sur la contribution africaine à la fondation de la pensée et de la littérature latines chrétiennes', in *Mélanges offerts à Léopold Sédar Senghor: langues – littérature – histoire ancienne* (Dakar: Nouvelles éditions africaines, 1977), pp. 356–74.

109 In *L'Unité culturelle de l'Afrique noire: Domaines du patriarcat et*

du matriarcat dans l'Antiquité classique (Paris: Présence africaine, 1959), C. A. Diop draws parallels between Osiris and Dionysus (p. 163).

110 Nkashama and Mudimbe, 'Remarques synthétiques sur la contribution africaine', p. 374.

111 François Hartog, *The Mirror of Herodotus: The Representation of the Other in the Writing of History*, translated by Janet Lloyd (Berkeley and Los Angeles: University of California Press, 1988 [1980]), p. xv.

112 I will refer here to the translation into English of 'Hérodote, le menteur' ('Herodotus the Liar') by Myles O'Byrne, to be published in 2014 in Pierre-Philippe Fraiture and Daniel Orrells (eds), *A V. Y. Mudimber Reader* (Virginia University Press).

113 Paul Veyne, *Comment on écrit l'histoire: Essai d'épistémologie* (Paris: Seuil, 1971).

114 On whom François Hartog wrote a book: *Le XIXe siècle et l'histoire: Le cas Fustel de Coulanges* (Paris: Presses universitaires de France, 1988).

115 Jules Zeller, *Histoire d'Allemagne: Origines de l'Allemagne et de l'Empire germanique* (Paris: Perrin, 1872).

116 V. Y. Mudimbe, 'Héritage occidental de la conscience nègre', *Congo-Afrique*, 26 (June–July 1968), pp. 2–14.

117 This echo is purely epistemological as the two men, at this stage, did not know one another's work. For a parallel between Said and Mudimbe, see Ali A. Mazrui, 'The Re-Invention of Africa: Edward Said, V. Y. Mudimbe, and Beyond', *Research in African Literatures*, 36(3) (2005), pp. 68–82.

118 Paul Ricœur, *History and Truth*, translated by Charles A. Kelbley (Evanston, Ill.: Northwestern University Press, 1998 [1955]), pp. 25–31.

119 Ibid., pp. 25–26. Italics in the original.

120 Henri-Irénée Marrou, *De la Connaissance historique* (Paris: Seuil, 1954), p. 272.

121 Pierre Nora (ed.), *Les Lieux de mémoire* (Paris: Gallimard, 1984–92).

122 See Edward Said, *Humanism and Democratic Criticism* (New York: Columbia University Press, 2004) and his introduction to the fiftieth anniversary edition of Erich Auerbach's *Mimesis: The Representation of Reality in Western Literature*, translated from German by Willard R. Trask (Princeton, NJ: Princeton University Press, 2003 [1953]); Assia Djebar, *L'Amour, la fantasia. Roman* (Paris: J. C. Lattès, 1985) and particularly where the narrator (a double of Djebar herself) affectionately reminisces about her relationship with her father, a primary school teacher who became a *de facto* spokesperson of French assimilation.

123 R. Bjornson, 'Alienation and Disalienation', in V. Y. Mudimbe (ed.), *The Surreptitious Speech: Présence africaine and the Politics of otherness, 1947–1987* (University of Chicago Press, 1992), pp. 147–56.

124 A. Hoschild, *King Leopold's Ghost: A Story of Greed, Terror, and Heroism in Colonial Africa* (Boston, Mass.: Houghton Miffin, 1998).

Chapter Two

1 Régis Debray, *Éloge des frontières* (Paris: Gallimard, 2010), p. 33.

2 V. Y. Mudimbe, *Autour de la 'Nation': Leçons de civisme. Introduction* (Kinshasa and Lubumbashi: 'Objectifs 80', Éditions du Mont Noir, 1972).

3 Since the conquest and unification of the country by Leopold II, the Belgian King, in 1885 as a result of the Berlin Conference (1884–85), the Congo has been renamed several times: État Indépendant du Congo (1885–1908), Congo Belge (1908–60), République du Congo-Kinshasa (1960–64), République Démocratique du Congo (1964–71), République du Zaïre (1971–97), and République Démocratique du Congo (since 1997).

4 See, among others, *Présence universitaire*, *Congo-Afrique*, *Cahiers économiques et sociaux*, *Zaïre-Afrique*, *Cahiers des religions africaines*, *Recherches, pédagogie et culture*.

5 See Bob W. White, *Rumba Rules: The Politics of Dance Music in Mobutu's Zaïre* (Durham, NC: Duke University Press, 2008).

6 See the two following monographs, exclusively devoted to the development of Zairean/Congolese literatures in colonial and postcolonial times: Mukala Kadima-Nzuji, *La Littérature zaïroise de langue française (1945–1960)* (Paris: ACCT/Karthala, 1984) and Silvia Riva, *Nouvelle histoire de la littérature du Congo-Kinshasa*, translated by Colin Fort (Paris: L'Harmattan, 2006 [2000]). See also Bernard Mouralis, *V. Y. Mudimbe ou le discours, l'écart et l'écriture* (Paris: Présence africaine, 1988), which provides a succinct overview of the cultural and literary context of Congo-Zaire from the colonial to the post-colonial period.

7 A point also confirmed to me by the author himself.

8 In *Rumba Rules* (p. 68), Bob White establishes a close link between censorship and the emergence of state-orchestrated cultural policy in Congo-Zaire. See also, Kasereka Kavwahirehi, *V. Y. Mudimbe et la ré-invention de l'Afrique: Poétique et politique de la décolonisation des sciences humaines* (Amsterdam and New York: Rodopi, 2006), pp. 127–28.

9 For a fictionalisation of censorship, see Georges Ngal, *Giambatista Viko ou le viol du discours africain* (Paris: Hatier, 1975).

10 Johannes Fabian, *Time and the Other: How Anthropology Makes its Objects* (New York: Columbia University Press, 2002 [1983]).

11 Aimé Césaire, *Une Saison au Congo* (Paris: Présence africaine, 1966). The play was significantly performed for the first time in Brussels at the Théâtre Vivant in March 1967. For a reading of the play against the backdrop of Césaire's other dramas, see J. Conteh-Morgan, *Theatre and Drama in Francophone Africa: A Critical Introduction* (Cambridge University Press, 1994).

12 See also Sylvain Bemba's novel *Léopolis* (Paris: Hatier, 1986). On the representation of political violence in Central Africa (and especially in Sony

Labou Tansi's works), see Dominic Thomas, *Nation-Building, Propaganda, and Literature in Francophone Africa* (Bloomington and Indianapolis: Indiana University Press, 2002), 'Performing Violence and Power' (pp. 71–85).

13 Joseph Kasa-Vubu was the first president of the République Démocratique du Congo (Democratic Republic of Congo) when the Belgian colony became independent on 30 June 1960. He remained in office until the military *coup* of 24 November 1965, a date which marks the end of the First Republic and the beginning of the Second Republic.

14 Cléophas Kamitatu-Massamba, *La Grande mystification du Congo-Kinshasa: Les Crimes de Mobutu* (Paris: François Maspero, 1971).

15 Jean-Luc Nancy, *La Communauté désœuvrée* (Paris: Christian Bourgois, 1986). The translation used here is *The Inoperative Community*, translated by Peter Connor, Lisa Garbus, Michael Holland, and Simona Sawhney (Minneapolis and Oxford: University of Minnesota Press, 1991).

16 Isidore Ndaywel è Nziem, *Histoire générale du Congo: De l'héritage ancien à la République démocratique* (Paris and Brussels: Duculot, 1998), p. 648.

17 Ibid., p. 649.
18 Ibid., p. 684.
19 Ibid., p. 675.
20 Ibid.
21 Ibid.
22 Ibid., p. 649.
23 Ibid., p. 675.

24 See Jean-Claude Kangomba, 'Mobutisme et mobutistes', *Congo-Meuse: Figures et paradoxes de l'histoire au Burundi, au Congo et au Rwanda*, 5 (2002), pp. 591–628 (595–96).

25 On this hugely influential figure, see Ludo Martens, *Pierre Mulélé ou la seconde mort de Lumumba* (Brussels: EPO, 1985) and *Une Femme du Congo* (Brussels: EPO, 1991).

26 Ndaywel è Nziem, *Histoire générale du Congo*, p. 671.

27 Ernest Wamba Dia Wamba, 'Struggles for the "Second Independence" in Congo-Kinshasa ', *UTAFITI*, 9(1) (1987), pp. 31–50.

28 Ndaywel è Nziem, *Histoire générale du Congo*, p. 628.

29 'The Congo: Death of a Rebel', *Time*, 18 October 1968 <www.time.com/time/magazine/article/0,9171,902443,00.html> (accessed 19 October 2010).

30 Benoît Verhaegen *Rébellions au Congo*, 2 vols (Brussels: CRISP, 1966).

31 As indicated by the author during a seminar held at the University of Warwick in November 2009.

32 See Bogumil Jewsiewicki, 'The Archaeology of Invention: Mudimbe and Postcolonialism', translated by François Manchuelle, in Manthia Diawara (ed.), *Callaloo*, special issue on V. Y. Mudimbe, 14(4) (1991), pp. 961–68 (p. 964).

33 V. Y. Mudimbe (ed.), *La Dépendance de l'Afrique et les moyens d'y remédier* (Paris: Berger Levrault, 1980).

34 V. Y. Mudimbe, 'La Culture', in Jacques Vanderlinden, with André Huybrechts, V. Y. Mudimbe, Leo Peeters, Daniel Van der Steen, and Benoît Verhaegen (eds), *Du Congo au Zaïre, 1960–1980: Essai de bilan* (Brussels: CRISP, 1980), pp. 310–98 (p. 331).

35 Ndaywel è Nziem, *Histoire générale du Congo*, p. 667.

36 H. Molongo Kalonda-Ba-Mpeta, *De la marginalisation à la nationalisation: un parcours authentique. Dictionnaire de littérature congolaise de langue française* (Lubumbashi: Celtram, 2009), pp. 31 and 113.

37 Kutumbagana Kangafu, *Discours sur l'authenticité: Essai sur la problématique idéologique du 'recours à l'authenticité'* (Kinshasa: Presses africaines, 1973).

38 Molongo Kalonda-Ba-Mpeta, *De la marginalisation à la nationalisation*, p. 31.

39 Kasereka Kavwariheri, *V. Y. Mudimbe et la ré-invention de l'Afrique: Poétique et politique de la décolonisation des sciences humaines* (Amsterdam and New York: Rodopi, 2006), p. 126.

40 The other texts referred to in the parentheses are by Pierre M'Buze-Nsomi Lobwanabi: *Révolution et humanisme: Essais* (Kinshasa: Presses africaines, 1974) and *Aux sources d'une révolution* (Kinshasa: Presses africaines, 1977).

41 Kangafu, *Discours sur l'authenticité*, p. 17.

42 L.-V. Thomas, *Le Socialisme et l'Afrique*, 2 vols. (Paris: Le Livre africain, 1966).

43 Kangafu, *Discours sur l'authenticité*, p. 25.

44 Ibid., p. 39.

45 Ibid., p. 41.

46 Karl Marx and Friedrich Engels, *The German Ideology*, in *Collected Works* (London: Lawrence and Wishart, 1976 [1845–7]).

47 Ibid., p. 59.

48 Ibid., p. 36.

49 Celia Britton, *The Sense of Community in French Caribbean Fiction* (Liverpool University Press, 2008). Nancy has also been used in other studies focusing on postcolonial literary materials. See Jane Hiddleston, 'The Specific Plurality of Assia Djebar', *French Studies*, 58(3) (2004), pp. 371–84, in which it is argued that Djebar's work offers a dialectics between the specific, the singular, and the plural; Peter Hallward, *Absolutely Postcolonial: Writing between the Singular and the Specific* (Manchester University Press, 2001), a book upon which Britton and Hiddleston partly draw in their analyses.

50 Britton, *The Sense of Community*, p. 4.

51 Nancy, *The Inoperative Community*, p. 45.

52 Ibid., p. 3.

53 Ibid., p. 9.

54 Ibid., p. 12.
55 Ibid., p. 10.
56 Ibid., p. 11.
57 Ibid., p. 48.
58 Ibid., p. 50.
59 Jean-Luc Nancy, *La Communauté désœuvrée* (Paris: Christian Bourgois Éditeur, 1986). The version used here is the 'Nouvelle édition revue et augmentée' (Paris: Christian Bourgois Éditeur, 1999), p. 117.
60 Nancy, *The Inoperative Community*, p. 46.
61 Ibid., p. 46.
62 Nancy uses the unusual adjective 'communiel'; he talks, for instance, of 'hantise communielle', in *La Communauté désœuvrée*, p. 63, translated in the English version as 'communal obsession' and 'haunting experience of [...] communality' (p. 25). 'Tissu communiel' (p. 75) is translated as 'communal fabric' (p. 30).
63 Nancy, *The Inoperative Community*, p. 63.
64 Ibid., p. 3.
65 Ibid., p. 4.
66 Ibid., p. 78.
67 Ibid., p. 26.
68 Ibid., p. 75.
69 Ibid., p. 80.
70 Ibid., p. 71.
71 Kangafu, *Discours sur l'authenticité*, p. 9.
72 Ibid.
73 Ibid., pp. 25–28.
74 Ibid., p. 26.
75 Ibid., p. 20.
76 Mobutu Sese Seko, *Paroles du Président* (Kinshasa: Éditions du Léopard, 1968). This small-sized book, modelled after Chairman Mao's *Little Red Book*, is a compilation of short extracts from speeches delivered by Mobutu between 1965 and 1968.
77 Kangafu, *Discours sur l'authenticité*, p. 27.
78 Ibid., p. 30.
79 Ibid., p. 47.
80 Ibid., p. 51.
81 Nancy, *The Inopertative Community*, p. 48.
82 Kangafu, *Discours sur l'authenticité*, p. 51.
83 Ibid., p. 53.
84 Stanislas Adotevi, *Négritude et négrologues*, Collection '10–18' (Paris: Union générale d'éditions, 1972).
85 Marcien Towa, *L. S. Senghor: Négritude ou servitude?* (Yaoundé: Clé, 1972).

86 Jean-Marie Abanda Ndengue, *De la négritude au négrisme: Essais polyphoniques* (Yaoundé: Clé, 1970).
87 Njoh-Mouelle Ebénézer, *Jalons* (Yaoundé: Clé, 1970).
88 'Aux sources des idéologies africaines' (chap. 4), pp. 43–59. This chapter is a revised version of an article published four years before: V. Y. Mudimbe, 'Héritage occidental et conscience nègre', *Congo-Afrique*, 26 (1968), pp. 2–14.
89 Kangafu, *Discours sur l'authenticité*, p. 53.
90 Ibid., p. 54.
91 Ibid., p. 55.
92 Ibid., p. 9.
93 Ibid., p. 32.
94 Ibid., p. 56.
95 Ibid. pp. 13–14.
96 Ibid., p. 13.
97 Ibid., p. 14.
98 Édouard Glissant, *Poétique de la Relation* (Paris: Gallimard, 1990).
99 Kangafu, *Discours sur l'authenticité*, p. 14.
100 Fabian, *Time and its Other*, p. 150.
101 Ibid., p. 46.
102 Ibid.
103 Ibid., p. 47.
104 Ibid., p. 156.
105 Kangafu, *Discours sur l'authenticité*, pp. 50–51.
106 Cited from Mobutu Sese Seko, *Paroles du Président*.
107 Kangafu, *Discours sur l'authenticité*, p. 57.
108 On this role played by the city, see the special issue of *Études Littéraires Africaines*, 27 (2009), edited by Pierre Halen, Maëline Le Lay, and Kabuya Rancy. See also Bogumil Jewsiewicki, D. Dibwe dia Mwembu, and R. Giordano (eds), *Lubumbashi 1910–2010: Mémoire d'une ville industrielle* (Paris: L'Harmattan, 2010).
109 On this oppressive climate of university life in Zaire during the 1970s, see P. Nkashama, *Le Pacte de sang. Roman* (Paris: L'Harmattan, 1984).
110 See Thierry Michel's documentary film, *Mobutu, roi du Zaïre* (1999).
111 Ndaywel è Nziem, *Histoire générale du Congo*, pp. 727–38.
112 Kangafu, *Discours sur l'authenticité*, p. 58.
113 See, for example, Gaston-Denys Périer's *Petite histoire des lettres coloniales de Belgique* (Brussels: Office de Publicité, 1942) in which 'colonialisme' is said to be a 'nouvel humanisme', p. 5. In *L'Idée coloniale en France de 1871 à 1962* (Paris: Éditions de la Table ronde, 1972), Raoul Girardet examines in a chapter entitled 'A la recherche d'un humanisme colonial' (pp. 175–90) the attempt, on the part of French colonial figures such as Albert Sarraut, Maurice Delafosse, and Robert Delavignette, to create the conditions for a colonial humanism.

114 Louis Althusser, *For Marx*, translated by Ben Brewster (London and New York: Verso, 1990 [1965]), p. 227. My emphasis.

115 See his soon to be published new monograph, *On African Fault Lines: Meditations on Alterity Politics*.

116 Nancy, *The Inoperative Community*, p. 80.

117 Ibid., pp. 80–81. The translator explains in brackets the ambiguity of the verb 'achever' that Nancy uses in the original (translated here as 'bring to completion').

118 Nancy, *La Communauté désœuvrée*, p. 198.

119 Ibid., p. 87.

120 Ibid., p. 35.

121 See, notably, 'Le Miroir des sciences humaines: remarques sur la signification de quelques leçons d'organisation' (*AF*, 123–48).

122 V. Y. Mudimbe, 'La Culture', in Jacques Vanderlinden, et al. (eds), *Du Congo au Zaïre, 1960–1980: Essai de bilan* (Brussels: CRISP, 1980), pp. 310–98 (p. 327).

Chapter Three

1 Philip Mitchell (late Governor of Kenya), article in *Africa*, vol. 3, no. 2 (April 1930), p. 217, cited by Bernard Porter in 'Wild Enthusiasts', *London Review of Books*, 10 May 2012, pp. 21–22.

2 Chinweizu, *The West and the Rest of Us: White Predators, Black Slavers, and the African Elite* (New York and Lagos: Random House/Nok Publishers, 1978).

3 Marshall Sahlins, *Culture and Practical Reason* (University of Chicago Press, 1976).

4 Jacques Lacan, *Le Séminaire de Jacques Lacan*, vol. 11, *Les quatre concepts fondamentaux de la psychanalyse, 1964*, edited by Jacques-Alain Miller (Paris: Seuil, 1973). See chap. 16, 'Le Sujet et l'Autre: l'Aliénation', pp. 185–96 and chap. 17, 'Le Sujet et l'Autre (II): l'Aphanisis', pp. 197–208. See also the version in English: *The Four Fundamental Concepts of Psychoanalysis*, edited by Jacques-Alain Miller, translated from French by Alan Sheridan (London: Karnac, 2004).

5 Lacan, *Les quatre concepts*, pp. 191–92.

6 Ibid., p. 193.

7 Roberto Harari, *Lacan's Four Fundamental Concepts of Psychoanalysis: An Introduction*, translated by Judith Filc (New York, Other Press, 2004), p. 257.

8 Lacan, *Les quatre concepts*, p. 194.

9 On this aspect of Mudimbe's thought, see Justin K. Bisanswa, 'V. Y. Mudimbe: Réflexion sur les sciences humaines et sociales en Afrique', *Cahiers d'Études Africaines*, 160 (2000), pp. 705–22.

10 On this tendency in other prominent postcolonial critics such as Edward Said, Chandra Mohanty, and Dipesh Chakrabarty, see Neil Lazarus, 'The Fetish of the West in Postcolonial Theory', in C. Bartolovich and Neil Lazarus (eds), *Marxism, Modernity and Postcolonial Studies* (Cambridge University Press, 2002), pp. 43–64.

11 Aimé Césaire, *Lettre à Maurice Thorez* (Paris: Présence africaine, 1956).

12 Notably in Kwame Nkrumah, *I Speak of Freedom: A Satement of African Ideology* (London: Heinemann, 1961) and *Consciencism: Philosophy and Ideology for Decolonization and Development with Particular Reference to the African Revolution* (London: Heinemann, 1964).

13 Patrice Nganang, *Manifeste d'une nouvelle littérature africaine: Pour une écriture préemptive* (Paris: Éditions Homnisphères, 2007), pp. 198–232.

14 V. Y. Mudimbe, *On African Fault Lines: Meditation on Alterity Politics* (Scottsville, South Africa: University of KwaZulu-Natal Press, 2013).

15 On the meaning of this metaphor, see Thomas Mpoyi-Buata, 'V. Y. Mudimbe ou le rêve du promontoir et le blocage dans l'ascenseur sur *L'Ecart'*, *Peuples noirs peuples africains*, 33(6) (1983), pp. 103–21.

16 As he told me during one of our meetings at the University of Warwick in November 2009.

17 Noureddine Lamouchi, *Jean-Paul Sartre et le Tiers Monde: Rhétorique d'un discours anticolonialiste* (Paris: L'Harmattan, 1996), p. 171. On this tension between ethics and politics, see also Christina Howells, *Sartre: The Necessity of Freedom* (Cambridge University Press, 1988).

18 Lamouchi, *Jean-Paul Sartre et le Tiers Monde*. See chap. 1, 'La découverte de l'histoire', pp. 29–36.

19 Jean-Paul Sartre, *What is Literature?*, translated by Bernard Fretchman (London; New York: Routledge, 2007 [1948]), p. 13.

20 Jean-Paul Sartre, 'Preface' to Frantz Fanon's *The Wretched of the Earth*, translated by Constance Farrington (London: Penguin Books, 2001 [1961]), p. 19.

21 See Jean-Paul Sartre's 'Le Colonialisme est un système', a speech that he delivered on 27 January 1956 at a rally convened at the Salle Wagram by the 'Comité d'Action des Intellectuels contre la Poursuite de la Guerre en Afrique du Nord'. First published in *Les Temps Modernes*, 123 (March–April 1956), pp. 1371–86 and subsequently reproduced in *Situations V* (Paris: Gallimard, 1964). On this speech and its genesis, see Todd Shepard, *The Invention of Decolonization: The Algerian War and the Remaking of France* (Ithaca, NY: Cornell University Press, 2006), pp. 63–68.

22 *La Pensée politique de Patrice Lumumba*, a volume of speeches by Lumumba collected and presented by Jean van Lierde, with a preface by Jean-Paul Sartre, pp. i–xlv (Paris: Présence africaine, 1963). The Preface was

later published as 'La Pensée politique de Patrice Lumumba' in *Présence africaine*, 47 (July–September 1963), pp. 18–58 and reprinted under the same title in *Situations V*.

23 See the translation of the essay to which I shall refer here: Jean-Paul Sartre, *Portrait of the Anti-Semite*, translated by Erik de Mauny (London: Secker and Warburg/Lindsay Drummond, 1948 [1946]). There is also a more recent translation of this text: *Anti-Semite and Jew: An Exploration of the Etiology of Hate*, translated by George J. Becker (New York: Schocken Books, 1995 [1946]). On this essay, its reception, and posterity, see Jonathan Judaken, *Jean-Paul Sartre and the Jewish Question: Anti-antisemitism and the Politics of the French Intellectual* (Lincoln and London: University of Nebraska Press, 2006).

24 See Jean-Paul Sartre, 'Le Noir et le Blanc aux États-Unis', *Combats*, 16 June 1949.

25 See T. C. Anderson, *Sartre's Two Ethics: from Authenticity to Integral Humanity* (Chicago, Ill.: Open Court, 1999).

26 See Patrick Williams, 'Roads to Freedom: Jean-Paul Sartre and Anti-colonialism', in Charles Forsdick and David Murphy (eds), *Postcolonial Thought in the French-Speaking World* (Liverpool University Press, 2009), pp. 147–56 (p. 149).

27 Sartre's indictment of anti-Semitism provides also an in-depth examination of the ways in which Jewish people in France have responded to their attackers. Although this point will not be developed here, it is worth noting that Sartre's line of argument with regards to the French Republic's tendency to ignore, in the name of universalist principles, ethnic, religious, and racial differences is still very current and echoes recent statements on this issue by Achille Mbembe: 'La République et l'impensé de la "race"', in Nicolas Bancel, Pascal Blanchard, and Sandrine Lemaire (eds), *La Fracture coloniale: La société française au prisme de son héritage colonial* (Paris: La Découverte, 2005), pp. 143–58; Didier Fassin and Eric Fassin, *De la Question sociale à la question raciale? Représenter la société française* (Paris: La Découverte, 2006); and Olivier Le Cour Grandmaison, *La République Impériale. Politique et racisme d'État* (Paris: Fayard, 2009).

28 Sartre, *Portrait of the Anti-Semite*, p. 115.

29 Ibid., p. 20.

30 Ibid., p. 22.

31 Here the translator is right to prefer this term to 'commitment' to translate the French 'engagement', Sartre, *Réflexions sur la question juive*, p. 12.

32 Sartre, *Portrait of the Anti-Semite*, p. 8.

33 Ibid., p. 12.

34 Ibid., p. 22.

35 Ibid., p. 44.

36 Ibid., p. 15.

37 Jean-Paul Sartre, *L'Être et le néant: Essai d'ontologie phénoménologique*, corrected edn, with index by Arlette Elkaïm-Sartre (Paris: Gallimard, 2003 [1943]). See 'Husserl, Hegel, Heidegger', pp. 271–91 and 'Le Regard', pp. 292–341. This question of the look is also theorised in Sartre's 'Réponse à Claude Lefort', *Les Temps Modernes*, 89 (April 1953), pp. 1571–629, reprinted in *Situations VII* (Paris: Gallimard, 1965), pp. 7–93.

38 Sartre, *Portrait of the Anti-Semite*, p. 66. My emphasis.

39 It is a well-known fact that *Réflexions sur la question juive* is one of Fanon's main inspirations for *Peau noire, masques blancs* (Paris: Seuil, 1952) and particularly for chap. 4, 'Du prétendu complexe de dépendance du colonisé'.

40 Edward Said, *Orientalism: Western Conceptions of the Orient* (London: Routledge and Kegan Paul, 1995 [1978]), p. 22.

41 Sartre, *Réflexions sur la question juive*, p. 194. This phrase was strangely left out of the English translation.

42 Anderson, *Sartre's Two Ethics: from Authenticity to Integral Humanity*, p. 118.

43 Régis Debray, *Révolution dans la révolution? Lutte armée et lutte politique en Amérique latine* (Paris: Maspero, 1967), pp. 13–44.

44 Jean-Paul Sartre, *Critique de la raison dialectique*, précédé de *Questions de méthode* (Paris: Gallimard, 1960).

45 Lamouchi, *Jean-Paul Sartre et le Tiers Monde*, pp. 112–14.

46 Jean-Paul Sartre, *Critique of Dialectical Reason*, vol. 1, *Theory of Practical Ensembles*, translated by Alan Sheridan-Smith (London: NLB, 1976 [1960]), p. 35.

47 See, among many others, Jacques Berque, *Dépossession du monde* (Paris: Seuil, 1964) and *L'Orient second* (Paris: Gallimard, 1970); Michèle Duchet, *Anthropologie et histoire au siècle des lumières: Buffon, Voltaire, Rousseau, Helvétius, Diderot* (Paris: Maspero, 1971); Jean Duvignaud, *Le Langage perdu: Essai sur la différence anthropologique* (Paris: Presses universitaires de France, 1973); Robert Jaulin, *La Paix blanche: Introduction à l'ethnocide* (Paris: Seuil, 1970); Gérard Leclerc, *Anthropologie et colonialisme: Essai sur l'histoire de l'Africanisme* (Paris: Fayard, 1972).

48 Robert Young, *White Mythologies: Writing History and the West* (London and New York: Routledge, 1990), pp. 28–47.

49 Johannes Fabian, 'Preface to the Reprint Edition', *Time and the Other: How Anthropology Makes its Objects* (New York: Columbia University Press, 2002 [1983]), pp. xxxv–xxxvii (p. xxxv).

50 Alongside books such as *Jamaa: A Charismatic Movement in Katanga* (Evanston, Ill.: Northwestern University Press, 1971) and *Power and Performance: Ethnographic Explorations through Proverbial Wisdom and Theater in Shaba, Zaire* (Madison and London: University of Wisconsin Press,

1990), which were informed by ethnographic work in Katanga. He also wrote studies of a more meta-discursive nature such as, among others, *Language and Colonial Power: The Appropriation of Swahili in the Former Belgian Congo* (Cambridge University Press, 1986) – the 1991 version (published by the University of California, Berkeley) is prefaced by Edward Said – and *Out of our Minds*, already mentioned in the Introduction to this book.

51 See Johannes Fabian, 'Preface and Acknowledgments', pp. xxxix–xlv (p. xliv) but also Anthony Mangeon, 'La Gnose africaine de V. Y. Mudimbe', in Justin K. Bisanswa (ed.), *Entre Inscriptions et Prescriptions: V. Y. Mudimbe et l'engendrement de la parole* (Paris: Champion, 2013), pp. 47–56; and, in the same collection of essays, V. Y. Mudimbe, 'Au nom de la gratitude, une méditation', pp. 395–441.

52 Fabian, *Time and the Other*, p. 17.
53 Ibid.
54 Ibid., p. 23.
55 Ibid.
56 Michel Foucault, Foreword to the English Edition, in *The Order of Things: An Archaeology of the Human Sciences* (London: Tavistock Publications, 1970 [1966], pp. ix–xiv (p. xiv).
57 See Michel Foucault, *L'Ordre du discours: Leçon inaugurale au Collège de France prononcée le 2 décembre 1970* (Paris: Gallimard, 1971), pp. 74–75.
58 Paul Ricœur, *Le Conflit des interprétations: Essais d'herméneutique* (Paris: Seuil, 1969). See the translation: Ricœur, *The Conflict of Interpretations: Essays in Hermeneutics* (London: Continuum, 2004), p. 49.
59 Ricœur, *The Conflict of Interpretations*, p. 49.
60 Ibid., p. 33.
61 Ibid., p. 32.
62 V. Y. Mudimbe, 'Anthropology and Marxist Discourse', *P&F*, 166–91.
63 Previously published as 'I as an Other: Sartre and Lévi-Strauss or an (Im)possible Dialogue on the Cogito', *American Journal of Semiotics*, 6(1) (1988–89), pp. 57–68.
64 See Christina Howells, in *The Cambridge Companion to Sartre* (Cambridge University Press, 1992): 'Sartre's constant tussle with the paradoxes endemic in the subject and the complexities of his evolving views might well have been of interest to those other philosophers who wished, in their various different ways, to deconstruct the classical humanist subject. But the polarization of French intellectual life led to a very different situation, in which Sartre's views were disregarded or dismissed by defiantly iconoclastic structuralists. This drove Sartre, in turn, to make polemical statements, at least in interviews, opposing Structuralism more strongly than his own philosophical positions should properly have allowed' (p. 342). See also, Young, *White Mythologies*, p. 37.
65 Michael Syrotinski, *Singular Performances: Reinscribing the Subject*

in *African Francophone Writing* (Charlottesville and London: University of Virginia Press, 2002), p. 6.

66 Fabian, *Time and the Other*, p. 57.
67 Ibid., p. 54
68 Ibid., p. 67.
69 Ibid.
70 Ibid., p. 86.
71 Ibid. p. 114.
72 Ibid., p. 115, cited from W. J. Ong's *Ramus: Method and the Decay of Dialogue* (Cambridge, Mass.: Harvard University Press, 1958).
73 Fabian, *Time and the Other*, p. 114.
74 Ibid., p. 121. The area of colonial and exotic exhibitions has generated a great deal of scholarly responses. See, for instance, Nicolas Bancel, et al. (eds), *Human Zoos: Science and Spectacle in the Age of Empires*, translations by Teresa Bridgeman (Liverpool University Press, 2008 [2002]).
75 Fabian, *Time and the Other*, p. 122.
76 Ibid., p. 52.
77 See Boris Wiseman's 'Structure and Sensation', in Boris Wiseman (ed.), *The Cambridge Companion to Lévi-Strauss* (Cambridge University Press, 2009), pp. 296–314 (p. 305).
78 Sartre, 'Orphée noir', p. ix.
79 As a school of thoughts, 'histoire immédiate' emerged in the 1950s. Until then, historical research focused chiefly on the distant past and it was generally accepted that a substantial chronological gap of at least three or four decades was needed between the historian's present and the studied historical period. In this respect, it is important to mention the pioneering article by René Rémond, 'Plaidoyer pour une histoire délaissée: La fin de la IIIe République', in *Revue française de science politique*, 2(7) (1957), pp. 253–70. In this article, Rémond was advocating the study of the end of the Third Republic, a period which, in his view, had been unduly neglected by contemporary historical research. At the beginning of the 1960s, the publisher Le Seuil created, under the editorship of the leftist foreign affairs journalist Jean Lacouture, a 'Histoire immédiate' series, which has until today explored contemporary history and specific cultural phenomena in France and elsewhere in the (postcolonial) world. See in this series: Claude Wauthier, *L'Afrique des Africains: Inventaire de la négritude* (Paris: Seuil, 1964); Norodom Sihanouk, *L'Indochine vue de Pékin: Entretiens avec Jean Lacouture* (Paris: Seuil, 1970); Alain Touraine, *Le Mouvement de mai ou le communisme utopique* (Paris: Seuil, 1968); Régis Debray, *La Guérilla du Che* (Paris: Seuil, 1974).
80 Catherine Coquery-Vidrovitch and Bogumil Jewsiewicki, 'Africanist Historiography in France and Belgium: Traditions and Trends', in Bogumil Jewsiewicki and David Newbury (eds), *African Historiographies: What History for Which Africa?* (London: Sage Publications, 1986), pp. 139–50 (p. 139).

81 See James Clifford: *The Predicament of Culture: Twentieth-Century Ethnography, Literature and Art* (Cambridge, Mass. and London: Harvard University Press, 1988), p. 26.

82 See Coquery-Vidrovitch and Jewsiewicki, 'Africanist Historiography in France and Belgium'.

83 Benoît Verhaegen, 'The Method of "Histoire Immédiate": Its Application to Africa', in Jewsiewicki and Newbury, *African Historiographies*, pp. 236–48 (p. 246). See also Benoît Verhaegen, in 'Méthode et problème de l'histoire immédiate', *Cahiers économiques et sociaux*, 8(3) (1970), pp. 471–86.

84 For a personal account on the circumstances and conditions behind the development of 'histoire immédiate in the Congo', see Laurent Monnier, '"Immediate History": Remembering the Golden Age of Research in Political Science at the University of Kinshasa', in Elisabeth Mudimbe-Boyi (ed.), *Remembering Africa* (Portsmouth, NH: Heinemann, 2002), pp. 283–301. Monnier is also the author of a 'histoire immediate'-inflected monograph published in as series whose Mudimbe was the general editor: *Ethnie et intégration régionale au Congo: Le Kongo central, 1962–1965* (Paris: EDICEF, 1971).

85 C. Coquery-Vidrovitch and Bogumil Jewsiewicki, 'Africanist Historiography in France and Belgium: Traditions and Trends', in Jewsiewicki and Newbury, *African Historiographies*, p. 141.

86 See, among many other titles, Benoît Verhaegen, *ABAKO (Association des Bakongo): 1950–1960; documents* (Brussels: Centre de Recherche et d'information socio-politiques, 1962); *Rébellions au Congo*, 2 vols (Brussels: CRISP, 1966); *La Décolonisation au Maniema (1958–1859)* (Brussels: Centre de Recherche et d'information socio-politiques, 1970); *Le Premier semestre de 1960* (Brussels: Centre de Recherche et d'information socio-politiques, 1970); Benoît Verhaegen and Herbert F. Weiss (eds), *Les Rébellions dans l'est du Zaïre (1964–1967)* (Brussels: Centre d'étude et de documentation africaines, 1997); Jean Tshonda Omasombo and Benoît Verhaegen, *Patrice Lumumba: Acteur politique: de la prison aux portes du pouvoir, juillet 1956–février 1960* (Paris and Tervuren: L'Harmattan, Musée royal de l'Afrique centrale, 2005).

87 Benoît Verhaegen, 'The Method of "Histoire Immédiate": Its Application to Africa', in Jewsiewicki and Newbury, *African Historiographies*, p. 236.

88 Ibid., p. 238.

89 Ibid.

90 Monnier, '"Immediate History"', p. 284.

91 On this dependency and inability to jettison Franco-French Higher Education models, see C. Coquery-Vidrovitch and Bogumil Jewsiewicki, 'Africanist Historiography in France and Belgium', in Jewsiewicki and Newbury, *African Historiographies*, p. 150.

92 Verhaegen, 'The Method of "Histoire Immédiate"', p. 237.

93 Ibid., p. 238.
94 Ibid., p. 242.
95 Ibid., p. 242.
96 Ibid., p. 242.
97 Ibid. p. 238.
98 Fabian, *Time and the Other*, p. 151.
99 See Monnier, '"Immediate History"', p. 287.
100 See D. A. Madolo, *African Philosophy in Search of Identity* (Bloomington and Indianapolis and Edinburgh: Indiana University Press/Edinburgh University Press, 1994).
101 Verhaegen, 'The Method of "Histoire Immédiate"', p. 238.
102 Sartre, *Critique of Dialectical Reason*, vol. 1, p. 69.
103 In *V. Y. Mudimbe et la ré-invention de l'Afrique*, Kasereka Kavwahirehi mentions this significant passage from one of Sartre's interviews: 'Je ne conteste pas l'existence des structures, ni la nécessité d'en analyser le mécanisme. Mais la structure n'est pour moi qu'un moment du pratico-inerte [...]. Toute création humaine a son domaine de passivité: cela ne signifie pas qu'elle soit de part en part subie [...]. L'homme est pour moi le produit de la structure, mais pour autant qu'il la dépasse' [I am not questioning the existence of structures nor the need to analyse their mechanism. But the structure is for me merely a moment of the practico-inert [...]. Every human creation has a dimension of passivity: this does not imply complete subjugation. Man is for me the product of the structure providing that he overcomes it] (*V. Y. Mudimbe et la ré-invention de l'Afrique: Poétique et politique de la décolonisation des sciences humaines* (Amsterdam and New York: Rodopi, 2006), p. 252).
104 Frantz Fanon, *Black Skins, White Masks*, Forewords to the 2008 edition by Ziauddin Sardar; Forewords to the 1986 edition by Homi K. Bhabha; translated by Charles Lam Markmann (London: Pluto Press, 2008 [1952]), p. 180.
105 Michel Foucault, *The Order of Things: An Archaeology of the Human Sciences*.
106 Fabian, *Time and the Other*, p. 156.
107 Ibid., p. 67.
108 Ibid., pp. 156–58.
109 Ibid., pp. 156–57.
110 Ibid., 159.
111 Ibid., p. 156.
112 Ibid., p. 159.
113 Ibid. p. 157.
114 Ibid., p. 163.
115 Ibid., p. 162.
116 Ibid., 163. In this, Fabian is very close to thinkers such as Dell Hymes, James Clifford, and George Marcus.

117 The translation used here is: V. Y. Mudimbe, *The Rift*, translated by Marjolijn de Jager (Minneapolis: Minnesota University Press, 1993).

118 See Kavwahirehi, *V. Y. Mudimbe et la ré-invention de l'Afrique*, pp. 178–86. In his analysis of the novel, Bernard Mouralis chooses to focus on the split, in fact the schizophrenic nature of the main character/narrator (*V. Y. Mudimbe ou le discours, l'écart et l'écriture* (Paris: Présence africaine, 1988), pp. 120–32). See also Daniel-Henri Pageaux, 'L'Ecart (1979) de Vumbi Yoka Mudimbe, nouveau roman africain, altérité impossible, écriture spéculaire', in Jean Bessière (ed.), *L'Autre du roman et de la fiction* (Paris: Lettres Modernes, 1997), pp. 131–38; Denis Ekpo, 'Schizophrénie et écriture avant-gardiste chez Mudimbe – une phénoménologie structurale de *L'Ecart*', *Neohelicon: Acta Comparationis Litterarum Universarum Amsterdam*, 18(1) (1991), pp. 99–116; Michael Syrotinski, '*L'écart:* Mad Writing?', in *Singular Performances*, pp. 32–39; Marie-Rose Abomo-Maurin, 'Mudimbe: de l'écriture de "L'Écart" à l'examen d'une mémoire', in Bisanswa, *Entre Inscriptions et Prescriptions*, pp. 139–49.

119 Syrotinski, *Singular Performances*, p. 33.

120 V. Y. Mudimbe, 'La Culture', in Jacques Vanderlinden, et al. (eds), *Du Congo au Zaïre, 1960–1980: Essai de bilan* (Brussels: CRISP, 1980), p. 328.

121 Jan Vansina, *Kingdoms of the Savannah* (Madison: University of Wisconsin Press, 1966).

122 Jan Vansina, *The Children of Woot: A History of* the *Kuba peoples* (Madison: University of Wisconsin Press, 1978).

123 Jan Vansina, *De la tradition orale: Essai de méthode historique* (Tervuren: Annales – Sciences Humaines, 1961).

124 See the tribute Mudimbe pays to Vansina's work in 'Préface. Quelle histoire? Une méditation de V.-Y. Mudimbe', in Bogumil Jewsiewicki, D. Dibwe dia Mwembu, and R. Giordano (eds), *Lubumbashi 1910–2010: Mémoire d'une ville industrielle* (Paris: L'Harmattan, 2010), pp. 7–22 (pp. 16–17).

125 Syrotinski, *Singular Performances*, p. 38.

126 Michael Hardt and Antonio Negri, *Empire* (Cambridge, Mass. and London: Harvard University Press, 2000).

127 See A. Etzioni, *Comparative Analysis of Complex Organizations* (New York: Free Press, 1975 [1961]).

128 Enrique D. Dussel, *The Invention of the Americas: Eclipse of the 'Other' and the Myth of Modernity*, translated by Michael D. Barber (London: Continuum, 1995).

129 A. Kuper, *The Invention of Primitive Society: Transformation of an Illusion* (London: Routledge, 1988).

130 G. Hofstede, *Cultures and Organizations: Software of the Mind* (London and New York: McGraw-Hill, 2005).

131 Ibid., p. 3. In italics in the original.

132 Ibid., p. x.

133 Ibid., p. 8.
134 Enrique D. Dussel, *Ética de la liberación en la edad de la globalización y de la exclusión* (Madrid: Trotta, 1998).
135 Monnier, '"Immediate History"', pp. 286–88.
136 I. Wallerstein, *Unthinking Social Science: The Limits of Nineteenth-Century Paradigms* (Cambridge: Polity Press, 1991), p. 128.
137 V. Y. Mudimbe, *Déchirures. Poèmes* (Kinshasa: Éditions du Mont Noir, 1971), p. 30.
138 Yambo Ouologuem, *Lettre à la France nègre* (Paris: E. Nalis, 1969).
139 François Furet, 'La France sauvage' (interview of Emmanuel Le Roy Ladurie by François Furet), *Le Nouvel Observateur*, 22 June 1966, pp. 28–29.

Chapter Four

1 Michel de Certeau, *The Practice of Everyday Life*, translated by Steven Rendall (Berkeley: University of California Press, 1984), p. 61.
2 Gayatri Chakravorty Spivak, 'Can the Subaltern Speak?', in Cary Nelson and Lawrence Grossbary (eds), *Marxism and the Interpretation of Culture* (Urbana: University of Illinois Press, 1988), pp. 271–313.
3 See Edward Said, 'Foucault and the Imagination of Power', in David C. Hoys (ed.), *Foucault: A Critical Reader* (Oxford: Blackwell, 1986), pp. 149–55; Gayatri Chakravorty Spivak, *In Other Words: Essays in Cultural Politics* (London and New York: Routledge, 1987) and 'Can the Subaltern Speak?'.
4 Ann Laura Stoler, *Race and the Education of Desire: Foucault's 'History of Sexuality' and the Colonial Order of Things* (Durham, NC and London: Duke University Press, 1995).
5 V. Y. Mudimbe, 'Et Dieu que devient-il?', OP, 156–63.
6 Paul Gilroy, *The Black Atlantic: Modernity and Double Consciousness* (London and New York: Verso, 1993), p. 208.
7 See Aedín Ní Loingsigh, 'Agoraphobic Travel? Mudimbe's *Cheminements: Carnets de Berlin (Avril-Juin 1999)*', *Studies in Travel Writing*, 13(4) (2009), pp. 357–67, where the author shows that Mudimbe deliberately chooses not to follow this conventional structure in *Carnets de Berlin*.
8 André Gide, *Voyage au Congo. Carnets de route* (Paris: Gallimard, 1927).
9 Aedín Ní Loingsigh, '"Alors, et l'Amérique?" Post-Independence African Travel to the United States', in *Forum for Modern Language Studies*, 45.2 (2009), pp. 129–39.
10 Ibid., p. 133.
11 For a sustained and observant analysis of other attempts on the part of African novelists (Ousmane Socé Diop and Bernard Dadié, notably) to

reverse the traditional ethnographic point of view, see Aedín Ní Loingsigh, *Postcolonial Eyes: Intercontinental Travel in Francophone African Literature* (Liverpool University Press, 2009).

12 See V. Y. Mudimbe: *Initiation au Français*, 2 volumes (Kinshasa: Celta, 1971); *Français: Les Structures fondamentales I* (Kinshasa: Centre de Recherches Pédagogiques, 1972); *Français. Les Structures fondamentales II* (Kinshasa: Centre de Recherches Pédagogiques, 1972).

13 Michel Crozier, *La Société bloquée* (Paris: Seuil, 1970).

14 Jean-Paul Sartre, 'Preface', in Frantz Fanon, *The Wretched of the Earth*, translated by Constance Farrington (London: Penguin Books, 2001 [1961]), p. 7.

15 Jean-Paul Sartre, *Colonialism and Neocolonialism*, translated by Azzedine Haddour, Terry McWilliams, and Steve Brewer (London: Routledge, 2001 [1964]), pp. viii–xix.

16 Richard Watts, 'Negritude, Présence africaine, Race', in Charles Forsdick and David Murphy (eds), *Postcolonial Thought in the French-Speaking World* (Liverpool University Press, 2009), pp. 227–37 (p. 236).

17 I will use here the translation into English of 'Avec L. G. Damas' ('A Meeting with L. G. Damas') by Myles O'Byrne, to be published in 2014 in Pierre-Philippe Fraiture and Daniel Orrells (eds) in *A V. Y. Mudimbe Reader* (Virginia University Press).

18 See Géza Róheim, *Psychoanalysis and Anthropology: Culture, Personality and the Unconscious* (New York: International University Press, 1950); Marie-Cécile Ortigues and Edmond Ortigues, *Œdipe* (Paris: L'Harmattan, 1984 [1966]).

19 Georges Devereux, *Essais d'ethnopsychiatrie générale*, translated by Tina Jolas and Henri Gobard (Paris: Éditions Gallimard, 1970).

20 John Colin Carothers, *The Psychology of the Mau Mau* (Nairobi: Government Printer, 1954).

21 Didier Fassin, 'Les Politiques de l'ethnopsychiatrie: La psyché africaine, des colonies africaines aux banlieues parisiennes', *L'Homme*, 153 (2000), pp. 231–50.

22 See Curtis M. Hinsley, *The Smithsonian and the American Indian: Making a Moral Anthropology in Victorian America* (Washington, DC and London: Smithsonian Institution Press, 1994 [1981]). First published, with the same publisher, under the following title: *Savages and Scientists: The Smithsonian Institution and the Development of American Anthropology, 1846–1910*.

23 This is how the Martin Luther King Jr. Center for Nonviolent Social Change describes itself on its website: 'Established in 1968 by Coretta Scott King, The King Center is the official, living memorial dedicated to advancing the legacy of Dr. Martin Luther King, Jr. Through various programs and partnerships, we strive to educate the world about his life and teachings, inspire

new generations to further his work, and strengthen causes and changemakers continuing his efforts today'. <www.thekingcenter.org/> (accessed 13 October 2011).

24 See Mark Christian, 'The State of Black Studies in the Academy: Introduction to the Special Issue', *Journal of Black Studies*, 36(5) (May 2006), pp. 643–45.

25 Laurent Monnier, '"Immediate History": Remembering the Golden Age of Research in Political Science at the University of Kinshasa', in Elisabeth Mudimbe-Boyi (ed.), *Remembering Africa* (Portsmouth, NH: Heinemann, 2002), p. 287.

26 See Deepika Bahri, 'Feminism In/And Postcolonialism', in Neil Lazarus (ed.), *The Cambridge Companion to Postcolonial Literary Studies* (Cambridge University Press, 2004), pp. 199–220.

27 See R. McAfee Brown, *Observer in Rome: A Protestant Report on the Vatican Council* (London: Methuen, 1964) and *The Ecumenical Revolution: An Interpretation of the Catholic-Protestant Dialogue* (London: Burns and Oats, 1973).

28 R. McAfee Brown, *Gustavo Gutiérrez: An Introduction to Liberation Theology* (Maryknoll, NY: Orbis Books, 1990).

29 See R. McAfee Brown, *Unexpected News: Reading the Bible with Third World Eyes* (Philadelphia, Pa.: Westminster John Knox Press, 1984).

30 Michel Foucault, *History of Madness*, translated by Jonathan Murphy and Jean Khalfa (London: Routledge, 2006 [1972]).

31 Ibid., p. 77.

32 Ibid., p. 14.

33 Ibid., p. 77.

34 Ibid., pp. 102–03.

35 Michel Foucault, *The Order of Things: An Archaeology of the Human Sciences*, translated from French (London: Tavistock Publications, 1970 [1966]), pp. 3–16.

36 Ibid., pp. 125–65.

37 See Edith Holden, *Blyden of Liberia: An Account of the Life and Labors of Edward Wilmot Blyden, LL.D., as Recorded in Letters and in Print* (New York: Vantage Press, 1967); Hollis Ralph Lynch, *Edward Wilmot Blyden: Pan-Negro Patriot 1832–1912* (London, Ibadan, and New York: Oxford University Press, 1967); Thomas W. Livingston, *Education and Race: A Biography of Edward Wilmot Blyden* (San Francisco, Calif.: Glendessary Press, 1975); Charles H. Lyons, *To Wash an Aethiop White: British Ideas about Black African Educability, 1530–1960* (New York: Teachers College Press, 1975); Edward Hulmes, 'Christian Attitudes to Islam: A Comparative Study of the Work of S. A. Crowther, E. W. Blyden and W. R. S. Miller in West Africa', D.Phil. thesis, Oxford University, 1981; Apollos Nwauwa, 'Empire, Race and Ideology: Edward Wilmot Blyden's Initiatives for an African University and

African-Centered Knowledge, 1872–1890', *International Journal of African Studies*, 2(2) (2001), pp. 1–22.

38 Edward Wilmot Blyden, *Selected letters of Edward Wilmot Blyden*, edited by Hollis Ralph Lynch (Millwood, NY: KTO Press, 1978).

39 L. H. Senghor, 'Edward Wilmot Blyden, Precursor of Negritude', in E. W. Blyden, *Selected Letters of Edward Wilmot Blyden*, edited by Hollis Ralph Lynch, pp. xix–xxii (p. xix). The original version in French, 'Edward Wilmot Blyden, Précurseur de la Négritude' (pp. xv–xvii), precedes the version in English, translated by David L. Schalk.

40 Ibid., p. xx.

41 Ibid.

42 Ibid., p. xxi.

43 Ibid., p. xx.

44 Ibid., p. xxi.

45 Ibid., p. xvii.

46 Ibid.

47 Edward Wilmot Blyden, 'The African Problem and the Methods of its Solution', in *The Voice of Black America: Major Speeches by Negroes in the Unites States, 1797–1971*, edited by Philip S. Foner (New York: Simon & Schuster, 1972), pp. 540–56 (p. 553).

48 This is a quote from Lyon's *To Wash an Aethiop White* (p. 108).

49 See '"Pure Negroes" for Africa', in Hollis Ralph Lynch's *Edward Wilmot Blyden: Pan-Negro Patriot 1832–1912*, pp. 105–39, where Lynch explores the strategies adopted by Blyden to persuade the American Colonization Society that it should only repatriate 'genuine Negroes' as opposed to Mulattoes (p. 105).

50 Ibid., p. 7.

51 Eric Burin, *Slavery and the Peculiar Solution: A History of the American Colonization Society* (Gainesville: University Press of Florida, 2005), p. 1.

52 Blyden, 'The African Problem and the Methods of its Solution', p. 556.

53 Ibid., p. 549.

54 Edward Wilmot Blyden, *The Jewish Question* (Liverpool: Lionel Hart, 1898).

55 See Hollis Ralph Lynch, *Edward Wilmot Blyden: Pan-Negro Patriot 1832–1912*, pp. 64–65; Benyamin Neuberger, 'Early African Nationalism, Judaism, and Zionism: Edward Wilmot Blyden', in *Jewish Social Studies*, 47(2) (1985), pp. 151–66; Michael J. C. Echeruo, 'Edward W. Blyden, "The Jewish Question" and the Diaspora: Theory and Practice', in *Journal of Black Studies*, 40(4) (2010), pp. 544–65.

56 Edward Wilmot Blyden, 'The African Problem and the Methods of its Solution', p. 550.

57 Ibid., p. 551.

58 M. J. C. Echeruo, 'Edward W. Blyden, "The Jewish Question," and the Diaspora, p. 546.

59 Hannah Arendt, *The Origin of Totalitarianism*, 3 vols (New York: Harcourt Brace and World, 1968).

60 V. Y. Mudimbe (ed.), *Nations, Identities, Cultures* (Durham NC: Duke University Press, 1997), p. 2.

61 Edward Wilmot Blyden, *Christianity, Islam and the Negro Race* (Edinburgh University Press, 1967 [1887]).

62 L. H. Senghor, 'Edward Wilmot Blyden, Precursor of Negritude', in Edward Wilmot Blyden, *Selected letters of Edward Wilmot Blyden*, p. xxi.

63 Foucault, *History of Madness*, p. 108.

64 Ibid.

65 Ibid.,

66 See, for instance, in the context of the Belgian Congo, the scholarly journal *Congo: Revue générale de la Colonie belge. Algemeen tijdschrift van de Belgische Kolonie*, which published on a variety of issues (literature, mythology, economics, geology, medicine, and agriculture) rather than in one specific scientific discipline. I studied this phenomenon in *La Mesure de l'autre*, pp. 64–70.

67 Michael Syrotinski, *Singular Performances: Reinscribing the Subject in African Francophone Writing* (Charlottesville and London: University of Virginia Press, 2002), p. 2.

68 Michel Foucault, *The Archaeology of Knowledge*, translated by Alan M. Sheridan Smith (London: Routledge 2002 [1969]), p. 154.

69 Ibid.

70 Foucault, *The Order of Things*, p. 345.

71 Ibid., p. 344.

72 Ibid., p. 352.

73 Ibid., p. 351.

74 See V. Y. Mudimbe and Anthony Appiah, 'The Impact of African Studies on Philosophy', in Robert H. Bates, V. Y. Mudimbe, and Jean O'Barr (eds), *Africa and the Disciplines: The Contributions of Research in Africa to the Social Sciences and Humanities* (University of Chicago Press, 1993), pp. 113–38, where the same Foucauldian reading grid is applied. See also *TF*, 39–40.

75 Foucault, *The Order of Things*, p. 357.

76 Ibid.

77 Ibid.

78 Ibid.

79 Ibid., p. 359.

80 Ibid., p. 360.

81 Ibid.

82 Ibid.

83 Ibid.
84 Ibid.
85 Émile Durkheim, *Les Formes élémentaires de la vie religieuse* (Paris: Alcan, 1912).
86 Marcel Mauss, *Essai sur le don: Forme et raison de l'échange dans les sociétés archaïques*: first published in the journal *L'Année sociologique* in 1923 and 1924 and republished later in Marcel Mauss, *Sociologie et anthropologie* (Paris: Presses universitaires de France, 1950).
87 Ibid., p. 148.
88 For a succinct but sustained exploration of the vexed relationship between anthropology, Foucault, and postcolonial studies, see David Richards, 'Postcolonial Anthropology in the French-speaking World', in Forsdick and Murphy, *Postcolonial Thought in the French-Speaking World*, pp. 173–84.
89 Foucault, *The Order of Things*, p. 378.
90 Ibid., p. 361.
91 Ibid.
92 On the intellectual and cultural overlaps between these movements, see Gary Wilder, *The French Imperial Nation-State: Negritude and Colonial Humanism between the Two World Wars* (Chicago University Press, 2005) and Anthony Mangeon, *La Pensée noire et l'Occident: De la bibliothèque coloniale à Barack Obama* (Cabris: Sulliver, 2010).
93 Paulin Hountondji, *African Philosophy: Myth and Reality*, translated by Henri Evans with the collaboration of Jonathan Rée (Bloomington: Indiana University Press, 1996 [1977]), p. 60.
94 Marcel Ntumba Tshiamalenga, 'Qu'est-ce que la "philosophie africaine"', in *La Philosophie africaine: Actes de la première semaine de philosophie de Kinshasa* (Kinshasa: Faculté de théologie catholique, 1977), pp. 33–36.
95 See Fabien Eboussi-Boulaga, 'Le Bantou problématique', *Présence africaine*, 66 (1968), pp. 4–40.
96 For a close reading of Eboussi-Boulaga's work, see also D. A. Masolo, *African Philosophy in Search of Identity* (Bloomington and Edinburgh: Indiana University Press/Edinburgh University Press, 1994), pp. 148–64.
97 Paulin Hountondji, *African Philosophy: Myth and Reality*, p. 34.
98 Ibid.
99 Quoted from M. Griaule and Germaine Dieterlen, *Le Renard pâle* (Paris: Institut d'ethnologie, 1965).
100 On this reversal and relationship between Griaule and Ogotemmêli, see James Clifford, *The Predicament of Culture: Twentieth-Century Ethnography, Literature and Art* (Cambridge, Mass. and London: Harvard University Press, 1988), p. 72.
101 Alexis Kagame, *La Philosophie bantu-rwandaise de l'être* (Brussels: Académie Royale des Sciences Coloniales, 1956). See also, by the same author,

La Philosophie bantu comparée (Paris: Présence africaine, 1976), which pursues the same objective.

102 For a close analysis of Kagame's theses, see Masolo, *African Philosophy in Search of Identity*, pp. 84–102 and Bernard Mouralis, *Littératures africaines et antiquité: Redire le face-à-face de l'Afrique et de l'Occident* (Paris: Honoré Champion, 2011), pp. 122–31.

103 Claude Lévi-Strauss, *Les Structures élémentaires de la parenté* (Paris: Presses universitaires de France, 1949).

104 Claude Lévi-Strauss, *Race et histoire* (Paris: Denoël, 1952).

105 Claude Lévi-Strauss, *La Pensée sauvage* (Paris: Plon, 1962).

106 See D. A. Masolo, *African Philosophy in Search of Identity*, pp. 53–56.

107 Quoted from Claude Lévi-Strauss, *The Savage Mind* (University of Chicago Press, 1966 [1962]). See, particularly, chap. 1, 'La Science du concret'.

108 Paul Ricœur, *Histoire et vérité* (Paris: Seuil, 1955); Paul Veyne, *Comment on écrit l'histoire: Essai d'épistémologie* (Paris: Seuil, 1971); Michel de Certeau, *L'Écriture de l'histoire* (Paris: Gallimard, 1975).

109 Beryl L. Bellman, *The Language of Secrecy: Symbols and Metaphors in Poro Rituals* (New Brunswick, NJ: Rutgers University Press, 1984).

110 Ibid., p. xii.

111 Ibid., p. xi.

112 Ibid., p. 144.

113 Frank Kermode, *The Genesis of Secrecy: On the Interpretation of Narrative* (Cambridge, Mass and London: Harvard University Press, 1979).

114 Bellman, *The Language of Secrecy*, p. 5.

115 Hans Georg Gadamer, *Truth and Method*, translation revised by Joel Weinsheimer and Donald G. Marshall (London: Continuum, 2004).

116 Bellman, *The Language of Secrecy*, p. 12.

117 R. Girardet, *L'Idée coloniale en France de 1871 à 1962* (Paris: Éditions de la Table ronde, 1972).

118 See, for instance, Ousmane Kane, *Non-Europhone Intellectuals* (Dakar: CODESRIA, 2012), p.1.

Chapter Five

1 Roy Wagner, *The Invention of Culture* (Chicago: University of Chicago Press, 1981 [1975]), pp. 13–14.

2 See V. Y. Mudimbe, 'La Diaspora et l'héritage culturel de l'impérialisme comme lieu de discours critique et de représentation du monde', *Revue Canadienne des Études Africaines*, 28(1) (1994), pp. 89–100, in which Mudimbe ascribes a politically and culturally transformative role to diasporas in the United States.

3 Achille Mbembe, *Sortir de la grande nuit: Essai sur l'Afrique décolonisée* (Paris: La Découverte, 2010), p. 100.

4 Patrice Nganang, *Manifeste d'une nouvelle littérature africaine: Pour une écriture préemptive* (Paris: Éditions Homnisphères, 2007).

5 See Achille Mbembe, *On the Postcolony* (Berkeley: University of California Press, 2001). A first version of this essay was published in French: *De la Postcolonie: Essai sur l'imagination politique dans l'Afrique contemporaine* (Paris: Karthala, 2000).

6 Mbembe, *Sortir de la grande nuit*, pp. 31–53.

7 This very autobiographical account is an amplification of a previously published article: Achille Mbembe, 'Ecrire l'Afrique à partir d'une faille', *Politique Africaine*, 51 (1993), pp. 69–97.

8 Mbembe, *Sortir de la grande nuit*, p. 37.

9 See Achille Mbembe, *La Naissance du maquis dans le Sud-Cameroun, 1920–1960: Histoire des usages de la raison en colonie* (Paris: Khartala, 1996) and notably 'De la mort de Ruben Um Nyobé' (chap. 12, pp. 377–96).

10 Mbembe, *Sortir de la grande nuit*, p. 39.

11 In *La République de l'imagination: Lettres au benjamin* (La Roque-d'Anthéron: Vents d'ailleurs, 2009), he also looks up to the figure of Ruben to find hope for a better future. See 'La Voix d'Um', pp. 45–69.

12 Nganang, *Manifeste*, p. 292.

13 Mongo Béti, *Main basse sur le Cameroun: Autopsie d'une décolonisation* (Paris: Maspero, 1972).

14 Nganang, *Manifeste*, p. 292.

15 Wim van Binsbergen, 'An Incomprehensible Miracle – Central African Clerical Intellectualism versus African Historic Religion: A Close Reading of Valentin Mudimbe's *Tales of Faith*', in *Reading Mudimbe*, special issue of the *Journal of African Cultural Studies*, edited by Kai Kresse, pp. 14–15.

16 Achille Mbembe, 'Necropolitics', translated by Libby Meintjes, *Public Culture*, 15 (2003), pp. 11–40.

17 Achille Mbembe, 'African Modes of Self-Writing', translated by Steven Rendall, *Public Culture* 14(1) (2002), pp. 239–73.

18 Mbembe, *Sortir de la grande nuit*, p. 58.

19 Jean-Loup Amselle, *L'Occident décroché: Enquêtes sur les postcolonialismes* (Paris: Stock, 2008).

20 Jean-François Bayart, *Les Études postcoloniales: Un carnaval académique* (Paris: Karthala, 2010).

21 Mbembe, *Sortir de la grande nuit*, pp. 75–76.

22 Ibid., p. 113.

23 Ibid.

24 Ibid., p. 62.

25 Ibid., p. 61.

26 Ibid., p. 62.

27 Jean-Paul Sartre, *Plaidoyer pour les intellectuels* (Paris: Gallimard, 1972).

28 See also V. Y. Mudimbe, *Réflexions sur la vie quotidienne* (Kinshasa: Éditions du Mont Noir, 1972), pp. 49–54, where rampant Zairian chauvinism is examined.

29 Frantz Fanon, *Les Damnés de la terre*, Preface by Jean-Paul Sartre (Paris: Maspero, 1961), p. 239. In 'Ecrire l'Afrique à partir d'une faille', Mbembe uses also the term 'nuit' to refer to the African postcolonial present.

30 Frantz Fanon, *The Wretched of the Earth*, translated by Constance Farrington (London: Penguin Books, 2001 [1961]), p. 251 (my italics).

31 Mbembe, *Sortir de la grande nuit*, p. 114.

32 Ibid., chap. 4: 'Le long hiver impérial français' (pp. 121–72).

33 Ibid., pp. 107–15.

34 Ibid., p. 104.

35 Ibid., pp. 149–61.

36 Ibid., p. 149.

37 Interestingly, Nicolas Sarkozy, during the presidential campaign of April and May 2012, would often come back to this idea of frontiers, via Régis Debray's *Éloge des frontières*, to capture the attention of electors on the far-right of the political spectrum.

38 Mbembe, *Sortir de la grande nuit*, p. 229.

39 See Fanon, *The Wretched of the Earth* and, more specifically, the chapter 'On National Culture', pp. 166–99.

40 Mbembe, *Sortir de la grande nuit*: 'Anciennes et nouvelles cartographies' (pp. 174–80).

41 Ibid., pp. 229–37.

42 See V. Y. Mudimbe, 'Ut Recte Valeant: Languages in 3rd Century Roman Africa', in Candido Mendes (ed.), *Latinité et identité haïtienne: Entre la tradition et la modernité* (Rio de Janeiro: Educam-Editora Universitária and Académie de la Latinité, 2005), pp. 296–317. I will refer here to a slightly revised (and unpublished) version of the same text which was presented by the author at a Research Seminar that he gave in November 2009 in the Department of Classic and Ancient History (University of Warwick). Same title, pp. 1–17.

43 Ibid., p. 1.

44 Ibid., p. 15.

45 Mbembe, *Sortir de la grande nuit*, pp. 180–91.

46 Reinhart Koselleck, *Futures Past: On the Semantics of Historical Time*, translated by Keith Tribe (Cambridge, Mass. and London: MIT Press, 1985), p. 77.

47 Mbembe, *Sortir de la grande nuit*, p. 180.

48 Ibid., p. 233.

49 Ibid., p. 226.

50 Ibid., p. 241.

51 Michael Syrotinski, *Singular Performances: Reinscribing the Subject*

in African Francophone Writing (Charlottesville and London: University of Virginia Press, 2002), p. 2.

52 Mbembe, *Sortir de la grande nuit*, p. 241.

53 On this text, see Michael Syrotinski, 'The Post-Genocidal African Subject: Patrice Nganang, Achille Mbembe and the Worldliness of Contemporary African Literature in French', in Charles Forsdick, Alec Hargreaves, and David Murphy (eds), *Transnational French Studies: Postcolonialism and Littérature-Monde* (Liverpool University Press, 2010), pp. 274–86.

54 It is however surprising that Nganang does not pay here any attention to Schmitt's murky past and support of National Socialism. I would like to thank Andreas Eckert for pointing this out to me.

55 And subsequently published as Patrice Nganang, *Interkulturalität und Bearbeitung: Untersuchung zu Soyinka und Brecht* (Munich: Iudicium Verlag, 1998).

56 Nganang, *Manifeste*, p. 27.

57 Ibid., p. 136.

58 Ibid.

59 '[t]o write poetry after Auschwitz is barabaric', in Adorno, *Prism*, translated by Samuel and Shierry Weber (Cambridge, Mass.: MIT Press, 1981), p. 34.

60 For a discussion on Adorno's oft-quoted (and misquoted) statement, see Michael Rothberg, *Traumatic Realism: The Demand of Holocaust Representation* (Minneapolis and London: University of Minnesota Press, 2000), pp. 25–58. For an introduction to Adorno's work, see Simon Jarvis, *Adorno: A Critical Introduction* (Cambridge: Polity, 1998); on the relationship between Adorno and postcolonial studies: Deepika Bahri, *Native Intelligence: Aesthetics, Politics, and Postcolonial Literature* (Minneapolis and London: University of Minnesota Press, 2003).

61 Nganang, *Manifeste*, p. 12.

62 Ibid., pp. 57–82.

63 Ibid., p. 63.

64 Jean-Paul Sartre, *Qu'est-ce que la littérature* (Paris: Gallimard, 1948). First published, in several instalments in *Les Temps Modernes* in 1947.

65 Nganang, *Manifeste*, p. 58.

66 Theodor Adorno, *Notes to Literature*, edited by Rolf Tiedemann; translated from the German by Shierry Weber Nicholsen, 2 vols. (New York: Columbia University Press, 1991–92).

67 Theodor Adorno, 'Commitment', translated by Frances McDonagh, in Ronald Taylor (ed.), *Aesthetics and Politics* (London: Verso, 1980 [1977]), pp. 75–89.

68 Cited by Adorno, in 'Commitment', p. 76.

69 Theodor Adorno, 'The Autonomy of Art', in Brian O'Connor (ed.), *The Adorno Reader* (Oxford: Blackwell, 2000), pp. 239–63 (p. 242).

70 Adorno, 'Commitment', pp. 77–79.
71 Nganang, *Manifeste*, p. 63.
72 Ibid., p. 83.
73 Ibid., pp. 130–31.
74 Ibid., p. 103.
75 Adorno, *Notes to Literature*, vol. 1, p. 39.
76 Nganang, *Manifeste*, p. 289.
77 Ibid., p. 295.
78 Ibid., p. 46.
79 Ibid., p. 67. This is based on a quote by Adorno, himself quoting Schoenberg, see Bahri, *Native Intelligence*, p. 29.
80 Nganang, *Manifeste*, pp. 46–47.
81 Mbembe, 'Necropolitics', p. 11. For an analysis of Mbembe's position (as put forward, notably, in *On the Postcolony*), see Dominic Thomas, *Nation-Building, Propaganda, and Literature in Francophone Africa* (Bloomington and Indianapolis: Indiana University Press, 2002). For an examination of sub-Saharan violence, see p. 190.
82 Ibid., p. 13.
83 Ibid.
84 Ibid., p. 14.
85 Ibid.
86 Ibid.
87 Nganang, *Manifeste*, pp. 68–72.
88 Ibid., p. 158.
89 Ibid., p. 159.
90 Ibid., p. 157.
91 Ibid., p. 115.
92 Ibid., p. 256.
93 Ibid., p. 296.
94 Ibid., p. 194.
95 Ibid., p. 202.
96 Ibid., pp. 38–39.
97 Ibid., p. 39.
98 Ibid., p. 36.
99 Ibid., p. 40.
100 Ibid., p. 41.
101 Achille Mbembe, 'À propos des écritures africaines de soi', *Politique africaine*, 77 (March 2000), p. 16.
102 Mbembe, 'African Modes of Self-Writing', p. 246.
103 Ibid., p. 249.
104 Ibid., p. 247.
105 Ibid., pp. 271–72.
106 Ibid., pp. 240–41.

107 Ibid., p. 239.
108 Ibid., p. 257.
109 Ibid., p. 262.
110 Mbembe, 'Ecrire l'Afrique à partir d'une faille', p. 84.
111 Nganang, *Manifeste*, p. 45.
112 Ibid.
113 Ibid., p. 42.
114 Ibid., p. 43.
115 Hannah Arendt, *The Jew as Pariah: Jewish Identity and Politics in the Modern Age* (New York: Grove, 1978).
116 Dominick LaCapra, *History and Memory after Auschwitz* (Ithaca, New York: Cornell University Press, 1998).
117 Anne Goldberg, *La Clepsydre: Essai sur la pluralité des temps dans le judaïsme* (Paris: Albin Michel, 2000).
118 See V. Y. Mudmbe, 'Physiologie de la négritude', *Études Congolaises*, 5 (September–October 1967), pp. 1–13.
119 Mbembe, 'African Modes of Self-Writing', p. 257.
120 D. A. Masolo, 'V. Y. Mudimbe: An Archaeology of African Knowledge', in D. A. Masolo, *African Philosophy in Search of Identity* (Bloomington and Edinburgh: Indiana University Press/Edinburgh University Press, 1994), pp. 178–99 (p. 188).
121 Mbembe, 'African Modes of Self-Writing', p. 242.
122 Ibid., p. 259.
123 Ibid.
124 Ibid., p. 269.
125 Ibid.
126 Ahmadou Kourouma, *Allah n'est pas obligé* (Paris: Seuil, 2000).
127 Mbembe, 'African Modes of Self-Writing', p. 269.
128 Nganang, *Manifeste*, p. 272: Ken Saro-Wiwa, *Sozaboy: A Novel in Rotten English* (Port Harcourt; Ewell: Saros 1985).
129 Mbembe, 'African Modes of Self-Writing', p. 262.
130 V. Y. Mudimbe, *On African Fault Lines: Meditation on Alterity Politics* (Scottsville, South Africa: University of KwaZulu-Natal Press, 2013), p. 75.
131 Michel de Certeau, Luce Giard, and Pierre Mayol, *L'Invention du quotidien* (Paris: Union Générale d'Éditions, 1980).
132 Michel de Certeau, Luce Giard, and Pierre Mayol, *The Practice of Everyday Life*, vol. 2, *Living and Cooking*, translated by Steven Rendall (Minneapolis: University of Minnesota Press, 1988), p. 141.
133 See Theodor Adorno, *Philosophy of New Music*, translated by Robert Hullot-Kentor (Minneapolis and London: University of Minnesota Press, 2006 [1949]).
134 On these two writers, see Nicki Hitchcott, *Women Writers in Francophone Africa* (Oxford: Berg, 2000) and Syrotinski, *Singular Performances*.

135 V. Y. Mudimbe, *Le Bel immonde* (original in French) (Paris: Présence africaine, 1976), p. 162.

136 See, in this respect, V. Y. Mudimbe, with Maliya Matumele, Nyunda ya Rubango, M. N. Losso Gazi, and Otshudiema Eloko a Nongo, *Le Vocabulaire politique Zaïrois: Une étude de sociolinguistique* (Lubumbashi: Celta, 1976).

137 There exists a very rich corpus of secondary literature on these issues. See, among many other publications, *Études Littéraires Africaines*, 'L'Enfant-soldat: Langages and images', 32 (2011), texts collected by Nicolas Martin-Granel, including Susanne Gehrmann, 'The Child Soldier's Soliloquy: Voices of New Archetypes in African Writing'(pp. 31–43); Nicki Hitchcott, 'Benjamin Sehene vs. Father Wenceslas Munyeshyaka: The Fictional Trial of a Genocide Priest', *Journal of African Cultural Studies*, 24 (1), 2012, pp. 21–34; Nicki Hitchcott, 'Writing on Bones: Commemorating Genocide in Boubacar Boris Diop's *Murambi*', *Research in African Literatures*, 40(3), 2009, pp. 48–61; Zoë Norridge, 'Writing against Genocide: Genres of Opposition in Narratives from and about Rwanda', in Patrick Crowley and Jane Hiddleston, *Postcolonial Poetics: Genre and Form* (Liverpool University Press, 2011), pp. 240–61; Audrey Small, 'The Duty of Memory: A Solidarity of Voices after the Rwandan Genocide', *Paragraph*, 30(1), 2007, pp. 85–100. See also the special issue dedicated to the representation of the Rwandan genocide by *French Cultural Studies*, 20(2) (2009).

138 A point also explored by Mbembe in 'The Aesthetics of Vulgarity' (*On the Postcolony*).

139 Bogumil Jewsiewicki, 'The Archaeology of Invention: Mudimbe and Postcolonialism', p. 964.

140 Syrotinski, *Singular Performances*, p. 128.

141 Mary Douglas, *Purity and Danger: An Analysis of the Concepts of Pollution and Taboo* (London: Routledge and Kegan Paul, 1966).

142 Mudimbe, *Le Bel immonde* (original in French), p. 49: 'Tu me perçois comme spectacle'.

143 Syrotinski, *Singular Performances*, p. 128.

144 Ibid., p. 130.

145 Neil Lazarus, 'Representation of Terror in V. Y. Mudimbe', in Kai Kresse (ed.), *Reading Mudimbe*, special issue on V. Y. Mudimbe, *Journal of African Cultural Studies*, 17(1) (2005), pp. 81–101 (p. 96).

146 For an interesting analysis of cannibalism with regards to colonialism and translation, see 'Introduction', in Susan Bassnett and Harish Trivedi (eds), *Post-colonial Translation: Theory and Practice* (London and New York: Routledge, 1999), pp. 1–19.

147 V. Y. Mudimbe, 'La Culture', in Jacques Vanderlinden, et al. (eds), *Du Congo au Zaïre, 1960–1980: Essai de bilan* (Brussels: CRISP, 1980), p. 324.

148 Syrotinski, *Singular Performances*, p. 131.

149 See V. Y. Mudimbe, '*The Politics of War: A* Meditation', in Einar Braathen, Morten Bøås, and Gjermund Sæther (eds), *Ethnicity Kills? The*

Politics of War: Peace and Ethnicity in Sub-Saharan Africa (Basingstoke: Macmillan, 2000), pp. 23–36.

150 Nganang, *Manifeste d'une nouvelle littérature*, p. 30.

151 See Bernard Mouralis, *V. Y. Mudimbe ou le discours, l'écart et l'écriture* (Paris: Présence africaine, 1988), pp. 109–15 and Kasereka Kavwahirehi, *V. Y. Mudimbe et la ré-invention de l'Afrique: Poétique et politique de la décolonisation des sciences humaines* (Amsterdam and New York: Rodopi, 2006), pp. 168–78.

152 Notably in an undergraduate seminar devoted to *Entre les eaux* that Mudimbe gave at the University of Warwick in November 2009.

153 Gustavo Gutiérrez, *A Theology of Liberation: History, Politics, and Salvation*, translated from Spanish and edited by Caridad Inda and John Eagleson (London: SCM Press, 1974).

154 See James H. Cone, *Black Theology and Black Power* (New York: Seabury Press, 1969) and, by the same author, *A Black Theology of Liberation* (Philadelphia: Lippincott, 1970). For investigations into the legacy of black theology, see Dwight N. Hopkins, *Heart and Head: Black Theology; Past, Present, and Future* (New York and Basingstoke: Palgrave Macmillan, 2002) and Linda E. Thomas, *Living Stones in the Household of God: The Legacy and Future of Black Theology* (Minneapolis, Minn.: Fortress Press, 2004).

155 Mudimbe summarises here (and quotes from) Verhaegen's article, 'Religion et politique en Afrique noire', in *Religions africaines et christianisme*, 1 (1979), pp. 179–94.

156 Gutiérrez, *A Theology of Liberation*, p. 211.

157 Ibid., p. 91.

158 Ibid.

159 Homi K. Bhabha, 'Articulating the Archaic', *The Location of Culture* (London: Routledge, 1983), pp. 123–38 (p. 137).

160 Mudimbe cites here from the volume edited by Joseph-Aurélien Cornet, Rémi De Cnodder, Ivan Dierickx, and Wim Toebosch: *Soixante ans de peinture au Zaïre* (Brussels: Les Éditeurs d'Art Associés, 1989). Cornet published another very influential book, referred to by Kutumbagana Kangafu – see Chapter 2 – to justify Mobutu's politics of authenticity: *L'Art de l'Afrique noire au pays du fleuve Zaïre* (Brussels: Éditions Arcade, 1972), with Preface by Joseph Désiré Mobutu.

161 For a similar process of resistance but in a Central American context, see William Hanks's analysis of the Spanish noun 'reducción' in *Converting Words: Maya in the Age of the Cross* (Berkeley and Los Angeles: University of California Press, 2009).

162 See, for instance, 'Anthropology and Marxist Discourse' *P&F*, 166–91, in which he reads Peter Rigby's *Persistent Pastoralists: Nomadic Societies in Transition* (London: Zed Books, 1985) against the background of this place/space opposition as developed by Michel de Certeau.

163 Certeau, *The Practice of Everyday Life*, p. 117.
164 Ibid.
165 On this artist, see Johannes Fabian, *Remembering the Present: Painting and Popular History in Zaire* (Berkeley: University of California Press, 1996).
166 *Temps de Chien: Chronique animale* (Paris: Le Serpent à plumes, 2003 [2001]) is, for instance, a diatribe against Paul Biya's dictatorship. The novel, seen from this angle, resonates with Nganang's regular assaults against the current Cameroonian regime's inability to treat all Cameroonian citizens equitably. His recent campaign against the arbitrary arrest of Enoh Meyomesse, described by Nganang as the 'Jean-Paul Sartre camerounais', is a clear example of the type of intellectual and political commitment that he embodies. On this last point, see Patrice Nganang, 'Cameroun: libérez Enoh Meyomesse' <www.afriquemonde.org/index1.php?id=2604> (consulted 21 May 2012).
167 Alan Sinfield, *Literature, Politics and Culture in Postwar Britain* (Berkeley and Oxford: University of California Press/Blackwell, 1989), p. 29.
168 Theodor Adorno, *Aesthetic Theory*, translated by Robert Hullot-Kentor (London: Continuum, 2004 [1970]), p. 3.
169 R. Hullot-Kentor, Translator's Introduction, ibid., pp. ix–xiii (p. xvi).
170 See van Binsbergen, 'An Incomprehensible Miracle'.
171 Hullot-Kentor, 'Translator's Introduction', p. xvii.
172 Ibid., p. xv.
173 van Binsbergen, 'An Incomprehensible Miracle, pp. 23–24.

Conclusion

1 Kai Kresse, 'Reading Mudimbe – An Introduction', in Kai Kresse (ed.), *Reading Mudimbe*, special issue on V. Y. Mudimbe, *Journal of African Cultural Studies*, 17(1) (2005), pp. 1–9 (p. 3).
2 'Afrocentrism' *à la* Molefi Asante being referred to as a 'slippery ideology', in Mudimbe's review of Stephen Howe's *Afrocentism* (1998): 'Race, Identity, Politics, and History', *Journal of African History*, 41(2) (2000), pp. 291–94 (p. 294).
3 V. Y. Mudimbe, 'Préface. Quelle histoire? Une méditation de V.-Y. Mudimbe', in Bogumil Jewsiewicki, D. Dibwe dia Mwembu, and R. Giordano (eds), *Lubumbashi 1910–2010: Mémoire d'une ville industrielle* (Paris: L'Harmattan, 2010), pp. 7–22.
4 Johannes Fabian, 'Keep Listening: Ethnography of Reading', in Jonathan Boyarin (ed.), *The Ethnography of Reading* (Berkeley: University of California Press, 1993), pp. 81–97 (p. 88). This text was so idiosyncratically written that it had to be read out and recorded in order to recover (part of) the meaning of the original: 'With untiring help from Kalundi Mango, a relatively simple and elegant solution was eventually found although not without many compromises as we shall see presently: Kalundi Mango was asked to read the text aloud and

this was recorded (1986 in Lubumbashi). The intonation patterns and other prosodic features on the recording made it possible to mark syntactic segments in the written text. Many passages remained doubtful and had to be corrected later with the help of semantics. Morphemes and sentence boundaries became clarified when we proceeded to translating the text' (p. 87).

   5 Johannes Fabian, *History from Below: The 'Vocabulary of Elisabethville' by André Yav: Text, Translations, and Interpretive Essay*, edited and translated with Commentary by Johannes Fabian, with assistance from Kalundi Mango; linguistic notes by W. Schicho (Amsterdam: John Benjamins Publishing Company, 1990).

   6 Mudimbe, 'Préface. Quelle histoire?', p. 8.

   7 Ibid., p. 12

   8 Ibid., p. 15.

   9 Fabian, 'Keep Listening: Ethnography of Reading', p. 90.

 10 Ibid., p. 94 n. 8.

 11 Mudimbe, 'Préface. Quelle histoire?', p. 12.

 12 V. Y. Mudimbe, *Études Congolaises*, 5 (September–October 1967), pp. 1–13 (p. 13).

 13 Mudimbe, 'Préface. Quelle histoire?', p. 21.

 14 Ibid., p. 8.

 15 Ibid., p. 21.

 16 Ibid., p. 8.

 17 Homi K. Bhabha, 'Articulating the Archaic', *The Location of Culture* (London: Routledge, 1983); see pp. 136–37.

 18 Michel de Certeau, *The Practice of Everyday Life*, translated by Steven Rendall (Berkeley: University of California Press, 1984), p. xiii.

 19 Michael Syrotinski, 'Reprendre: Mudimbe's Deconstructions', in *Deconstruction and the Postcolonial: At the Limits of Theory* (Liverpool University Press, 2007), p. 82.

 20 At a meeting at the University of Leiden in January 2006, he told me that he wasn't an Africanist, a word used in this case in its modern sense (i.e., expert in Africa).

 21 Homi K. Bhabha, 'Dissemination: Time, Narrative and the Margins of the Modern Nation', *The Location of Culture*, pp. 139–70 (p. 139).

 22 Michael Hardt and Antonio Negri, *Empire* (Cambridge, Mass. and London: Harvard University Press, 2000), p. xiii.

 23 Ibid., pp. 139–41.

 24 Ibid., p. 141.

 25 Ibid., p. 134.

 26 Achille Mbembe, *On the Postcolony* (Berkeley: University of California Press, 2001), p. 11.

 27 Patrice Nganang, *Temps de Chien: Chronique animale* (Paris: Le Serpent à plumes, 2003 [2001]), p. 43.

28 Patrice Nganang, *Mont Plaisant. Roman* (Paris: Philippe Rey, 2011).
29 Ibid., p. 28.
30 Ibid., p. 15 (in French).
31 Patrice Nganang, 'J'ai écrit pour le Cameroun qui souffre d'une stagnation historique' <www.jeuneafrique.com/Article/ARTJAWEB20110119164143/> (consulted 22 May 2012).
32 Jean-Paul Sartre, 'Preface', in Frantz Fanon, *The Wretched of the Earth*, translated by Constance Farrington (London: Penguin Books, 2001 [1961]), p. 7.
33 Bogumil Jewsiewicki, 'The Archaeology of Invention: Mudimbe and Postcolonialism', translated by François Manchuelle, in Manthia Diawara (ed.), *Callaloo*, special issue on V. Y. Mudimbe, 14(4) (1991), pp. 961–68 (p. 962).

Select Bibliography

Works by V. Y. Mudimbe Consulted

'Physiologie de la négritude', *Études Congolaises*, 5 (September–October 1967), pp. 1–13.
'Héritage occidental et conscience nègre', *Congo-Afrique*, 26 (June–July 1968), pp. 2–14.
Déchirures: Poèmes (Kinshasa: Éditions du Mont Noir, 1971).
Initiation au français, 2 vols (Kinshasa: Celta, 1971).
Français: Les structures fondamentales I (Kinshasa: Centre de Recherches Pédagogiques, 1972).
Français: Les structures fondamentales II (Kinshasa: Centre de Recherches Pédagogiques, 1972).
Autour de la 'Nation': Leçons de civisme. Introduction (Kinshasa and Lubumbashi: 'Objectifs 80', Éditions du Mont Noir, 1972).
Réflexions sur la vie quotidienne (Kinshasa: Éditions du Mont Noir, 1972).
Entre les eaux (Paris: Présence africaine, 1973).
L'Autre Face du royaume: Une introduction à la critique des langages en folie (Lausanne: L'Âge d'homme, 1973).
'Les Intellectuels zaïrois', *Zaïre-Afrique*, 88 (1974), pp. 451–63.
Carnets d'Amérique, septembre – novembre 1974 (Paris: Éditions Saint-Germain-des-Prés, 1976).
(with Pius Ngandu Nkashama), 'Remarques synthétiques sur la contribution africaine à la fondation de la pensée et de la littérature latines chrétiennes', in *Mélanges offerts à Léopold Sédar Senghor: langues – littérature – histoire ancienne* (Dakar: Nouvelles éditions africaines, 1977), pp. 356–74.
(with Maliya Matumele, Nyunda ya Rubango, M. N. Losso Gazi, and Otshudiema Eloko a Nongo), *Le Vocabulaire politique Zaïrois: Une étude de sociolinguistique* (Lubumbashi: Celta, 1976).
Le Bel immonde (Paris: Présence africaine, 1976).
Air: Étude sémantique (Vienna: Acta ethnologica et linguistica, 1979).
L'Écart (Paris: Présence africaine, 1979).
(ed.), *La Dépendance de l'Afrique et les moyens d'y remédier* (Paris: Berger Levrault, 1980).

'La Culture', in Jacques Vanderlinden, with André Huybrechts, V. Y. Mudimbe, Leo Peeters, Daniel Van der Steen, and Benoît Verhaegen (eds), *Du Congo au Zaïre, 1960–1980: Essai de bilan* (Brussels: CRISP, 1980), pp. 310–98.

L'Odeur du père: essai sur des limites de la science et de la vie en Afrique noire (Paris: Présence africaine, 1982).

The Invention of Africa: Gnosis, Philosophy, and the Order of Knowledge (Bloomington and Indianapolis: Indiana University Press, 1988).

Before the Birth of the Moon, translated by Marjolijn de Jager (New York: Simon & Schuster, 1989 [1976]).

Shaba Deux: Les carnets de Mère Marie-Gertrude (Paris: Présence africaine, 1989).

Parables and Fables: Exegesis, Textuality and Politics in Central Africa (Madison: University of Wisconsin Press, 1991).

'"Reprendre": Enunciations and Strategies in Contemporary African Arts', in Susan Vogel (ed.), *Africa Explores: Twentieth-Century African Art* (Munich: The Center for African Art and Prestel, 1991), pp. 276–87.

Between Tides, translated by Stephen Becker (New York: Simon & Schuster, 1991[1973]).

(ed.), *The Surreptitious Speech: Présence africaine and the Politics of otherness, 1947–1987* (University of Chicago Press, 1992).

Robert H. Bates and Jean O'Barr (eds), *Africa and the Disciplines: The Contributions of Research in Africa to the Social Sciences and Humanities* (University of Chicago Press, 1993).

The Rift, translated by Marjolijn de Jager (Minneapolis: Minnesota University Press, 1993, [1979]).

(with Bogumil Jewsiewicki), *History Making in Africa* (Middletown, Conn.: Wesleyan University Press, 1993).

The Idea of Africa (Bloomington and Indianapolis: Indiana University Press, 1994).

Les Corps glorieux des mots et des êtres: Esquisse d'un jardin africain à la bénédictine (Paris and Montreal, Présence africaine/Humanitas, 1994).

'La Diaspora et l'héritage culturel de l'impérialisme comme lieu de discours critique et de représentation du monde', *Revue Canadienne des Études Africaines*, 28(1) (1994), pp. 89–100.

'The Idea of Luba', Afterword to Mary Nooter Roberts and Allen Roberts (eds), *Memory: Luba Art and the Making of History* (New York: Prestel and the Museum for African Art, 1996).

Tales of Faith: Religion and Political Performance in Central Africa (London and Atlantic Highlands, NJ: The Athlone Press, 1997).

(ed.), *Nations, Identities, Cultures* (Durham NC: Duke University Press, 1997).

'*The Politics of War*: A Meditation', in Einar Braathen, Morten Bøås, and Gjermund Sæther (eds), *Ethnicity Kills? The Politics of War: Peace and Ethnicity in Sub-Saharan Africa* (Basingstoke: Macmillan, 2000), pp. 23–36.

'Race, Identity, Politics, and History', *Journal of African History*, 41(2) (2000), pp. 291–94.

'De la cosmologie dogon: Une méditation', Ponti/*Ponts*, 4 (2004), pp. 235–48.

'Ut Recte Valeant: Languages in 3rd Century Roman Africa', in Candido Mendes (ed.), *Latinité et identité haïtienne: Entre la tradition et la modernité* (Rio de Janeiro: Educam-Editora Universitária and Académie de la Latinité, 2005), pp. 296–317.

Cheminements: Carnets de Berlin (avril–juin 1999) (Quebec: Humanitas, 2006).

'Et Nunc ... Per Hoc Signum: A Meditation on Genitives in Everyday Life Stories', *South Atlantic Quaterly*, 108(3) (2009), pp. 419–47.

'In the House of Libya: A Meditation', in Daniel Orrells, Gurminder K. Bhambra, and Tessa Roynon (eds), *African Athena: New Agendas* (Oxford University Press, 2011), pp. 191–209.

(with Susan Mbula Kilonzo), 'Philosophy of Religion on African Ways of Believing', in Elias Kifon Bongmba (ed.), *The Wiley-Blackwell Companion to African Religions* (Oxford: Wiley-Blackwell, 2012), pp. 41–61.

'Au nom de la gratitude, une méditation', in Justin K. Bisanswa (ed.), *Entre Inscriptions et Prescriptions: V. Y. Mudimbe et l'engendrement de la parole* (Paris: Champion, 2013), pp. 395–441.

On African Fault Lines: Meditation on Alterity Politics (Scottsville, South Africa: University of KwaZulu-Natal Press, 2013).

Other Works Consulted

Adelman, Kenneth Lee, 'The Recourse to Authenticity and Negritude in Zaire', *Journal of Modern African Studies*, 13(1) (1975), pp. 134–39.

Adorno, Theodor, *Aesthetic Theory*, translated by Robert Hullot-Kentor (London: Continuum, 2004 [1970]).

——, *Prism*, translated by Samuel and Shierry Weber (Cambridge, Mass.: MIT Press, 1981).

Adotevi, Stanislas, *Négritude et négrologues*, Collection '10–18' (Paris: Union générale d'éditions, 1972).

Agamben, Giorgio, *Homo Sacer: Sovereign Power and Bare Life*, translated by Daniel Heller-Roazen (Stanford, Calif.: Stanford University Press, 1998 [1995]).

Althusser, Louis, *For Marx*, translated by Ben Brewster (London and New York: Verso, 1990 [1965]).

Althusser, Louis, and Étienne Balibar, *Reading Capital*, translated by Ben Brewster (London: NLB, 1970 [1968]).

Amselle, Jean-Loup, *L'Occident décroché: Enquêtes sur les postcolonialismes* (Paris: Stock, 2008).

Amselle, Jean-Loup, and Emmanuelle Sibeud (eds), *Maurice Delafosse: Entre orientalisme et ethnographie, l'itinéraire d'un africaniste (1870–1926)* (Paris: Maisonneuve et Larose, 1998).

Antonio, Edward P., *Inculturation and Postcolonial Discourse in African Theology* (New York: Peter Lang, 2006).

Appiah, Anthony Kwame, *In My Father's House: Africa and the Philosophy of Culture* (New York: Oxford University Press, 1992).

Apter, Andrew, *Beyond Words: Discourse and Critical Agency in Africa* (University of Chicago Press, 2007).
Arendt, Hannah, *The Origin of Totalitarianism*, 3 vols. (New York: Harcourt Brace and World, 1968).
——, *The Jew as Pariah: Jewish Identity and Politics in the Modern Age* (New York: Grove, 1978).
Auerbach, Erich, *Mimesis: The Representation of Reality in Western Literature*, translated from German by Willard R. Trask, with a new Introduction by Edward W. Said (Princeton, NJ: Princeton University Press, 2003 [1953]).
Baaz, Maria Eriksson, and Mai Palmberg (eds), *Same and Other: Negotiating African Identity in Cultural Production* (Stockholm: Elanders Gotab for the Nordiska Afrikainstitutet, 2001).
Bachelard, Gaston, *La Poétique de l'espace* (Paris: Presses universitaires de France, 1998 [1957]).
Bahri, Deepika, *Native Intelligence: Aesthetics, Politics, and Postcolonial Literature* (Minneapolis and London: University of Minnesota Press, 2003).
——, 'Feminism In/And Postcolonialism', in Neil Lazarus (ed.), *The Cambridge Companion to Postcolonial Literary Studies* (Cambridge University Press, 2004).
Bancel, Nicolas, Pascal Blanchard, and Sandrine Lemaire (eds), *La Fracture coloniale: La société française au prisme de son héritage colonial* (Paris: La Découverte, 2005).
Bancel, Nicolas, Pascal Blanchard, Gilles Boëtsch, Eric Deroo, Sandrine Lemaire, and Charles Forsdick (eds), *Human Zoos: Science and Spectacle in the Age of Empires*, translations by Teresa Bridgeman (Liverpool University Press, 2008 [2002]).
Bartolovich, Crystal, and Neil Lazarus (eds), *Marxism, Modernity and Postcolonial Studies* (Cambridge University Press, 2002).
Bassnett, Susan, and Harish Trivedi (eds), *Post-colonial Translation: Theory and Practice* (London and New York: Routledge, 1999).
Bayart, Jean-François, *Les Études postcoloniales: Un carnaval académique* (Paris: Karthala, 2010).
Bellman, Beryl L., *The Language of Secrecy: Symbols and Metaphors in Poro Rituals*, Foreword by James W. Fernandez (New Brunswick, NJ: Rutgers University Press, 1984).
Bemba, Sylvain, *Léopolis* (Paris: Hatier, 1986).
Bénabou, Marcel, *La Résistance africaine à la Romanisation* (Paris: Maspero, 1976).
Bénot, Yves, *Idéologies des indépendances africaines* (Paris: François Maspero, 1969).
Bernal, Martin, *Black Athena: The Afro-Asiatic Roots of Classical Civilization*, vol. 1, *The Fabrication of Ancient Greece, 1785–1995* (New Brunswick, NJ: Rutgers University Press, 1987).
——, *Black Athena: the Afro-Asiatic Roots of Classical Civilization*, vol. 2, *The Archaeological and Documentary Evidence* (New Brunswick, NJ: Rutgers University Press, 1991).

——, *Black Athena: the Afro-Asiatic Roots of Classical Civilization*, vol. 3, *The Linguistic Evidence* (London: Free Association Books, 2006).
Berque, Jacques, *Dépossession du monde* (Paris: Seuil, 1964).
——, *L'Orient second* (Paris: Gallimard, 1970).
Béti, Mongo, *Main basse sur le Cameroun: Autopsie d'une décolonisation* (Paris: Maspero, 1972).
Bhabha, Homi K., *The Location of Culture* (London: Routledge, 1994).
Bimwenyi, Oscar, *Discours théologique négro-Africain: Problèmes des fondements* (Paris: Présence africaine, 1981).
Binsbergen, Wim van, 'An Incomprehensible Miracle – Central African Clerical Intellectualism versus African Historic Religion: A Close Reading of Valentin Mudimbe's *Tales of Faith*', in *Reading Mudimbe*, special issue of the *Journal of African Cultural Studies*, edited by Kai Kresse, pp. 11–65.
Bisanswa, Justin K., 'V. Y. Mudimbe: Réflexion sur les sciences humaines et sociales en Afrique', *Cahiers d'Études Africaines*, 160 (2000), pp. 705–22.
——, *Conflits de mémoire: V. Y. Mudimbe et la traversée des signes* (Frankfurt: IKO-Verlag für Interkulturelle Kommunikation, 2000).
—— (ed.), *Entre Inscriptions et Prescriptions: V. Y Mudimbe et l'engendrement de la parole* (Paris: Champion, 2013).
Blyden, Edward Wilmot, *Christianity, Islam and the Negro Race*, with an Introduction by Christopher Fyfe (Edinburgh University Press, 1967 [1887]).
——, 'The African Problem and the Methods of its Solution', in *The Voice of Black America: Major Speeches by Negroes in the Unites States, 1797–1971*, edited with Commentary by Philip S. Foner (New York: Simon & Schuster, 1972), pp. 540–56.
——, *Selected Letters of Edward Wilmot Blyden*, edited with Introduction by Hollis Ralph Lynch; Foreword by Léopold Sédar Senghor (Millwood, NY: KTO Press, 1978).
Bongie, Chris, *Friends and Enemies: The Scribal Politics of Post/Colonial Literature* (Liverpool University Press, 2008).
Bontinck, Franz (ed.), *Aux Origines de la Philosophie bantoue: La correspondance Tempels-Hulstaert (1944–1948)*, Bibliothèque du Centre d'études des religions africaines, 10 (Kinshasa: Faculté de théologie catholique, 1985).
Bouveignes, Olivier de, *Les Anciens rois de Congo* (Namur: Grands Lacs, 1948).
Bragard, Véronique, and Stéphanie Planche, 'Museum Practice and the Belgian Colonial Past: Questionning the Memories of an Ambivalent Metropole', in Dominic Thomas (ed.), *Museums in Postcolonial Europe*, special issue of the *African and Black Diaspora: An International Journal*, 2(2) (2009), pp. 181–91.
Britton, Celia, *The Sense of Community in French Caribbean Fiction* (Liverpool University Press, 2008).
Bruyère, Vincent, 'Mudimbe cartographe: Essai sur le corps transculturel des mots et des êtres', in Désiré K. Wa Kabwe-Segatti and Pierre Halen (eds), *Du Nègre bambara au Négropolitain: Les littératures africaines en contexte transculturel* (Metz: Centre Ecritures, 2009), pp. 31–44.

Burin, Eric, *Slavery and the Peculiar Solution: A History of the American Colonization Society* (Gainesville: University Press of Florida, 2005).
Butler, Judith, *Gender Trouble: Feminism and the Subversion of Identity* (New York: Routledge, 1990).
Cailler, Bernadette, 'The Impossible Ecstasy: An Analysis of V. Y Mudimbe's *Déchirures*', *Research in African Literatures*, 24(4) (1993), pp. 15–28.
Carothers, John Colin, *The Psychology of the Mau Mau* (Nairobi: Government Printer, 1954).
Certeau, Michel de, *L'Écriture de l'histoire* (Paris: Gallimard, 1975).
Certeau, Michel de, Luce Giard, and Pierre Mayol, *L'Invention du quotidien* (Paris: Union Générale d'Éditions, 1980).
——, *The Practice of Everyday Life*, translated by Steven Rendall (Berkeley: University of California Press, 1984).
——, *The Practice of Everyday Life*, vol. 2, translated by Steven Rendall (Minneapolis: University of Minnesota Press, 1998).
Césaire, Aimé, *Discours sur le colonialisme* (Paris: Présence africaine, 1950).
——, *Lettre à Maurice Thorez* (Paris: Présence africaine, 1956).
——, *Une Saison au Congo* (Paris: Présence africaine, 1966).
Chinweizu, *The West and the Rest of Us: White Predators, Black Slavers, and the African Elite* (New York and Lagos: Random House/Nok Publishers, 1978).
Christian, Mark, 'The State of Black Studies in the Academy: Introduction to the Special Issue', *Journal of Black Studies*, 36(5) (May 2006), pp. 643–45.
Clifford, James, *The Predicament of Culture: Twentieth-Century Ethnography, Literature and Art* (Cambridge, Mass. and London: Harvard University Press, 1988).
Cone, James, H., *Black Theology and Black Power* (New York: Seabury Press, 1969).
——, *A Black Theology of Liberation* (Philadelphia, Pa.: Lippincott, 1970).
Conteh-Morgan, John, *Theatre and Drama in Francophone Africa: A Critical Introduction* (Cambridge University Press, 1994).
Cooper, Frederick, *Colonialism in Question: Theory, Knowledge, History* (Berkeley: University of California Press, 2005).
Cornet, Joseph-Aurélien, *L'Art de l'Afrique noire au pays du fleuve Zaïre*, Preface by Joseph Désiré Mobutu (Brussels: Éditions Arcade, 1972).
Cornet, Joseph-Aurélien, Rémi De Cnodder, Ivan Dierickx, and Wim Toebosch, *Soixante ans de peinture au Zaïre* (Brussels: Les Éditeurs d'Art Associés, 1989).
Coulon, Virginia, 'Étude bibliographique de l'œuvre de V. Y. Mudimbe', in Mukala Kadima-Nzuji and Sélom Komlan Gbanou, *L'Afrique au miroir des littératures, des sciences de l'homme et de la société: Mélanges offerts à V. Y. Mudimbe* (Paris: L'Harmattan, 2003), pp. 557–89.
Crowley, Patrick, and Jane Hiddleston (eds), *Postcolonial Poetics: Genre and Form* (Liverpool University Press, 2011).
Crozier, Michel, *La Société bloquée* (Paris: Seuil, 1970).
Davies, Ioan, 'Negotiating African Culture: Towards a Decolonization of the

Fetish', in Frederic Jameson and Masao Miyoshi (eds), *The Cultures of Globalization* (Durham NC and London: Duke University Press, 1998), pp. 125–45.
Davis, Whitney, *Queer Beauty: Sexuality and Aesthetics from Winckelmann to Freud and Beyond* (New York: Columbia University Press, 2010).
De Craemer, Willy, *The Jamaa and the Church: A Bantu Catholic Movement in Zaire* (Oxford: Clarendon Press, 1977).
Debray, Régis, *Révolution dans la révolution? Lutte armée et lutte politique en Amérique latine* (Paris: Maspero, 1967).
——, *La Guérilla du Che* (Paris: Seuil, 1974).
——, *Éloge des frontières* (Paris: Gallimard, 2010).
Derrida, Jacques, *Writing and Difference*, translated, with an Introduction and additional notes by Alan Bass (Chicago University Press, 1978 [1967]).
Devereux, Georges, *Essais d'ethnopsychiatrie générale*, translated from English by Tina Jolas and Henri Gobard; Preface by Roger Bastide (Paris: Éditions Gallimard, 1970).
Diawara, Manthia (ed.), *Callaloo*, special issue on V. Y. Mudimbe, 14(4) (1991), pp. 929–1035.
——, 'Reading Africa through Foucault: V. Y. Mudimbe's Reaffirmation of the Subject', in Anne McClintock, Aamir Mufti, and Ella Shohat (eds), *Dangerous Liaisons: Gender, Nation, and Postcolonial Perspectives* (Minneapolis: University of Minnesota Press, 1997), pp. 456–65.
Dieterlen Germaine, and Marcel Griaule, *Le Renard pâle* (Paris: Institut d'ethnologie, 1965).
Diop, Cheikh Anta, *Nations nègres et culture: De l'antiquité nègre égyptienne aux problèmes culturels de l'Afrique noire d'aujourd'hui* (Paris: Présence africaine, 1999 [1954]).
——, *L'Unité culturelle de l'Afrique noire: Domaines du patriarcat et du matriarcat dans l'Antiquité classique* (Paris: Présence africaine, 1959).
——, *Antériorité des civilisations nègres: Mythe ou vérité historique?* (Paris: Présence africaine, 1967).
Djebar, Assia, *L'Amour, la fantasia. Roman* (Paris: J. C. Lattès, 1985).
Douglas, Mary, *Purity and Danger: An Analysis of the Concepts of Pollution and Taboo* (London: Routledge and Kegan Paul, 1966).
Duchet, Michèle, *Anthropologie et histoire au siècle des lumières: Buffon, Voltaire, Rousseau, Helvétius, Diderot* (Paris: Maspero, 1971).
Durkheim, Émile, *Les Formes élémentaires de la vie religieuse* (Paris: Alcan, 1912).
Dussel, Enrique D., *The Invention of the Americas: Eclipse of the 'Other' and the Myth of Modernity*, translated by Michael D. Barber (London: Continuum, 1995).
——, *Ética de la liberación en la edad de la globalización y de la exclusión* (Madrid: Trotta, 1998).
Duvignaud, Jean, *Le Langage perdu: Essai sur la différence anthropologique* (Paris: Presses universitaires de France, 1973).
Ebénézer, Njoh-Mouelle, *Jalons* (Yaoundé: Clé, 1970).

Eboussi-Boulaga, Fabien, 'Le Bantou problématique', *Présence africaine*, 66 (1968), pp. 4–40.
——, *La Crise du muntu: Authenticité africaine et philosophie* (Paris: Présence africaine, 1977).
——, *Christianity without Fetishes: An African Critique and Recapture of Christianity*, translated from French by Robert R. Barr (Maryknoll, NY: Orbis Books, 1984 [1981]).
Echeruo, Michael J. C., 'Edward W. Blyden, "The Jewish Question" and the Diaspora: Theory and Practice', in *Journal of Black Studies*, 40(4) (2010), pp. 544–65.
Ekpo, Denis, 'Schizophrénie et écriture avant-gardiste chez Mudimbe – une phénoménologie structurale de *L'Écart*', *Neohelicon: Acta Comparationis Litterarum Universarum Amsterdam*, 18(1) (1991), pp. 99–116.
Engels, Friedrich, and Karl Marx, *The German Ideology*, in *Collected Works*, edited by Roy Pascal; translated by William Lough and C. P. Magill (London and New York: Lawrence and Wishart/International, 1976 [1845–7]).
Etzioni, Amitai, *Comparative Analysis of Complex Organizations* (New York: Free Press, 1975 [1961]).
Eze, Emmanuel Chukwudi, *On Reason: Rationality in a World of Cultural Conflict and Racism* (Durham, NC and London: Duke University Press, 2008).
Fabian, Johannes, 'Charisma and Cultural Change: The Case of the Jamaa Movement in Katanga (Congo Republic)', *Comparative Studies in Society and History*, 11(2) (1969), pp. 155–73.
——, *Jamaa: a Charismatic Movement in Katanga* (Evanston, Ill.: Northwestern University Press, 1971).
——, *Time and the Other: How Anthropology Makes its Objects*, with a Foreword by Matti Bunzl (New York: Columbia University Press, 2002 [1983]).
——, *Power and Performance: Ethnographic Explorations through Proverbial Wisdom and Theater in Shaba, Zaire* (Madison and London: University of Wisconsin Press, 1990).
——, *History from Below: The 'Vocabulary of Elisabethville' by André Yav: Text, Translations, and Interpretive Essay*, edited and translated with Commentary by Johannes Fabian, with assistance from Kalundi Mango; linguistic notes by W. Schicho (Amsterdam: John Benjamins Publishing Company, 1990).
——, *Language and Colonial Power: The Appropriation of Swahili in the Former Belgian Congo* (Cambridge University Press, 1986; repub., with a Foreword by Edward Said: Berkeley, University of California Press, 1991).
——, 'Keep Listening: Ethnography of Reading', in Jonathan Boyarin (ed.), *The Ethnography of Reading* (Berkeley: University of California Press, 1993), pp. 81–97.
——, *Remembering the Present: Painting and Popular History in Zaire* (Berkeley: University of California Press, 1996).
——, *Out of our Minds: Reason and Madness in the Exploration of Central Africa* (Berkeley: University of California Press, 2000).
Fanon, Frantz, *Peau noire, masques blancs* (Paris: Seuil, 1952).

——, *Black Skins, White Masks*, Foreword to the 2008 edition by Ziauddin Sardar; Foreword to the 1986 edition by Homi K. Bhabha; translated by Charles Lam Markmann (London: Pluto Press, 2008 [1952]).

——, *Les Damnés de la terre*, Preface by Jean-Paul Sartre (Paris: Maspero, 1961).

——, *The Wretched of the Earth*, Preface by Jean-Paul Sartre, translated by Constance Farrington (London: Penguin Books, [1961] 2001).

Fassin, Didier, 'Les Politiques de l'ethnopsychiatrie: La psyché africaine, des colonies africaines aux banlieues parisiennes', *L'Homme*, 153 (2000), pp. 231–50.

Fassin, Didier, and Eric Fassin, *De la Question sociale à la question raciale? Représenter la société française* (Paris: La Découverte, 2006).

Forsdick, Charles, and David Murphy (eds), *Postcolonial Thought in the French-Speaking World* (Liverpool University Press, 2009).

Forsdick, Charles, Alec Hargreaves, and David Murphy (eds), *Transnational French Studies: Postcolonialism and Littérature-Monde* (Liverpool University Press, 2010).

Foucault, Michel, *The Order of Things: An Archaeology of the Human Sciences*, translated from French (London: Tavistock Publications, 1970 [1966]).

——, *The Archaeology of Knowledge*, translated by Alan M. Sheridan Smith (London: Routledge 2002 [1969]).

——, *L'Ordre du discours: Leçon inaugurale au Collège de France prononcée le 2 décembre 1970* (Paris: Gallimard, 1971).

——, *History of Madness*, edited by Jean Khalfa; translated by Jonathan Murphy and Jean Khalfa (London: Routledge, 2006 [1972]).

Fraiture, Pierre-Philippe, *La Mesure de l'autre: Afrique subsaharienne et roman ethnographique de Belgique et de France, 1918–1940* (Paris, Éditions Honoré Champion, 2007).

——, 'V. Y. Mudimbe's "Long Nineteenth Century"', in Charles Forsdick and David Murphy (eds), *Postcolonial Thought in the French-Speaking World* (Liverpool University Press, 2009), pp. 136–46.

——, 'Mudimbe's Fetish of the West and Epistemological Utopianism', *French Studies*, 63(3) (2009), pp. 308–22.

Furet, François, 'La France sauvage' (interview of Emmanuel Le Roy Ladurie by F. Furet), *Le Nouvel Observateur*, 22 June 1966, pp. 28–29.

Gadamer, Hans Georg, *Truth and Method*, translation revised by Joel Weinsheimer and Donald G. Marshall (London: Continuum, 2004).

Gehrmann, Susanne, 'The Child Soldier's Soliloquy: Voices of New Archetypes in African Writing', *Études Littéraires Africaines*, special issue 'L'Enfant-soldat: Langages and images', collected by Nicolas Martin-Granel, 32 (2011), pp. 31–43.

Gérard, Jacques E., *Les Fondements syncrétiques du Kitawala* (Brussels: Collection Études Africaines, 1969).

Giddens, Anthony, *The Consequences of Modernity* (Cambridge: Polity, 1990).

Gide, André, *Voyage au Congo: Carnets de route* (Paris: Gallimard, 1927).

Gilroy, Paul, *The Black Atlantic: Modernity and Double Consciousness* (London and New York: Verso, 1993).

Girardet, Raoul, *L'Idée coloniale en France de 1871 à 1962* (Paris: Éditions de la Table ronde, 1972).
Goff, Barbara (ed.), *Classics and Colonialism* (London: Duckworth, 2005).
Goff, Barbara, and Michael Simpson (eds), *Crossroads in the Black Aegean: Oedipus, Antigone, and Dramas of the African Diaspora* (Oxford University Press, 2007).
Goldberg, Anne, *La Clepsydre: Essai sur la pluralité des temps dans le judaïsme* (Paris: Albin Michel, 2000).
Granesse, Anke, and Kai Kresse (eds), *Sagacious Reasoning: H. Odera Horuka in Memoriam* (Frankfurt am Main: Peter Lang, 1997).
Greenwood, Emily, *Afro-Greeks: Dialogues between Anglophone Caribbean Literature and Classics in the Twentieth Century* (Oxford University Press, 2010).
Greschat, Hans-Jürgen, *Kitawala: Ursprung, Ausbreitung und Religion der Watch-Tower-Bewegung in Zentralafrika* (Marburg: Elwert, 1967).
Gutiérrez, Gustavo, *A Theology of Liberation: History, Politics, and Salvation*, translated from Spanish and edited by Caridad Inda and John Eagleson (London: SCM Press, 1974).
Halen, Pierre, Maëline Le Lay, and Kabuya Rancy (eds), *Lubumbashi, épicentre littéraire*, special issue of *Études Littéraires Africaines*, 27 (2009).
Hallward, Peter, *Absolutely Postcolonial: Writing between the Singular and the Specific* (Manchester University Press, 2001).
Hanks, William, *Converting Words: Maya in the Age of the Cross* (Berkeley and Los Angeles: University of California Press, 2009).
Harari, Roberto, *Lacan's Four Fundamental Concepts of Psychoanalysis: An Introduction*, translated from Spanish by Judith Filc (New York: Other Press, 2004).
Hardt, Michael, and Antonio Negri, *Empire* (Cambridge, Mass. and London: Harvard University Press, 2000).
Hardwick, Lorna, *Translating Worlds, Translating Cultures* (Oxford University Press, 2000).
Harrow, Kenneth W., *Threshold of Change in African Literature: The Emergence of a Tradition* (Portsmouth, NH and London: Heinemann/James Currey, 1994).
Hartog, François, *The Mirror of Herodotus: The Representation of the Other in the Writing of History*, translated by Janet Lloyd (Berkeley and Los Angeles: University of California Press, 1988 [1980]).
——, *Le XIXe siècle et l'histoire: Le cas Fustel de Coulanges* (Paris: Presses universitaires de France, 1988).
Hebga, Meinrad, *Emancipation d'églises sous-tutelle: Essai sur l'ère post-missionnaire* (Paris: Présence africaine, 1976).
Heusch, Luc de, *Le Roi ivre ou l'origine de l'État* (Paris: Gallimard, 1972).
——, 'The King Comes from Elsewhere', in A. Jacobson-Widding (ed.), *Body and Space: Symbolic Models of Unity and Division in African Cosmology*

and *Experience*, Acta Universitalis Upsaliensis, *Uppsala Studies in Cultural Anthropology*, 16 (1991), pp. 109–17.

Hiddleston, Jane, 'The Specific Plurality of Assia Djebar', *French Studies*, 58(3) (2004), pp. 371–84.

——, *Understanding Postcolonialism* (Stocksfield: Acumen, 2009).

Hinsley, Curtis M., *Savages and Scientists: The Smithsonian Institution and the Development of American Anthropology, 1846–1910* (Washington, DC and London: Smithsonian Institution Press, 1981).

Hitchcott, Nicki, *Women Writers in Francophone Africa* (Oxford: Berg, 2000).

——, 'Writing on Bones: Commemorating Genocide in Boubacar Boris Diop's *Murambi*', *Research in African Literatures*, 40(3) (2009), pp. 48–61.

——, 'Benjamin Sehene vs. Father Wenceslas Munyeshyaka: The Fictional Trial of a Genocide Priest', *Journal of African Cultural Studies*, 24(1) (2012), pp. 21–34.

Hodgen, Margaret T., *Early Anthropology in the Sixteenth and Seventeenth Centuries* (Philadelphia: University of Pennsylvania Press, 1971).

Hofstede, Geert, *Cultures and Organizations: Software of the Mind* (London and New York: McGraw-Hill, 2005).

Holden, Edith, *Blyden of Liberia: An Account of the Life and Labors of Edward Wilmot Blyden, LL.D., as Recorded in Letters and in Print*, Foreword by Nnamdi Azikiwe (New York: Vantage Press, 1967).

Hopkins, Dwight N., *Heart and Head: Black Theology; Past, Present, and Future* (New York and Basingstoke: Palgrave Macmillan, 2002).

Hountondji, Paulin, *African Philosophy: Myth and Reality*, translated by Henri Evans with the collaboration of Jonathan Rée; Introduction by Abiola Irele (Bloomington: Indiana University Press, 1996 [1977]).

Howe, Stephen, *Afrocentrism: Mythical Past and Imagined Homes* (London: Verso, 1998).

Howells, Christina, *Sartre: The Necessity of Freedom* (Cambridge University Press, 1988).

——, *The Cambridge Companion to Sartre* (Cambridge University Press, 1992).

Huddart, David Paul, *Postcolonial Theory and Autobiography* (London: Routledge, 2008).

Hulmes, Edward, 'Christian Attitudes to Islam: A Comparative Study of the Work of S. A. Crowther, E. W. Blyden and W. R. S. Miller in West Africa', D.Phil. thesis, Oxford University, 1981.

Hymes, Dell (ed), *Reinventing Anthropology* (New York: Pantheon Books, 1972).

Jarvis, Simon, *Adorno: A Critical Introduction* (Cambridge: Polity, 1998).

Jaulin, Robert, *La Paix blanche: Introduction à l'ethnocide* (Paris: Seuil, 1970).

Jewsiewicki, Bogumil, 'The Archaeology of Invention: Mudimbe and Postcolonialism', translated by François Manchuelle, in Manthia Diawara (ed.), *Callaloo*, special issue on V. Y. Mudimbe, 14(4) (1991), pp. 961–68.

Jewsiewicki, Bogumil, and David Newbury (eds), *African Historiographies: What History for Which Africa?* (London: Sage Publications, 1986).

Jewsiewicki, Bogumil, Donatien Dibwe dia Mwembu, and Rosario Giordano

(eds), *Lubumbashi 1910–2010: Mémoire d'une ville industrielle*, Preface by V. Y. Mudimbe (Paris: L'Harmattan, 2010).
Johnson, Christopher, *Claude Lévi-Strauss: The Formative Years* (Cambridge University Press, 2003).
Judaken, Jonathan, *Jean-Paul Sartre and the Jewish Question: Anti-antisemitism and the Politics of the French Intellectual* (Lincoln and London: University of Nebraska Press, 2006).
Jules-Rosette, Bennetta, 'Speaking about Hidden Times: The Anthropology of V. Y. Mudimbe', *Callaloo*, special issue on V. Y. Mudimbe, 14(4) (1991), pp. 944–60.
Kadima-Nzuji, Mukala, *La Littérature zaïroise de langue française (1945–1960)* (Paris: ACCT/Karthala, 1984).
Kagame, Alexis, *La Philosophie bantu-rwandaise de l'être* (Brussels: Académie Royale des Sciences Coloniales, 1956).
——, *La Philosophie bantu comparée* (Paris: Présence africaine, 1976).
Kalanda, Mabika, *La Remise en question, base de la décolonisation mentale* (Brussels: Éditions remarques africaines, n.d. [1966]).
Kamitatu-Massamba, Cléophas, *La Grande mystification du Congo-Kinshasa: Les crimes de Mobutu* (Paris: François Maspero, 1971).
Kane, Ousmane, *Non-Europhone intellectuals* (Dakar: CODESRIA, 2012).
Kangafu, Kutumbagana, *Discours sur l'authenticité: Essai sur la problématique idéologique du 'recours à l'authenticité'* (Kinshasa: Presses africaines, 1973).
Kangomba, Jean-Claude, 'Mobutisme et mobutistes', *Congo-Meuse: Figures et paradoxes de l'histoire au Burundi, au Congo et au Rwanda*, 5 (2002), pp. 591–628.
Kasende, Jean-Christophe, *Le Roman africain face aux discours hégémoniques: Étude sur l'énonciation et l'idéologie dans l'œuvre de V. Y. Mudimbe* (Paris: L'Harmattan, 2001).
Kaumba, Lufunda, 'Dimensions de l'identité: Approche phénoménologique de l'univers romanesque de Mudimbe', unpublished thesis, University of Louvain (Belgium), 1986.
Kavwahirehi, Kasereka, *V. Y. Mudimbe et la ré-invention de l'Afrique: Poétique et politique de la décolonisation des sciences humaines* (Amsterdam and New York: Rodopi, 2006).
Kermode, Frank, *The Genesis of Secrecy: On the Interpretation of Narrative* (Cambridge, Mass. and London: Harvard University Press, 1979).
Koselleck, Reinhart, *Futures Past: On the Semantics of Historical Time*, translated by Keith Tribe (Cambridge, Mass. and London: MIT Press, 1985).
Kresse, Kai (ed.), *Reading Mudimbe*, special issue on V. Y. Mudimbe, *Journal of African Cultural Studies*, 17 (1) (2005), pp. 1–129.
Kuper, Adam, *The Invention of Primitive Society: Transformation of an Illusion* (London: Routledge, 1988).
Lacan, Jacques, *Le Séminaire de Jacques Lacan*, vol. 11, *Les quatre concepts fondamentaux de la psychanalyse, 1964*, edited by Jacques-Alain Miller (Paris: Seuil, 1973).

——, *The Four Fundamental Concepts of Psychoanalysis*, edited by Jacques-Alain Miller, translated from French by Alan Sheridan (London: Karnac, 2004).

LaCapra, Dominick, *History and Memory after Auschwitz* (Ithaca, NY: Cornell University Press, 1998).

Lagae, Johan, Luce Beeckmans, and Sofie Boonen, 'Decolonizing Spaces: A (Visual) Essay on Strategies of Appropriation, Transformation and Negotiation of the Colonial Built Environment in Postcolonial Congo', *HAGAR: Studies in Culture, Polity and Identities*, 9(2) (2010), pp. 49–88.

Lamouchi, Noureddine, *Jean-Paul Sartre et le Tiers Monde: Rhétorique d'un discours anticolonialiste*, Foreword by Jack Cornazi; Preface by Geneviève Idt (Paris: L'Harmattan, 1996).

Landau, Paul, *Popular Politics in the History of South Africa, 1400–1948* (Cambridge University Press, 2010).

Lazarus, Neil (ed.), *The Cambridge Companion to Postcolonial Literary Studies* (Cambridge University Press, 2004).

——, 'Representation of Terror in V. Y. Mudimbe', *Journal of African Cultural Studies*, 17(1) (2005), pp. 81–101.

Le Cour Grandmaison, Olivier, *La République impériale: Politique et racisme d'État* (Paris: Fayard, 2009).

Leclerc, Gérard, *Anthropologie et colonialisme: Essai sur l'histoire de l'Africanisme* (Paris: Fayard, 1972).

Lévi-Strauss, Claude, *Les Structures élémentaires de la parenté* (Paris: Presses universitaires de France, 1949).

——, *Race et histoire* (Paris: Denoël, 1952).

——, *Tristes tropiques* (Paris: Plon, 1955).

——, *La Pensée sauvage* (Paris: Plon, 1962).

——, *The Savage Mind* (University of Chicago Press, 1966 [1962]).

——, *Structural Anthropology*, vol. 1, translated by Claire Jacobson and Brooke Grundfest Schoepf (Harmondsworth: Penguin Books: 1963).

——, *Le Regard éloigné* (Paris: Plon, 1983).

——, *Regarder, écouter, lire* (Paris: Plon, 1993).

——, *Myth and Meaning: Cracking the Code of Culture* (New York: Schocken Books, 1995).

Lévi-Strauss, Claude, with Didier Eribon, *De Près et de loin* (Paris: Plon, 1988).

Livingston, Thomas W., *Education and Race: A Biography of Edward Wilmot Blyden* (San Francisco, Calif.: Glendessary Press, 1975).

Lufuluabo, François-Marie, *La Notion Luba-bantoue de l'être* (Tournai: Casterman, 1964).

Lynch, Hollis Ralph, *Edward Wilmot Blyden: Pan-Negro Patriot, 1832–1912* (London, Ibadan, and New York: Oxford University Press, 1967).

Lyons, Charles H., *To Wash an Aethiop White: British Ideas about Black African Educability, 1530–1960* (New York: Teachers College Press, 1975).

M'Buze-Nsomi Lobwanabi, *Révolution et humanisme: Essais* (Kinshasa: Presses africaines, 1974).

——, *Aux sources d'une révolution* (Kinshasa: Presses africaines, 1977).

McAfee Brown, Robert, *Observer in Rome: A Protestant Report on the Vatican Council* (London: Methuen, 1964).
——, *The Ecumenical Revolution: An Interpretation of the Catholic–Protestant Dialogue* (London: Burns and Oats, 1973).
——, *Unexpected News: Reading the Bible with Third World Eyes* (Philadelphia, Pa.: Westminster John Knox Press, 1984).
——, *Gustavo Gutièrrez: An Introduction to Liberation Theology* (Maryknoll, NY: Orbis Books, 1990).
McClintock, Anne, Aamir Mufti, and Ella Shohat (eds), *Dangerous Liaisons: Gender, Nation and Postcolonial Perspectives* (Minneapolis: University of Minnesota Press, 1997).
MacGaffey, Wyatt, *Modern Kongo Prophets: Religion in a Plural Society* (Bloomington: Indiana University Press, 1983).
MacGregor, Neil, *A History of the World in 100 Objects* (London: Allan Lane, 2010).
Mamdani, Mahmood, 'The Invention of the Indigène', *London Review of Books*, 20 January 2011, pp. 31–33.
Mangeon, Anthony, 'Lumières noires, discours marrons: Indiscipline et transformations du savoir chez les écrivains noirs américains et africains; itinéraires croisés d'Alain Leroy Locke, V. Y. Mudimbe et leurs contemporains', unpublished thesis, Université de Cergy-Pontoise (France), 2004.
——, *La Pensée noire et l'Occident: De la bibliothèque coloniale à Barack Obama* (Cabris: Sulliver, 2010).
——, 'La Gnose africaine de V. Y. Mudimbe', in Justin K. Bisanswa (ed.), *Entre Inscriptions et Prescriptions: V. Y. Mudimbe et l'engendrement de la parole* (Paris: Champion, 2013), pp. 47–56.
Marrou, Henri-Irénée, *De la Connaissance historique* (Paris: Seuil, 1954).
Martens, Ludo, *Pierre Mulélé ou la seconde mort de Lumumba* (Brussels: EPO, 1985).
——, *Une Femme du Congo* (Brussels: EPO, 1991).
Martin-Granel, Nicolas, *Études Littéraires Africaines*, 'L'Enfant-soldat: Langages and images', 32 (2011).
Masolo, D. A., *African Philosophy in Search of Identity* (Bloomington and Indianapolis and Edinburgh: Indiana University Press/Edinburgh University Press, 1994).
Massenzio, Marcello, 'An Interview with Claude Lévi-Strauss, *Current Anthropology*, 42 (2001), pp. 419–25.
Mauss, Marcel, *Sociologie et anthropologie*, Introduction by Claude Lévi-Strauss (Paris: Presses universitaires de France, 1950).
Mazrui, Ali A., 'The Re-Invention of Africa: Edward Said, V. Y. Mudimbe, and Beyond', *Research in African Literatures*, 36(3) (2005), pp. 68–82.
Mbembe, Achille, 'Ecrire l'Afrique à partir d'une faille', *Politique Africaine*, 51 (1993), pp. 69–97.
——, *La Naissance du maquis dans le Sud-Cameroun, 1920–1960: Histoire des usages de la raison en colonie* (Paris: Khartala, 1996).

——, *De la Postcolonie: Essai sur l'imagination politique dans l'Afrique contemporaine* (Paris: Karthala, 2000).
——, 'À propos des écritures africaines de soi', *Politique africaine*, 77 (March 2000), p. 16.
——, *On the Postcolony* (Berkeley: University of California Press, 2001).
——, 'African Modes of Self-Writing', translated by Steven Rendall, *Public Culture* 14(1) (2002), pp. 239–73.
——, 'Necropolitics', translated by Libby Meintjes, *Public Culture*, 15 (2003), pp. 11–40.
——, 'La République et l'impensé de la "race"', in Nicolas Bancel, Pascal Blanchard, and Sandrine Lemaire (eds), *La Fracture coloniale: La société française au prisme de son héritage colonial* (Paris: La Découverte, 2005), pp. 143–58.
——, *Sortir de la grande nuit: Essai sur l'Afrique décolonisée* (Paris: La Découverte, 2010).
Mbiti, John S., *Concepts of God in Africa* (London: SPCK, 1970).
Mélice, Anne, 'La Désobéissance civile des Kimbanguistes et la violence coloniale au Congo Belge (1921–1959)', in *Les Temps Modernes*, 658/659 (April–July 2010), pp. 218–50.
Michel, Thierry, *Mobutu, roi du Zaïre* (1999) [film].
Miller, Christopher L., *Blank Darkness: Africanist Discourse in French* (University of Chicago Press, 1985).
Mobutu, Sese Seko, *Paroles du Président* (Kinshasa: Éditions du Léopard, 1968).
Molongo Kalonda-Ba-Mpeta, Huit, *De la marginalisation à la nationalisation: un parcours authentique. Dictionnaire de littérature congolaise de langue française* (Lubumbashi: Celtram, 2009).
Monnier, Laurent, *Ethnie et intégration régionale au Congo: Le Kongo central, 1962–1965* (Paris: EDICEF, 1971).
——, '"Immediate History": Remembering the Golden Age of Research in Political Science at the University of Kinshasa', in Elisabeth Mudimbe-Boyi (ed.), *Remembering Africa* (Portsmouth NH: Heinemann, 2002), pp. 283–301.
Morlighem, Henri, and Tiarko Fourche, *Une Bible noire* (Paris: Max Arnold, 1973).
Moudileno, Lydie, *Littératures africaines francophones des années 1980 et 1990* (Dakar: Conseil pour le développement de la recherche en sciences sociales en Afrique, 2003).
Mouralis, Bernard, *V. Y. Mudimbe ou le discours, l'écart et l'écriture* (Paris: Présence africaine, 1988).
——, *Littératures africaines et antiquité: Redire le face-à-face de l'Afrique et de l'Occident* (Paris: Honoré Champion, 2011).
Mpoyi-Buata, Thomas, 'V. Y. Mudimbe ou le rêve du promontoir et le blocage dans l'ascenseur sur L'Ecart', *Peuples noirs peuples africains*, 33(6) (1983), pp. 103–21.
Mudimbe-Boyi, Elisabeth, 'Testi e Immagini. La Missione del "Congo" nelle Relazioni dei Missionari Cappucini Italiani 1645–1700', unpublished thesis, Lubumbashi, 1977.

—— (ed.), *Remembering Africa* (Portsmouth, NH: Heinemann, 2002).
Mulago, Vincent, *La Religion traditionnelle des Bantu et leur vision du monde* (Kinshasa: Faculté de théologie catholique, 1980).
Mveng, Engelbert, *Les Sources grecques de l'histoire négro-africaine depuis Homère jusqu'à Strabon* (Paris: Présence africaine, 1972).
——, *L'Afrique dans l'Église: Paroles d'un croyant* (Paris: L'Harmattan, 1986).
Nancy, Jean-Luc, *The Inoperative Community*, edited by Peter Connor; translated by Peter Connor, Lisa Garbus, Michael Holland, and Simona Sawhney; Foreword by Christopher Fynsk (Minneapolis and Oxford: University of Minnesota Press, [1986] 1991).
Ndaywel è Nziem, Isidore, *Histoire générale du Congo: De l'héritage ancien à la République démocratique* (Paris and Brussels: Duculot, 1998).
Ndengue, Jean-Marie Abanda, *De la négritude au négrisme: Essais polyphoniques* (Yaoundé: Clé, 1970).
Neuberger, Benyamin, 'Early African Nationalism, Judaism, and Zionism: Edward Wilmot Blyden', in *Jewish Social Studies*, 47(2) (1985), pp. 151–66.
Nganang, Patrice, *Interkulturalität und Bearbeitung: Untersuchung zu Soyinka und Brecht* (Munich: Iudicium Verlag, 1998).
——, *Temps de Chien: Chronique animale* (Paris: Le Serpent à plumes, 2003 [2001]).
——, *Manifeste d'une nouvelle littérature africaine: Pour une écriture préemptive* (Paris: Éditions Homnisphères, 2007).
——, *La République de l'imagination: Lettres au benjamin* (La Roque-d'Anthéron: Vents d'ailleurs, 2009).
——, *Mont Plaisant. Roman* (Paris: Philippe Rey, 2011).
——, 'Cameroun: Libérez Enoh Meyomesse' <www.afriquemonde.org/index1.php?id=2604> (accessed 21 May 2012).
Ní Loingsigh, Aedín, '"Alors, et l'Amérique?" Post-Independence African Travel to the United States', in *Forum for Modern Language Studies*, 45(2) (2009), pp. 129–39.
——, 'Agoraphobic Travel? Mudimbe's *Cheminements: Carnets de Berlin (Avril–Juin 1999)*', *Studies in Travel Writing*, 13(4) (2009), pp. 357–67.
——, *Postcolonial Eyes: Intercontinental Travel in Francophone African Literature* (Liverpool University Press, 2009).
Nkashama, Ngandu Pius, *Le Pacte de sang. Roman* (Paris: L'Harmattan, 1984).
Nkrumah, Kwame, *I Speak of Freedom: A Satement of African Ideology* (London: Heinemann, 1961).
——, *Consciencism: Philosophy and Ideology for Decolonization and Development with Particular Reference to the African Revolution* (London: Heinemann, 1964).
Norridge, Zoë, 'Writing Against Genocide: Genres of Opposition in Narratives from and about Rwanda', in Patrick Crowley and Jane Hiddleston (eds), *Postcolonial Poetics: Genre and Form* (Liverpool University Press, 2011), pp. 240–61.

Nwauwa, Apollos, 'Empire, Race and Ideology: Edward Wilmot Blyden's Initiatives for an African University and African-Centered Knowledge, 1872–1890', *International Journal of African Studies*, 2(2) (2001), pp. 1–22.

O'Connor, Brian (ed), *The Adorno Reader* (Oxford: Blackwell, 2000).

Obenga, Théophile, *L'Afrique dans l'Antiquité: Égypte pharaonique, Afrique noire* (Paris: Présence africaine, 1973).

——, *L'Égypte, la Grèce et l'école d'Alexandrie: Histoire interculturelle dans l'Antiquité. Aux sources égyptiennes de la philosophie grecque* (Paris: L'Harmattan, 2005).

Olakunle, George, *Relocating Agency: Modernity and African Letters* (Albany: State University of New York Press, 2003).

Ong, Walter J., *Ramus: Method and the Decay of Dialogue* (Cambridge, Mass.: Harvard University Press, 1958).

Orrells, Daniel, Gurminder K. Bhambra, and Tessa Roynon (eds), *African Athena: New Agendas* (Oxford University Press, 2011).

Ortigues, Marie-Cécile, and Edmond Ortigues, *Œdipe* (Paris: L'Harmattan, 1984 [1966]).

Ouologuem, Yambo, *Le Devoir de violence* (Paris: Seuil, 1968).

——, *Lettre à la France nègre* (Paris: E. Nalis, 1969).

Oyèníyì Okùnoyè, 'Ewì, Yorùbá Modernity, and the Public Space', *Research in African Literatures*, 41(4) (2010), pp. 43–64.

Pageaux, Daniel-Henri, 'L'Ecart (1979) de Vumbi Yoka Mudimbe, nouveau roman africain, altérité impossible, écriture spéculaire', in Jean Bessière (ed), *L'Autre du roman et de la fiction* (1996), pp. 131–38.

Parry, Benita, *Postcolonial Studies: A Materialist Critique* (London: Routledge, 2004).

Périer, Gaston-Denys, *Petite histoire des lettres coloniales de Belgique* (Brussels: Office de Publicité, 1942).

Pirotte, Jean, *Périodiques missionnaires belges d'expression française: Reflets de cinquante années d'évolution d'une mentalité, 1889–1940* (Louvain: Bibliothèque de l'Université, 1973).

Porter, Bernard in 'Wild Enthusiasts', *London Review of Books*, 10 May 2012, pp. 21–22.

Quaghebeur, Marc, Émile Van Balberghe, et al. (eds), *Papier blanc, encre noire: Cent ans de culture francophone en Afrique centrale (Zaïre, Rwanda et Burundi)*, 2 vols (Brussels: Édition Labor, 1992).

Quayson, Ato, *Postcolonialism: Theory, Practice, or Process?* (Oxford: Polity, 2000).

Rémond, René, 'Plaidoyer pour une histoire délaissée: La fin de la IIIe République', in *Revue française de science politique*, 2(7) (1957), pp. 253–70.

Rey, Alain, 'Remarques sémantiques', in *Langue Française*, 4 (1969), pp. 5–29.

Richards, David, 'Postcolonial Anthropology in the French-speaking World', in Charles Forsdick and David Murphy (eds), *Postcolonial Thought in the French-Speaking World* (Liverpool University Press, 2009), pp. 173–84.

Ricœur, Paul, *Histoire et vérité* (Paris: Seuil, 1955).
——, *History and Truth*, translated by Charles A. Kelbley (Evanston, Ill.: Northwestern University Press, 1998 [1955]).
——, *The Conflict of Interpretations: Essays in Hermeneutics*, Introduction by Don Ihde (London: Continuum, 2004 [1969]).
Rigby, Peter, *Persistent Pastoralists: Nomadic Societies in Transition* (London: Zed Books, 1985).
Riva, Silvia, *Nouvelle histoire de la littérature du Congo-Kinshasa*, Preface by V. Y. Mudimbe and Marc Quaghebeur, translated from Italian by Colin Fort (Paris: L'Harmattan, 2006 [2000]).
Róheim, Géza, *Psychoanalysis and Anthropology: Culture, Personality and the Unconscious* (New York: International University Press, 1950).
Rothberg, Michael, *Traumatic Realism: The Demands of Holocaust Representation* (Minneapolis and London: University of Minnesota Press, 2000).
——, *Multidirectional Memory: Remembering the Holocaust in the Age of Decolonization* (Stanford, Calif.: Stanford University Press, 2009).
Sahlins, Marshall, *Culture and Practical Reason* (University of Chicago Press, 1976).
Said, Edward, *Orientalism: Western Conceptions of the Orient* (London: Routledge and Kegan Paul, 1995 [1978]).
——, *Humanism and Democratic Criticism* (New York: Columbia University Press, 2004).
——, 'Introduction to the Fiftieth Anniversary Edition' of Erich Auerbach's *Mimesis: the Representation of Reality in Western Literature*, translated from German by Willard R. Trask (Princeton, NJ; Oxford: Princeton University Press, 2003 [1953]), pp. ix–xxxii.
Sartre, Jean-Paul, *L'Être et le néant: Essai d'ontologie phénoménologique*, corrected edn, with index by Arlette Elkaïm-Sartre (Paris: Gallimard, 2003 [1943]).
——, *Portrait of the Anti-Semite*, translated by Erik de Mauny (London: Secker and Warburg/Lindsay Drummond, 1948 [1946]).
——, *Anti-Semite and Jew: An Exploration of the Etiology of Hate*, translated by George J. Becker, Preface by Michael Walzer (New York: Schocken Books, 1995 [1946]).
——, *Réflexions sur la question juive* (Paris: Paul Morihien, 1946).
——, *Qu'est-ce que la littérature ?* (Paris: Gallimard, 1948).
——, 'Orphée noir', in Léopold Sédar Senghor, *Anthologie de la nouvelle poésie nègre et malgache de langue française*, Foreword by C.-André Julien (Paris: Presses universitaires de France, 1948), pp. ix–xliv.
——, *What is Literature?*, translated by Bernard Fretchman, with an Introduction by David Caute (London; New York: Routledge, 2007 [1948]).
——, 'Réponse à Claude Lefort', *Les Temps Modernes*, 89 (April 1953), pp. 1571–629.
——, 'Le Colonialisme est un système', *Les Temps Modernes*, 123 (March–April 1956), pp. 1371–86.

———, *Critique of Dialectical Reason*, vol. 1, *Theory of Practical Ensembles*, translated by Alan Sheridan-Smith, edited by Jonathan Rée (London: NLB, 1976 [1960]).

———, *Colonialism and Neocolonialism*, Preface by Robert Young; Introduction by Azzedine Haddour; translated by Azzedine Haddour, Terry McWilliams, and Steve Brewer (London: Routledge, 2001 [1964]).

Schmidt, Wilhelm, *Der Ursprung der Gottesidee*, 12 vols. (Münster: Aschendorff, 1926–55).

Schmitt, Carl, *Political Theology: Four Chapters on the Concept of Sovereignty*, translated by George Schwab; Foreword by Tracy B. Strong (University of Chicago Press, 2005).

Schrevel, Michel de, *Les Forces politiques de la décolonisation congolaise jusqu'à la veille de l'indépendance* (Louvain: Imprimerie M. and L. Symons, 1970).

Sebag, Lucien, *Marxisme et Structuralisme* (Paris: Payot, 1964).

Senghor, Léopold Sédar, *Anthologie de la nouvelle poésie nègre et malgache de langue française*, Preface, 'Orphée noir', by Jean-Paul Sartre; Foreword by C.-André Julien (Paris: Presses universitaires de France, 1948).

Shepard, Todd, *The Invention of Decolonization: The Algerian War and the Remaking of France* (Ithaca; NY: Cornell University Press, 2006).

Shohat, Ella, and Robert Stam, *Unthinking Eurocentrism: Multiculturalism and the Media* (London: Routledge, 1994).

Sibeud, Emmanuel, *Une Science impériale pour l'Afrique: La construction des savoirs africanistes en France (1878–1930)* (Paris: EHESS, 'Recherches d'histoire et de sciences sociales', 2002).

Sihanouk, Norodom, *L'Indochine vue de Pékin: Entretiens avec Jean Lacouture* (Paris: Seuil, 1970).

Small, Audrey, 'The Duty of Memory: A Solidarity of Voices after the Rwandan Genocide', *Paragraph*, 30(1) (2007), pp. 85–100.

Smet, A. J., 'Placide Tempels et son œuvre publiée', *Revue Africaine de Théologie*, 1 (1977), pp. 77–128.

———, *Histoire de la philosophie africaine contemporaine: Courants et problèmes* (Kinshasa: Faculté de théologie catholique, 1980).

Spivak, Gayatri Chakravorty, *In Other Words: Essays in Cultural Politics* (London and New York: Routledge, 1987).

———, 'Can the Subaltern Speak', in Cary Nelson and Lawrence Grossbary (eds), *Marxism and the Interpretation of Culture* (Urbana: University of Illinois Press, 1988), pp. 271–313.

Spleth, Janice, 'The Dynamics of Power in Mudimbe's *Before the Birth of the Moon*', in Phanuel Akubueze Egejuru and Ketu H. Katrak (eds), *Nwanyibu: Womanbeing and African Literature* (Trenton, NJ: Africa World Press, 1997), pp. 69–82.

Stenger, Friedrich, *White Fathers in Colonial Central Africa: A Critical Examination of V. Y. Mudimbe's Theories on Missionary Discourse in Africa* (Münster, Hamburg, and London: LIT Verlag, 2001).

Stengers, Jean, *Congo, mythes et réalités: 100 ans d'histoire* (Paris and Louvain-la-Neuve: Duculot, 1989).
Stoler, Ann Laura, *Race and the Education of Desire: Foucault's 'History of Sexuality' and the Colonial Order of Things* (Durham, NC and London: Duke University Press, 1995).
Syrotinski, Michael, *Singular Performances: Reinscribing the Subject in African Francophone Writing* (Charlottesville and London: University of Virginia Press, 2002).
——, *Deconstruction and the Postcolonial: At the Limits of Theory* (Liverpool University Press, 2007).
——, 'The Post-Genocidal African Subject: Patrice Nganang, Achille Mbembe and the Worldliness of Contemporary African Literature in French', in Charles Forsdick, Alec Hargreaves, and David Murphy (eds), *Transnational French Studies: Postcolonialism and Littérature-Monde* (Liverpool University Press, 2010), pp. 274–86.
Tempels, R. P. Placide, *Bantu Philosophy*, translated by Colin King; with a Foreword to the English edition by Margaret Read (Paris: Présence africaine, 1959).
Thomas, Dominic, *Nation-Building, Propaganda, and Literature in Francophone Africa* (Bloomington and Indianapolis: Indiana University Press, 2002).
—— (ed.), *Museums in Postcolonial Europe*, special issue of the *African and Black Diaspora: An International Journal*, 2(2) (2009), pp. 125–269.
Thomas, Linda E., *Living Stones in the Household of God: The Legacy and Future of Black Theology* (Minneapolis, Minn.: Fortress Press, 2004).
Tilley, Helen, *Africa as a Living Laboratory: Empire, Development and the Problem of Scientific Knowledge, 1870–1950* (University of Chicago Press, 2011).
Touraine, Alain, *Le Mouvement de mai ou le communisme utopique* (Paris: Seuil, 1968).
Towa, Marcien, *L .S. Senghor: Négritude ou servitude?* (Yaoundé: Clé, 1972).
Tshiamalenga, Marcel Ntumba, 'Qu'est-ce que la "philosophie africaine"', in *La Philosophie africaine: Actes de la première semaine de philosophie de Kinshasa* (Kinshasa: Faculté de théologie catholique, 1977), pp. 33–36.
Van Reybrouck, David, *Congo, une histoire*, translated from Dutch by Isabelle Rosselin (Arles: Actes Sud, 2012).
Vansina, Jan, *De la tradition orale: Essai de méthode historique* (Tervuren: Annales – Sciences Humaines, 1961).
——, *Kingdoms of the Savannah* (Madison: University of Wisconsin Press, 1966).
——, *The Children of Woot: A History of the Kuba Peoples* (Madison: University of Wisconsin Press, 1978).
Verhaegen, Benoît, *ABAKO (Association des Bakongo): 1950–1960; documents* (Brussels: Centre de Recherche et d'information socio-politiques, 1962).
——, *Rébellions au Congo*, 2 vols (Brussels: CRISP, 1966).
——, *La Décolonisation au Maniema (1958–1859)* (Brussels: Centre de Recherche et d'information socio-politiques, 1970).

——, 'Méthode et problème de l'histoire immédiate', *Cahiers économiques et sociaux*, 8(3) (1970), pp. 471–86.

——, *Le Premier semestre de 1960* (Brussels: Centre de Recherche et d'information socio-politiques, 1970).

——, *Introduction à l'histoire immédiate: Essai de méthodologie qualitative* (Gemboux: Duculot, 1974).

——, 'Religion et politique en Afrique noire', *Religions africaines et christianisme*, 1 (1979), pp. 179–94.

——, 'The Method of "Histoire Immédiate": Its Application to Africa', in Bogumil Jewsiewicki and David Newbury (eds), *African Historiographies. What History for Which Africa?* (London: Sage Publications, 1986), pp. 236–48.

Verhaegen, Benoît, and Jean Tshonda Omasombo, *Patrice Lumumba: Acteur politique ; de la prison aux portes du pouvoir, juillet 1956–février 1960* (Paris; Tervuren: L'Harmattan, Musée royal de l'Afrique centrale, 2005).

Verhaegen, Benoît, and Herbert F. Weiss (eds), *Les Rébellions dans l'est du Zaïre (1964–1967)* (Brussels: Centre d'étude et de documentation africaines, 1997).

Veyne, Paul, *Comment on écrit l'histoire: Essai d'épistémologie* (Paris: Seuil, 1971).

Wagner, Roy, *The Invention of Culture* (Chicago University Press, 1981[1975]).

Wallerstein, Immanuel, *Unthinking Social Science: The Limits of Nineteenth-Century Paradigms* (Cambridge: Polity Press, 1991).

Wamba Dia Wamba, Ernest, 'Struggles for the "Second Independence" in Congo-Kinshasa', *UTAFITI*, 9(1) (1987), pp. 31–50.

Watts, Richard, 'Negritude, Présence africaine, Race', in Charles Forsdick and David Murphy (eds), *Postcolonial Thought in the French-Speaking World* (Liverpool University Press, 2009), pp. 227–37.

Wauthier, Claude, *L'Afrique des Africains: Inventaire de la négritude* (Paris: Seuil, 1964).

Wehrs, Donald R., *Pre-colonial Africa in Colonial African Narratives: From Ethiopia Unbound to Things Fall Apart, 1911–1958* (Aldershot: Ashgate, 2007).

White, Bob W., *Rumba Rules: The Politics of Dance Music in Mobutu's Zaïre* (Durham, NC: Duke University Press, 2008).

Wilder, Gary, *The French Imperial Nation-State: Negritude and Colonial Humanism between the Two World Wars* (Chicago University Press, 2005).

Williams, Patrick, 'Roads to Freedom: Jean-Paul Sartre and Anti-colonialism', in Charles Forsdick and David Murphy (eds), *Postcolonial Thought in the French-Speaking World* (Liverpool University Press, 2009), pp. 147–56.

Wiseman, Boris (ed.), *The Cambridge Companion to Lévi-Strauss* (Cambridge University Press, 2009).

Young, Robert, *White Mythologies: Writing History and the West* (London and New York: Routledge, 1990).

Zeller, Jules, *Histoire d'Allemagne: Origines de l'Allemagne et de l'Empire germanique* (Paris: Perrin, 1872).

Index

Abraham, W.E. 140
adaptation theology 23–4, 29–30, 198n56
Adorno, Theodor W. 15, 156, 157, 159, 161, 164, 166, 179, 180
Adotevi, Stanislas 64, 118, 150
African, literature 160–1
Afro-radicalism 163–4
Ahidjo, Ahmadou 149
allochronism 91–2, 94, 95, 97, 101–3, 107
Althusser, Louis 12, 73–4, 81, 82, 102, 174
Amselle, Jean-Loup 151
anthropological methodology 31–2, 34–5, 45, 68
    critique of social anthropology 83, 89–92, 94–5, 101–2, 106
    informed by Western principles 1–2, 51–2, 76–7, 100, 162
aphanisis, concept of 79–81
Arendt, Hannah 3, 130, 164
authenticity of Zaire *see* Congo-Zaire, Zairianisation
autobiography 4, 15

Bachelard, Gaston 16
Bakounine, Michel 81
Balandier, Georges 96
Baluba ontology 142–3
Bantu culture 38, 49, 75, 139–40, 142, 171, 195n20
    ontology 21, 22–3
Bataille, Georges 59
Bayart, Jean-François 151
Beardsley, Grace H. 40
Bellman, Beryl 143–4
Bénabou, Marcel 40

Benedict, Ruth 68
Benjamin, Walter 156
Bernal, Martin
    Black Athena 12, 40, 41
Béti, Mongo 151
Bhabha, Homi 9–10, 176–7, 185, 186
Bimwenyi, Oscar 23, 138
Bisanswa, Justin 9
Bjornson, Richard 48
Bloch, Marc 45
Blondel, Charles 136–7
Blyden, Edward Wilmot 14, 114–15, 128–32, 140, 183
Boas, Franz 35
Bosch, Hieronymus 14, 114, 127
Bourgeois, Alain 40
Braudel, Fernand 34, 45
Brecht, Bertolt 156–7
Brenner, Louis 10
Britton, Celia 59
Brown, Nicholas 11
Brown, Sterling 128
Burgkmair, Hans 127
Butler, Judith 171

Cabral, Amilcar 123
Cameroon 148–9
Carothers, John Colin 121
Cartesianism 93
Cendrar, Blaise 140
Césaire, Aimé 3, 21, 52, 64, 81, 83, 122, 156, 160, 160–1, 188, 203n11
Chakrabarty, Dipesh 9–10
Che Guevara, Ernesto 88, 13, 174–5
Chinweizu 79
chose du texte 8, 13, 143–4, 154, 171

Christianity
    attempts to find vocations among indigenous converts 21–2, 29
    indigenization of biblical messages by missions 19, 23–5, 124–5, 196n25
    missionary orders' role in education 18, 194n11
    overlap between missionary and anthropologist 18, 22, 96
    propagation of faith fuelled by need for imperial expansion 19–21
    role in shaping African modernity 17–18, 48, 77
coevalness 97–9, 102, 110–11, 146, 198–9n64
Congo-Zaire 17, 36, 46, 47, 48–9, 96, 197n38, 203n3
    censorship 51, 70
    Zairianisation 12, 50, 51, 55–64, 183, 186
    see also Bantu culture; Kasai; Katanga; Kinshasa; Luba culture; Lubumbashi; Mobuto regime
Copans, Jean 141
Crahay, Franz 138
Crowther, Samuel Ajayi 21, 23
Crozier, Michel, *La Société bloquée* 118
Cullen, Countee 128

Damas, Léon Gontran 14, 118, 150, 160–1
de Beauvoir, Simone 171
de Certeau, Michel 32, 33, 40, 142, 154, 166, 177, 185–6
de Chardin, Teilhard 128
de Coulanges, Fustel 44
de Heusch, Luc 38
de Tracy, Destutt 58
Debray, Régis 47, 50, 88, 174
decolonisation 3, 22–3, 47, 79–80, 85, 95–6, 104, 144–6, 150–6, 176, 185
    as an unfinished process 81
Delafosse, Maurice 66
Democratic Republic of Congo *see* Congo-Zaire

Derrida, Jacques 11, 33
Devereux, Georges 119–20
Diawara, Manthia 10
Diop, Cheikh Anta 40, 41, 66–7, 68, 129–30, 138, 177
Djebar, Assia 47–8
Dogon ontology 139–40, 143
Du Bois, W.E.B. 3, 128
Dumézil, Georges 136, 137
Duras, Marguerite 3
Dürer, Albrecht 127
Durkheim, Émile 136–7
Dussel, Enrique 107–8, 173–4

Ebénézer, Njoh-Mouelle 64
Eboussi-Boulaga, Fabien 23, 29, 138, 139, 143, 151
    Christianity without Fetishes 29–30
Engels, Friedrich 81
ethnophilosophy 138–9, 140–1
ethnopsychiatry 119–21
Etzioni, Amitai 107–8
ethnocentrism 29, 35, 44, 69, 83, 95, 99, 106, 116, 121, 130–1, 138–9, 141–2, 146
eurocentrism 10–11, 34, 98, 104, 113
existentialism 100, 101

Fabian, Johannes 1–2, 13, 24, 51, 67, 68, 83, 90–3, 94–5, 99, 101–2, 104, 107, 109, 113, 183, 199n64
Fanon, Frantz 85, 86, 100–1, 118, 119, 123, 145, 150, 151, 169, 182, 184–5
Fantouré, Alioum 103
Fassin, Didier 121
Febvre, Lucien 34
feitiços, Western perceptions of 19, 127
feminist rewriting of history 123–4
Foucault, Michel 23, 44, 58, 89, 101, 133, 142, 143, 146, 151, 162, 180–1, 182, 187
    Histoire de la folie à l'âge classique 19
    History of Sexuality 113–14
    Les Mots et les choses 18–19, 57, 92, 120–1
    postcolonial criticism 113–14

The History of Madness 125–6, 132
The Order of Things 114–15, 134–9
Fourche, Tiarko 32–3, 36
Freud, Sigmund 137, 180–1
Frobenius, Leo 32, 66, 140
Furet, François 111

Gadamer, Hans-Georg 143, 144
Geertz, Clifford 95
Gide, André, *Voyage au Congo* 115, 116, 117
Gilroy, Paul 114, 153
Girardet, Raoul 145–6
Glissant, Édouard 67, 155
gnosis 125, 131, 156
Godelier, Maurice 81
Goldberg, Anne 164
Goldmann, Lucien 81
Goldstein, Kurt 136, 137
Grasser, Erasmus 127
Griaule, Marcel 9, 32, 68, 115, 138, 139, 142–3
Guiraud, Pierre 41
Gutiérrez, Gustavo 124, 173–5

Haneke, Michael 3
Harari, Roberto 80
Hardt, Michael 106, 186–7
Hazoumé, Romuald 186
Hebga, Meinrad 23
Hegel, Georg Wilhelm Friedrich 89, 92, 102, 152, 156, 159, 162
Heger, Klaus 41
Heidegger, Martin 59, 156
Herodotus 12, 40, 42–3, 45, 48, 59, 123
Herskovits, Melville 9
historicism 4, 15, 19, 59, 76
historiography, African and Western 33–5, 44
Hjelmslev, Louis 41
Hodgen, Margaret 19
Hofstede, Geert 13, 108–9
Holocaust, the 3, 13, 15, 85, 88, 110, 157, 164–5, 180
Hoschild, Adam 48
Hountondji, Paulin 14, 22, 115, 138–9, 143
Houston, Drusilla D. 40
Hullot-Kentor, Robert 180

'Ideology' 7, 9, 48, 50, 52, 57–9, 64, 69, 71, 73, 88, 127, 154, 179
immanentism 60–4, 66
inculturalisation *see* indigenization
indigenization, of Christianity 19, 23–5, 29
Irele, Abiola 80

Jahn, Janheinz 138
Jamaa movement 24–5
Jones, Ernest 79

Kadima-Nzuji 52
Kagame, Alexis 14, 23, 138, 140, 163
Kalanda, Mabika 33
Kanda-Matalu, Tshibumba 178
Kane, Cheikh Hamidou 151
Kangafu, Kutumbagana 12–13, 56–78, 88
Kasa-Vubu, Joseph 52, 72, 168, 204n13
Kasai 37
Kasende, Jean Christophe 9
Kavwariheri, Kasereka 9, 56
Kenyatta, Jomo 123
Kermode, Frank 144
Kimbanguism 24, 77
Kinshasa 70
Kongo (Kingdom of) 5, 20
Koselleck, Reinhart 3, 155
Kourouma, Ahmadou 82, 103, 166, 167
Kresse, Kai 10, 11, 182
Kristeva, Julia 171
Kuper, Adam 108

Labov, William 119
Lacan, Jacques 79–80
LaCapra, Dominick 164
Laing, Ronald 89
Lamouchi, Noureddine 85, 88
Lazarus, Neil 10, 171
Lebbe, Frédéric 29
Lévi-Strauss, Claude 16, 45, 46, 92–4, 140, 142–3, 146, 180–1
   The Savage Mind 17, 33–5, 92
   views on anthropological fieldwork 35, 95
   Western historiography 34–5, 36, 44
Lévy-Bruhl, Lucien 136–7, 139, 196n34
Liberia 128, 129, 130, 131, 151
Liking, Werewere 11, 167

linguistic analysis of translations 32–3, 41
Locke, Alain 128
Lopès, Henri 103
Luba culture
    mythemes 36–7, 46
    mythology 17
    study of 31–9
    use of colour 37
Lubumbashi (Elisabethville) 4, 8, 25, 56, 70, 90, 117, 183–4
Lufuluabo, F.M. 23
Lukász, Georg 81
Lumumba, Patrice 52, 53, 54, 72–3, 96, 122, 123, 183
Lynch, Hollis Ralph 132

McAfee Brown, Robert 124–5, 173–4
Marrou, Henri-Irénée 45–6
Marx, Karl 81, 82, 102, 180–1
Marxism 81–2, 88, 99, 101, 145, 153, 165
Masolo, D.A. 10, 165
Maspero, François 52
Maurier, Henri 32–3
Mauss, Marcel 136, 137
Maximum Illud (1919) 22
Mbembe, Achille 14–15, 147–56, 159–60, 162–6, 176–7, 179–80, 181, 186, 187, 188
Mbiti, John 23, 138, 140
Mead, Margaret 68
Mels, Bernard 163
Memmi, Albert 85
Mercier, Ernest 40
Métreaux, Rhoda 68
Mobuto regime 12, 50–78, 82, 104, 168, 172, 178, 183
    Mouvement Populaire de la Révolution (MPR) 52, 53, 57, 70–1, 78
    Nsele manifesto 53–4, 55, 58–9, 63, 71–2, 77
Monénembo, Tierno 11, 82
Monnier, Laurent 96–7, 110, 123
monotheism 22
Morgenstern, Christian 119
Morlighem, Henri 33, 36
Mouralis, Bernard 9, 39

Mudimbe, V.Y. 16
    academic position in United States 13, 50, 113, 114
    'Air: Étude sémantique' 41
    analysis of black figures in classical art 14, 126, 127, 151, 163, 166
    analysis of term 'revolution' 71–2
    Autour de la 'Nation' 50, 56–63, 67, 69, 70–8, 81, 106, 183
    Carnets d'Amérique 27, 67, 114–25, 145
    Carnets de Berlin 7, 27, 46, 48
    Entre les eaux 24, 26–7, 55, 81, 88, 151, 164, 166, 167, 172–4
        Landu character analysis 26–7, 29
    Frère Mathieu 25
    'In the House of Libya' 39–40
    L'Autre Face du royaume 42–4, 45, 47, 50, 51, 52, 57, 63, 66, 69, 70, 74, 76, 78, 118, 119, 132, 145, 152, 173, 175
        analysis of colonisation and alienation 79–81, 84–5, 89–90, 100, 183
    Le Bel immonde 26, 31, 95, 151, 164, 166, 167–72
    L'Écart 81, 95, 102–6, 171, 185, 197n49
    Les Corps glorieux 4, 23, 25, 27, 32–3, 41–2, 117, 152–3, 182
    L'Odeur du père 47, 50, 65, 70, 74–5, 76, 79, 120–1, 132, 145, 175, 181
        analysis of colonisation and alienation 81, 88–90, 98–9, 100, 183
    On African Fault Lines 83, 106–9, 166, 178–9, 181
    Parables and Fables 18, 21, 23, 24–5, 31, 37, 47, 81, 93, 107, 150
    preface to the *Vocabulaire* 183–4
    'Reprendre' 164, 176–7
    Shaba Deux 17, 26, 27–30, 49, 152–3, 168, 183, 198n59
        Marie-Gertrude character analysis 27–30
    stylistic abstruseness 70
    Tales of Faith 6, 16, 18, 25, 48, 180

The Idea of Africa 4–8, 16, 18, 19–20, 25, 37, 77–8, 117, 124, 151, 161, 176–8
The Invention of Africa 16, 19, 20–1, 31, 44, 57, 82, 92, 106, 113, 114, 125–46, 151, 154–6, 161, 163, 185
The Surreptitious Speech 24
Une Bible noire 31–9, 150, 168, 182
'Ut Recte Valeant' 154
Western-style education 11, 17, 25, 42, 47, 52, 55, 118
see also themes
Mudimbe-Boyi, Elisabeth 20
Mulago, Vincent 23, 24–5, 138, 140
Mulélé, Pierre 12, 54–5, 58, 72–3, 96
Mulongo, Huit 56
Mveng, Engelbert 14, 23, 41, 66–7, 115, 138, 143

Nambikwara ontology 142–3
Nancy, Jean-Luc 12–13, 53, 59–62, 64, 66, 67–8, 69, 75–6, 180
see also immanentism
nativism 163–4
Ndaywel, Isidore è Nziem 53, 56
Ndengue, Jean-Marie Abanda 64
Negri, Antonio 106, 186–7
negritude 14, 64–7, 114, 118, 121–3, 130–1, 132, 158–9, 161
Ngal, Georges 52, 56, 103
Nganang, Patrice 14–15, 82, 147–8, 156, 158–9, 160–2, 166, 168, 172, 179–80, 181, 186, 187, 188
Ní Loingsigh, Aedín 116
Nietzsche, Friedrich 156
Nkashama, Pius 41, 52, 70
Nkrumah, Kwame 57, 82, 123, 165
Nyerere, Julius 123, 165

Obenga, Théophile 41, 138
Ogotemmêli 140
Ong, Walter J. 95
ontology
    Baluba 142–3
    Bantu 21, 22–3
    Dogon 139–40, 143
    Luba 31–9
    Nambikwara 142–3

Ortigues, Edmond 120
Otherness 22–3, 34, 68, 79–80, 83, 85–6, 88–9, 110–11
Ouologuem, Yambo 111, 151
Ousmane, Sembène 167
Oyono, Ferdinand 184

paganism, perceptions of 21
Pedagogy: 82, 94, 102, 110, 119–120, 144
Picasso, Pablo 140

Rajkumar, Deepa 107
Ramism 94–5
'Reprendre' 30, 40, 42, 48, 63, 81, 177, 184, 186
Rey, Alain 41
Ricœur, Paul 45, 92–3, 142, 143
Rigby, Peter 198–9n64
Riva, Silvia 56
Róheim, Géza 120
Romain-Desfossés, Pierre 176, 177–8, 182
Romano, Giovanni 20–1, 23
Rothberg, Michael 3, 7
Rouch, Jean 3
Rousseau 93
Rwanda, genocide 157, 159, 161, 164

Sahlins, Marshall 79
Said, Edward 8, 9–10, 16, 19, 45, 47–8, 87, 113, 133, 151, 186
    Orientalism 8, 16, 19, 45
Sartre, Jean Paul 16, 26, 45, 46, 81, 98, 99, 100, 122, 145, 146, 152, 157–8, 169
    analysis of anti-semitism 86–8, 100, 104, 210n24;28
    concept of the self 93
    Critique of Dialectical Reason 17, 33–4
    post-war antiracist activism 82–3, 85–6, 90, 122, 158–9
    Western historiography 34–5
Saussure 41
Schmidt, Wilhelm 22, 140, 195–6n22
Schmitt, Carl 156, 226n54
Sembène, Ousmane 11
Senghor, L.S. 14, 40, 41, 57, 64, 67, 80, 85, 114, 128–30, 131–2, 133, 138, 150, 151, 160–1

Smet, A.J. 195n17
Smith, Faith 10
Snowden, Frank 40
Soyinka, Wole 40, 156–7, 160, 188
Spivak, Gayatri Chakravorty 9–10, 113, 133, 169, 186
Stengers, Jean 48
Stanley, Henry Morton 169
Stoler, Ann Laura 113–14
structuralism 92, 100, 144, 212n65
Suret-Canale, Jean 96
Syrotinski, Michael 11, 26, 94, 103, 133, 171, 186

Tadjo, Véronique 11, 167
Tansi, Sony Labou 11, 82, 103
Tati-Loutard 82
Tempels, Placide F. 9, 14, 21–3, 32, 68, 75, 115, 138–9, 142–3, 163
  La Philosophie bantoue 23–4, 68, 139, 163, 182
  see also indigenization; Jamaa movement
themes
  coevalness 97–9, 102, 110–11, 146, 198–9n64
  concept of 'aphanisis' 79–81
  Congolese misogyny 17, 152–3, 167, 169, 171
  critique of human sciences 83, 84–5, 89–90, 106, 110, 133–46, 150
  epistemological dependency and neo-colonialism 84, 86–7, 95–9, 103–4, 110
  ethnic violence 17
  gender politics 26, 27, 37, 46, 123–4, 183
  Greco-Latin cultures, insight into African history 40–2, 46, 49, 57
  inter-subjectivity 107–8, 109–10, 150
  links between history and myth 39–40, 46
  Mobuto-led politics of authenticity 50–78, 104
  negritude 14, 64–7, 114, 118, 121–3, 130–1, 132, 158–9, 161
  notion of 'Otherness' 22–3, 34, 68, 79–80, 83, 85–6, 88–9, 110–11

  notions of race 30–1, 121–3
  relationship between theory and praxis 88–9, 92–3, 99, 101
  religious symbolism 37–8
  sense of alienation 48, 79–80
  significance of aid 106–7
  subjectivity of historians 45–6, 47, 104
  Third-Worldism 111–12
  'West and the Rest' 79–112
  Western culture, role in shaping African modernity 17, 44, 46, 91, 100
Thomas, Louis-Vincent 57
Thorez, Maurice 81, 83
Tobie, Nathan 121
Touré, Ahmed Sékou 82
Towa, Marcien 64, 118, 138, 150
Tshiamalenga, Marcel 33, 138, 139, 143
Tshombe, Moïse 53, 72
Tutuola, Amos 156, 160, 188

Ullmann, Stephen 41
Um Nyobé, Ruben 149, 224n11

van Binsbergen, Wim 10, 17–18, 25, 150, 180
Vansina, Jan 105
Vellut, Jean-Luc 48
Verhaegen, Benoît 13, 17, 55, 83, 95, 96–100, 104, 107, 109, 166–7, 172–5, 183, 184
Veyne, Paul 40, 43–4, 45, 142
visualism 95
von Helmholtz, Hermann 89

Wagner, Roy 147, 178, 185
Walker, Margaret 123
Wallerstein, Immanuel 111
Western culture, role in shaping African modernity 17, 44, 46, 91, 100
Wiredu, Kwasi 32–3, 140

Yav, André (pseudonym) 183–4
Yém Mback, Pierre 149
Young, Robert 118

Zaire see Congo-Zaire
Zeller, Jules 44